get better!
the pursuit of better health and better healthcare design
at lower costs per capita

33rd UIA /PHG International Seminar on Public Healthcare Facilities
Toronto, Canada. September 24-28, 2013

Proceedings
edited by Romano Del Nord

Conference organized by:

UIA/PHG International Union of Architects / Public Health Group

IIDEX Canada
National Design + Architecture Expo and Conference

Published by
TESIS Inter-University Research Centre
Systems and Technologies for Social and Healthcare Facilities
University of Florence

Scientific Editor:
Prof. Romano Del Nord
Director of TESIS Inter-University Research Centre
University of Florence

Session introductions (pp. 23, 111, 221, 299) and volume layout:
Francesca Nesi
Arch. PhD
University of Florence

Proofreading:
Rebecca Milner

Published by

TESIS Inter-University Research Centre "Systems and Technologies for Social and Healthcare Facilities"

Department of Architecture DIDA
University of Florence

Via San Niccolò 93
info@tesis.unifi.it
+ 39 055 275 5348
Florence 50125
Italy

ISBN 978-88-907872-2-5
First Print 2014

The editors of the volume wish to thank Cliff Harvey as the Canada contact and for coordination, Vivian Lo for her support in collecting the papers and reports from the authors, and Tracy Bowie, the Vice President of IIDEXCanada, Canada's National Design + Architecture Expo & Conference, for acting as the representative in the organization of the conference in Toronto.

Cover photograph by Romano Del Nord, Peter Gilgan Centre for Research and Learning in Toronto designed by Diamond Schmitt Architects. Background image courtesy of Perkins Eastman Black/IBI Group Architects in joint venture, Women's College Hospital in Toronto, ON.

TESIS Inter-University Research Centre "Systems and Technologies for Social and Healthcare Facilities"
University of Florence, Italy

Index

Planning, Design and Construction Improvement Process

Design Issues for Healthcare Buildings

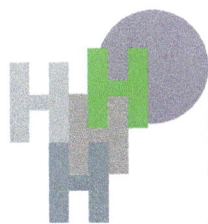

Environmental Quality: Comfort, Humanization, Evidence-Based Design

Planning and Design of Facilities for Specific Service Providers

Foreword

Welcome to Toronto, welcome to Ontario, and welcome to Canada – that is how on September 24th, 2013 we began the 33rd Annual Meeting and Forum of the International Union of Architect's Public Health Group (UIA-PHG) and the Global University Programs in Healthcare Architecture (GUPHA); and now a warm welcome to you as an extended participant of the Forum as you read through these proceedings.

The Forum's theme was to *get better! the pursuit of better health and better healthcare design at lower costs per capita.* The participants included architects and other designers, as well as clinicians, government officials and senior administrators from over 20 different countries. The keynote speaker was David Webster from IDEO who spoke of how design thinking could improve the healthcare ecosystem. Other events included tours of projects highlighting how design improved the patient and family experience, their health outcomes, as well as contributed to a healthy workplace for staff.

The challenge for delegates, and which is now extended to you – was to actively integrate the proceedings which covered a wide range of experiences, knowledge, and understanding of designing for health in the different care environments. To take this information and create an intelligent story of how design contributes to improving health and the environments of care; and to share this story with your community to help them achieve better health and care through the built environment. Now with your extended participation, we hope the messages and challenge outlined in the proceedings will help you to get better in helping others get better. We are very thankful to the UIA-PHG for bringing their knowledge community to Toronto. I know the UIA-PHG is looking forward to your future participation wherever you can catch up with them around the world as they continue to share their experiences, knowledge and understanding of designing for health.

Enjoy and be challenged!
Cliff Harvey, OAA, FRAIC

TESIS Inter-University Research Centre "Systems and Technologies for Social and Healthcare Facilities"
University of Florence, Italy

Foreword to the UIA PHG Proceedings, Toronto, 2013

Participants attending the UIA Public Health Group Seminar held in Toronto, Canada, 24-28 September 2013.

On behalf of all the participants who attended our annual seminar in Toronto, Canada, I am delighted to be able to pen a few words for the Foreword to these proceedings. As is apparent on the faces of those present, this was an enjoyable opportunity for those in the international community represented by the UIA Public Health Group to get together to share the latest knowledge pertaining to the planning and design of health facilities around the world.

Although Cliff Harvey appears in the back left-hand corner of this photograph, it was his efforts and those of his team that were responsible for this highly successful UIA PHG Seminar held in September 2013. He and his team should have been front and centre in this photograph to acknowledge their excellent efforts. They even arranged for beautiful weather throughout the duration of the Seminar!

If Cliff Harvey and his IIDEX team provided the setting, then those who presented the papers demonstrated the food for the mind that can be consumed at forums of this nature. The table of contents for these proceedings demonstrates the range of topics and the breadth of knowledge exhibited by those giving presentations – everything from the globalisation of healthcare to the design of specific healthcare facilities, from rethinking the healthcare delivery model to rethinking how best to reuse heritage healthcare facilities.

All of these topics fit within the compendium of knowledge and experience that healthcare architects around the world need to be constantly updating if they are to provide contemporary professional services to clients in both the public and private sectors.

Annual gatherings such as this held in Toronto play a vital part in fostering the intellectual enquiry and structured learning that are a necessary part of exploring alternative options to solving common problems.

I therefore commend the efforts of Professor Romano Del Nord and his TESIS team for preserving these learnings by compiling this compendium of the proceedings. Their efforts mean that we can continue to experience the joyful acquisition of knowledge that all those who attended were able to gain over three magical days in September 2013.

Enjoy the contents

Adjunct Professor Warren Kerr AM
Director UIA PHG

Facilities for Research and Training as an Added Value of the Hospital of Excellence: the Peter Gilgan Centre for Research and Learning in Toronto

Romano Del Nord

13

The primary purpose of the PHG (Public Health Group) seminars has always been to encourage discussion of experiences acquired in different geographical and cultural contexts and to spread the culture of sustainable projects through a description of operating methodologies deriving from the results of research in the healthcare facilities sector.

In this institutional context, the study visits programme offers an important knowledge-based and contemplative contribution, which is systematically associated with conference activities to more clearly illustrate the specific characteristics of the country hosting the seminar.

The group of facilities included in the study visits are usually very diversified so as to meet the multidisciplinary and multi-purpose requirements needed considering the professions of those participating in the seminars (PHG members and professionals interested in the different interpretative readings of the projects presented).

The programme of study visits put together by the organizers of the 33rd PHG seminar held in Toronto in September 2013 certainly helped to confirm this approach. It included visits to Bridgepoint Active Healthcare, Centre for Addiction and Mental Health (CAMH), Princess Margaret Hospital, Rotman School of Management (University of Toronto), Yorkdale Shopping Centre, and Peter Gilgan Centre for Research and Learning PGCRL.

As it is not possible to analytically specify the innovative characteristics of each building included in the programme, I will focus on just one building complex I consider particularly interesting for the quality of the innovative solutions used, the degree of sustainability achieved, its close interaction with the adjacent paediatric hospital and its architectural value in terms of an urban landmark.

The Peter Gilgan Centre for Research and Learning, the focus of one of the visits, is a particularly innovative building in functional and technological terms: designed by Diamond Schmitt Architects Inc., it was built in Toronto in three years and it was opened in September 2013.

14

Figure 1. *Peter Gilgan Centre for Research and Learning, external views of the building (left) and main entrance (right).*

Figure 2. *Detail of bow windows.*

The complex, intended to house laboratories for biomedical research on childhood illnesses, was conceived by interpreting the most advanced principles of the multidisciplinary research approach and in full compliance with the environmental sustainability imperatives that such a complex facility requires. For its size and the number of researchers it enables to coexist in a single facility, the PGRCL is one of the most advanced centres of research on childhood illnesses in the world, conceived in compliance with environmental sustainability principles.

It accommodates more than 2000 expert researchers in different disciplines organized into 6 scientific areas. The construction of the new facility meant that distinct research groups previously spread throughout several buildings could be concentrated into one, and a functional connection could be created with the adjacent Hospital For Sick Children (Sick Kids) to maximize the principle of "integration" between assistance, research and training.

The guiding principle characterizing the layout of the complex is the "system of spatial interdependences that encourage and stimulate spontaneous interaction" between researchers and research groups. This goal was achieved through the planning of large spaces acting as focal points between the laboratories, which foster opportunities for meetings and interdisciplinary exchanges through the attractiveness of comfortable settings and the provision of facilities for relaxation. These spaces have been designed to be open, pervaded by natural light, free of visual barriers, equipped with all the services necessary for a pleasant stay and to be stimulating for communicative exchanges.

Figure 3. The skywalk provides a functional connection between PGCRL and SickKids.

15

Figure 4. Collaborative spaces connected by stairs.

16

*Figure 5. Spaces for interaction and scientific col-
laboration, different levels of privacy.*

Figure 6. Open plan space pervaded with natural light.

The lower floors of the building have been designed to become as permeable as
possible to the community and open to initiatives and events of public interest
so that they encourage respect and passion for research.
The presence of shops and restaurants on the ground floor helps to demystify
this simulacrum of research.

The initial reception spaces, which are completely transparent, are integrated
with areas used for advance training and conference activities, communicating – with advanced systems – the research areas of interest, the most innovative projects and the high degree of allegiance to the centre which is conveyed,
moreover, by the high number of contributions from donors. The training areas
are made even more efficient by the presence of technological devices that encourage distance learning and openness to internationalization.

The most stimulating part of the building in terms of perfect correspondence
between architectural quality and functional innovation, as already mentioned,
is the area with dedicated spaces for interaction and scientific collaboration.

On the basis that innovation research is increasingly fostered by spontaneous exchanges between different disciplinary areas and that the environmental psychophysical well-being of researchers helps to accelerate scientific productivity, the new complex features a large bow window volumetrically open on several floors with precise distinctions of the meeting spaces contained within.

Different levels of privacy up to the total absence of barriers, different spatial dimensions in the comfortably furnished areas, different lighting levels and different visual relationships with the context of the surrounding urban structure of the city find their counterpoint in the curvilinear form of the façade, the landings, the connection spaces and the furnishings themselves.

17

Figure 7. Space interacts with the panorama of the entire city of Toronto.

TESIS Inter-University Research Centre "Systems and Technologies for Social and Healthcare Facilities"
University of Florence, Italy

18

Figure 8. Large bow window volumetrically open on several floors.

A second characteristic concerns the relationship between the researchers' work spaces located in the 17 floors of laboratories and the continuous development of the curtain wall forming the transparent façade.

The type of interface conceived through the relationship between the façade elements and the ends of the laboratory counters ensures that each whole floor can be totally reconfigured, highlighting the strategic importance attributed to the flexibility requirement and leaving all the work

19

areas flooded with natural light. In this regard, it is emblematic that the source of natural light reaches around 90% of the entire operational surface of the complex.

The mandatory requirement that each floor be reconfigurable is met by the flexibility of the installed equipment systems, thanks to which each "wet" workbench can be substituted by a "dry" workbench depending on the needs of the specific research in progress. The modular nature of the workbenches integrates with the mod-

TESIS Inter-University Research Centre "Systems and Technologies for Social and Healthcare Facilities"
University of Florence, Italy

TESIS

20

Figure 9. Laboratories.

ularity of the false ceilings and that of the floor in order to better satisfy the principle of versatility in the daily, monthly and long-term variations.

Numerous technologically advanced solutions have been used to attain the "Leed Gold" certification for sustainable design. These include the sophisticated treatment of the translucent façade of the laboratory floors, used to maximize the diffusion of natural light inside the work spaces and at the same time to contain the effect of solar radiation; all the glass panels are covered with a ceramic treatment in horizontal bands with a progressively variable density and, consequently, with differentiated behaviour in relation to the angle of the sun's rays.

The solutions chosen to reduce the use of water by 50% and energy consumption by 38%, to use 22.5% of recycled materials to make maximum use of products with low VOC emissions and to process 75% of waste diverted from land fills also help to increase sustainability performances.

Figure 10. Panels of donors.

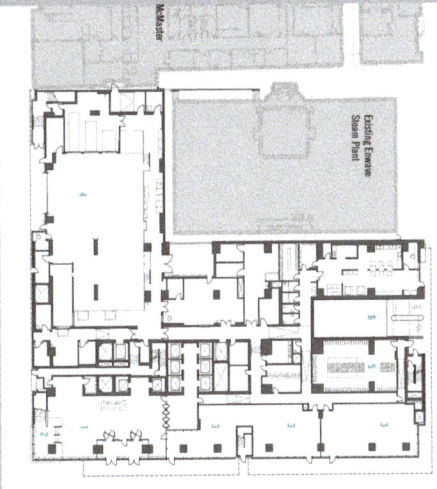

Figure 1. Ground floor plan.

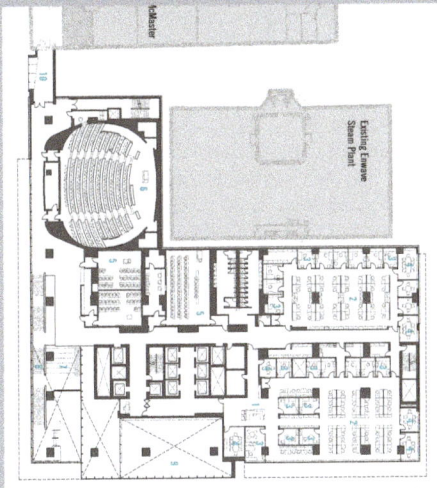

Figure 2. Third floor plan.

Figure 3. Typical dry lab floor.

COLLABORATIVE SPACE

• Collegial 'neighbourhoods' in six thematic research precincts overcome the isolation inherent in the high rise form by providing two-and three-storey collaborative spaces;
• Connected by stairs, these working lounges have kitchenettes, white boards, soft furnishings and incomparable views of the city through low-iron glazing with crystal clear transparency;
• The curvilinear form of the glass bay windows differentiates these spaces as a defining feature of the façade and the form continues inside to create a dynamic hub space.

FLEXIBLE LABORATORY SPACE

• Long, open, flexible lab space accommodates diverse research needs and interaction;
• Modular mobile benching converts from web lab to dry lab as research demand requires;
• Support spaces are located in the core for permanent facilities such as lab sinks and fume-hoods;
• Concealed overhead services provide a plug-in network of utility ports for additional flexibility.

EDUCATIONAL SPACE

• A three-storey learning concourse is publicly accessible with conference and meeting rooms;
• State-of-the-art teleconferencing and distance learning technologies allow for information exchange around the world;
• A 250-seat tele-educational auditorium provides intimacy, excellent sightlines and acoustics.

21

PETER GILGAN CENTRE FOR RESEARCH AND LEARNING

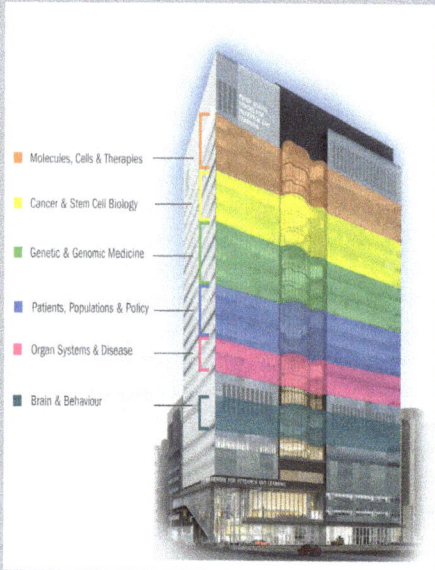

- Molecules, Cells & Therapies
- Cancer & Stem Cell Biology
- Genetic & Genomic Medicine
- Patients, Populations & Policy
- Organ Systems & Disease
- Brain & Behaviour

BRAIN & MENTAL HEALTH

A team of basic scientists, clinicians-scientists and health professionals address issues such as pain management, brain injury and repair – including traumatic brain injury, vision and auditory perception, epilepsy, cognitive and neuropsychiatric disorders such as ADHD, autism, obsessive compulsive disorder and schizophrenia.

ORGAN SYSTEMS & DISEASE

Tens of thousands of Canadian children suffer from congenital birth defects and complex and chronic diseases of the cardiovascular, immune, endocrine, respiratory and musculoskeletal systems – and retain these problems as adults. Early intervention is key in preventing a lifetime of health challenges and starts with understanding how disease begins before birth and in childhood. SickKids focuses on the development of new diagnostic techniques such as imaging technologies and new treatments to bring transformative new approaches to respiratory diseases, tissue reconstructive surgery, cardiac anomalies and joint disease in children.

PATIENTS, POPULATIONS & POLICY

Focusing on outcomes and impacts, SickKids researchers seek to improve the health and quality of life of children and their families. Undertaking studies on issues that matter to Canadians, SickKids scientists are developing evidence-based methods to ensure research findings lead to the more effective and efficient delivery of health-care, including the management of asthma, obesity, eating disorders and Type 1 diabetes, as well as access to primary care, evaluation of the effectiveness of new health technologies, injury prevention and effective health promotion strategies for youths at risk of mental illness.

GENETIC & GENOMIC MEDICINE

There has been an explosion of knowledge in human genetics and genetic diseases in the past decade, which will increasingly influence prevention, treatment and cures for diseases. SickKids has been a leader in this research, and will continue to focus on the identification of genes and genomic variants impacting on child health, the translation of genetic findings into clinical diagnostic tests, the development of novel therapies based on these findings and the evaluation of the efficacy and social impact of new genetic tests and therapies.

CANCER & STEM CELL BIOLOGY

Despite enormous advances in the past 20 years, cancer is the most common cause of disease-related death in children. SickKids is the largest childhood cancer treatment centre in Canada and a major contributor to international paediatric clinical trials. SickKids researchers leading studies in cancer stem cells are poised to identify new predictors and are working to develop innovative therapies.

MOLECULES, CELLS & THERAPIES

SickKids is uniquely placed to identify new targets for therapeutic interventions in disease that begin in childhood and affect adult life, developing new molecular therapies and carrying them through to clinical impact. An interdisciplinary approach unites researchers in the development of an innovative pipeline approach to target discovery and drug development for childhood diseases.

Text and images on pages 19 and 20 courtesy of Diamond Schmitt Architects Inc.

PLANNING, DESIGN AND CONSTRUCTION IMPROVEMENT PROCESS
Session introduction

This session reveals that the common goal of those involved in designing healthcare buildings worldwide is to improve the process of planning, designing and constructing healthcare facilities in order to provide the best care to the greatest number of people at the lowest possible cost. To achieve this objective it is necessary to put in place a series of measures to improve not only the design of individual buildings but also the whole system of buildings and relationships that affect the delivery of care.

To improve all phases in the construction of healthcare buildings, the body of knowledge developed by designers over the course of their professional experience should be made available to decision makers so they have the tools with which to ponder the best choices to make in order to produce long-term benefits. Planning is the most critical phase as it is here that the choices can be more affected by contingent aspects such as the search for political consensus or the availability or lack of funds.

By reading the articles it is clear that research and the education of professionals should be strengthened through the establishment of post-graduate courses in healthcare design and the development of research activities related to this specific topic. Professionals should be trained to acquire a more detailed view of the problem and adopt a systematic methodology aimed at improving the design process and user involvement. The research should provide new tools to improve the planning of healthcare facilities.

The process of designing healthcare buildings should be improved by working on procurement procedures that can reduce the time between the decision to construct and the effective use of the building. Collaboration between different professionals is an important part of the improvement process and can be facilitated through the use of technological supports that allow the rapid sharing of information and connections between people involved in the design even when they are located in different parts of the world.

In this scenario, communication plays a key role not only in facilitating the necessary relationships between professionals in the design phase but also in identifying user needs. Due to the globalization of the market the most advanced prefabricated technologies can be moved or manufactured in emerging countries to create state-of-the-art healthcare facilities. On the other hand, due to the ease of communication and transport, facilities of excellence can be accessed from anywhere in the globe. Where different cultures meet, user involvement becomes essential to determine the current needs and find appropriate answers to different care demands.

In conclusion, preparation for the future includes research and education, the creation of platforms for sharing knowledge, and the creation of centres of research excellence in the implementation of study programs relating to the planning and design of social and healthcare facilities aimed at improving expertise and knowledge resources for planners and decision makers. Improvement is possible where professionals can acquire a specialist vision of healthcare design coupled with a comprehensive picture of the hospital's relationship with the community and market.

Master Plans and Target Planning to Avoid Wrong Investments in Healthcare

Eggert U.[1], Eggert-Muff G.[2], Meyer A.[3]

u.eggert@iod-aep.de

[1] Institute of Development for Infrastructure and Healthcare, Owner, Stuttgart, Germany
[2] Architekten Eggert und Partner GmbH, Partner, Stuttgart, Germany
[3] Institute of Development for Infrastructure and Healthcare, Consultant, Stuttgart, Germany

Significant cost savings can be achieved for hospital campuses with careful target planning. The Institute of Development for Infrastructure and Healthcare (IOD) has selected five case studies to demonstrate examples and the importance of masterplanning and target planning:

1. Project with master plans since 1865: Hotel Dieu De Paris, France;
2. Project with master plans since 1926: Lorenz-Ring University Hospital, Freiburg, Germany;
3. Project without master plans since 1820: Katharinen Hospital, Stuttgart, Germany;
4. Project with master plans since 1995: Friedrich-Schiller-University Clinic, Jena, Germany;
5. Project with master plans since 1991: Virngrund Clinic, Ellwangen, Germany.

The aim of this paper is to provide an understanding of the importance of masterplanning on healthcare campuses for long term cost-efficiency (low cost per capita), and the negative implications if masterplanning is neglected. It will provide an awareness of the need to set up master plans and target plans, and how to continue and update them at certain stages. Only in this way can wrong investments be avoided. The overall aim of such plans is to minimize the costs of the healthcare system in the long run.

Keywords: *healthcare masterplanning, target planning, hospital campus development*

HISTORICAL DEVELOPMENT OF NURSING AND MEDICAL SCIENCE

The spread of medical science started in Greece around 300 BC. It derived from theories developed in 1000-500 BC in Baghdad and gradually spread to Asia Minor. It reached Monte Casino and from there Central Europe around 1000 AD (Curschmann H., Annette Nicolas-Benduski A.) (Figure 1).

HÔSPITAL HÔTEL-DIEU, PARIS

Juxtaposition of Today's Aerial Photograph and the Old Masterplan from 1865

The old Hôtel Dieu was entirely demolished and replaced by a significantly larger new building. Prior to that, several master plans had been developed but aborted.

TESIS Inter-University Research Centre "Systems and Technologies for Social and Healthcare Facilities"
University of Florence, Italy

TESIS

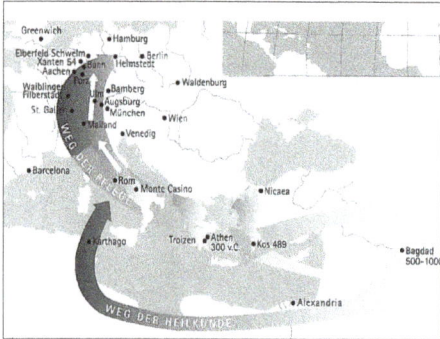

Figure 1. Central Europe over 2300 years. © Dr. Curschmann, H., Berlin.

26

The first modern master plan of the Hôtel Dieu de Paris from 1865 is impressive. At present the complex stands on the Ile de la Cité, at right angles to Notre Dame (Figure 2).

Hôtel Dieu now shows an impressive expanded development structure and its external appearance reveals a longstanding building arrangement (Figure 3).

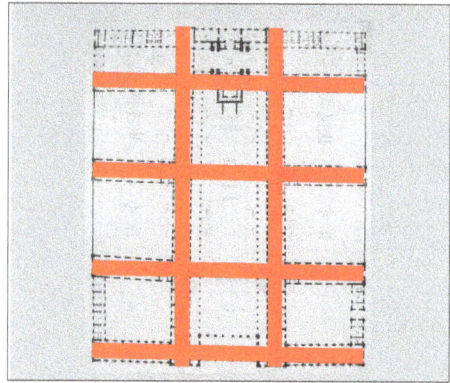

Figure 2. Juxtaposition of today's aerial photograph and the first master plan from 1865. Sources: Google Maps. Assistance Publique-Hôpitaux de Paris.

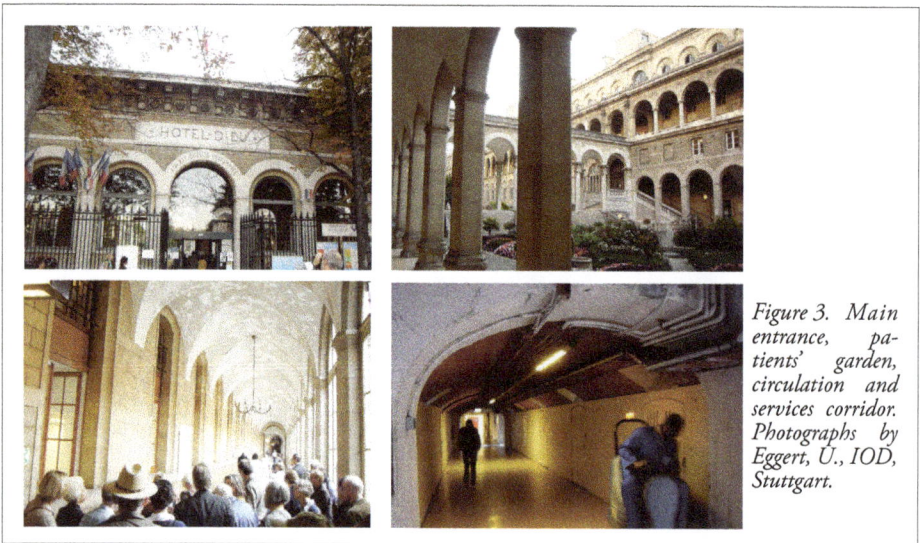

Figure 3. Main entrance, patients' garden, circulation and services corridor. Photographs by Eggert, U., IOD, Stuttgart.

Master Plan Update (1980)

It is remarkable how this master plan is still consistent today. The update of the master plan in 1980 contains only minor changes (Figure 4).

The new operating theatres were added underneath the patients' garden (Figure 5, above). The external view shows the characteristics of the building interlocking with the blocks and courtyards of the city. It is wonderful to see the generous distances between the building wings (Figure 5, below).

LORENZRING UNIVERSITY-CLINIC, FREIBURG

1st Master Plan (1920s) and 2nd Master Plan (1960s)

Freiburg's chief town planner Lorenz was commissioned in the 1920s to create a master plan for the hospital. The hospital largely survived the Second World War. The spacious ring system proved to be efficient and sustainable for later developments. With the continuation of the master plan in the 1960s the first part of the head clinic for ENT and eyes was added (Figure 6).

3rd Master Plan (1987)

In 1987 the first architectural competition for the completion of the head clinics was announced by the county's building authority. The advocate for this tender was Prof. Architect M. D. Fecker, head of the building department at the Ministry of Finance in Baden-Wüerttemberg. The 1st prize (Figure 7) was awarded to the architects Gerhard

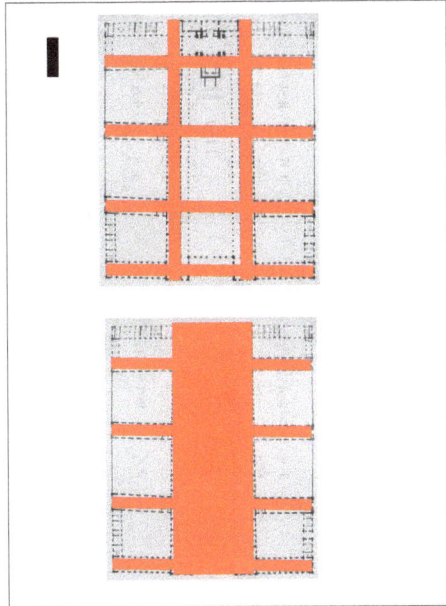

Figure 4.   1st master plan from 1865 and 2nd master plan from 1980. Source: Assistance Publique-Hôpitaux de Paris, illustrated by IOD.

Figure 5.   Patients' garden above the operating theatres and external view. Photographs by Eggert, U., IOD, Stuttgart.

27

28

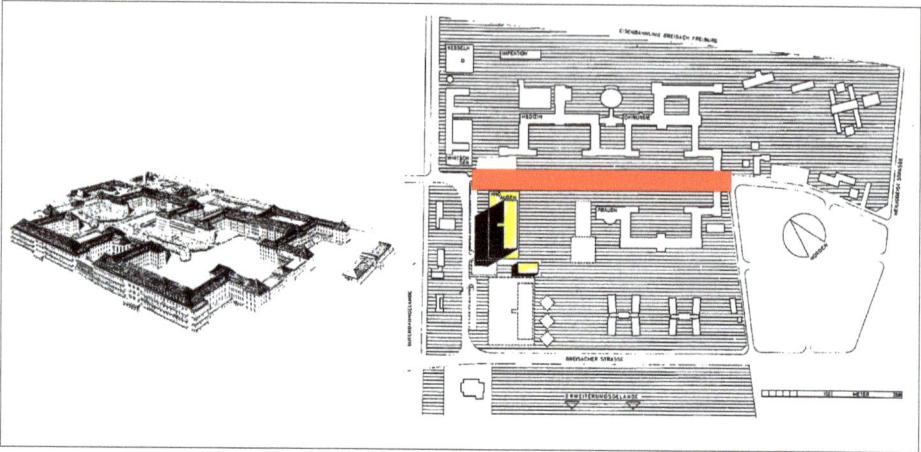

Figure 6. 1st master plan from the 1920s and 2nd master plan from the 1960s. Sources (left): University Clinic, Freiburg. Source (right): University Clinic, Freiburg, incl. illustration by authors.

Laage and Uwe Eggert. The clinic was to accommodate neurology, neuro-surgery, stereotactic surgery, diagnostic radiology, radiology, neuropathology and institutes for students. At the same time it was to be independent from its outpatient department. A bridge connection was suggested to enable communication between the new ENT department and the old ENT clinic above ground and also underground by AGV.

4th Master Plan (1994)

The opening of the project towards Hugstetter Street with its spacious entrance to the university hospital was a crucial contribution. The 1994 site plan by the building authority of Freiburg (Figure 8) left plenty of space for a generous main entrance, providing a new dimension to the Lorenz-ring. It opened up and enlarged the campus to the south. The construction of the neuroscience centre was awarded in 1996 by the Senate of Berlin.

Figure 7. 3rd master plan from 1987 and its integrated routing of services. Sources: AEP / Laage.

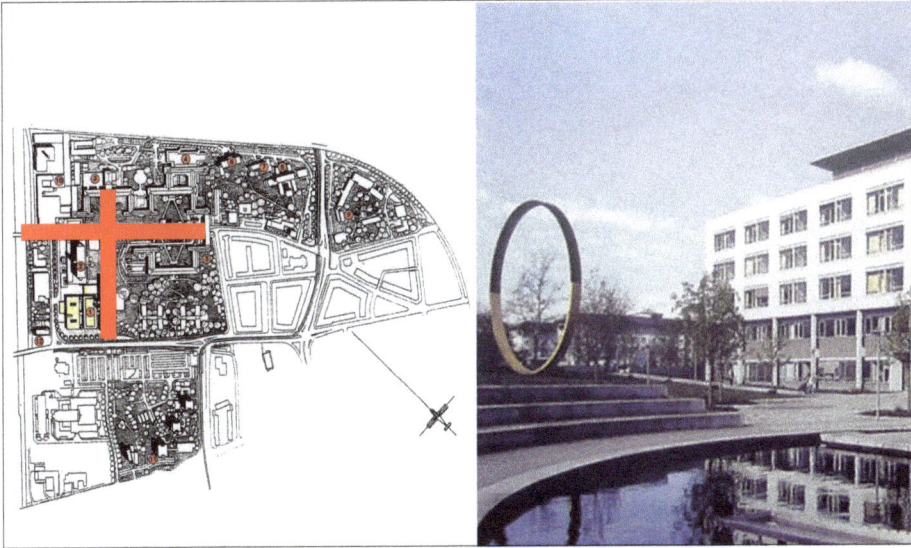

Figure 8. 4ᵗʰ master plan from 1994 with a view of the neuroscience centre. Source (left): AEP / Laage. Source (right): University Clinic, Freiburg

29

Summary and Findings of the Campus Development

The recognizable scheme of the Lorenz-Ring with its meandering landscape and central-axis is impressive. The opening of the ring creates open spaces for further specialist clinics and institutes so that several medical functions could be seamlessly integrated within the ring. The supply of the various clinics is facilitated by the AGV rail system in the underground level.

KATHARINEN HOSPITAL, STUTTGART

Queen Katharina von Württemberg founded the clinic in 1820. Following its construction, in the years 1820-28 the Katharinen Hospital was altered and extended several times.

Replacement Buildings of the Original Katharinen Hospital (1955)

Following the city council's visit to Sweden in the 1950s, Prof. Architect Döcker extended the hospital to approximately 1000 beds (Figure 9). The city's own hospitals, however, had a problem. Several hospital sites owned by the city co-existed, and each had its own history. At the beginning of the 1970s the desire was to unite all these hospitals to form a university clinic in Stuttgart Bad Cannstatt.

The senior planning officer Fahrenholtz (from Hamburg) was the initiator. Fahrenholtz was not re-elected and thus a potential master plan was overturned for the site in Stuttgart Bad Cannstatt.

30

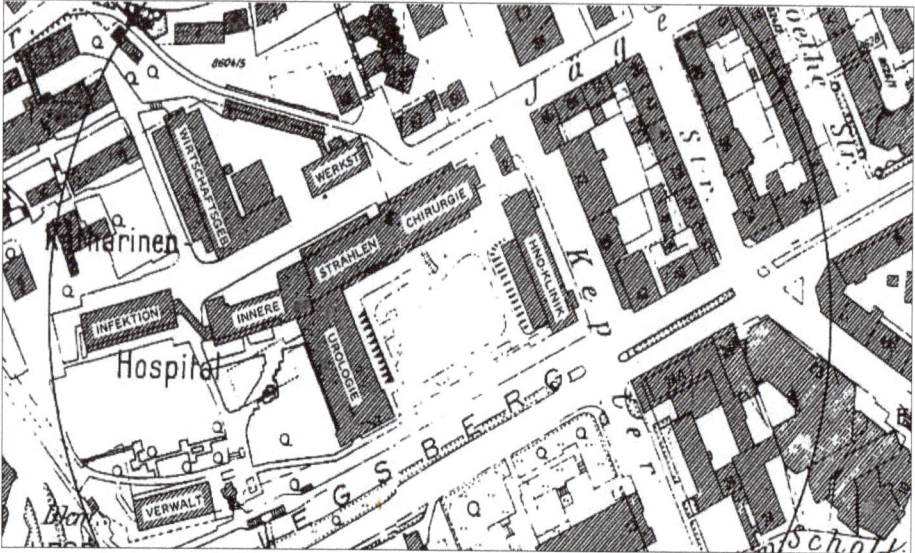

Figure 9. Replacement buildings from 1955 for the original Katharinen Hospital. Source: City of Stuttgart.

2nd Large Expansion by Architectural Competition (1984 – 1992)

The second large expansion between 1984 and 1992 was again tendered without a prior master plan. The architectural competition, tendered in 1984, focused on only a part of the site covering a net area of 11,500 sq m: the 1st prize went to the architecture firm Heinle & Wischer (Figure 10). The main focus of the brief was:

1. essential operational units for diagnostics and therapy;

2. a new main entrance for the entire complex;

3. a neurosurgical clinic with 44 beds, 24 intensive care beds and 24 intensive therapy beds;

4. various other functions and administration areas.

All functions were to be connected to their respective operational areas in the old building. The result could only be a patchwork.

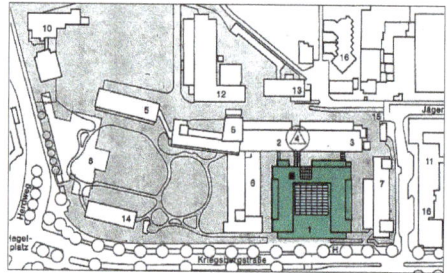

Figure 10. 2nd large expansion at the main entrance, by Heinle Wischer Architekten. Source: City of Stuttgart.

Figure 11. Generous main entrance hall. Source: City of Stuttgart.

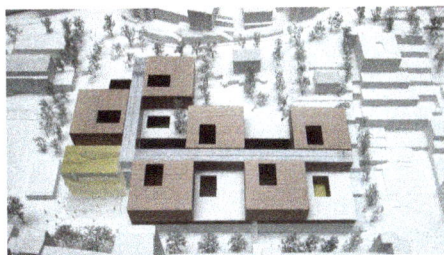

31

Figure 12. Mother & Child Centre by Sorg & Frosch + HPP. (left), and subsequent site investigation (right). Source: wettbewerbe aktuell, Stuttgarter Zeitung.

Generous Entrance Atrium (1992)

The prize-winning design by Heinle & Wischer (Figure 9) suggested a convincing main entrance building, called the "Katharinenhof" (Figure 11), although at the wrong location. The main entrance lies asymmetrically within the entire site and is far too low in relation to the surrounding buildings as a result of the brief. The architects were bound by the brief and cannot be held responsible for the result.

Further Expansion and Site Investigation (2004)

In May 2004 a further architectural competition for the Mother-Child Centre, the Olgäle, was won by architects HPP and Laage. Only few months later, in Decem-

ber 2004, a site investigation was filed after the architectural competition had been decided, see the article from the Stuttgarter Zeitung (Figure 16, above). Here further new plans were announced such as:

1. a new head centre – existing buildings date from 1991, see 2nd extension;
2. an internal medicine centre;
3. a surgical centre;
4. a new heart centre as a replacement for the old Sana site;
5. a new mental health centre.

The request by the county's architecture forum to tender an urban design competition was answered as follows:
"We do not consider an urban design competition necessary given the result elaborated so far." (source: letter from the mayor Dr. Wolfgang Schuster to Mr U. Eggert of the Architektur-Forum Baden-Württemberg).

Master Plan by AEP as an Additional Part of the Competition Entry

Several options in a master plan or targeted planning bring unforeseen qualities that have not been thought of before. An example of this is the master plan by AEP from May 2004 (Figures 12 and 13) which was prepared prior to the city's site investigation and foresaw:

1. the utilization of the entire site with all the clinics and functional locations (Figure 12, left);

2. optical features, e.g. wayfinding aides, such as the Vineyard Hill (Figure 13) and the urban link with the city's park (Figure 12, left);

3. a central entrance for lying-down patients in all clinics (Figure 12, right).

These qualities are today irrevocably lost.

3ʳᵈ enlargement by framework, abandoning the site investigation (2005)

In 2005 the municipal council decided to modernize the clinic of Stuttgart, as detailed in the "structural framework" (Figure 15). It envisages the concentration of the clinic onto the two sites Stuttgart Centre and Bad Cannstatt.

The modernization should be complete by 2016 (Source: City of Stuttgart). Having decided to leave and expand the Sana heart centre at its current location, the municipal council combined the head centre with the mental health centre: "There is now simply no space left for a separate head centre" (Stuttgarter Zeitung, 2005).

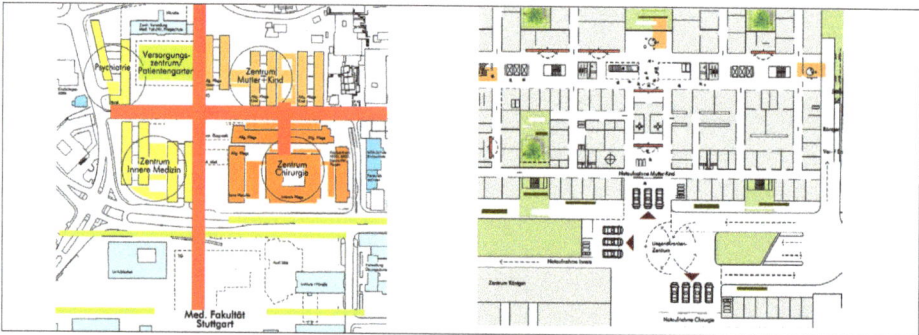

Figure 13. The master plan suggested by AEP (left) provides a single A&E entrance for 3 buildings (right). Source: AEP (2004).

Figure 14. Artist's view of the main entrance to the paediatric clinic, as suggested by AEP. Source: AEP (2004).

In 2010 a new architectural competition was tendered for internal medicine and a surgical medicine centre. The brief covered a total net area of 39,000 sq m and specified restructuring with 40% for conversion and rehabilitation, and 60% for a new built area.

The architects Arcass won first prize (Figure 15, below). It was decided to use the remaining area between the heart centre and the old ENT building by keeping the old west wing. This meant that it was not possible to achieve an urban vista between Vineyard Hill and the city's garden, and the large investment of the Olgäle children's hospital was therefore relegated to the backyard.

Demolition of the Main Entrance by Heinle & Wischer

The current planning status was summarized by the Stuttgarter Zeitung (Figure 16): "as a last step the Katharinenhof can be demolished and also replaced by a new building by 2022." The building, which was only commissioned in 1991 and served as a main entrance and prime address for the Central Stuttgart site, will now be demolished. This is the result of a lack of masterplanning and target planning.

33

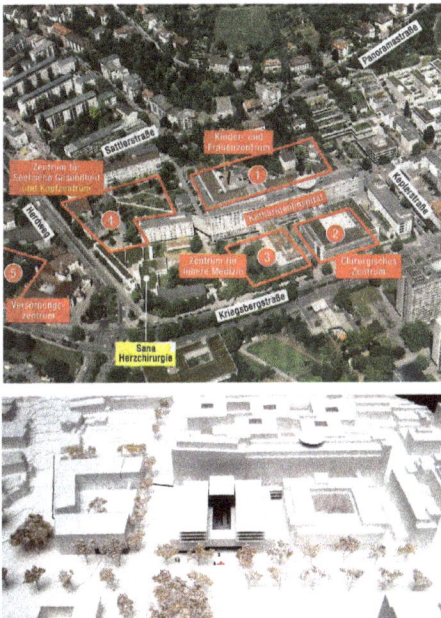

Figure 15. New proposal (above), abandoning the site investigation, and 3rd enlargement (below) by Arcass. Source: Stuttgarter Zeitung, wettbewerbe aktuell.

Figure 16. Press article making the demolition official and new main entrance subject to demolition. Source: Stuttgarter Zeitung (2012).

34

Figure 17. Urban planning competition site in 1995. Source: wettbewerbe aktuell (1996).

THE FRIEDRICH-SCHILLER-UNIVERSITY CLINIC, JENA

Urban Planning Competition (1995)

The first measure was an urban planning concept competition, with the construction part carried out in a second stage, for the Friedrich-Schiller-University Clinic in Jena, Germany.

This was the progressive thinking of the client and it delivered good results. The clinic's situation was studied and examined within its urban context. A framework was developed as a basis for the second stage construction competition. The task was to bring together six clinic sites. For the extension of the medical facility, the site of the internal medicine clinic in Jena-Lobeda emerged as the appropriate location, measuring 31 ha in total, of which 11 ha are a landscape conservation area.

The brief called for a clinic with a 133,000 sq m net usable area, to be realized in 4 phases. The first and largest phase was to be completed in eight to ten years. The further phases were to follow in two-year steps.

Once completed the clinic would provide 1,350 beds, with the first phase providing 980. Five architect's entries (Figure 18) were shortlisted in part one of the competition:

- Dr. Worscheck und Partner, Erfurt;
- Koch und Partner, Munich / Leipzig;
- HPP Hentrich-Petschnigg u. Partner, Leipzig;
- Prof. Gerber und Partner, Dortmund;
- AEP Eggert und Partner, Stuttgart.

Master Plan Competition Entry by AEP (1996)

The entry by AEP shows the urban integration of the University of Jena, the residential quarter Lobeda, and the clinic (Figure 19). The solution integrated a traffic system with the shared park and ride system.

Master plan by Dr. Worschech und Partner, Erfurt, as built

The entry chosen came Dr. Worscheck, later cooperating with HWP (Figure 20).

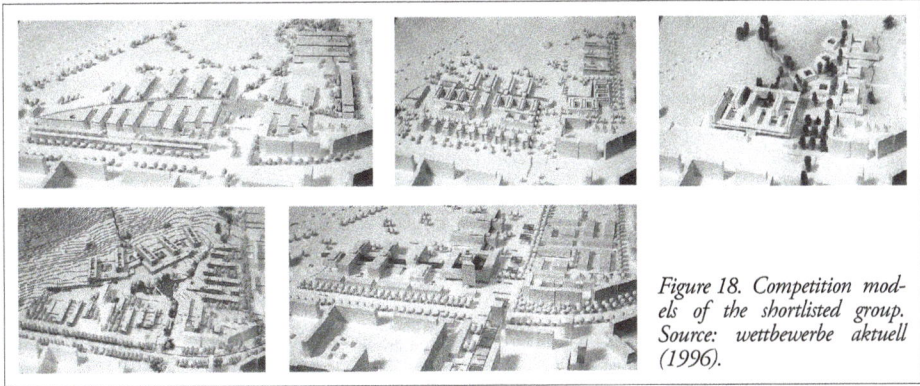

Figure 18. Competition models of the shortlisted group. Source: wettbewerbe aktuell (1996).

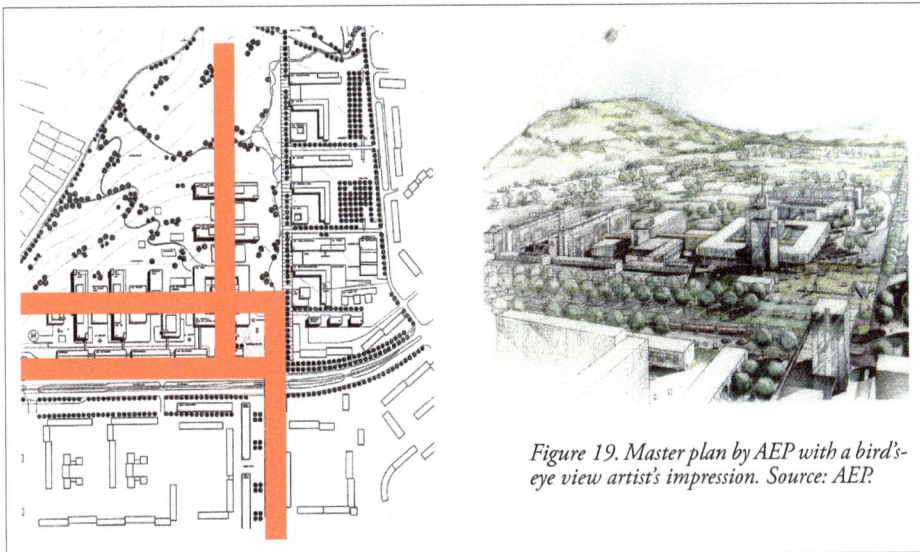

Figure 19. Master plan by AEP with a bird's-eye view artist's impression. Source: AEP.

Figure 20. Aerial photograph as built today by Dr. Worschech und Partner with HWP. Source: Google Maps (2013).

VIRNGRUND CLINIC, ELLWANGEN

Existing Situation (1990)

In 1991 a limited architectural competition was tendered for the rehabilitation and extension of the General Hospital Ellwangen (Figure 21). The commission went to the architects Eggert+Partner (today AEP). The architects' idea was a clinic with a main axis running north-south, to which all individual buildings and functions would be connected and which would create a central main entrance (Figure 21, above). With this the basis for a master plan was set up, although only an architectural competition was tendered.

The brief asked for the retention of the individual ward blocks with the installation of new sanitary units for each bedroom. The new build included an intensive care department, psychiatry, as well as a café and technical areas. Attention had to be paid to the underground vaults under Dalking Street and the site for the new clinic buildings. During the Second World War these were used as shelters and underground military hospitals, but also as a basement for a brewery for storing ice, beer and bottling.

1st Master Plan, 1st Prize by AEP

Providing appropriate access for lying-down patients, visitors, ambulances, deliveries, pathology and central storage was one of the most important criteria. The existing parking spaces along Dalkinger Street/Garden Street were to be extended as two-level parking to minimize further ground sealing on the clinic site.

The basis for the first phase was target planning and the brief approved by the Social Ministry. The clinic's circulation axis was newly created from the north to the main entrance across levels 1 to 5. All new facilities are located alongside it. The entrance hall was designed as light-flooded centre point with open staircases and three lifts to all levels. Its large glass walls open it up to the patient garden to the west and the city of Ellwangen to the southeast. The prayer room with vestry was newly designed at the entrance level. A new recovery room and the anaesthesia department were positioned on level 5, on same level as the existing operating theatres.

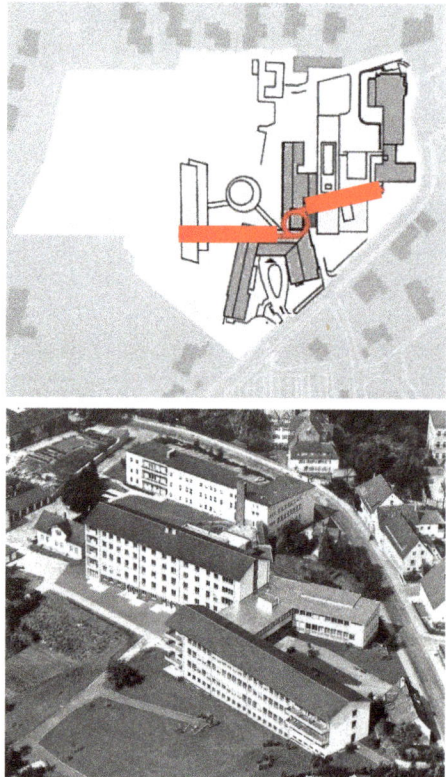

Figure 21. Existing situation and 1st masterplan (1st prize by AEP). Sources: Vierngrund Clinic.

1st Phase (1996 – 1999)

A new longitudinal building was created between the old surgery and the urology building (Figure 22). It was connected to the existing buildings on the lower levels by the new clinic's main axis: level 0 (technical spaces), level 1 (technical spaces), level 2 (pathology, changing rooms, central storage), and level 3 (ambulances). Ambulances for surgery and internal medicine were planned on level 3. Levels 4 and 5 respectively accommodate the intensive care department and laboratories, and conferences.

2nd Master Plan by AEP, 2nd Phase (2002 – 2003)

Due to new considerations by the Social Ministry the parameters from the 1st target planning changed. Instead of having the psychiatry department in an east-west orientation a new adult psychiatry department with 45 beds and an additional children's and youth psychiatry department with 20 beds were required. With the 2nd target planning, AEP developed a new main axis for the clinic (Figure 23), and the second phase for the psychiatry department had to be re-developed due to spatial, functional and site specific reasons. The result was two trapezoidal buildings along the southern axis, linked to the clinic across all levels. Both buildings have their individual external spaces.

3rd Phase (2004 – 2008)

Due to new requests from the client the previous idea to re-use the old operating theatre building as a maternity unit was abandoned. AEP subsequently prepared several options for the clients, the Higher Finance Directorate and the Social Ministry. The surgical ward with maternity unit was united with the remaining diagnostics and therapy units in the surgical ward (Figure 24).

The first section of the third phase is comprised of an 8-storey ward, operational specialist areas and delivery rooms. The second section is comprised of the administration building and entrance hall. By merging the St. Anna Clinic with the Virngrund Clinic the original scope of the brief was enlarged by 40 beds, 3 delivery rooms, 1 emergency autopsy room as well as several examination and doctors' rooms.

37

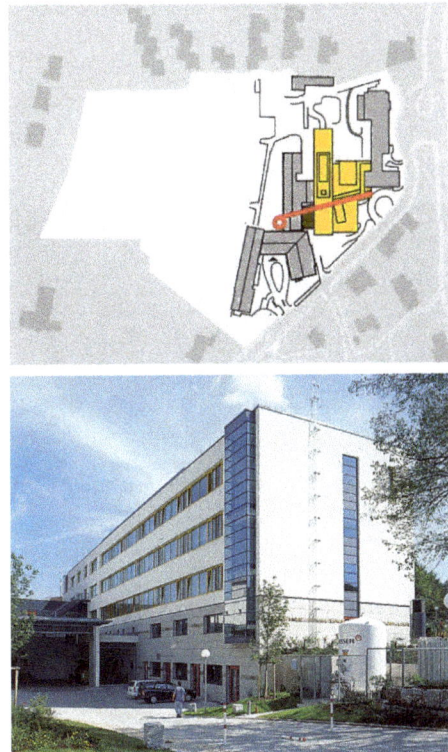

Figure 22. 1st phase and external view of nursing wards with offices, supplies and waste facilities. Source: AEP (2012).

38

A helideck was designed but not constructed. Research conducted by AEP showed that the clinic in Aalen could accommodate such a function. The old surgery building was demolished. The cleared site allowed the target plan to be pursued further. Larger wards and site boundaries resulted in a building shape that opens up to the west and allows a dual-corridor system in the rear part of the building.

The adult psychiatry department served as an interim building during the third construction phase and was used as a ward for the surgical unit, as well as during the fourth construction phase when it was used as a ward for internal medicine.

The second section of the third ded the target to create a direct link in the fourth phase with the east-west and north-south axis as well as with the main entrance hall (Figure 25). The old department of Internal Medicine, a building from the 1950s, was demolished. Pre-examinations showed that preservation with the extension and fit out of the sanitary units was not economically viable.

On the cleared site a new ward was created with 72 beds on levels 6 and 7, with 1-bed, 2-bed and 4-bed rooms. Specialist facilities such as physical therapy moved to level 5. For the entrance level AEP suggested suggested the client let spaces for ambulances. This was well received.

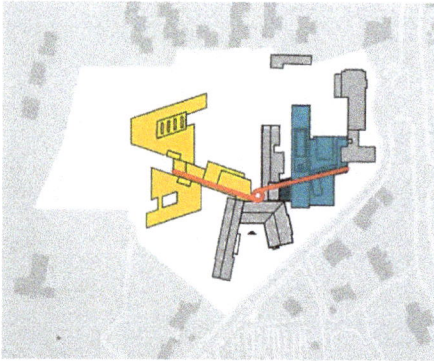

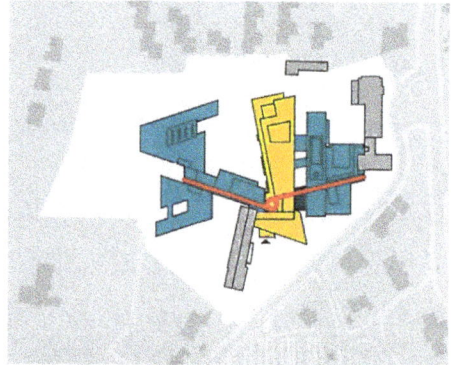

Figure 23. 2ⁿᵈ master plan by AEP, 2ⁿᵈ phase. Aerial view of the new psychiatry department. Source: AEP (2012).

Figure 24. 3ʳᵈ phase. Aerial view of the theatres, wards, delivery areas, diagnostics, administration and teaching. Source: AEP (2012).

Summary and Findings of the Project Development (1990 – 2012)

With a development time of 21 years, an entirely new clinical complex was developed at the site of the former district hospital Ellwangen: the St. Anna Virngrund Clinic with a total volume of 157,550 m3. Planning with cost-efficient materials without compromising on quality or the safety of the building was the top priority for the architects. Almost 50% of the costs were allocated to technical areas, which will have a positive effect on operating costs in the future.

The three target plans from the years 1991/2000 and 2004 could be realized entirely in functional terms. With the help of timely new target plans (and resulting master plans) interim costs could be kept to a minimum. New buildings and sections were not demolished. Instead, for instance, the old glass windows from the old vestry were saved and re-used in the entrance hall. The development cycle looked like this:

1. the idea for a master plan came from AEP;
2. talks were held with the owner and the Social Ministry was involved;
3. the situation was explained;
4. the new master plan was obtained;
5. sometimes additional money was given for its implementation;
6. this led to the next commission.

CONCLUSIONS

Historic hospitals, e.g. the Hôtel Dieu in Paris, are concrete evidence of successful master plans. In addition they are often valuable urban structures. This should be a reminder for today's decision makers in current hospital developments.

Individual planners and mayors want to build themselves a 'memorial' of their own short term in office in order to be remembered in the future as investors in useful infrastructure. This ego-driven and short-term thinking often has the opposite effect as these buildings don't respond to long-term demands. Hence they will need to make way for costly new buildings or significant redevelopments, and the incapability of the original planners is blamed.

Producing a master plan need not be an expensive feat, especially in relation to the long-term cost savings for smart campus developments. This is of particular interest to society when public money is involved.

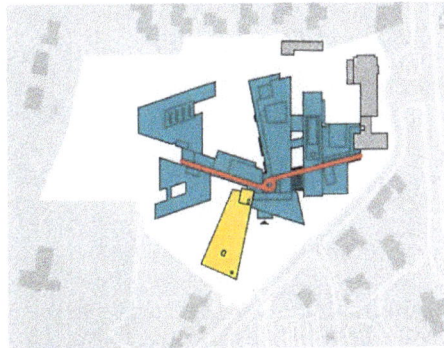

Figure 25. 3rd master plan by AEP, 4th phase. Aerial view of wards, physiotherapy, medical shopping mall. Source: AEP (2012).

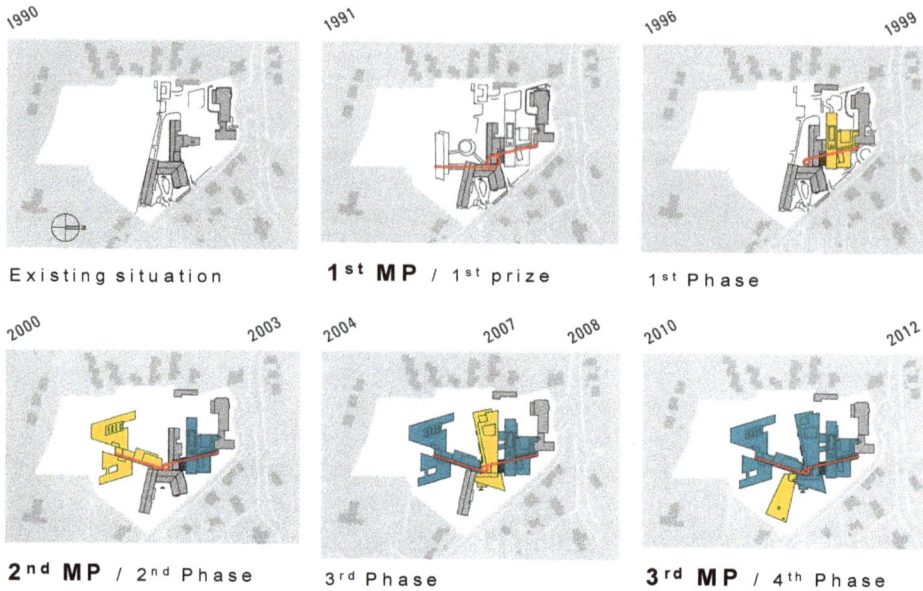

Figure 26. Overview of master plans and phases. Source: AEP (2012).

Further investigation should be done on how to initiate master plans. The authors have experience in being the initiators as architects, but they cannot be everywhere. The difficult part is triggering the process of producing a master plan on the client's side early on in a project phase, and communicating the long-term benefits. Master plans are beneficial for all stakeholders, except demolition companies.

REFERENCES

AEP Architekten Eggert Generalplaner GmbH, (2004). *Wettbewerbsbeitrag Mutter Kind Zentrum Stuttgart.* Stuttgart.

AEP Architekten Eggert Generalplaner GmbH, (2012). *Phasendiagramm Klinik Ellwangen.* Stuttgart.

Google Maps (2013), https://maps.google.com, 2013.

Senatsverwaltung für Bauen, Wohnen und Verkehr (1999). Wege der Pflege und Heilkunde nach Mitteleuropa und betrachtete Krankenhausstandorte. In Curschmann H., Nicolas-Benduski A., *Krankenhäuser für Berlin Historische Entwicklung der Krankenhäuser.* Berlin: Senatsverwaltung für Bauen, Wohnen und Verkehr, 3/1999.

Stuttgarter Zeitung, (2005). Nr. 274. 26.11.2005. Stuttgart: Stuttgarter Zeitung Verlagsgesellschaft mbH.

Stuttgarter Zeitung. Bury M., (2012). *Am Klinikum wird noch bis 2022 gebaut.* Nr. 143. 23.06.2012. Stuttgart: Stuttgarter Zeitung Verlagsgesellschaft mbH.

Wettbewerbe Aktuell (1996). *Neubau Klinikum 2000 der Friedrich-Schiller-Universität Jena.* Freiburg: Wettbewerbe Aktuell Verlagsgesellschaft mbH. 1/1996.

Planning and Procuring Today's Hospitals for Tomorrow's Needs

Nedin P.[1], Wood K.[2]

Katie.Wood@arup.com
[1]Ove Arup and Partners Ltd., United Kingdom
[2]Arup Canada Inc.

This paper reviews the drivers in healthcare that will require change in hospital design. These include the changing disease burden, the needs of the patient of the future, the home as the new hospital department and the pressures placed on the individual to remain unhealthy! The paper will then identify the key areas where hospitals being planned and procured today must respond in order to provide value for money over the long term. It will consider these requirements in the context of PPP procurement and identify a series of lessons learnt from Arup's global experience.

INTRODUCTION TO ARUP

Arup is an independent firm of designers, planners, engineers, consultants and technical specialists offering a broad range of professional services. The firm has 90 offices in 37 countries and over 11,000 staff worldwide. The firm has delivered a wide range of healthcare projects across 160 countries. Arup's independence means a proportion of the profits can be reinvested into research including a series of healthcare design topics.

TOMORROW'S HEALTHCARE

There are a wide range of drivers which means that healthcare will continue to change at a fast pace. The following themes were explored:
– Shift in approach to healthcare delivery;
– Rising cost of the delivery of healthcare services;
– Changing patient expectations;
– The needs of elderly patients;
– Public health and chronic illness;
– Rapidly changing technology;
– How hospitals can respond.
Long-term value for money for hospitals was explored under three main themes:
– Supporting good health outcomes;
– Flexibility;
– Operational efficiency.

Significant change is ahead, some of which can be predicted and much that cannot. The life of the primary systems of a hospital can be expected to be at least 50 years.

Designing only for current needs could result in sub-optimal value for money over the life of the building.

Three case studies concerned the achievement of long-term value for money for health services through the Public Private Partnership mechanism. In each case, Arup acted as the government's advisor and was therefore involved in the development of the requirements around long-term value.

Figure 1. Arup: 90 offices in 37 countries.

42

Figure 2. Altnagelvin Hospital clinical block, Northern Ireland.

Figure 3. Ysbyty Aneurin Bevan. South Wales, UK.

Figure 4. Richard Desmond Children's Eye Centre in Moorfields Eye Hospital, London.

Figure 5. Basildon Cardiothoracic Hospital, Essex UK.

Figure 6. Medicover Hospital, Poland.

Figure 7. Alfred ICU, Melbourne, Australia.

Figure 8. Kenema Clinic, Sierra Leone.

Figure 9. Hospital Del Norte, Madrid.

Figure 10. Pembury Hospital, Kent, UK.

Figure 11. St Helens PFI Hospital, UK.

Figure 12. OASTSIH, Australia

Figure 13. Kaiser – Antioch, USA.

In conclusion, Arup sets out its recommendations for the process of planning, designing and procuring hospitals for the future. A sustainable approach means balanced consideration of:
– Whole-life costing;
– Future needs;
– Low carbon;
– Innovation;
– Therapeutic or healing environment.

43

Current View	Evolving Model of Care
Geared towards acute conditions	Geared towards long term conditions
Hospital-centric	Embedded in communities
Doctor-dependent	Team-based
Episodic care	Continuous care
Disjointed care	Integrated care
Reactive care	Preventative care
Patient as passive recipient	Patient as partner
Self-care infrequent	Self-care encouraged and facilitated
Carers undervalued	Carers supported as partners
Low-tech	High-tech

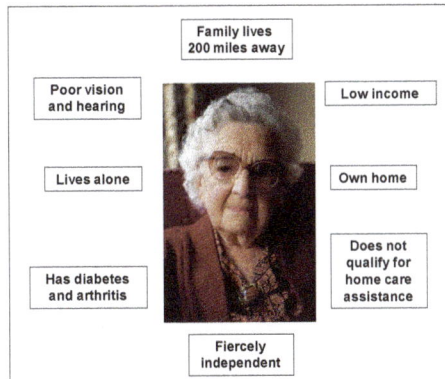

Figure 14. Caring for our elderly.

Figure 15. A shift in the approach to delivery.

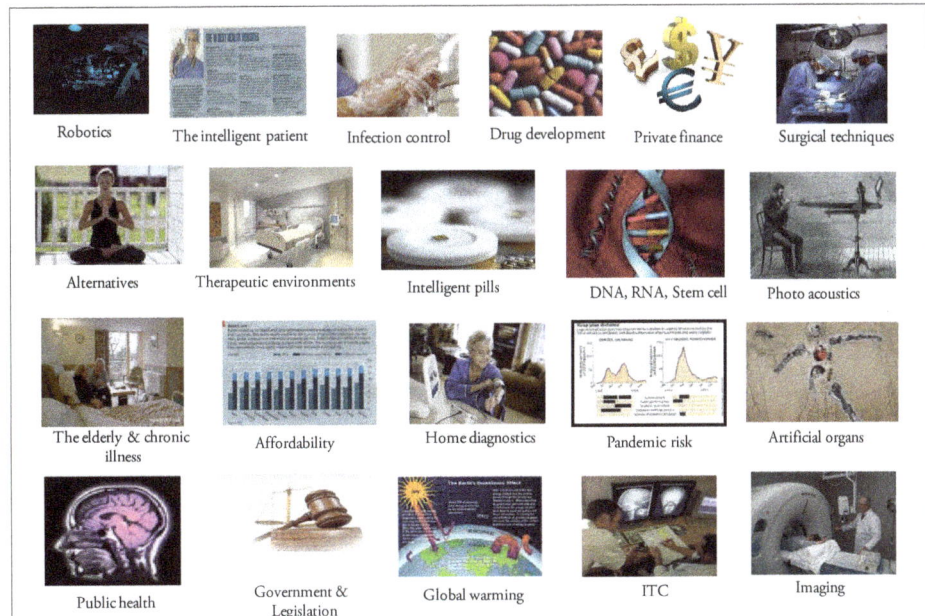

Robotics   The intelligent patient   Infection control   Drug development   Private finance   Surgical techniques

Alternatives   Therapeutic environments   Intelligent pills   DNA, RNA, Stem cell   Photo acoustics

The elderly & chronic illness   Affordability   Home diagnostics   Pandemic risk   Artificial organs

Public health   Government & Legislation   Global warming   ITC   Imaging

Figure 16. Healthcare drivers.

TESIS Inter-University Research Centre "Systems and Technologies for Social and Healthcare Facilities" University of Florence, Italy

44

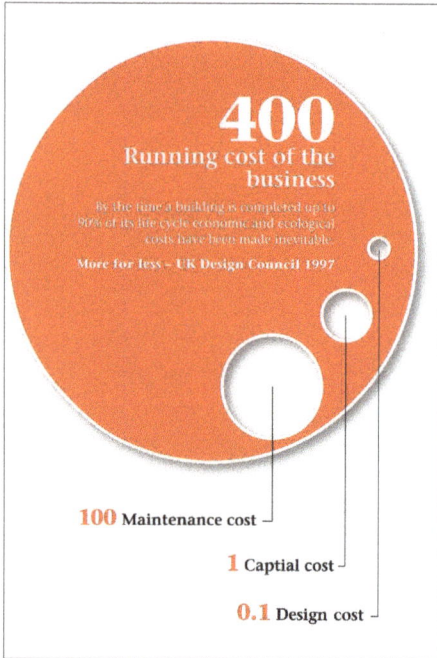

Figure 17. Long term value for money means: good health outcomes, flexibility, and operational efficiency.

The project also needs to be considered in the context of the broader health system it operates in, involving a complex set of inter-relationships.

An integrated team including the owner, staff, stakeholders, functional planners, the design team, and specialists has the best chance of achieving this.

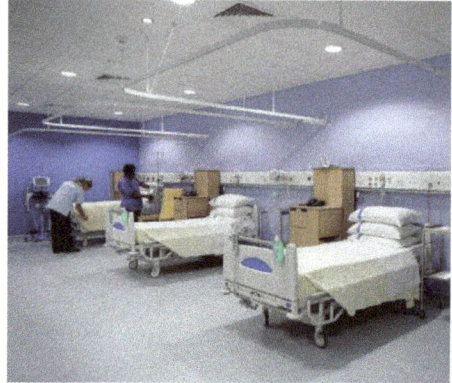

Figure 18. Example of operational efficiency: independent sector treatment centres, UK.

Figure 19. Example of operational efficiency: New Royal Adelaide Hospital, Australia.

Designing For Better Healthcare – The Singapore Perspective

Lai R.[1]

ruby.lai@cpgcorp.com.sg
[1] Senior Consultant, CPG Consultants Private Limited, Singapore

Singapore experiences similar problems to most developed countries in the world, i.e. how to provide good healthcare at a lower cost. This paper explores the various ways it tries to tackle this problem.
Singapore is a tiny island in South East Asia, with a population of less than 5.5 million. The World Health Organisation (WHO) has ranked Singapore's Healthcare system as the sixth best in the world, and Singapore's expenditure on healthcare is only four percentage of its Gross Domestic Product – which is less than a quarter of that paid by the United States, and half that paid by many Western European countries. Despite this success, the government still faces many challenges in trying to ensure affordable healthcare for everyone.
The fact is that good architecture is not enough to ensure good healthcare. A whole system must be developed in order to achieve good healthcare. From the early days of nationhood, almost fifty years ago, Singapore's government has considered healthcare development to be an integrated and inseparable part of the overall development planning for the country, and expended great efforts in providing good housing, clean water and food, unpolluted air, effective sanitation and waste disposal, and the development of parks and tree planting to enhance the environment and living conditions.

In Singapore, healthcare services are provided by both the public and private sectors. Eighty percent of outpatient services in Singapore are provided by private general practitioners, while on the other hand, eighty percent of inpatient services are provided by public hospitals.

Public hospitals in Singapore are not strictly speaking government hospitals as they were restructured almost twenty years ago. Although they are wholly-owned by the government, they are autonomous and are run like private hospitals. They are allowed to keep their income and have considerable freedom in their operations, although they are subjected to broad policy guidance by the government through the Ministry of Health. The infrastructure is fully funded by the government, then leased to the hospitals. They are managed like not-for-profit organisations and receive an annual government subvention or subsidy for the provision of subsidised medical services to the patients. They thus have the flexibility to introduce innovative and cost-effective management systems to motivate and retain good staff. Being funded by the government, they are also encouraged to concentrate on research.

SINGAPORE'S HEALTHCARE CHALLENGES

The healthcare challenges faced by Singapore are probably similar to those faced by many developed countries. The main challenges are:

1. With urbanisation and increased wealth, non-communicable diseases caused by high blood pressure, high blood glucose, physical inactivity and obesity have gained prominence.

2. Apart from the common lifestyle-related diseases, however, the advent of the Severe Acute Respiratory Syndrome (SARS) which badly affected countries like Singapore, Hong Kong and Toronto, and new emerging diseases like the Middle East respiratory syndrome coronavirus, show that communicable diseases are still a threat and cannot be ignored.

3. In addition, the aging population also brings with it new healthcare problems.

All this puts a greater strain on the healthcare services – not only on the infrastructure, but also on the healthcare manpower, and with the increased complexity the challenge of affordability is also increased.

SINGAPORE'S HEALTHCARE STRATEGIES

Singapore's strategies to overcome the problems are:

– Invest more in healthcare and research infrastructures, placing greater emphasis on design to enhance the healing process and the work environment;
– Create different types of facilities to address the different requirements of the aged;
– Increased training to up the number of professional medical and allied health staff;
– Reduce dependency by encouraging individuals to take greater responsibility and tapping on the resources of the private sector.

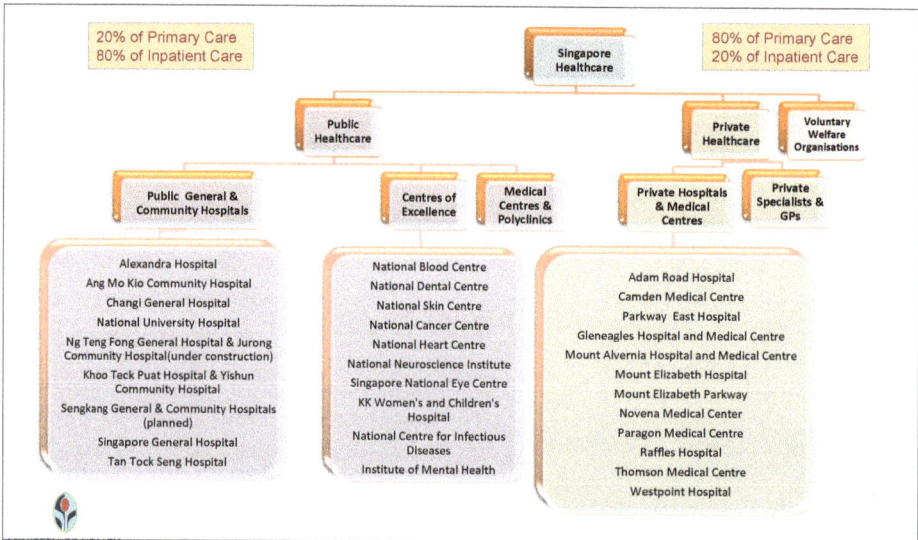

Figure 1. Singapore healthcare.

46

Strategy 1 - Enhancing Accessibility to Healthcare, with Greater Emphasis on Design

Singapore's population has increased sharply over the last ten years, largely due to the growth of the expatriate workforce – many of whom became permanent residents. The government has thus had to embark on aggressive investment in healthcare and research facilities, while paying great attention to design.

In the 1990s, most of the hospitals were rebuilt when they were restructured. In recent years, more new hospitals are being built, and by 2020 there will be an increase of over 3,700 beds including beds in community hospitals for step-down care.

An example of a recently completed hospital is the Khoo Teck Puat Hospital, an acute hospital with 550 beds. This project has won many awards for its beautiful environment and sustainable design. In Singapore, over sixty percent of the patient rooms are heavily subsidised and are cohort rooms with natural ventilation. Great care was taken in the design of the patient rooms to ensure good natural ventilation and great views of the garden and landscaped reservoir beyond.

Figure 2. Khoo Teck Puat Hospital.

Figure 3. The new Ng Teng Fong General Hospital and Jurong Community Hospital.

Another example is the Ng Teng Fong General Hospital and Jurong Community Hospital, which are currently under construction. This is the first hospital to be built where a community hospital is integrated with the acute hospital. The special feature of this hospital is that every bed is designed with a window – so even patients in the cohort rooms have their own window looking out onto landscaped planters, and have a degree of separation and privacy from each other.

The public hospital in Singapore is seen not only as a place to treat illness but also as a place for health education. The public are encouraged to come for health talks and obtain information from the learning centres within the hospital. Exhibitions are held to educate the public on health screening and healthy living.

There is ever-increasing use of sophisticated technology in modern hospitals. Public hospitals are fortunate in that the government is generous in its funding of high-tech medical equipment, thus enhancing medical diagnosis, treatment and research.

It is important to design the hospitals so that new equipment can be adopted in the future. The hospitals are designed with larger rooms, higher structural loading, and higher mechanical and electrical provisions to enable future growth.

As manpower is scarce, technology is used to enhance medical services. Integrated patient information systems are installed and can be shared between hospitals to ensure the doctor has the full medical record of the patient on hand.

47

Figure 4. *The new Ng Teng Fong General Hospital and Jurong Community Hospital.*

48

Technology can also help improve efficiency and reduce manpower. All public hospitals are equipped with automated guided vehicles to transport food and clean linen, pneumatic chute systems for the disposal of waste and dirty linen, and pneumatic tube systems for the transportation of specimens and medication.

In addition, great emphasis is placed on green technology for buildings in Singapore, and all public buildings are required to attain the Greenmark Platinum Award, which is the highest award for energy efficiency in Singapore. Careful design to enhance day lighting reduces the need for artificial lighting, and the detailed design of sun shading reduces the heat load on the air-conditioning system in Khoo Teck Puat and Ng Teng Fong General Hospitals.

In Singapore with its high urban density, most developments tend to be multi-storey and tall. It is rare for hospitals to obtain a large site with natural landscaping. The Khoo Teck Puat Hospital is eight storeys and the Ng Teng Fong General Hospital is sixteen storeys high. The hospital thus has to create its own gardens and sanctuaries on roof tops to

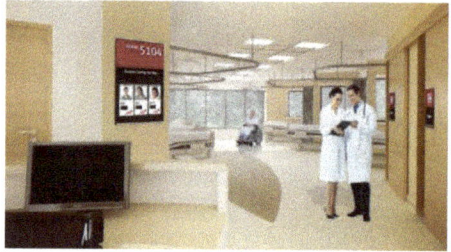

Figure 5. *Every patient has a window even in cohort wards in Ng Teng Fong General Hospital.*

Figure 6. Beautiful courtyards enhance the environment for Khoo Teck Puat Hospital.

49

Figure 7. Carefully designed sunshades cut out glare and heat for Khoo Teck Puat Hospital.

compensate for the lack of natural scenery, bringing gardens closer to the patients and staff.

Great emphasis is also placed on collaboration between clinicians and researchers to encourage translational and clinical research. Informal meeting places are designed for people to meet and congregate.

Aside from hospitals, there has also been an increase in the construction of research facilities. One example is The Academia – a recently completed research facility for the Singapore General Hospital featuring a tower for service laboratories with a Bio-safety Level 3 laboratory, and a tower for research. It also has significant areas for training, including skills laboratories and an animal vivarium. Singapore, like Toronto, was badly affected by SARS in 2003. Post SARS, all public hospitals were upgraded to add isolation wards, and their emergency departments were redesigned to separate and isolate "suspect" infectious cases. A new hospital for infectious diseases will be constructed to be completed in 2018.

Strategy 2 – Address the Needs of the Aging Population

As for most developed countries, family sizes are reducing, resulting in fewer children to look after the elderly parents. As the number of elderly patients increases, there is a reduced community capability in caring for the frail.

The healthcare needs of the elderly are different from those of younger patients. With an aging population, chronic diseases become more prevalent. There is thus greater demand for sub-acute and rehabilitative care, rather than acute hospital care. With older patients, when they get sick, their length of stay in hospital is longer – thus creating a greater demand for hospital beds. In addition, they also require a longer period for sub-acute care, which is costly if managed in an acute setting. The Community Hospital is

thus evolving to provide sub-acute care for patients. In order to ensure continuity of service for the patients, new acute hospitals are built with a community hospital attached to allow for the seamless transfer of the patient from the acute hospital to the community hospital.

For those who require longer-term care, the government is building more nursing homes which will be managed by volunteer welfare organisations, while more healthcare practitioners are being trained to provide home-based care.

The Singapore Healthcare System has thus developed into a hub and spoke system where an acute hospital is partnered with a community hospital. These are built and distributed through the Singapore island to serve about one million people per cluster. The community hospital and acute hospital will func-

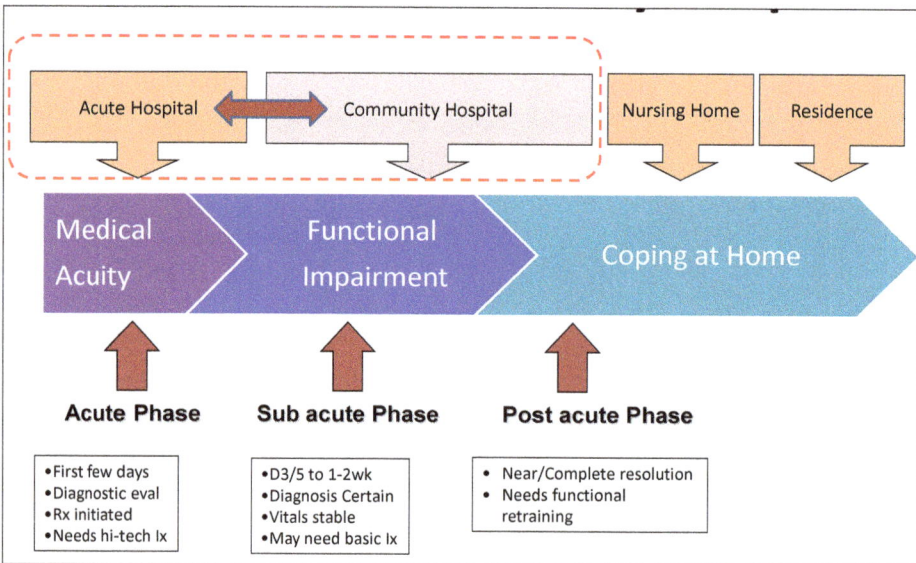

Figure 8. Evolution of a community hospital.

Figure 9. Mobility Park designed for the Jurong Community Hospital.

tion almost as one entity, and are built within the same complex, with the doctors from the acute hospital also serving the community hospital. There are to be nursing homes in the community which will have links to the community hospital and acute hospital so that if patients deteriorate they can be transferred back to the acute hospital.

The first public hospital to be built with an integrated community hospital is the 700-bed Ng Teng Fong General Hospital with the 400-bed Jurong Community Hospital which will be completed by 2014/2015. The hospital staff for both hospitals is under the Jurong Health System, and there will be a seamless transfer of patients from the acute hospital to the community hospital. While at the community hospital patients will be seen by the same doctors who were caring for them in the acute hospital. The community hospital is designed with facilities for sub-acute and step-down care with greater emphasis on rehabilitation. A mobility park is provided for rehabilitating patients to practice boarding the bus or car, and walking along footpaths.

Strategy 3 – Addressing the Needs Relating to the Greater Demand for Healthcare Staff

With the swell in hospitals and other healthcare institutions, it is necessary to increase the number of medical and allied health staff. This is achieved by upping the number of medical and allied health schools, and expanding training facilities within hospitals.

One example is the Yong Loo Lin School of Medicine which was established in the National University of Singapore (NUS) in 1905. To increase its intake, extra buildings are being constructed, providing additional education and research facilities for the students. The Centre of Translational Medicine, a 42,000 sq m laboratory and teaching facility was completed in 2011, and the MD1 building for the Faculty of Medicine, a 37,000 sq m building providing medical education, research and campus amenities, will be completed in 2014.

In addition to the Medical School at the National University of Singapore, new medical schools were introduced. One of these is the Duke-NUS Graduate Medical School. A major collaboration in Academic Medicine between Duke-NUS and Singapore Health Services (SingHealth) – the largest healthcare group in Singapore, it is Singapore's first US-style graduate-entry medical school. The key to the partnership's success is the integration of cutting-edge clinical and translational research and patient care.

Another new medical school will be the Lee Kong Chian School of Medicine. which is a collaboration between the Nanyang Technological University of Singapore and Imperial College in London.

51

52

Figure 10. Centre of Translational Medicine, NUS.

Figure 11. Duke-NUS Graduate Medical School.

Strategy 4 – Addressing the Problem of Affordability

The issue of affordability is probably one of the most difficult problems to address. Regardless of how much the government spends, people will still complain it is not enough. The government in Singapore made a conscientious decision long ago that while the state will subsidise the cost of healthcare, individuals should still bear some responsibility for their healthcare expenditure. This has become the guiding principle in the government's healthcare policies.

The government provides a tiered subsidy for healthcare expenses for Singapore citizens. This ranges from patients in the C-class wards (cohort wards with natural ventilation) who receive up to 80 percent subsidy, to those in the A-class wards who are treated as private patients and do not receive any subsidy.

The Central Provident Fund (CPF) is a comprehensive social security savings plan where it is mandatory for employees to deposit twenty percent of their salary into the CPF, and the employer deposits fifteen percent. To ensure each individual has the funds to pay for their healthcare needs, a portion of this is set aside for Medisave. Medisave will be used to pay for the individual's hospital bills, and some approved outpatient costs. As the funds in Medisave are actually the individual's savings, they tend to be careful about spending them, and will avoid unnecessary and wasteful expenditure. Singaporeans who want to stay in a higher class ward if they get hospitalised can purchase additional private insurance to complement Medisave. In addition, individuals can use funds from their Medisave account to purchase insurance under Medishield to cover catastrophic illnesses. For older Singaporeans, there is Eldershield, an affordable severe disability insurance scheme that provides insurance coverage to those who require long-term care. All Singaporeans and permanent residents who are CPF members are automatically covered under Eldershield when they turn 40 years old. Those who have insufficient Medisave to pay their medical bills can seek assistance from Medifund, an endowment fund set up by the government. Recently, the government has introduced means testing which accesses the household income of the patient so that patients from the lower income bracket will have higher subsidies.

To ensure high standards, there is keen competition between private and public hospitals. All hospitals have to publish their price lists so that patients can make an informed decision on whether to use a public or private hospital.

In recent years, due to the bed crunch in public hospitals as the population growth outstripped the provision of new public hospitals, the government has made arrangements to lease beds from private hospitals for subsidised healthcare, and to help supplement the facilities required to make up for the shortfall in public facilities. In addition, the government has established a pool of approved private general practitioners to provide subsidised outpatient services. The government also funds the construction of nursing homes which are then managed by voluntary welfare organisations. In this way, there is a good partnership between the public and private sector in the provision of healthcare services for the people.

In order to keep healthcare costs down, it is important to try to keep people healthy. People are encouraged to undergo preventive screening. There are many anti-smoking campaigns, and smoking is banned from most public areas. There is also great emphasis on keeping the elderly active and healthy. People are trained to be Health Ambassadors to promote healthy living, and activity centres are being set up for senior citizens to meet and socialize and keep active.

53

THE HEALTHCARE SCENE IN SINGAPORE

Currently there are many healthcare projects going on in Singapore, comprising acute hospitals, community hospitals, nursing homes, etc. Two parcels of land were tendered out for the development of private hospitals, and an integrated healthcare facility is under construction.

The new infrastructure will cost over 2 billion SGD (about 1.6 billion USD). This will increase accessibility to healthcare for the people. To enable a more equitable distribution of subsidies means testing is being implemented more widely so that those from the lower bracket will have greater subsidies. The government meanwhile continues to look for more innovative ways to meet the patients' needs by diversifying the facilities and partnering the private sector. At the same time, the public sector is continuing to lead in medical research and the training of healthcare staff to provide improved health outcomes. This has the added advantage of making Singapore a world-class research centre and thus encourages Health Tourism.

In summary, the principle of co-sharing and self-reliance is the mainstay of Singapore's Healthcare System. The key to Singapore's efficient healthcare system lies in its emphasis on individuals to make a significant contribution towards their own healthcare costs. With this focus, the government has been able to maintain a relatively low level of public expenditure on healthcare for many years. The government continues to try to improve the healthcare facilities and the coverage of Medisave and other insurance schemes, and has recently announced that it will be increasing expenditure on healthcare to further improve its provisions. Essentially though, it relies on individuals to try to keep themselves healthy and to seek appropriate healthcare services.

With the dedicated efforts of providing good healthcare facilities and sufficient subsidies while educating the population to stay healthy and make responsible healthcare choices, the government aims to continue providing good healthcare for Singapore.

Research-Based Design: Practice – Options – Value

Harvey C.[1], Smith R.[2]

rsmith@designattheintersection.com
Clifford.Harvey@ontario.ca
[1] Ontario Ministry of Health and Long-Term Care, Canada
[2] Design At The Intersection, LLC

55

Healthcare Architects in the US and Canada are working together to share knowledge about how to integrate Research into our practice to inform design and foster innovation. This paper will feature an update on what RAIC Ontario Healthcare Architects and AIA AAH Healthcare Architects are each doing in their respective Research Committees to develop a relevant research agenda and disseminate knowledge that practitioners can use and apply in design. Future scenarios will be considered with an emphasis on how greater impact and value can be provided to enable research to inform design (and inform client user groups) for the purpose of stimulating innovation.

ONTARIO'S HEALTHCARE TRANSFORMATION AGENDA: FROM INNOVATIVE PRACTICES TO SUSTAINABLE PRACTICES. THE REGULATOR'S DILEMMA

Ontario has a public healthcare system which is really a system of systems. On one scale, the meta-scale, it is a public healthcare system regulated and funded by the Ministry of Health and Long-Term Care (MOHLTC). It uses a number of levers to guide the quality of care received by the 13+ million Ontarians through a number of health service organizations. Similarly to many public healthcare systems, the cost of healthcare in Ontario is increasing to the point of breaking not only the health-

care system but other social systems as well, such as education. In response, the Ontario Government introduced its Transformation Agenda through Ontario's Action Plan for Health Care. The aim of the agenda is to transform innovative practices into sustainable practices. These innovative practices have demonstrated better quality care at lower costs.

The first lever available to the MOHLTC to control costs and the quality of care is regulations. The Ministry introduced the Excellent Care for All Act in 2010. The Act clearly places the responsibility for delivering quality care to Ontarians on the health service organization (i.e. the hospital).

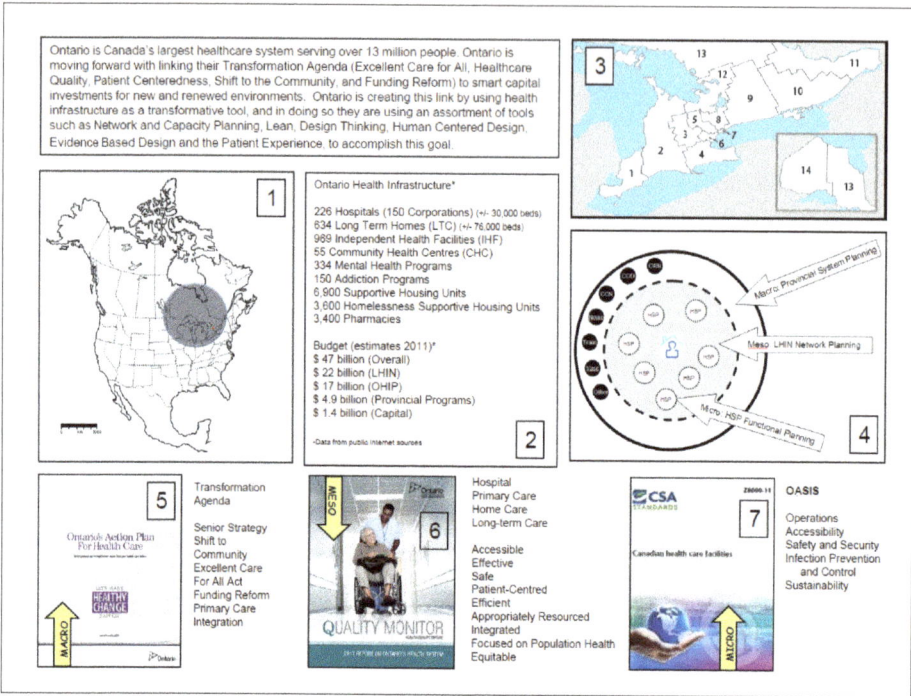

Figure 1. Healthcare system in Ontario, Canada.

The Act strengthened the role of Health Quality Ontario (HQO) in the system; as an agency of the MOHLTC, HQO monitors and reports on the quality indicators for healthcare organizations. These indicators are now tied directly to the compensation that health service organizations receive and are publicly reported.

The second lever available to the MOHLTC to control costs and the quality of care is funding. Health System Funding Reforms (HSFR) are policies developed as part of the MOHLTC transformation agenda. While hospitals once received only global funding, to be budgeted based on a hospital's determination of the needs of its community, now their funding is tied to a percentage of Quality-Based Procedures (QBP) and the Health-Based Allocation Model (HBAM). HBAM funding is tied to the statistical demographics of the hospital's community. QBP funding pays for known procedural outcomes based on best clinical practices; as such the ministry through QBP will no longer pay for adverse events in hospitals, including errors or hospital acquired infections (HAI).

The third lever available to the MOHLTC to control costs and the quality of care is the channels through which Ontarians receive their public healthcare. Traditionally these channels beyond primary care have been the hospital. However, new channels in the form of new organizations have been created to deliver speciality care, such as new ambulatory clinics or birth centres that only provide one type of service.

These are major and significant policy shifts for the Ontario healthcare system and a challenge to the healthcare designer. The regulator's dilemma is that if the government wants to initiate these changes at the meta-scale of a social system, and have them filter down into the built environment, the levers have to shift macro-level thinking at the level of the organization's design, swing down to the meso-level of service design, and finally transfer into the micro-level of traditional architectural design.

It is clear that traditional design is not necessarily prepared for this challenge. Often we continue to design our environments based on one model of healthcare captured in a traditional design process.

Healthcare is changing fast and the design industry needs to change with it to serve all levels of services. This is not a threat to the traditional designer, but an opportunity to bring new creativity and design processes to all levels of the healthcare system.

We need to develop new research design tools and processes to explore the complexity of health at the different scales of the care environments.

57

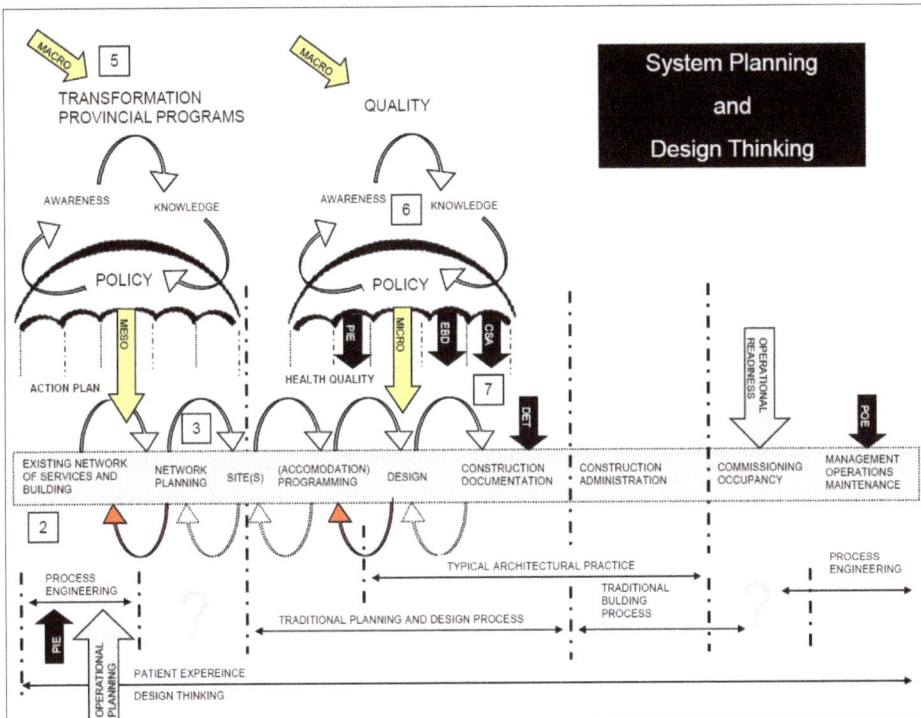

Figure 2. System planning and design thinking.

TESIS Inter-University Research Centre "Systems and Technologies for Social and Healthcare Facilities"
University of Florence, Italy

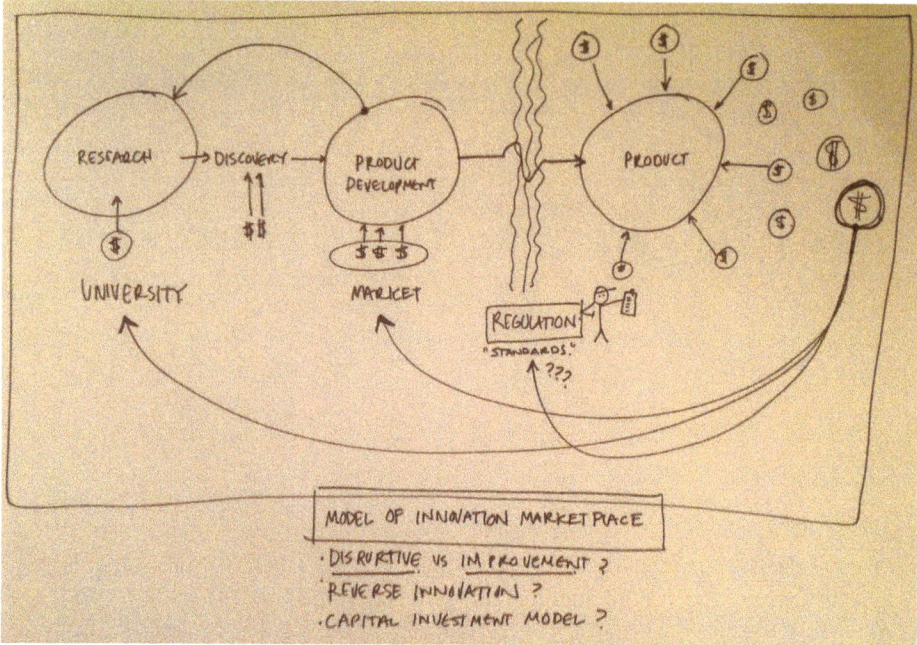

Figure 3. The regulator's dilemma.

RESEARCH-BASED DESIGN: PRACTICE – OPTIONS – VALUE

Research is a key element of the scientific process. In Healthcare design it brings an element of reliability to a project, and when one is investing scarce healthcare capital into a project, consistent and predictable outcomes matter. But does reliability outweigh the value of intuitive thinking? Roger Martin, the author of the Design of Business, would argue it does not. One is retrospective; the other prospective. One is based on observations and measurements; the other is based on exploring and testing an idea or concept of what might be. Healthcare environments require high performance in both technical and human systems. Design for healthcare environments requires research and

Figure 4. Designing by complexity.

Figure 5. Traditional design.

Figure 6. Product / service.

development that is both retrospective and prospective, to inform future applications of design concepts in a changing environment.

Evidence-Based Design (EBD), and Post Occupancy Evaluation (POE) studies have emerged as a way of conducting research about what works and why, but they can take many years to record and disseminate the results. To complement this process, feedback can be obtained through innovation and continuous improvement methodologies. The new healthcare research agenda should focus on discovery and exploration. There are many topics that rise to the top of this new research agenda. Some of these topics are: emerging building typologies for new clinical practices, new services design for better patient experiences, and innovative design and construction strategies.

The framework of this research can take the form of case studies, prototyping and simulation (design lab experiments), and process improvement programs (stakeholder involvement). Knowledge gained from research and development that is then disseminated to a wide audience for feedback and further development benefits all stakeholders.

A key catalyst for dissemination is the "Knowledge Repository" found at the Center for Health Design website, which is supported by the American Institute of Architects/Academy of Architecture for Health (AIA/AAH), American Society of Healthcare Engineering (ASHE), and the Facility Guidelines Institute (FGI).

Working across borders, the AIA/AAH is also partnering with the Royal Architectural Institute of Canada

(RAIC) and the Canadian Standards Association (CSA) to share information and resources. The RAIC/CSA work includes a roundtable and a conference to explore how research can support innovative practices and continuous improvement in the design process. It is well recognized, as with many traditional research practices, that the time it takes current basic research to move through the process and become applied research and then standards can take years.

Healthcare on the other hand is not standing still, and by the time the design research findings are codified into standards, it can be 10 to 15 years after the initial discovery had been observed. In many instances the healthcare practices have changed but the resultant building will be around for another 50 years.

In many cases, these environments now entrench and reinforce traditional practices, constraining healthcare and design from moving forward to better quality patient experiences and care. This new research design agenda supports Ontario's Healthcare transformation agenda of turning innovative practices into sustainable practices.

The solution may lie in better understanding that both observation and discovery are important aspects of basic research as is design, and new research tools can be found in simulation, prototyping and storytelling to help translate observation and discovery into new environments through an enhanced design process.

Figure 7. Organizational issues.

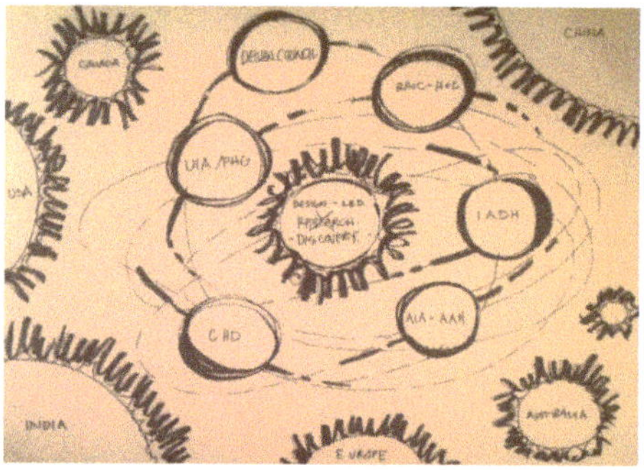

Figure 8. Design-led discovery.

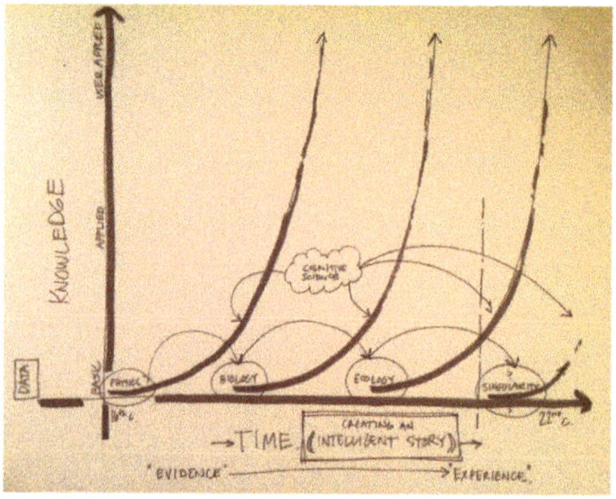

Figure 9. Evolution of knowledge over time.

Planning Solutions by Design: Reuniting Healthcare Programming and Design

Epstein N.[1], Patterson M.[2]

nepstein@nycum.com
Mark.Patterson@smithgroupjjr.com
[1] William Nycum & Associates Limited, M. Arch, NSAA, Halifax NS, Canada
[2] SmithGroupJJR, AIA, ACHA, EDAC, LEED AP BD+C, Phoenix AZ, USA

Hospital planning and programming can take years and involve a number of incremental and often very politicized steps. When significant cultural and operational change is desired, the disconnect that ensues from separate and distinct programming and design phases can be difficult to overcome. Some major pitfalls of this disconnect include an underestimation of architectural and tangential impacts during the programming and planning stages. This often includes restrictions imposed by the building site and a lack of awareness of the inputs users are making to the program without corresponding architectural visualization. As healthcare facilities and systems are increasingly attempting to optimize efficiencies and reduce costs, LEAN process integration, the development of multi-functional spaces and alternate means of delivering services are increasingly being pursued. These issues benefit greatly from a less sequential, more visual and more iterative process of programming and schematic design in parallel.

For a new 200-bed/20-OR facility project, Capital Health (Halifax) and the Nova Scotia Department of Health and Wellness recognized the pitfalls of this traditional "program first, then plan, then design" sequence and decided to combine the phases into one 7-month fast-tracked combined and simultaneous Programming/Planning/Schematic Design process. The result was a highly iterative, understandable and interactive process that forced major internal and external conflicts inherent in the project to the front of the room. This process increased the frequency of confrontation aimed at the early resolution of issues and the promotion of patient outcomes through space and not just square footage and adjacencies. Benefits included better understanding and buy-in by stakeholders in the process that ultimately would establish the budget for the project going forward.

Keywords: *programming, planning, design, hospitals, canada*

BACKGROUND

Space programming and functional programming are not part of all project types, but are critical steps in most medium and large scale healthcare planning and design projects. Healthcare programming evolved through a need to organize the project before starting the design process. It allows discussions about a facility's requirements and how it is intended to operate. Programming aims to review, summarize and convey a vast amount of complex project information at the earliest stages of a project. Programming represents a critical planning step and serves to translate information generally from the client/clinical/operations team to the consultant team.

Modern healthcare projects are increasingly complex. In an effort to improve operational efficiencies, reduce wait-times and lower the cost of healthcare delivery, issues as wide-ranging as culture change, LEAN process optimization, emerging technologies and new models of care delivery are being discussed at the planning and programming stages. How these issues can be addressed, let alone translated into built form is oftentimes too complex to be adequately conveyed through typical programming tools.

Traditionally, publically-funded healthcare projects in Canada – and to varying degrees in other jurisdictions in North America and around the world – have proceeded in a fairly linear fashion (Figure 1).

Often, project briefs or preliminary space programs are compiled based on a needs assessment and submitted to government for funding consideration. In many cases, it is at this very early stage – before a significant number of users or stakeholders have been consulted – that funding is secured and the project budget approved (Figure 2). Different jurisdictions have varying resources for putting together these briefs and the input is often provided without consideration of site location, impact to adjacent facilities or existing operations.

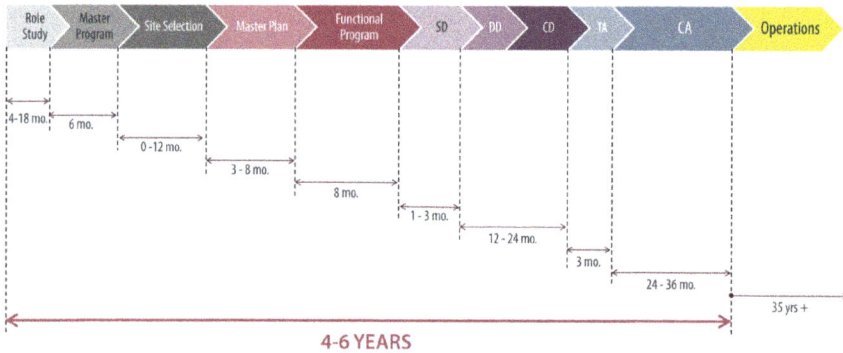

Figure 1. *Traditional (simplified) sequence, phases & timeline for large healthcare projects.*

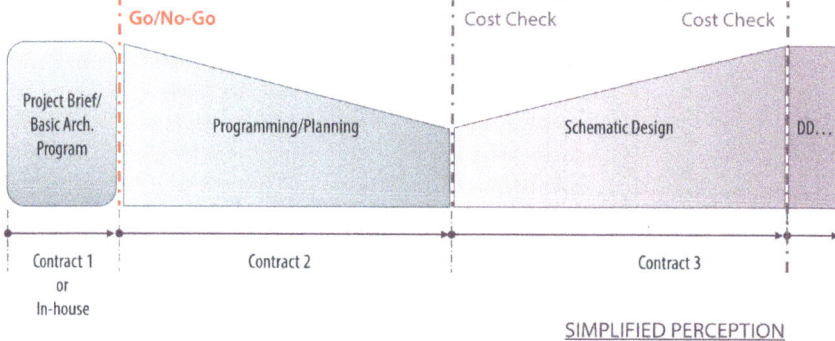

Figure 2. *Traditional Programming/Planning/Design Sequence.*

Benefits	Drawbacks
• Least money spent on design/consultant fees before financial/regulatory approval received. • Provides early snapshot of costs and opportunities • Can be undertaken by internal facilities/planning staff on smaller projects at large organizations. • Does not necessarily occupy end-user and staff time or raise hopes until a project is a reasonable possibility. • Rational and orderly sequence.	• Difficult for stakeholders, end users and the public to understand programming in the absence of visualization. • Difficult to implement significant culture or organizational change through programming alone (tendancy to fall back on the status quo). • Leads to discontinuity between Programming and Design (intent can be misinterpreted). Input can be "lost in translation" between program and design. • Program alone drives the approved project budget. • Overall time for the process is lengthened due to discreet packaging and procurement of work. • Time elapsed between Pre-design and Design phases can see significant changes in processes, standards and technology.

Table 1. Benefits and Drawbacks of Traditional/Sequential PreDesign | Design Process.

Healthcare programming and planning have traditionally been procured and executed as part of a discreet pre-design phase of large healthcare projects. This work is often tied to feasibility studies, financing requests, business case development and/or stakeholder engagement processes. These vital processes aim to determine the fundamental requirements of a project – Why? Where? What? When? How Many? How Long? How Much? – before pen is put to paper designing any spaces. On large healthcare projects, these tasks are typically performed by specialized healthcare programming and planning consultants who are often separate and distinct from the designers engaged on subsequent phases of the project. In fact, often the pre-design phase of a project is a separate contract entirely from the ultimate design contract with several years separating them. Some of the main factors that drive this ordering and separation of work include: a desire for early financial planning (i.e. cost estimates), a desire to more closely/accurately define the scope of the design work, a desire to quickly get the project scope to a level that can be benchmarked against other/past projects, and jurisdictional requirements and public procurement regulations. In a publicly-funded healthcare system, changing priorities, partisan policies and economic realities oftentimes impact a project in the time elapsed between the pre-design and design phases of a project. Table 1 highlights some of the benefits and drawbacks to this sequential approach.

While it is generally accepted that programming decisions should not predetermine design solutions (Adams, 1990), it is a reality that if a project budget is determined on the basis of the program alone before design begins, the design solutions moving forward are significantly impacted by the earlier program decisions. In an effort to mitigate some of the negative consequences of this sequential approach, some clients have proposed overlapping the Pre-Design and Design phases (Figure 3), requiring that the Design Team be brought on board midway through the Pre-Design

63

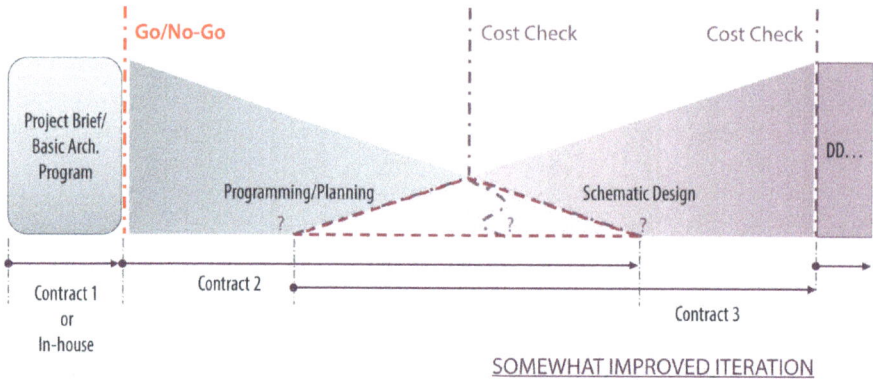

Figure 3.   Sequential Programming/Planning/Design Process with Contractual Overlap.

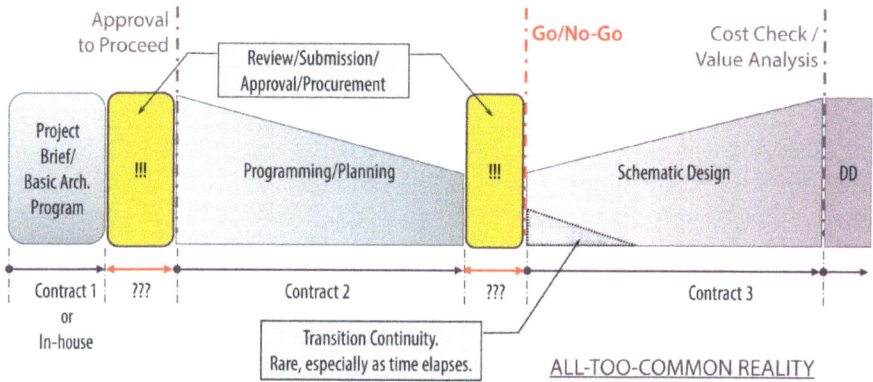

Figure 4.   The All-Too-Common Reality of Healthcare Planning/Design Projects.

phase and requiring the Programmers/ Planners to continue to be involved partway into the Design Phase of the project. This is aimed at reducing the disconnect between these two portions of the project, helping to ensure that the rationale behind Pre-Design decisions is properly conveyed and understood by the design team.

While holding good potential to reduce or eliminate many of the issues inherent in the purely sequential format, this scenario comes with its own set of issues, including scope ambiguity between programming/planning tasks and design tasks during the period of overlap. This contractual set-up becomes highly problematic in a government-controlled capital funding system. Within the Canadian healthcare system, significant delays are common between pre-design and design phases, as multiple levels of government review submissions, assess priorities, establish budgets and authorize capital expenditures. Delays of several years are not uncommon before an RFP for design services is ultimately released. With delays and uncertainty of this magnitude, the design consultants are rarely engaged during the pre-design phase. (On occasion, a one-sided overlap is seen where the pre-design consultant is engaged to assist with the transition into design.) In practice, the process resembles something much more like that shown in Figure 4.

Over the years, the rate of change in operational requirements (e.g. equipment, technology, processes) within healthcare facilities has increased significantly. When paired with lengthy review/approval processes and delays, this has led to programming/planning work being increasingly outdated once projects move into design.

REUNITING PROGRAMMING AND DESIGN

Many institutional healthcare clients have begun to consider new ways of working through the early stages of new capital projects in order to improve the alignment of planning, programming and design with the larger institutional goals of culture and operational change, and reduced operating costs. In addi-

tion, many clients are seeking ways to shorten the overall timeframe from initial project conception to construction. Simultaneously, new technologies have made new ways of working through planning, programming and early design phases possible. For example:

• New methods of digital representation such as SketchUp have allowed for the rapid development of compelling three-dimensional visual representations of concepts. Concepts can now be revised in near real-time and digital working models can be utilized in early concept work.

• Building Information Modelling (BIM) software allows programming data to readily take physical form in the planning and programming process. Additionally, the ability for programming information and metadata to be tagged to spaces in building models allows space and functional program data to be continually updated as design concepts are tested, effectively shortening the feedback/iteration loop between programming and schematic design.

• Web-based collaboration tools and Telehealth equipment allow wider client/user involvement in the design process

65

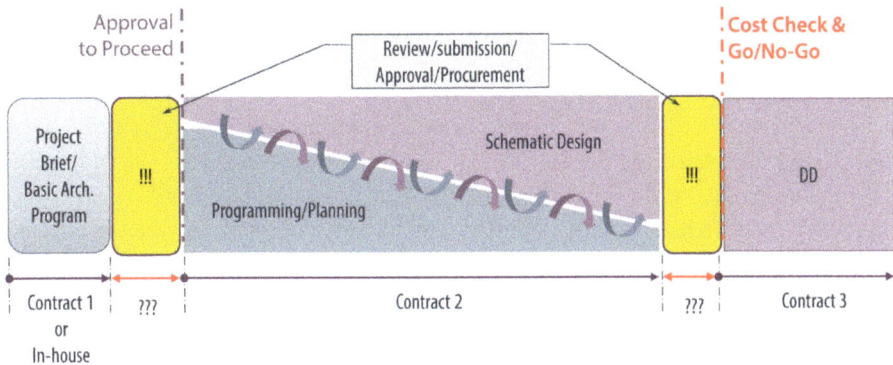

Figure 5. *Merging Programming, Planning and Schematic Design.*

TESIS Inter-University Research Centre "Systems and Technologies for Social and Healthcare Facilities"
University of Florence, Italy

and allow virtual facility tours and collaboration for facilitating culture change and organizational change during early planning and design.

• On-line surveys can facilitate data gathering and the tracking of large, physically dispersed user groups and stakeholders.

• Social media allows wider informal engagement and feedback.

• The ubiquity of modern mobile communication technologies (email, text, mobile, social media) allows for near constant & immediate touch-points with project team members, stakeholders and the general public.

Figure 5 represents an alternative to the traditional sequential program/plan/design method commonly seen in large capital healthcare projects in Canada. In this approach, programming, planning and schematic design are combined into one contract, awarded to a multidisciplinary team capable of delivering and coordinating the required expertise. In this approach, these tasks proceed in parallel through a series of iterative cycles where concepts are conceived, developed and evaluated from a programming and design perspective.

THE MODEL IN PRACTICE - INNOVATIVE CARE FLEXIBLE FACILITIES PROJECT (HALIFAX, NS)

The Capital District Health Authority (CDHA) is the largest provider of health services in the province of Nova Scotia, Canada. CDHA operates hospitals, health centres and community-based services serving the 400,000+ residents of the city of Halifax and provides specialist services to the rest of Nova Sco-

tia and Atlantic Canada. Earlier role studies, facility assessments and master plans had identified the need for the replacement of a significant amount of the aging clinical infrastructure. In 2012, CDHA issued an RFP for the "Innovative Care Flexible Facilities" (ICFF) project with the overall aim of replacing this aging infrastructure through new additions to other more modern tertiary and quaternary care hospitals in Halifax/Dartmouth. The project scope included planning, programming, concept design, schematic design as well as business case development and submission to government, for facilities housing roughly 200 inpatient beds, 24 operating theatres and associated support facilities. Importantly, the project was to be completed in roughly seven months with an anticipated submission to government in June 2013.

The project also included the following objectives for the process:

• In-depth user input and consensus-building in the planning and design process;

• Organizational change & increased efficiency of operations;

• Alignment with concurrent clinical services planning work being undertaken internally;

• Patient-centred and cost effective solutions;

• Alignment with concurrent clinical services planning work;

• Collaborative, humble process;

• Public engagement throughout the process.

This client realized that to meet the project objectives in the very tight timeframe allowed, it would be impossible

Benefits	Drawbacks
• VISUALIZATION: Issues can be visualized as they evolve.	• PROCESS can feel foreign to those used to the "traditional" sequential model
• RAPID TESTING: Can test questions and show not just areas but <u>form.</u>	o Can feel like putting cart before the horse
• SPATIAL REALITIES: Addresses site realities in the Programming phase.	o Starting designing before you know the total area of the building can be uncomfortable
• INNOVATIVE THINKING: Gets everyone thinking critically.	• SCOPE CREEP: If rough budget unknown at beginning of the phase, tendency toward blue-sky thinking and scope/budget creep.
• COSTING: More accurate costing for submission for project funding.	• DETAIL: Can get bogged down in higher level of detail than is warranted due to early introduction of drawings
• SUPPORTS CHANGE: Can more readily implement desired culture change and organizational change.	• EMOTION/ATTACHMENT: The process risks clients getting "emotionally" attached to a design that is abandoned due to still-evolving programmatic needs.
• CONTINUITY: Continuity of vision between programming, concept development and design.	• MISINTERPRETATION: Drawings can be interpreted as decisions being made, rather than points of discussion. The process requires frequent reassurance of users/ stakeholders.
• ENGAGEMENT & UNDERSTANDING: Better user buy-in, engagement and understanding. The process allows meaningful Public Engagement during the earliest planning and design stages.	• CONFLICT: Process inherently brings conflict to the fore early in the planning process, as implications are more clearly visualized. This, however, often results in better and more informed decision making.
• SPEED: Faster than sequential/separate Pre-Design and Schematic Design.	
• ENJOYMENT: More enjoyable!	

Table 2. Benefits and Drawbacks of the Merged Programming/Planning/Schematic Design Model.

Figure 6. Process and production images from the ICFF project.

TESIS Inter-University Research Centre "Systems and Technologies for Social and Healthcare Facilities"
University of Florence, Italy

to break the process down into separate sequential steps or contracts. CDHA decided to implement the merged process described above and after a lengthy public RFP process, a team led by William Nycum & Associates Limited (Halifax) and SmithGroupJJR (Phoenix, AZ) was awarded the contract in October 2012. Table 2 lists the benefits and drawbacks of this process as evidenced by the design team, and as stated by various stakeholders involved in the ICFF project.

Ultimately, the format of the ICFF project resulted in a highly enjoyable and productive process that engaged the various stakeholders in very meaningful discussions on how to improve patient outcomes, increase health system productivity, more readily respond to evolving future needs, reduce operating costs and best meet the needs of patients, family members and staff.

CONCLUSIONS

Merging programming, planning and schematic design results in a highly iterative, understandable and interactive process. With good client and stakeholder participation and engagement in the process, it can be a highly effective, enjoyable and time-efficient method of delivering a project that is best suited to the unique needs and goals of individual healthcare providers. The process pushes critical issues to the fore early in the project and can lead to a more holistic approach to programming through more relatable discussions of space utilization and not merely square footage and adjacencies.

ACKNOWLEDGMENTS

The authors wish to thank Capital District Health Authority for trying this innovative method of early project delivery. Many thanks to all the hardworking staff, volunteers and public stakeholders who took part in the Innovative Care Flexible Facilities project and to the entire project team for all their hard work and dedication.

REFERENCES

Adams, J. (1990). The Role of the Architect in Healthcare Facilities Programming: The Hospital Administrator's Point of View. *Royal Architectural Institute of Canada* (RAIC) Seminar Proceedings, 24 May 1990.

Feasibility of Mobile Hospitals in Japan

Okamoto K.[1]

dr@okamoto-kazuhiko.com
[1] University of Tokyo, Japan

In order to discuss the feasibility of mobile hospitals in Japan, three examples from Japan, India and the US were taken. It was found that the core function of the mobile hospital is to bring medical equipment, while screening and/or accommodation are available on-site.

Keywords: *depopulated area, disaster, hospital ship, hospital train, mobile hospital.*

BACKGROUND AND OBJECTIVE

Medical services in Japan are now covered by a fully insured and free access system and, according to a WHO report [1], they were top-ranked in the attainment of an overall health system. However, it is easy to understand that this system costs too much and reconstruction that concentrates limited medical resources into acute hospitals will soon be needed. This change might accelerate a shortage of medical services in rural areas which suffer from a lack of medical doctors even now.

The concept of introducing mobile hospitals into Japan does not miss the point, though such hospitals are often thought to be necessary only in war time or disaster situations. This research discusses the feasibility of this approach by exploring the merit and demerit of mobile hospitals through a survey of three examples in the world.

METHOD

Interview with the directors and staff of mobile hospitals, measuring the rooms and medical equipment, and observing the medical activities carried out.

HOSPITAL SHIP IN JAPAN

This ship (Fig. 1) is owned and operated by a private hospital chain to whom prefectural ownership and operation was transferred due to the shrinkage of its budget. It delivers basic medical checkups to people living on small islands that have no hospital, performed by doctors and nurses. Five permanent ship crew members live on the ship. All are employed by the hospital.

Feasibility of Architectural Technology

Physical barriers such as door frames and stairs (Fig. 2) will be improved on

70

the new ship due to come into operation in a few years. A capacity expansion system is necessary as the number of patients varies from 1 to 255 per day.

Feasibility of Hospital Management

Although they say it is impossible to link the paper medical chart on the ship to the electronic medical chart in the hospital, a united medical chart system involving clinics on the islands should be established. This ship is too small to accommodate the medical staff and resources to cover the risks that could occur with medical treatment. The more islands they cover, the more cooperative hospitals will be needed to supply medical staff as the ship can only accommodate ship crews.

Feasibility of Cost Management

The annual budget of this operation is 120 million JPY, almost half of which is covered by the government and 4 prefectures.

The hospital will have difficulty negotiating with the local medical society over the territory on which to execute medical treatment for profit.

Feasibility of Sustainability

In terms of "hospital growth and change," the replacement of medical equipment is essential for this ship; this however has never been done in the 22 years since its completion due to the lack of a wide entrance.

Figure 1. The hospital ship.

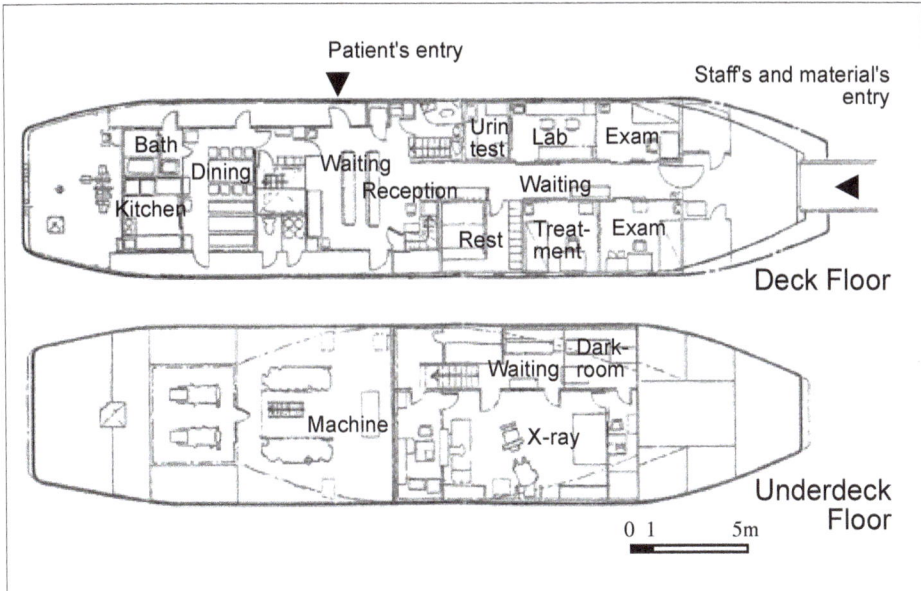

Patient's entry

Staff's and material's entry

Bath

Dining

Kitchen

Waiting

Reception

Urin test

Lab

Exam

Waiting

Rest

Treat-ment

Exam

Deck Floor

71

Dark-room

Waiting

Machine

X-ray

0 1   5m

Underdeck Floor

Figure 2.   Floor plan of the hospital ship.

HOSPITAL TRAIN IN INDIA

This train (Fig. 3) is owned and operated by an NPO which delivers surgical operations for cleft lips, cataracts and polio-related orthopedic conditions performed by volunteer doctors and nurses. There are 11 permanent non-medical staff living in the train (Fig. 4). 5,000 patients were screened and 500 underwent a surgical operation in 2 weeks of activity.

Feasibility of Architectural Technology

The main concept could be applied to Japan, namely that medical resources on the hospital train concentrate on surgical operations and other areas of the existing medical and architectural resources such as the screening room and recovery beds are left in the city. Having enough local support for hospital logistics also

means the resources in the train carriage can be streamlined. Water, mineral water and food are delivered by local shops, medical trash and laundry are sent to local facilities, and electricity cables are connected to the station. However in terms of controlling cleanliness, a clean air flow in the operating theatre is not guaranteed due to the structure of the carriage.

Feasibility of hospital management

Although the drugs given and the medical skills and styles of the dispatched medical staff from many different places may vary, they can be unified by lectures given at Lifeline express. Hygiene management, including practices such as fumigation and changing shoes, may be confusing because the concepts differ from Japanese ones. A medical chart should be given to each patient for their future local treatment.

TESIS

Feasibility of Cost Management

One operation costs 75,000 USD, while voluntary medical staff are enlisted each time.

Feasibility of Sustainability

The medical equipment can easily be replaced every few years as it is small, for example anesthesia instruments or microscopes. One operating theatre carriage was added in 2007 to realize the NPO's original concept of "disaster mitigation." One car equipped with an operating theatre and an autoclave can be separated and dispatched even if a medical procedure is in progress.

MOVING HOSPITAL IN THE US

This mobile hospital (Fig. 5) regularly delivers a dental, vision and basic medical check-up service to uninsured people mainly in Tennessee, while it occasionally dispatches aircraft to disaster areas.

This time a registration and screening area was set up in temporary tent in a parking lot, the dental area in a church gym, the vision area in the church's backyard and the medical check-up area in the church's office so that over 1,000 patients could be seen in 2 days.

Figure 3. The hospital train with a temporary ramp.

Feasibility of Architectural Technology

Operational space is borrowed from community buildings such as schools or churches, where the medical equipment is set up on similarly borrowed desks. Some vehicles are modified to accommodate glass lens cutters while others and aircraft are used as originally planned to carry medical equipment, collapsible dental chairs and other supplies. The equipment is always stored in vehicles and this system saves storage space at the headquarters. Only in emergencies are water and generators brought.

Feasibility of Hospital Management

The director of the NPO encouraged many state governors to eliminate the medical doctor's license barrier which doesn't allow unpaid activity across borders. This was achieved in 10 states so doctors are now able to come from many other states. There are only 6 full-time non-medical staff, the others are volunteers. As the maximum number of dental chairs is 100 and dental equipment requires the assembly of vacuum tubes, 100-150 student volunteers are needed to set up. All the staff stay in the nearest motel even if the operation is held in the neighboring city in order to save time. All the patients' paper medical charts are kept at the headquarters.

Feasibility of Cost Management

The only subsidy received from the public sector is the rent for the headquarters premises, an old county building with a rental fee of 1 USD per year.

73

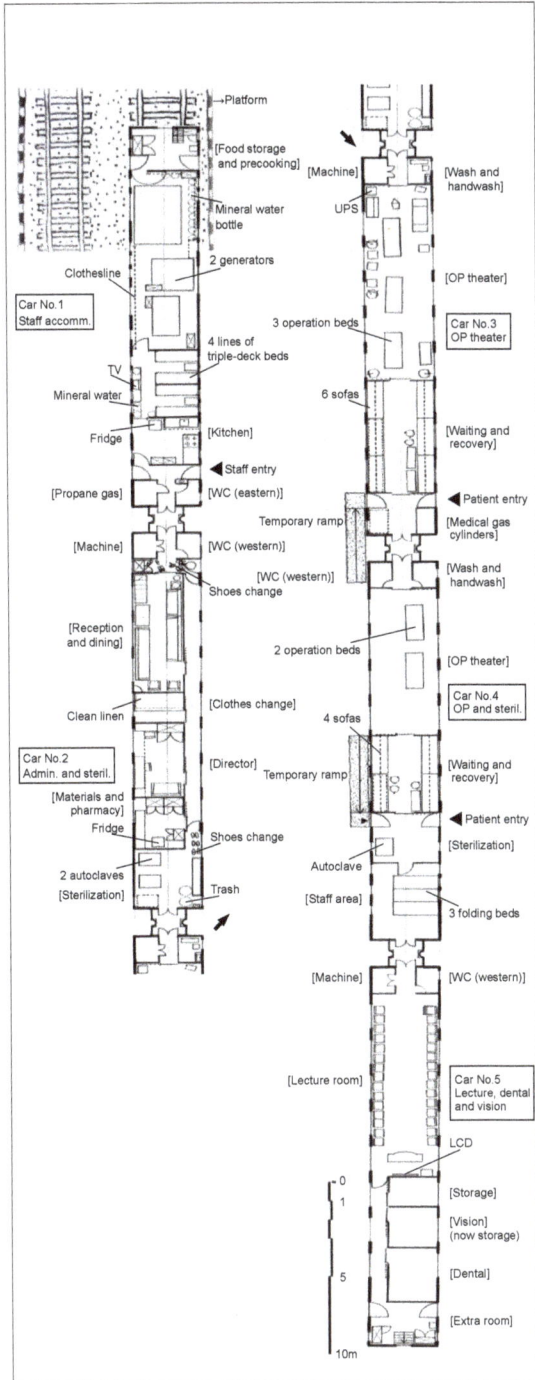

Figure 4. Floor plan of the hospital train.

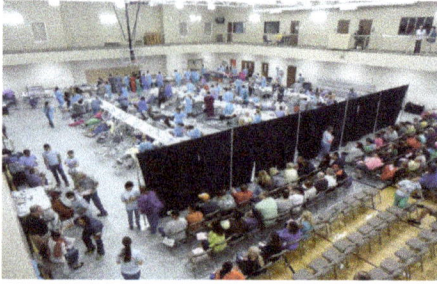

Figure 5. Dental treatment in a gym.

74

Feasibility of Sustainability

Medical equipment can easily be replaced because almost none of it is fixed to architecture or vehicles.

INTERIM CONCLUSIONS

Though this study is still ongoing, these three examples allow interim conclusions to be drawn with regard to the creation of mobile hospitals in Japan:

1) Mobile hospitals should only carry medical equipment;

2) Space for outpatient, minor treatment and inpatient areas can be provided in public buildings in town;

3) Electricity, water and food are available in town (except in disaster situations);

4) Full-time staff should concentrate on operations while doctors or nurses should be volunteers;
5) Targeting diseases should be limited because mobile hospitals do not have the facilities of acute hospitals, and the gaps between volunteer doctors with different skills and backgrounds should be filled.

REFERENCES

[1] WHO (2000). The WORLD HEALTH REPORT 2000 Health Systems: Improving Performance.

[2] Harvey, J. Y. (2001). Mercy Trains - Australia Army Ambulance Trains in World War II, Iron Horse Press.

[3] Wiltse, C. M. (1965). The Medical Department: Medical Service in the Mediterranean and Minor Theaters, United States Army in World War II, Department of the Army.

[4] Hospitals on Wheels. Railroad Magazine, 1945 September.

[5] Stemen, C. (1890). Railway Surgery, J. H. Chambers and Co.

Get Better: Integrating the Care Delivery, Planning and Construction Model. Excitement, Surprises, Lessons and Rewards

Sun P.P.[1]

ppsun@aol.com
[1]AIA/ACHA/NCARB, United States

The fundamental basis of planning, design and construction has been undergoing transformation. Using integrated processes some projects have been able to add value and reduce cost and time in their delivery. The modifications in management and approach have changed the dynamics in delivering care models, both operational and physical, which may represent solutions for the future.

The delivery of healthcare projects and programs today relies on teams and multiple specialists. We can start by asking who they are and what their relationship is in today's world. They can be reduced to a few major groups: engineer, architect, program manager, and owner.

The following statements represent the groups:
- Engineer: architects just don't want to do anything logical.
- Architect: engineers just don't have an imagination.
- Program manager: we protect owners from architects and engineers.

Architects and engineers: program managers keep us from working effectively by getting between us and the owner.

Owners: no one seems to be able to control the costs or schedule.
- It's my money; why isn't it my building?
- Why doesn't it work the way you promised it would?

To move ahead effectively we must integrate our approach and services. We must change.

If you do not change, you may end up
where you are heading
Lao Tsu

The transition to affecting change can come from adapting thoughts taken from "Thriving on Chaos" by Tom Peters. "Thriving on Chaos" identified milestones in change occurring in major industries, many of which have meant the difference between success, failure and survival. The following is a comparison between current behavior patterns and a future approach for five major areas:

1. Production – Currently there is an emphasis on volume, cost and functional integrity, while the future needs to concentrate on quality, responsiveness, innovation, short intervals, flexibility, people and automation.

2. Innovation – Current innovation is focused on central research and development, cleverness rather than determined customer-driven value, while the future should encourage innovation by working in small autonomous units which make large and small customers notice improvements.

3. Structure – Organizational structure is currently focused on hierarchical and functional integrity, while the future should bring about flat functional organizations breaking down barriers, supervisors should create self-managed teams and managers should facilitate rather than guard the turf.

4. Information – Currently information is centralized for consistency and control and is internally aimed, while the future should focus on information for all and customer-based systems managed by the "line" and decentralized for maximum flow.

5. Finance and Cost – Currently finance is generally centralized and finance staff act as "cops" while the future requires the decentralized deployment of finance people to the field and "business team members." Costs are known from the start and are managed by the team.

These tenants helped establish new behaviour patterns which were used in the development of approaches geared towards building more responsively and for the future.

Excellence does not come from believing in excellence – only in constant improvement and constant change.
Tom Peters

The design team also used Integrated Project Delivery (IPD) and LEAN methods. These methods have proven effective in breaking down the "independent silos" which create the attitudes addressed earlier between groups. While IPD is now generally known as a way of working together and using Building Information Management (BIM), a more definitive definition is as follows:

Integrated Project Delivery:

An approach that aligns project objectives with the interests of key participants. It creates an organization able to apply the principles and practices of Lean.
Matthews and Howell 2005

And LEAN is described as follows:

LEAN:
A methodology to manage and improve construction processes with minimum cost and maximum value by considering customer needs.
Koskela et al. 2002

An additional communications method was developed from a process called "Bioteaming" gleaned from the "Bioteaming Manifesto" by Ken Thompson and Robin Good. Bioteaming framed the idea that communications should be open among all groups and fed in "blasts" so that all were informed at all stages. This method and the philosophy behind it represent nature's way of organizing and managing teams to achieve results.

While these elements framed the approach to the work, the project and subject of the case study is the Delta Health Center's clinical expansion. The

Delta Health Center is at the core of a nationwide approach to try to control increasing costs in healthcare delivery in the USA.

Understanding the basics of healthcare metrics in the USA is fundamental to understanding the new approach to healthcare delivery. The USA has transitioned from a predominantly cost-free faith-based and community-based hospital system in the early 1900s, to the development of national reimbursement systems in the 1960s and the inclusion of for profit hospitals beginning in the 1970s. More recently non-profit chains, university systems and for profit chains have grown through the phases of large hospitals into smaller models in an attempt to correct for market demand and economic sustainability. The overall cost, however, has been dramatic and dramatically increasing.

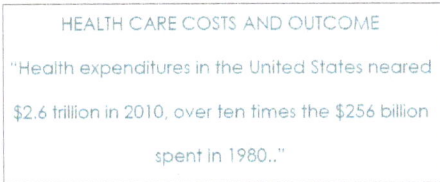

HEALTH CARE COSTS AND OUTCOME

"Health expenditures in the United States neared $2.6 trillion in 2010, over ten times the $256 billion spent in 1980.."

Figure 1. Issue one: High Cost. Source Martin A. B. et al., "Growth in US Health Spending Remained Slow in 2010; Health Share of Gross Domestic Product Was Unchanged from 2009." Health Affairs, 2012.

The next three charts show the cost of healthcare compared to other countries. The USA spends two and a half times the OECD average.

The rising cost for the individual and for a family are shown in the following two charts. The premiums for a family have risen to more than $16,000 and the total cost with deductibles to more than $22,000.

When these costs are compared with median household income the cost of healthcare is dramatic.

As a result there are many who cannot afford healthcare insurance or prefer to not have healthcare insurance. It is estimated that the number of people without healthcare insurance rose from 49 million in 2009 to almost 49.9 million in 2010. Graphically the dark area below represents the uninsured.

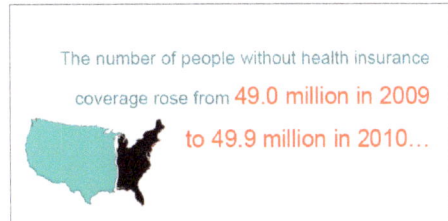

77

The number of people without health insurance coverage rose from 49.0 million in 2009 to 49.9 million in 2010…

Figure 2. Issue Two: Coverage and Access. Source: US Census 2010 news release 9-13-2011; http://www.census .gov.

Who are the uninsured? The following chart shows the estimated distribution.

With such high costs one must ask about the quality of care. Unfortunately this care system ranks 37th according to the World Health Organization.

As healthcare relates to longevity the cost of healthcare and longevity comparisons are shown in the following two charts where several countries spend dramatically less and have equivalent life spans of approximately 78 years.

It was also found that the USA was not performing well with Primary Care and spends much more for ambulatory care and administrative costs.

As a result the major legislation passed in 2010 was the "Patient Protection Affordable Care Act," often spoken of as "ObamaCare."

This new system is intended to increase

the number of people covered by insurance, increase access to care, reduce impediments to care and to include new services previously not covered such as mental health. One emphasis is Primary Care, the focus of this paper. Indeed, keeping people healthy is a novel idea.

It is a lot harder to keep people well than it is just get them over a sickness.
DeForest Clinton Jarvis

The world of hospitals has dominated our attention, but it is now believed that keeping people out of hospital is one solution to the high price of healthcare. As such, the PPACA has dedicated a significant share of resources towards primary care and community health centres. In fact $11 billion was dedicated in the first phase to community health centres.

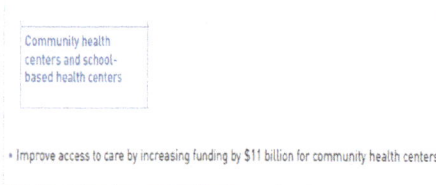

Figure 3. Kaiser Foundation: Analysis of the Health Care Reform Plan.

Our subject facility is the Delta Health Center, the first and therefore oldest primary care centre in the USA. The Delta Health Center is in the Mississippi Delta, some six to seven hours north of the Gulf of Mexico. It is situated in one of the most fertile areas of the North American Continent. It is served by major river systems that allowed for early development but as rail and highway transportation became dominant it became less of a focus for agricultural product markets.

This area is also known as one of the most dangerous due to tornados, which cause destruction in a surprising and unpredictable manner.

Over the past half century the region suffered an economic decline which resulted in a significant part of the population facing poverty in many counties. The three counties of Bolivar, Washington and Sunflower, served by the Delta Health Center, show some of the highest poverty rates in the country.

In these counties the poverty and mortality rates are significant.

In the midst of this, the Delta Health Center was formed by Dr. H. Jack Geiger and several founding members including Dr. Hatch and Dr. Andrew James. It was as much a solution for illness as it was a social experiment and a response to the neglect shown to this area, which originally profited from the economic system founded on slavery.

The Delta Health Center was unique because it reached beyond a simple clinic. It created education opportunities and helped train some of the first doctors and nurses from the area. It developed a farm that grew crops which could add to the nutritional base of the population. It created a water system so that potable water could be available to the population. It created a transportation system to be able to bring patients and the community to the Delta Health Center.

Thus from its roots in 1964 and modest beginnings, it developed into a small system of care.

It is here that the concept of building a new model for primary care for the 21st century began. It is here that the system of planning using IPD and LEAN methods sought to bring about new solutions for old problems. It was here that the beginnings of planning began to take root.

The planning started with the operations staff, including doctors and nurses. Forming the right operations model is critical in any plan, and functionality can only be created through those who will ultimately use the facility. The cost of operations and outcomes are the real problems and not the architectural aspects of design.

If design represents 10% of the overall construction costs, facility operations represent 4.2 times the cost of the building. More importantly though, the cost of functional operations is 42 times the cost of the building. These costs, however, are insignificant with respect to the real objective: patient outcome.

With this in mind the planning process began using an integrated model of plan-

ners and engineers. Keeping true to the basis for IPD and LEAN methods as well as Bioteaming, the communications model was interdisciplinary and eventually the addition of subcontractors was anticipated.

Appropriately, the basis of the primary care service was defined as part of the initial processes that take place in the exam or treatment room. The care components were defined and standards were developed. Each room was standardized and, as standardization worked, manufacturing resources were contacted. After a search for compatibility, the Herman Miller group offered several models for exam and treatment room equipment and options.

The most exciting room type featured a portion of the room used for clinical work and a portion for patient education. Thus keeping the patient healthy took on the role it needed in the development of the facility.

79

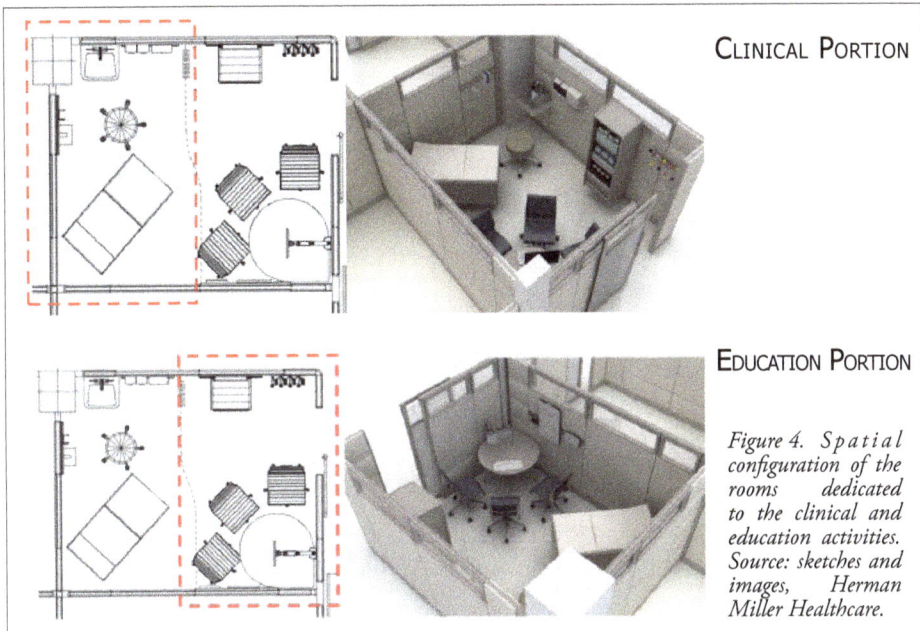

CLINICAL PORTION

EDUCATION PORTION

Figure 4. Spatial configuration of the rooms dedicated to the clinical and education activities. Source: sketches and images, Herman Miller Healthcare.

Thus the new room was born. But what about the organization of these rooms and their relationship to operations?

Three major planning and design criteria were developed while working with physicians and nursing staff.

1. The ratio of exam rooms to physician offices was 3:1.

2. Patients should not pass a physician's office while going to the exam room. The distraction of seeing a physician and the distraction to the physician being encountered meant it was better to have these areas naturally sheltered from one another.

3. The layout of most clinics does allow natural light to penetrate the core of the facility. This makes for a stressful environment for both patients and staff.

Thus the basic plan was developed. The relationship between patient flows and offices is shown in the lower diagram where patients do not pass physicians' offices on their way to the exam rooms. Offices are naturally separated.

The desire not to replicate dark and anonymous corridors led to the development of the concept of small courtyards. These could be replicated to create larger floor areas. The tradition of natural light and natural space within a building is well known in many cultures.

The Mississippi Delta was a predominant agricultural area. Construction workers in this area represented a small portion of the work force, and the general population was much smaller than most urban areas.

Thus the concept of using modular construction arose. The modules could be built off-site, brought to the site and "plugged in" to the pre-constructed courtyards and corridors. Other facilities were researched and this concept showed promise. Thus using the dimensional characteristics of modular construction and transportation limits led to the development of dimension-based

plans. Three plans were developed which fitted with the demographics of the region. A small plan for 20-30,000 visits, a mid-sized plan for 40-60,000 visits, and a large plan for 60-90,000 visits.

While the planning process proceeded, the project was submitted for a grant worth as much as $5 million. The Delta Health Centre won the full $5 million; they were heady times. "Bridging documents" were developed with the intent of having a modular manufacturer complete the product as a "design build" type of arrangement since their expertise was in developing the "product."

Procedures to bring on board a full design team were quickly completed. Thus the plan for IPD was taking full shape. Work sessions with various vendors began to help mould the project. Soon a complete set of documents and specifications was ready for modular manufacturing bidders. The plan followed the functional aspects developed earlier, as did the rooms. Detailed bridging documents were carefully completed and released for bidding. But disaster struck: the offers from modular manufacturing bidders were unaffordable even though they provided budget profiles and guidelines.

We felt like we were trapped, not unlike the following quote:

I have six locks on my door, all in a row. When I go out I lock every other one. I figure no matter how long somebody stands there picking the locks, they are always locking three.

Elavane Booster

The project was rebid with assurances from the modular manufacturers, but the results were even worse.

It was a dark day:

80

A day without sunshine is like, you know, night.
Steve Martin

From this point it was necessary to change and proceed:

It takes considerable knowledge just to realize the extent of your own ignorance.
Thomas Sowell

And:

A fanatic is one who can't change his mind and won't change the subject.
Winston Churchill

The objective is still to be able to provide care to those in need. The method, however, may change. As such the project provided an option to allow any form of construction process. This was known as allowing "stick construction," also called conventional construction.

As such the owner entertained "conventional" construction as an alternative. After the contracting process had been revised a new contractor was hired as a "design-builder" and the redesign began. The intent remained the same and consequently the room arrangement (plan) stayed the same. The dimensional characteristics were kept but all the detailing had to be changed. The modular to conventional process proved to be critical in one area: integration.

With a solid process map for clinic operations, and an integrated planning and design team, the next step was to assimilate the new design-builder into the project. This was by and far the largest project in the Mississippi Delta at the time, yet there was little participation from constructors in any of the bidding procedures. The final design-build contractor came from the Jackson Mississippi area about two hours away. Most of the sub-contractors came from the Mississippi area, a major plus for the project.

While the project was being converted from modular to conventional construction in detail, approvals from the Environmental Protection Agency were taking longer than expected. Eight Native American groups were contacted to see if they had any objections to the project. Two responded and desired more information. This was completely out of the hands of the project team since Native American groups are considered sovereign states. They had to deal with the Federal government directly. The entire Mississippi Delta is on a flood plain, of different degrees. This makes the area a fertile basin for agriculture, but it also meant the project had to prove the level of the flood plain at the site and the agencies that carried out this type of investigation never had the funding to map the entire area. Nevertheless, the project site is about three feet higher than the surrounding area and, since another recent Federal project had been built nearby and was over three feet lower in terms of floor elevation, it was not denied.

The new team did not share the basis of either the Lean methods or the integrated project delivery techniques, but since the owner insisted on "at least trying" integrated meetings were held and the subcontractors were allowed to meet and work directly with the design team and the owner. The floor plan was secured, equipment was incorporated as before, furnishings were confirmed and systems were revisited. A major change was the roof design and roofing system. The seven courtyards offered a challenge, but one which resulted in an elegant solution. The conversion to conventional construction allowed for an all-brick exterior. Once all the drawings had been redeveloped the project received a building permit from the local authority.

81

82

Since this was one of the first Primary Care facilities of its kind and one of the first to receive Affordable Care Act funding, the project needed an appropriate launch. On June 7, 2013 a "ground breaking" event was held attended by local, state and national representatives who were in the shadow of the "greats," namely those who founded the concept of Primary Care and the FQHC (Federally Qualified Health Center): Drs. H Jack Gieger, John Hatch and Andrew James.

Site preparation and site mobilization began immediately. At 2:00 AM on July 10, 2013 the first major concrete pour began. The need to pour concrete in the early morning relates to the extreme heat topping 100 degrees Fahrenheit during the day. Lighting for the pour was provided by three "light plants" comprised of independent generators and banks of high intensity lights. The second and last pour was on July 29, also starting at 2:00 AM. The crisp air, dark nights, rumbling of almost 100 concrete mixers, major pumpers, and dozens of squawking walky-talkies made for exciting evenings.

There were mixed emotions over the switch from a "modular" concept to "conventional" construction. With closer consideration we can question whether there really was a significant shift from the "modular" ideal. The plan disciplined by dimensional characteristics and governed by modular transportation and efficiencies worked well and was maintained.

The equipment and systems furnishings were factory built and added to the modularity. The roof was comprised of repeated roof trusses manufactured off-site and delivered. With the plan incorporating highly repeated elements the framers developed a process of "wall sections" which were built on site and stacked, awaiting the completion of the concrete foundations and slabs for installation.

Thus much of the modularity, ease of construction and quality control carried over. The project was not built in a climate-controlled factory and shipped to the site, but it was built in an integrated manner and in a repetitive pattern thus allowing for a cost which is estimated to be 30% below the comparable market cost, and at least that much lower than the cost of the modular bids.

The project is now nearing completion. A series of terrible weather conditions delayed the project completion for over four months, but achieving a project of this scope in the Mississippi Delta in less than a year is testimony to the planning, design and construction methodology.

The lessons learned from this demonstration project for healthcare came from many principles borrowed and slightly modified from "the Bioteaming Manifesto" by Thompson and Good. These lessons included the following:

Leadership - Every team member is treated as a leader;

Connectivity - Connect team members, partners and networks synergistically;

Execution - The team experiments, co-operates and learns (together);

Organization - The team establishes sustainable self-organization;

Movement and Change - Trust replaces blame. The discovery of problems is celebrated because it is "better now than later."

To conclude, the following two quotes added to the inspiration for this project:

To improve is to change; to be perfect is to change often.
Winston Churchill

And

You must be the change you wish to see in the world.
Mahatma Gandhi

Globalization of Health Care: Designing, Developing and Implementing a Just World-Class Health System in a Frontier Market

Waruingi M.[1,2], Downing K.[1], Amos I.[3], Waritu S.[1], Amos O.[3], Peiffer S. [1], Ademodi T.[1], Agunbiade S.[1], Ekanem U.[1,4], and Fellows of Ustawi Research Institute's Fellowship for Globalization of Health Care

macharia@kdnc.org
[1] Ustawi Research Institute
[2] Center for Health Systems & Design, College of Architecture, Texas A&M University
[3] Thompson & Grace Investment Limited
[4] Uyo University Teaching Hospital

The focus of this paper is the approach to the design, development and implementation of a world-class healthcare system (WCHS) in Akwa Ibom State, an oil producing state in the South-South region of Nigeria. It reports the Ustawi Research Institute's emerging paradigm for the design, development and implementation of a WCHS in a frontier market. This report draws on rich experience gained in the design, development and implementation of a world-class academic medical centre developed as part of a master-planned medical city and connected to a franchised system of ambulatory, tertiary care medical centres located in the state of Akwa Ibom, Nigeria.

A qualitative method was used to gather inductive data from stakeholders of health and human development in Nigeria. The grounded theory design facilitated the theoretical sampling of key concepts about the state of health services in Nigeria. Comparative analysis yielded a grounded theory that a WCHS in a frontier market has three distinct structures: (a) a community engagement structure, (b) a payment structure, and (c) a health services delivery structure. The three structures are necessary subsystems of a complete system that forms a comprehensive entity for health production in a frontier market. Planners, designers, and architects of healthcare systems and facilities must be aware of the working principles of the three necessary structures for community engagement, payment and health services delivery when designing, developing and implementing world-class health projects in frontier markets.

Keywords: *health; medicine; health finance; health policy; health care quality*

This paper reports the effort to generate a theoretical model for high quality health services in a traditionally marginalized market. A qualitative approach helped to collect inductive data about the design, development and imple- mentation of world-class health care system (WCHS) in Akwa Ibom State, an oil producing state in the South-South region of Nigeria. Recent economic indicators qualify Akwa Ibom, and indeed Nigeria, as a frontier market that

84

has registered phenomenal growth over the past five years. Furthermore, Nigeria is projected to sustain an accelerated growth pattern in the foreseeable future. Unprecedented rapid economic growth has converted the traditional notion of the Third World into the new notion of a frontier market. The switch from Third World to frontier market has caught many an unprepared global health practitioner by surprise. The unpreparedness of global health practitioners presents a unique problem in which the globalization of healthcare lags behind the general globalization of industrial manufacturing and consumer services such as mobile phones and automobiles. High quality health service delivery systems, such as preventative medicine and primary care clinics, general hospitals, and specialty medical centres, are not emerging at a rate close to any other business in the frontier markets.

The mismatch between the globalization of manufacturing and consumer services, and the globalization of healthcare has left a large gap in health services in frontier markets, leading to a serious clamor for health services. Consequently, there is an enormous demand for high quality medical services. Meeting this demand places a tall order on global health practitioners. At the heart of this tall order is the role of healthcare planners, healthcare architects, healthcare systems engineers, healthcare systems developers, healthcare systems implementers, and healthcare leaders.

This paper reports on the work carried out at Ustawi Research Institute to fulfill a certain aspect of this enormous demand for world-class health services in Nigeria, one of the fastest growing frontier economies. It attempts to respond to

the following key questions:
• How can we facilitate the globalization of affordable and accessible, high quality healthcare to a frontier market?
• Reverse question: How can we create the conditions for the emergence of affordable and accessible, high quality care in a traditionally marginalized market?

To respond to these questions, the paper will first examine the concept of globalization to help anchor the idea of the emergence of frontier markets. It will then examine the current state of the globalization of healthcare in order to learn from its present working principle. Finally, it reports on the Ustawi Research Institute's approach to the emerging paradigm for the design, development and implementation of a world-class health system in a frontier market. This report draws on rich experience gained in the design, development and implementation of a world-class health system designed for a master-planned medical city, and connected to a franchised system of ambulatory medical centres distributed thoughout the state of Akwa Ibom, Nigeria.

BACKGROUND

The problem of the design, development and implementation of a WCHS in a frontier market relies on comprehension of the inner workings of globalization in general terms, and the globalization of healthcare in specific terms. This section examines the two terms (i.e. globalization and the globalization of healthcare) as the central phenomena critical to comprehend the design, development and implementation of world-class healthcare systems in frontier markets.

Globalization

Globalization as economic and social connection across the world has been growing for centuries. However, the present model of globalization fundamentally differs from its traditional notion as the pace of global integration has picked up dramatically, but it is secondary to the inexorable acceleration of the speed of the trans-border transfer of knowledge through the information superhighway.

Recent reports indicate that the pace of economic growth in the so-called Third World countries far outstrips growth in the so-called First World. In a complete departure from the traditional economic structure that had the Third World countries traditionally pegged as producers of agricultural products and raw materials, these countries are now the producers of completely manufactured products. Indeed, the rapid economic progress in the traditionally labeled Third World comes from the intensive export of finished products and services, rather than raw materials.

The growth in the emerging and frontier markets is down to the speed of communication, the exchange of knowledge, goods and services, and transportation. With advanced information and communication technologies, money instantly traverses national boundaries through electronic money sending and receiving systems that range from individual level remittance systems and real-time web-based electronic billing and payment systems to global interbank electronic funds transfer systems.

The consequence of these events is the emergence of new ways of organizing business entities, regulations, economies, and human movement on a global scale. Places traditionally classified as low-income developing countries are rising up and connecting directly to the global capital and technical pool (Belton, 2010). Indeed, far beyond the emergence of these nations is the empowerment of the people local to them.

Yawning Gap

Even with the evident dramatic rise in tempo, globalization remains limited. The globalization of healthcare lags far behind the globalization of manufacturing. As companies open up in new markets, their employees are left without access to healthcare services.

Granted, medical services are local by nature. Most medical services require direct contact between the provider and the consumer. Certain medical services (e.g. invasive surgical procedures) are sophisticated and still very expensive to provide by remote means over the information superhighway. Advances in medical science and technology could rapidly yield refined robotic surgeries carried out transnationally. However, such services are still very pricey, account for a large part of the total expenditure, and cannot be directly traded internationally, at least for now.

Globalization of Healthcare

The globalization of healthcare refers to the increasing globalization of the health sector (Craig & Beichl, 2009; Reading, 2010; Schroth & Khawaja, 2007). Traditionally, the health sector has been closed and nationally focused. The globalization of healthcare operates at three distinct levels of reality: (a) the level of the consumers of care, (b) the level of the healthcare professionals, and (c) the level of the organization.

85

Transnational Consumers

Health and medical tourism are two distinct forces that fuel the movement of consumers across national boundaries in search of care. The major distinction is that health tourism involves the restoration of wellbeing, while medical tourism involves the restoration of health by medical means. Consumers travel to seek healthcare where they can find it. Consumers from low-income countries move to high-income countries to find care. African elite consumers have traditionally travelled to Europe and the United States to seek care. More recently, tens of thousands of Africans travelled to Asian countries such as India for medical care. Another recent phenomenon is the travel of consumers from developed countries to developing countries to seek care. On the one hand, the local people are not the target consumers of medical and health tourism. As such, promoters of medical tourism create structures for the delivery of care with little or no attention to the needs of the local people in the destination countries. The promise of financial rewards from health and medical tourism distracts local health providers from paying attention to the local people. The effect of the inattention to distributive, deliberative and social justices remains uncertain and unexplored.

Transnational Individual Providers

The transnational migration of health professionals has historically been the main pathway of the health services trade. Professional migration followed colonial and linguistic ties. Physicians and nurses migrate for economic reasons such as better pay and financial security.

The migration of healthcare professionals can create health equity concerns especially in developing countries, which suffer from the brain drain caused when health professionals leave. In addition, these countries lose the investment that they made when educating these health professionals as well as their potential contributions to the healthcare field (Adams & Stilwell). Such loses also affect health service delivery because some areas may have inadequate health professionals and health services.

Transnational Medical Systems

At the level of the organization are private companies involved in hospital building projects. For example in March 2013, Johns Hopkins Medicine International (JHMI) signed an agreement with Sun Yat-sen University (SYSU) and affiliates in Guangzhou, China, to create a long-term platform for exchanges among clinical and translational investigators, research professionals and administrators. Although the transnational medical facilities help to introduce high-tech, high-touch medicine in the destination countries, they lack critical elements of structural equity that would ascertain social and related deliberative and distributive justices for the local communities. Indeed, social, deliberative and distributive justices are not the motivators for the emerging transnational medical systems. The implementation of high technology medical facilities that lack the critical elements of structural equity poses serious challenges for sustainability in the long term. The design, development and implementation of sustainable world-class health services in Akwa Ibom, Nigeria, called for these critical elements of structural equity to be considered.

Transnational Health Insurance

Transnational health insurance involves selling health insurance products in multiple countries. In Europe, a new European Union Directive on cross-border healthcare was passed in 2011.

The EU Directive gives European citizens the right to access healthcare services in other European Economic Area (EEA) countries as long as the treatment is medically necessary and available under the NHS.

Transnational Operations

The operational level of reality involves the cross-border supply of services. One example is the use of new telemedicine technologies to provide health services across borders and to remote regions within countries and between countries.
Commercially available devices are able to stream video from the patient's home to a healthcare provider via the Internet.

Gap in Effectiveness

The globalization of health and medicine has had little impact on health indicators. The process of the effective globalization of such knowledge and skills from U.S. healthcare organizations to the frontier markets remains elusive. The design, development and implementation of a world-class health system (WCHS) in Akwa Ibom state could help to define some of the processes that would facilitate the globalization of healthcare services in a frontier market.

Statement of the Problem

The general problem is the production and delivery of high quality health services that ensure the critical elements of structural equity in frontier markets. The system for health delivery in Akwa Ibom, a frontier market, is in a severe state of disrepair. Health services in Akwa Ibom are unsafe, of low quality, and inaccessible to the majority of the people (Jacob & Akpan, 2009). The people of Akwa Ibom, afraid to use health services in the nation, seek medical care in other countries such as India, South Africa, England, and the United States. Indeed healthcare consumers in Akwa Ibom would be willing to pay more for better high-value care with an improved supply of drugs, better technical quality, better maintained health facilities, and shorter wait times.

Globalization opens up economic opportunities for well-developed healthcare systems to export their knowledge and technical expertise to new markets. The specific problem is that the process for creating the conditions for economically viable high-quality care services in traditionally marginalized geopolitical locations in the frontier market is not certain. There is a dearth of literature on the structural features of a sustainable healthcare organization in a frontier market.

Statement of Purpose

The purpose of this project was to discover elements critical to the production and delivery of high quality health services in the frontier market in the state of Akwa Ibom, Nigeria.

87

The objective was to engage the community in an inductive dialogue that would facilitate the emergence of knowledge relevant to the design, development, planning, and implementation of a world-class health system in Akwa Ibom state. The specific communities involved were Eket, the location of future clinical laboratories and an imaging centre for the world-class health system; Uyo, the present location of a federal teaching hospital; and Afaha Obong, the future location of the world-class health system complex. The direct engagement of the three communities helped to shape many questions that guided further data collection.

Significance of the Problem

This project is significant for the stakeholders of the globalization of healthcare. The stakeholders fall into two categories: salient or core stakeholders, and fringe stakeholders (Hart & Sharma, 2004). The core stakeholders are the visible and "readily identifiable parties with a stake in an organization's existing operations." Examples of core stakeholders of the globalization of healthcare include the leaders of healthcare organizations, the designers of health systems, healthcare planners, architects, engineers, hospital builders, governmental organizations, and non-governmental organizations. Other core stakeholders include the manufacturers and suppliers of equipment used in healthcare organizations, community leaders in developed and frontier markets, other businesses, employees, and investors.

Examples of fringe stakeholders include the adversarial, divergent, non-legitimate, the poor, the weak, the illiterate, and the disinterested, such as rural folks. Non-humans such as plants, animals, etc., occupying the frontier regions as their natural habitats, are fringe stakeholders of the globalization of healthcare.

Theoretical Underpinnings

A second purpose of the project was to communicate to the stakeholders the vision of creating a world-class health system in the heart of Africa. Effectiveness in communicating a vision is a function of co-creating, which in turn relies on the ability to put the last first.

Co-creating

Co-creating as the most effective way of communicating a vision formed a theoretical basis for the project procedures (Senge, Kleiner, Roberts, Ross, & Smith, 1994). Co-creating arises from community engagement, which is paramount to building a shared vision (Issel, 2009). The strategy for community engagement must be well defined before the project begins. Involving the community leads to participation that empowers the local stakeholders and enhances "their capacity to assist in the assessment and their ownership of the data gathered and results produced by the assessment" (Issel, p. 125). Co-creating involves three major steps: (a) strategic analysis; (b) strategic formulation; and (c) strategic choice. Some people like to refer to co-creation as co-operative collaboration. In implementation, members of the group work together to conduct a thorough strategic analysis. This involves a through market audit to gain a fundamental understanding of the strengths and weaknesses of the organization vis-a-vis the competition in the health systems ecosystem. In strategic formulation, members of the group work together to identify all the possible choices of health systems and their corresponding applications in an organization. In strategic choice, the members of the group make choices about which objectives to implement. The priority plan helps to set the implementation goals, and then the objectives for each goal.

Putting the Last First

The goal was to involve the community members in building a shared vision, because when there is a shared vision people excel and learn because they want to, not because they are forced to.

The goal of community participation in this project was continuous and permanent with a view to generating a good understanding of the community members. Continued community involvement was critical to the establishment of opportunities for deliberative justice, which is the centerpiece of the ascertainment of healthcare equity in the WCHS. This participatory approach was empowering to both men and women, and allowed them to share their knowledge freely (Chambers, 1997). Local people living in villages were knowledgeable about the local conditions and willing to make huge sacrifices just to eke out their survival. The will to make huge sacrifices accumulates as massive tacit knowledge which can remain unknowable to an outsider who is unwilling to listen and learn. This project was founded on the theoretical principle that access to crucial knowledge in the tacit dimension is reliant on absolute humility and putting the local people first.

METHOD

The qualitative method adopted for this purpose helped to obtain inductive data from multiple stakeholders of health and human development in several sites in Nigeria (a frontier market), and the United States (a developed market). The qualitative method was appropriate because data on the sustainable structures for the delivery of health services in a traditionally marginalized healthcare market is lacking. The qualitative approach meant the the stakeholders could be approached with an open mind and an open heart, and a willingness to listen to their needs. The inductive approach helped to do away with preconceived notions of how healthcare should be organized. Such an open approach helped to entertain multiple points of view from a diverse group of stakeholders.

The emerging grounded theory design helped to explore concepts shared by the stakeholders of global health and human development, and to formulate a theoretical model for the design, development and implementation of a world-class health system in a frontier.

Comparative analysis helped to generate a theoretical model for the production and delivery of affordable and accessible, high quality health services in frontier markets. The grounded theory was appropriate because it helped in the discovery of the properties and dimensions of key categories of elements critical to sustainable entry into a frontier market. The data analysis involved the coding of data to allow a new theory to emerge (Glaser, 1998). The coding consisted of naming and categorizing data, and required going back and forth to the data (Brown, 2002). Thus, the processes involved the constant review and re-review of the data to allow concepts to emerge (Goulding, 2006).

89

Geographical Location

Nigeria was the specific country of focus in this project. Located in West Africa, Nigeria borders Chad and Cameroon to the east, the Republic of Benin to the west, and Niger to the north. To the south lies the coast of the Gulf of Guinea on the Atlantic Ocean.

Nigeria's economic outlook is promising, and the World Bank reports it as a mixed economy that has already reached middle-income status. The country has an abundant supply of natural resources. In addition, Nigeria has an advanced financial, legal, communications, and transport infrastructure.

The stock exchange is active and picking up. According to the World Bank, Nigeria ranked 31 in global purchasing power parity as of 2011. This economic growth comes from oil exports, as Nigeria is the 7th largest trade partner with the U.S., supplying 20% of oil consumed in the United States.

Oil trade notwithstanding, the country enjoys a positive outlook from the global financial sector. Citigroup projected Nigeria to have the highest average GDP growth in the world between 2010 and 2050. Accordingly, Citigroup classified Nigeria as among the 11 Global Growth Generators countries.

This positive economic outlook makes Nigeria a great candidate for world-class health services.

Participants

The participants in the study hailed from four distinct locations: Akwa Ibom state, Rivers state, Cross-Rivers state, and Lagos state. The majority of the participants hailed from Akwa Ibom state (one of Nigeria's 36 states, with an estimated population of between 4 and 5 million people. The Akwa Ibom state is located between longitudes 7°3 and 8°3 East, and latitudes 4°3 and 5°3 North. On the continent of Africa, Akwa Ibom State is in the coastal South-South region of Nigeria.

Data Collection

The data collection involved in-depth interviews with stakeholders of health and human development in the states visited. The focus of the study was ten thematic areas (Table 1).

The procedure for collecting data from the participating individuals was co-creating in *open space large group processes* (Waruingi, 2010); it involved various types of open group processes such as direct interviews and focus group discussions. Theoretical sampling involved a careful line-by-line review of the interview notes seeking emerging concepts from each interview. The emerging concepts were used to determine the next plan of action, or to indicate where to focus additional interviews. The additional interviews allowed concepts identified in preceding interviews to be compared with concepts emerging from the subsequent interviews. The comparative analysis yielded key categories showing specific properties and dimensions.

90

Type of needs assessed	Examples of Topics
Community needs assessment	Nutrition, infectious diseases, injury prevention, drugs, alcohol, tobacco, housing, oral health, violence prevention, chronic diseases, environmental health, mental health, occupational safety
Programmatic needs assessment	Allergy, asthma and clinical immunology; anesthesiology; cardiothoracic surgery; cardiovascular medicine; dermatology; emergency medicine; endocrinology, metabolism and clinical nutrition; family and community medicine; gastroenterology and hepatology; geriatrics and gerontology; hematology and oncology; infectious diseases; physical medicine and rehabilitation; medicine; nephrology; psychiatry and behavioral medicine; neurology; pulmonary, critical care and sleep medicine; neurosurgery; oncology; obstetrics and gynecology; radiology; ophthalmology; rheumatology; oral and maxillofacial surgery; surgery; orthopedic surgery; otolaryngology; pathology; transplant surgery; paediatric surgery; trauma and critical care; paediatrics; urology.
Facilities needs assessment	Physical plant, elevations, architecture, engineering, construction.
Technology needs assessment	Clinical technologies, administrative technologies, building technologies, health information technologies.
Quality needs assessment	Accreditation, Joint Commission International, International Standards Organization, Continuous quality improvement, Deming cycle, FOCUS-PDCA, Lean-Six sigma, risk assessment, risk mitigation.
Franchising needs assessment	Franchising, business models, collectivism, individualism.
Health care cooperative needs assessment	Equity: distributive justice, deliberative justice, social justice.
Governance needs assessment	Leadership, people, money.
Legal needs assessment	Legal structures.
Financing needs assessment	Capital acquisition, capital allocation.

Table 1.   Ten Thematic Areas.

RESULTS

The aim of this project was to discover how design principles could be used to create the conditions for the emergence of affordable and accessible high quality care in a traditionally marginalized market. Interviews with key informants identified a huge need for medical services and healthcare in general, which is completely mismatched with other areas of development in the state.

The major finding was that healthcare in Akwa Ibom state, and Nigeria in general, has remained at a rudimentary level.

The delivery system is completely inadequate to deal with local medical conditions.

The majority of the people do not have access to care, do not seek care, or seek care in other countries.

91

People Do Not Access Care

Basic care is lacking across the state. Primary and secondary healthcare facilities are under-funded, under-staffed, and under-equipped. At the heart of this problem is the lack of an organized system to manage payment for healthcare services. Preventative health practices and medicine are also lacking with minimal attention to maintaining wellness. Health insurance organizations are few, and many self-employed people without formal employment do not participate in insurance schemes. Patients needing tertiary care either die at home or raise funds to travel to India, Germany, the United Kingdom, the United States, or other destinations for medical care.

People Do Not Seek Care

Many people do not seek care from the healthcare system. Health literacy and trust in the healthcare system is generally low. Many people do not have a correct understanding of disease, the role of proper nutrition, lifestyle, and behavior in disease causation.

Many people attribute illness to evil spirits and prefer to consult traditional healers. People only show up at the hospital when they are quite ill or at the point of death. By that stage, healthcare providers are unable to treat the condition effectively.

People Seek Care in Other Countries

Most providers in the tertiary centres refer their patients to India for laboratory diagnosis, imaging, treatments, and surgeries. Common diagnostic investigations referred to India include genetic studies and immunohistochemistry. Some Akwa Ibom people needing CT scans and MRI are able to get tests in Port Harcourt and Enugu, but both cities are more than two hours away by road. The imaging centres in these two cities are crowded and have long waiting lists. People needing recurrent tertiary care due to chronic diseases are in serious trouble as they would have to travel to India very frequently.

Abstraction of Grounded Theory

The results indicate an unjust health system in Akwa Ibom. Despite the extreme abundance of natural resources and exuberant economic growth in this frontier market, people do not have access to care, they do not trust the quality of care, and they seek care elsewhere. Given these findings we examined the data closely to discover the intrinsic story line. A comparative analysis of the expressed needs yielded the grounded

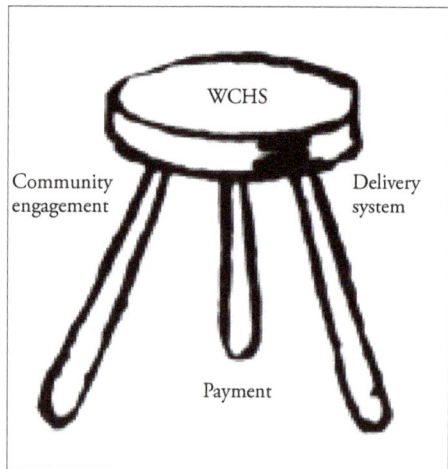

Figure 1. Phenomenal structure of a WCHS.

theory that a just WCHS is a comprehensive entity with three sub-entities: (a) community engagement, (b) services delivery, and (c) payment ascertainment (Figure 1). This analysis gave rise to a grounded theory that:
• the phenomenal structure of the world-class health system in frontier markets has three distinct sub-entities;
• the successful execution of the three sub-entities is reliant upon the careful implementation of affordable pieces in a neat sequence, with regular monitoring and evaluation.

The three elements are the subsystems of a world-class health system in a frontier market. The subsystems co-operate under an overarching umbrella organization providing business governance and oversight to ascertain complete justice in the sustainable design of a WCHS for a frontier market in a rapidly globalizing planet. Each subsystem serves a specific function to contribute to a world-class health system. The community engagement subsystem operates through a healthcare co-operative (HCC) with specific functions and forms the platform for deliberative justice. The payment subsystem operates through an organized health insurance scheme that forms an avenue for access to care, ensuring social justice. The delivery subsystem operates through a hospital system and the affiliated ambulatory medical centres that form the pathway for the distribution of health and medical services, ascertaining distributive justice. Thus, the community engagement element helps to meet deliberative justice, the payment element helps to meet social justice, and the delivery element helps to meet distributive justice.

Deliberative Justice

Deliberative justice focuses on policy formulation through dialogue. Dialogue ensures the participation of all stakeholders in the design of the services that matter to them (Isaacs, 1993). In the deliberative conception of justice, the legitimacy and value of healthcare decision-making will be enhanced if local people and community representatives take advantage of opportunities to engage in dialogue and discussion about matters of public concern.

In a WCHS, an organized healthcare cooperative represents the operational principle of deliberative justice. The healthcare co-operative will enroll members of the local community in a manner that will enable less privileged people at risk to gain access to the services provided at the WCHS.

Distributive Justice

The distributive justice component is related to the needs of the individuals in the community and the WCHS's response to those needs. Thus, the attributes and behaviors of each individual form the ultimate unit of analysis of distributive justice. As such, distributive justice at the WCHS will emphasize the equity of medical care delivery, preventative medicine, and wellness for all the people of Akwa Ibom state.

The WCHS in Nigeria will deliver its services efficiently and effectively compared to the other healthcare institutions in Nigeria. Overall, the WCHS brand must maintain modern laboratories, advanced equipment, an effective electronic medical system, and clean healthcare facilities.

93

Franchising

In franchising, the approach is to delineate the delivery of ambulatory services from hospital services in order to produce operational efficiency in the WCHS in Akwa Ibom state. In the franchise model, emphasis is placed on promoting the creation of private outpatient clinics by individual franchisees as part of a comprehensive approach that addresses the entire continuum of care. Such clinics would offer preventive and curative services.

Hospitals would be reserved for sicker patients requiring inpatient care. Such triage would help to reduce costs while providing the most appropriate care possible at each level, and serve as a disincentive for providers withholding patients in order to maximize financial returns. The idea is to shift the focus from the traditional illness model to a wellness model.

Social Justice

The social justice component explicitly acknowledges the environmental determinants of disease. Environmental factors are physical, social and economic. The physical environment in Akwa Ibom contributes to diseases incident to the local people. Factors affecting the environment range from the tropical climate, which encourages the proliferation of mosquitoes that transmit the malaria parasite, to extreme environmental pollution from the oil and gas industry.

In a WCHS, social justice is reflected in public health actions aimed at health promotion within communities in Akwa Ibom. The goal of social justice is to contribute to the improvement of health thus minimizing disparities among subgroups of the Akwa Ibom population.

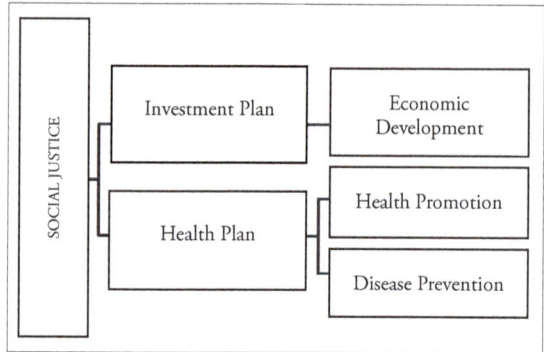

Figure 2. Functional structure of a healthcare co-operative, the social justice ascertainment arm of a world-class health system.

In a WCHS, social justice takes the community as the unit of measurement, and is concerned with population health. Social and economic factors are key determinants of population health. Social justice calls for a population health oriented perspective to design and assess the production of health. Two ways that the WCHS would address population health are the creation of an investment plan and a healthcare insurance plan (Figure 2). The investment plan will focus on economic development, while the health plan will focus on health promotion and disease prevention activities.

Investment Plan. In a WCHS, an investment plan will enable members to participate through the purchase of shares. The focus of the investment plan is economic development. A WCHS must be built with the express intent of formulating innovative strategies to nurture the social and economic development of the local people. Members of the healthcare cooperative will contribute to a common pool of funds through the purchase of co-operative shares.

Prepaid Health Insurance Plan.

In the WCHS, a Health Insurance Plan, a prepaid health-plan, would aim for health promotion and disease prevention. The WCHS would engage in health promotion activities for its members. The completed needs assessment of this project identified many opportunities for health promotion such as health literacy, diet, exercise, and healthy living.

The healthcare cooperative will also engage in disease prevention activities such as vaccination against common diseases, and monitoring the general health of individuals. The completed needs analysis published in module 4 of this project identifies opportunities for disease prevention in Akwa Ibom.

Health Insurance Program will provide expanded access to healthcare for millions of Nigerians at affordable costs. For the WCHS, financing will be accomplished by means of consumer payment for the services through an established insurance system. The focus of the prepaid payment system is to increase access to healthcare.

This also includes insurance for non-formally employed residents such as those whose income is dependent on subsistent crops. These people have no consistent income, and in fact their income depends on the weather conditions (rain or drought) and excess farming for sale or consumption.

The engagement of this group is important for two reasons; primarily to increase access to healthcare at the grassroots level, and secondly for sustainability and the expansion of the WCHS across Nigeria.

CONCLUSIONS

A just WCHS is a comprehensive entity with three sub-entities of (a) community engagement, (b) services delivery, and (c) payment ascertainment. The three elements are the subsystems of a world-class health system in a frontier market. The subsystems co-operate under an overarching umbrella organization providing business governance and oversight to ascertain complete justice in the sustainable design of a WCHS for a frontier market in a rapidly globalizing planet. Each subsystem serves a specific function to contribute to a world-class health system. The community engagement subsystem operates through a healthcare co-operative with specific functions that form the platform for deliberative justice. The payment subsystem operates through an organized health insurance scheme that forms an avenue for access to care, ensuring social justice. The delivery subsystem operates through a hospital system and the affiliated ambulatory medical centres that form the pathway for the distribution of health and medical services, ascertaining distributive justice. Thus, the community engagement element helps to meet deliberative justice, the payment element helps to meet social justice, and the delivery element helps to meet distributive justice.

REFERENCES

Adams, O., and Stilwell, B. (2004). Health professionals and migration. *Bulletin of the World Health Organization*, 82(8), 560-560.
Belton, K. A. (2010). From cyberspace to offline communities: Indigenous peoples and global connectivity. *Alternatives: Global, Local, Political*, 35(3), 193-215.

95

Brown, S. C., Stevenson, R. A., Troiano, P. F., and Schneider, M. K. (2002). Exploring complex phenomena: Grounded theory in students' affairs research. *Journal of College Student Development*, 43(2), 173-183.

Chambers, R. (1997). *Whose reality is it? Putting the last first.* London, UK: Intermediate Technology Publications.

Couper, I. D. (2004). Seeking quality: some experiences in South Africa. *Rural and remote health*, 4(2), 271.

Craig, K., and Beichl, L. (2009). *Globalization of healthcare: case management in a 21st-century world.*

Gail, S. T. (2011). Healthcare in the Emerging Markets: A New Frontier for Economic Growth. *The Whitehead Journal of Diplomacy and International Relations*, 12(2), 7.

Glaser, B. G. (1998). *Doing grounded theory: Issues and discussions.* Mill Valley, CA: Sociology Press.

Goulding, C. (2006). *Grounded theory: A practical guide for management, business and market researchers.* London, UK: Sage Publications.

Hart, S. L., and Sharma, S. (2004). Engaging fringe stakeholders for competitive imagination. *Academy of Management Executive*, 18(1), 1-13.

Isaacs, W. (1993). Taking flight: Dialogue, collection thinking, and organization learning. *Organizational Dynamics*, 22(2), 24-39.

Issel, L. M. (2009). *Health program planning and evaluation: A practical, systematic approach for community health.* Sandbury, MA: Jones & Bartlett.

Jacob, A., and Akpan, P. A. (2009). Spatial distribution and accessibility of health facilities in Akwa Ibom state, Nigeria. *Ethiopian Journal of Environmental Studies and Management*, 2(2), 49-57.

Jiaming, S., and Xun, W. (2007). Personal Global Connectivity and Consumer Behavior: A Study in Shanghai. *Journal of International Consumer Marketing*, 19(3), 103.

John, M. (2009). Globalisation. *Appropriate Technology*, 36(1), 52.

Lotfi, C., Ravinder, M., Mohammed, H. A.-T., Al-Anoud, M. A.-T., Marco, A., and Javaid, I. S. (2011). Medical education and research environment in Qatar: a new epoch for traslational research in the Middle East. *Journal of Translational Medicine*, 9(1), 16.

Patel, A., Gauld, R., Norris, P., and Rades, T. (2012). Quality of generic medicines in South Africa: perceptions versus reality - a qualitative study. B*MC health services research*, 12(1), 297-297.

Peter, T. (1999). Globalization. *Oxford Review of Economic Policy*, 15(4), 76-89.

Reading, J. P. (2010). Who's Responsible for This? The Globalization of Healthcare in Developing Countries. *Indiana Journal of Global Legal Studies*, 17(2), 367-387.

Schroth, L., and Khawaja, R. (2007). Globalization of healthcare. *Frontiers of health services management*, 24(2), 19.

Senge, P. M., Kleiner, A., Roberts, C., Ross, R., and Smith, B. (1994). *The fifth dicsipline field book: strategies and tools for building a learning organization.* New Youk, NY: Currency/Doubleday.

Tache, S., Kaaya, E., Omer, S., Mkony, C. A., Lyamuya, E., Pallangyo, K., and Macfarlane, S. B. (2008). University partnership to address the shortage of healthcare professionals in Africa. *Global public health*, 3(2), 137-148.

Wang, L., and Lo, L. (2007). Global connectivity, local consumption, and Chinese immigrant experience. *GeoJournal*, 68(2), 183-194.

Waruingi, M. (2010). Emergencing: Discovering the tacit dimension of global health leadership. *Journal of Global Health Care Systems*, 1(3), 1-41.

From Reactive to Proactive Management of the South African Healthcare Estate

De Jager P.[1], Abbott G.[2]

pdejager@csir.co.za, gabbott@csir.co.za

[1] Pr. Arch, M.A., Research group leader, Architectural Engineering, Building Science and Technology, Built Environment, CSIR, Pretoria, South Africa
[2] Health Facilities, Architectural Engineering Research Group, Building Science and Technology, Built Environment, CSIR, Pretoria, South Africa

Healthcare spending in South Africa is inequitably distributed across the private and public sectors. The treasury reports that 49% of expenditure is attributable to the private sector serving 16% of the population (National Treasury 2012, Fiscal Review for 2011). This expenditure pattern has undermined aspirations of equity, access to care and social justice. Furthermore it has been widely acknowledged that much of the public health architecture represents a legacy estate with poor replacement rates and a generally weak culture of facility maintenance.

In light of this, there has been a commitment to transform the healthcare sector through the introduction of a national health insurance system, which is to be phased in over a 14-year period. This, coupled with a renewed focus on infrastructure investment by government, will surely lead – over time – to a substantially transformed healthcare estate. Historical implementation partners – public works departments – are increasingly being displaced by the introduction of cadres of built environment specialists employed by the respective provincial health departments wishing to meet their own specialised needs more directly. As the core mandate and skill is not built environment-related this transition is posing interesting challenges.

The National Department of Health has elected to take a proactive stance to address this by introducing a multi-pronged programme. A collaborative partnership titled Infrastructure Unit System Support (IUSS) has been established. This is mandated to improve the planning, procurement, design, construction, operation and disposal of healthcare facilities across all tiers of health service delivery. Various working groups have embarked on a series of activities: developing a comprehensive set of infrastructure guidelines, norms, and standards (specifically tailored to the resource constraint environment); implementing cost modelling tools; establishing a project monitoring support unit; and introducing a computerised project management information system. All are being developed with a very high level of stakeholder engagement to encourage participation, leverage and cultivate expertise, promote early uptake, and to ensure compatibility with constitution-mandated provincial autonomy.

TESIS Inter-University Research Centre "Systems and Technologies for Social and Healthcare Facilities"
University of Florence, Italy

TESIS

The approach incorporates a series of transformation agendas, recognition of the resource constraints (both human and material) and a commitment to principles of sustainable development. Several decision support tools of interest address – in an integrated manner – the optimisation of infrastructure at a strategic planning level, and the streamlining and automated benchmarking of room requirements and generic assemblies for the purpose of briefing consultants. These are linked to cost estimator tools.

In the primary levels of care, emerging guidelines are promoting the use of low-technology solutions which are easy to operate and maintain, but are not simplistic. They need to address the mandatory performance requirements, such as achieving the necessary air quality for TB transmission mitigation.

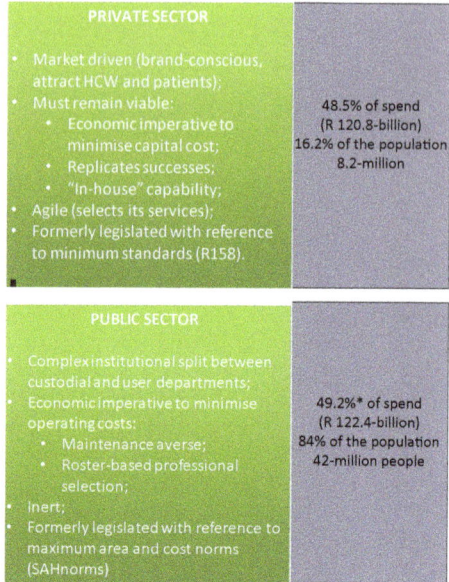

Figure 2. *The sectorisation of healthcare provision with distinctive characteristics: private and public sector.*

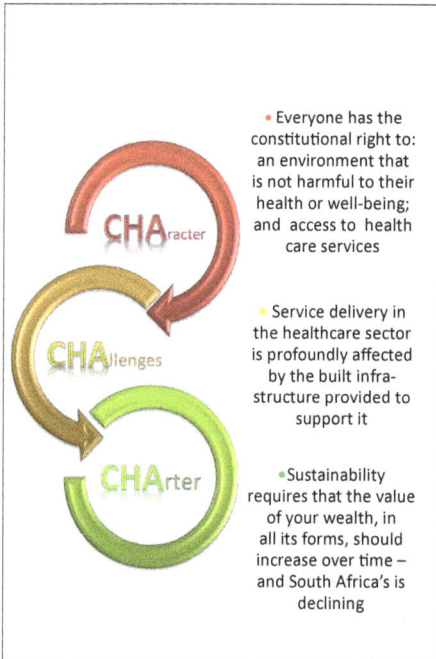

Figure 1. *Rights, service delivery and sustainability.*

Figure 3. *Fourways Private Hospital – Gauteng. Fourways Life Hospital (private), A3 Architects.*

98

This may require some fundamental re-thinking of the compensation structures for built environment professionals which currently incentivise engineering and design methods that may not optimise life-cycle and operational functionality or address environmental concerns.

In the majority of cases the existing health infrastructure portfolio will remain in service for the foreseeable future given that wholesale rapid replacement is unaffordable. Additional work is needed in addressing brown-field building projects and the maintenance of existing facilities. Failure to decisively remove failing infrastructure from service or constructively upgrade it into useful active service can demonstrably increase risks and costs. The IUSS programme has consequently identified a focus area to address maintenance and ensure that conditions are maintained at a more affordable, and hence sustainable, level. More research on evidenced-based decision support in the retrofitting and refurbishing, as well as decommissioning, of existing buildings is sorely needed to ensure that buildings are efficiently and effectively initiated into and removed from service at the appropriate time.

Work planned for the future is to consider the impact on architecture of alternative service modalities such as telemedicine, and examine the role of construction technology (such as open-building technologies) in providing flexible future-proof healthcare buildings. Although it is too early to determine the impact of the full programme, the early signs are that the quality of the infrastructure is improving and underspending is reducing.

99

Figure 4. Khayelitsha Public Hospital – Western Cape. Khayelitsha District Hospital (public), Western Cape. ACG Architects.

Figure 5. Left: Khotsong TB Hospital, Eastern Cape. Right: Hamburg Clinic, Eastern Cape.

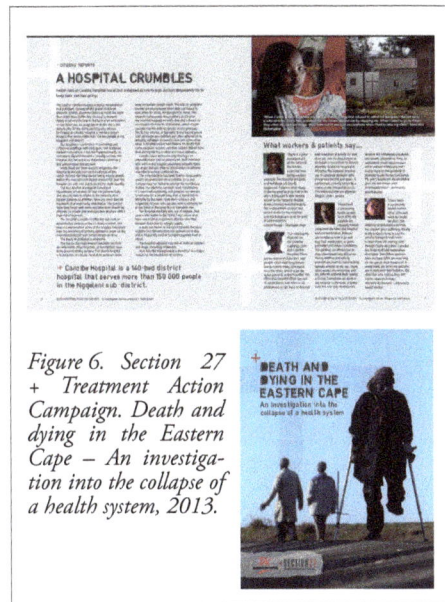

Figure 6. Section 27 + Treatment Action Campaign. Death and dying in the Eastern Cape – An investigation into the collapse of a health system, 2013.

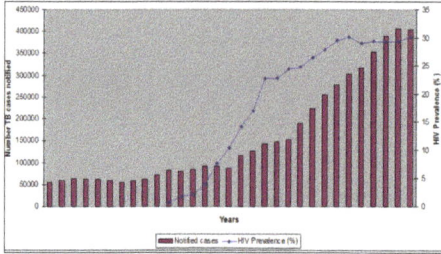

Figure 7. Challenge 1: Quadruple burden of disease. South Africa's life expectancy has dropped, WHO.

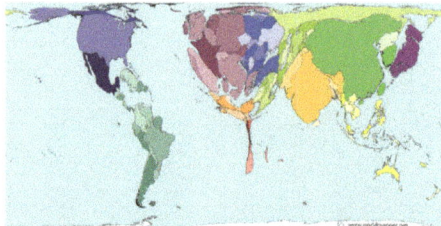

Figure 8. Challenge 2: Resource constraints. © Copyright Sasi Group (University of Sheffield) and Mark Newman (University of Michigan).

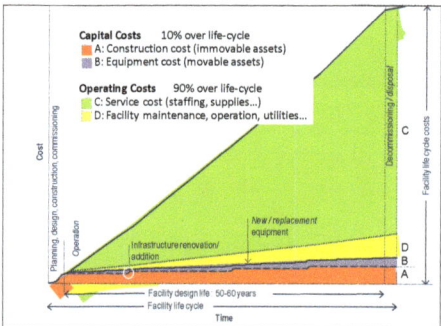

Figure 9. Challenge 3: Healthcare infrastructure lifecycle costs.

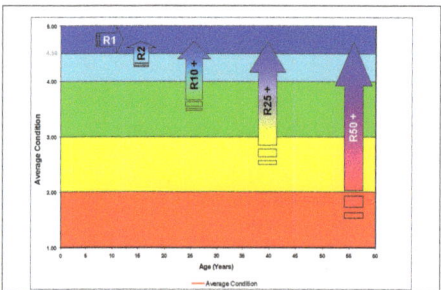

Figure 10. Challenge 3: Neglecting maintenance is very costly = unsustainable (vs cost to retain in "very good" condition).

Figure 11. Challenge 4: Buildings are fixed assets – but healthcare services must be flexible to address technology developments and needs.

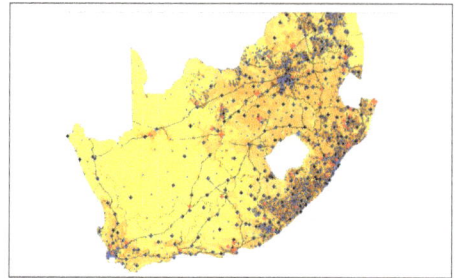

Figure 12. Challenge 5: 9 autonomous provinces and a national government: client department and public works. (Abbott G., 2009).

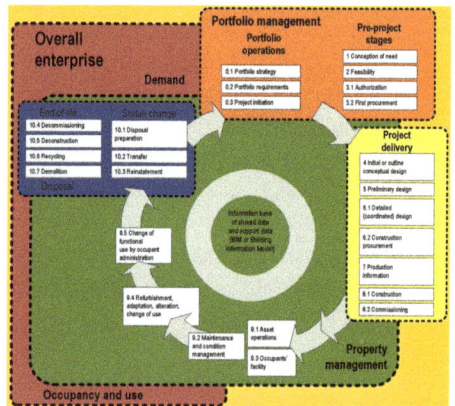

Figure 13. Schematic diagram of phases and stages in the whole life. Source: BSI ISO Buildings and constructed assets, 2010. Redrawn by P. de Jager.

Through this initiative, it is hoped that healthcare infrastructure management will move away from the reactive state of the past few decades, towards a more proactive state, and that a more dependable, equitable and sustainable estate will result.

Rethinking the Health Delivery Model for an Aging Population to Improve Patient-Centered Outcomes and Focus on Wellness and Prevention

Clement L.[1], Juma H.[2]

hjuma@dsai.ca
[1]M.D., CCFP, Medical Advisor, MSSS – Quebec
[2]MSC, Arch., MRAIC, PMP, LEED, Diamond Schmitt Architects

Care collaboration is the process by which the patient and the care team are cooperatively involved in ongoing health care management towards the goal of high quality and cost-effective medical care. The primary care team knows the patient's history and can integrate new information and decisions from a whole-patient perspective and is responsible for coordinating the care with other healthcare professionals. Technology can facilitate the timely transfer of medical information and access to specialty care for an aging population. Wellness and prevention founded on outcomes and measured results are not simply functional factors but actually improve the quality of life for all users.

This presentation highlights 3 key messages: Canada has an aging population; care delivery models must change to respond to today's reality; the care environment must adapt accordingly.

THE FACTS – HEALTHCARE LANDSCAPE

Canada's elderly population is increasing, and is seen as a significant burden on the Canadian health system, especially on emergency departments and the demand for acute inpatient beds. In addition to the aging population, other emerging requirements should be taken into consideration, such as multicare in multi-sites, patient-centered care, prevention and the management of chronic diseases.
The care delivery model must take into account the following impacts and factors: social care and healthcare must provide effective solutions for multiple problems; in order to improve the quality of care, patients must be treated as a whole and there must be proper care environments and physical buildings adapted to the needs of the population; patient and family expectations for quality safe care are increased; chronic diseases management; self-management with multi-disciplinary support; IT can be used to enable communication, education, and telehealth; focus on wellness and prevention; healthcare costs need to be contained, efficient, effective, and appropriate; resources and workforces need to share skills across organizations.
Striving for value: innovative care models embrace the philosophy of "total quality management and continuums of care."

TESIS Inter-University Research Centre "Systems and Technologies for Social and Healthcare Facilities"
University of Florence, Italy

TESIS

102

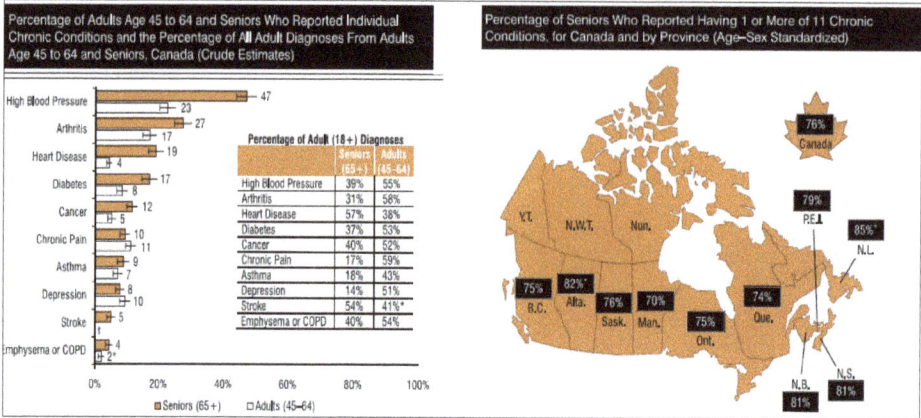

Figure 1. *Aging population and chronic conditions in Canada. Sources: 2008 Canadian Survey of experiences with primary Health Care, Statistics Canada, Canadian Institute for Health Information.*

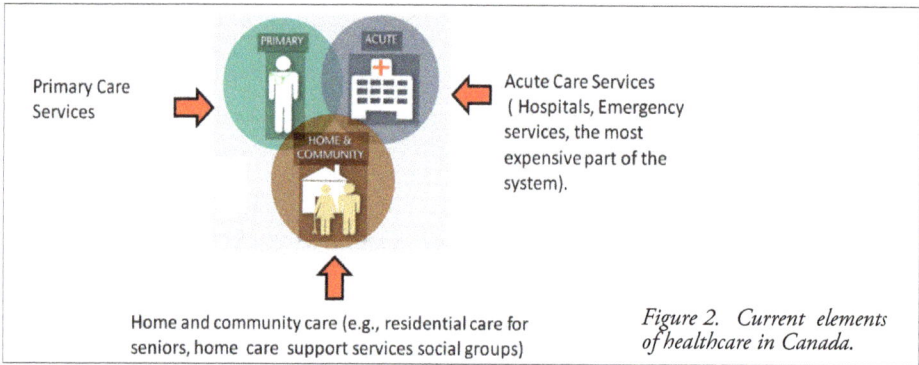

Primary Care Services

Acute Care Services (Hospitals, Emergency services, the most expensive part of the system).

Home and community care (e.g., residential care for seniors, home care support services social groups)

Figure 2. *Current elements of healthcare in Canada.*

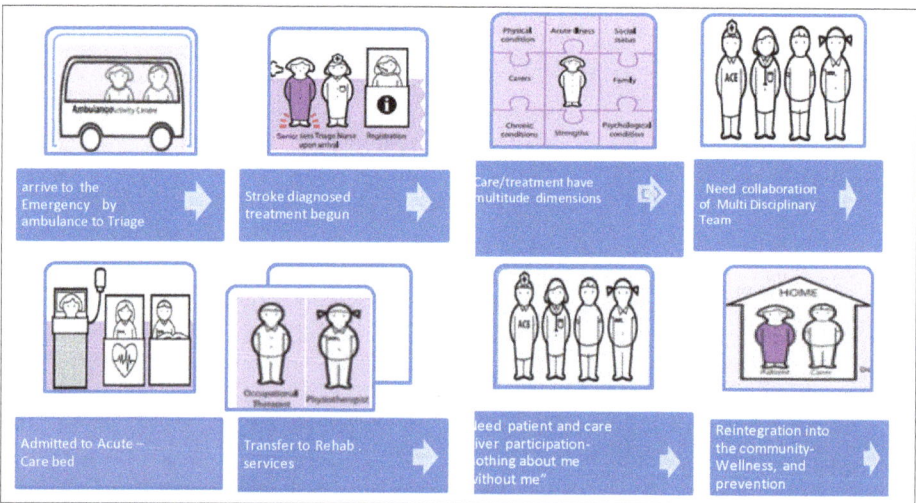

arrive to the Emergency by ambulance to Triage

Stroke diagnosed treatment begun

Care/treatment have multitude dimensions

Need collaboration of Multi Disciplinary Team

Admitted to Acute Care bed

Transfer to Rehab services

Need patient and care giver participation- "nothing about me without me"

Reintegration into the community- Wellness, and prevention

Figure 3. *A story: 75-year old stroke patient, care environment and people.*

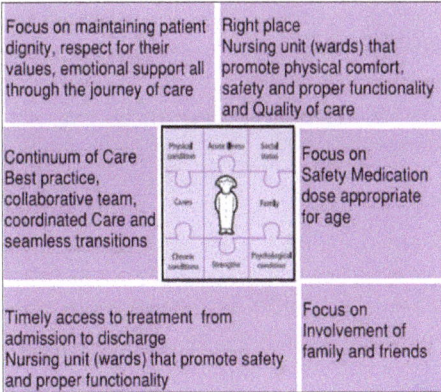

Figure 4. Quality of care. Nursing units (wards) should promote integrated care.

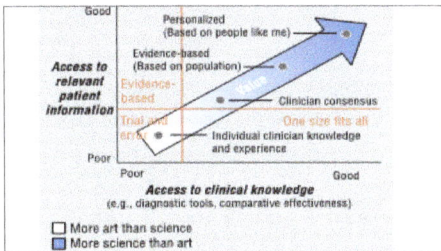

Figure 5. Increasing value requires higher information intensity. Source: IBM Global Business Services and IBM Institute for Business Value.

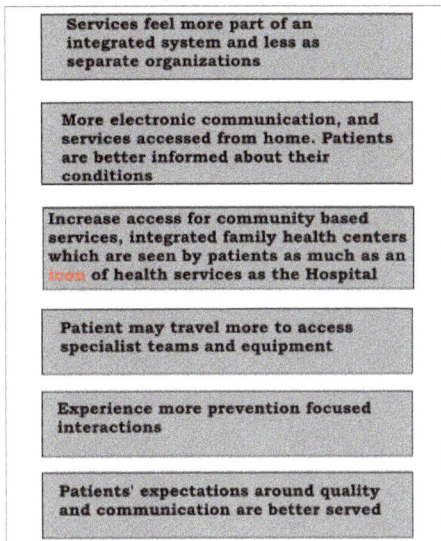

Services feel more part of an integrated system and less as separate organizations

More electronic communication, and services accessed from home. Patients are better informed about their conditions

Increase access for community based services, integrated family health centers which are seen by patients as much as an icon of health services as the Hospital

Patient may travel more to access specialist teams and equipment

Experience more prevention focused interactions

Patients' expectations around quality and communication are better served

Figure 6. Paradigm shift — looking forward. Source: Trends in Service Redesign, August 2010, Ministry of Health, New Zealand.

COLLABORATIVE TEAM BUILDING

Collaborative team building is characterized by the following features: multidimensional assessment and multiagency management teams; multidisciplinary input from physiotherapists, occupational therapists, and community nurses; domain for comprehensive geriatric assessment, care coordination; front-loaded senior decision-making process, including primary care, acute care, self-dependence and wellness; early discharge planning liaison with GP.

103

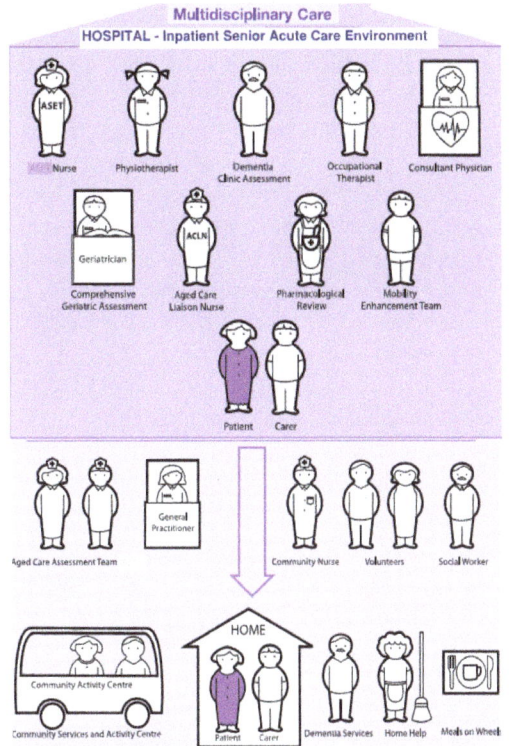

Figure 7. Collaborative team.

CARE ENVIRONMENT "REDESIGN"

Healthcare design must break out of the traditional linear process. Building design processes must support patients, families, and caregivers in a truly human way that impacts patient outcomes.

Ideal healthcare environments can be achieved by integrating architectural products and technology for more functional and pleasant patient experiences; incorporating medical processes, ergonomics and efficiency.

Quality design in buildings: safety is a priority user requirement; design thinking, relationship between users, space and technology requirement; human-centered design interrelationship between performance materials and space (efficiency, safety, effective, timely); patient, caregiver and user satisfaction; research-backed design outcomes provide better quality of care.

Elements that impact the design thinking for senior acute care inpatient units and space planning considerations for an acute care inpatient (senior) adult ward encompass: levels of acuity, and whether there would be multiple levels of acuity; specialties: whether the rooms would be flexible or designed for a specific acuity, i.e. medical, surgical, etc.; the clinical care model, the nurse-to-patient ratio and how it would be implemented; whether clinical care on the unit would be centralized or decentralized; which aspects would increase staff productivity and satisfaction; the supply distribution model: how and where medical supplies and pharmaceuticals would be distributed, stored, and tracked, and by whom; healing environment; patient family amenities; safety/flexibility; visibility versus privacy.

EVIDENCE-BASED DESIGN; RESEARCH-BACKED FINDINGS

A research-based design process requires observation; a safety-driven design goal must be backed by quantifiable scientific findings. It is imperative that the patient, family, nursing staff, environmental services, and facilities management personnel be involved in this process.

Improved building efficiency can help to dramatically increase quality, and in particular it can help to reduce infection and operating costs and increase patient/staff and family satisfaction.

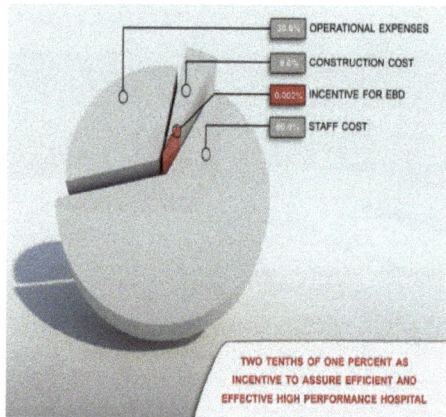

Figure 8. Research cost compared to the life cycle cost of a building. Source: Healthcare Design Magazine 2013 – HKS.

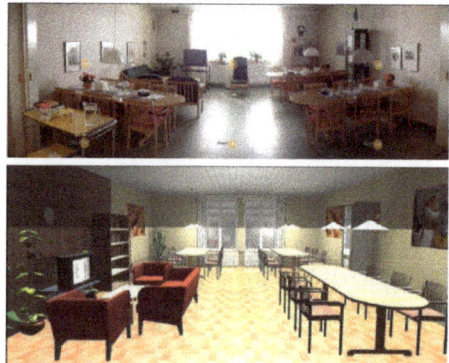

Figure 9. Psychosocially supportive design by Géza Fischl.

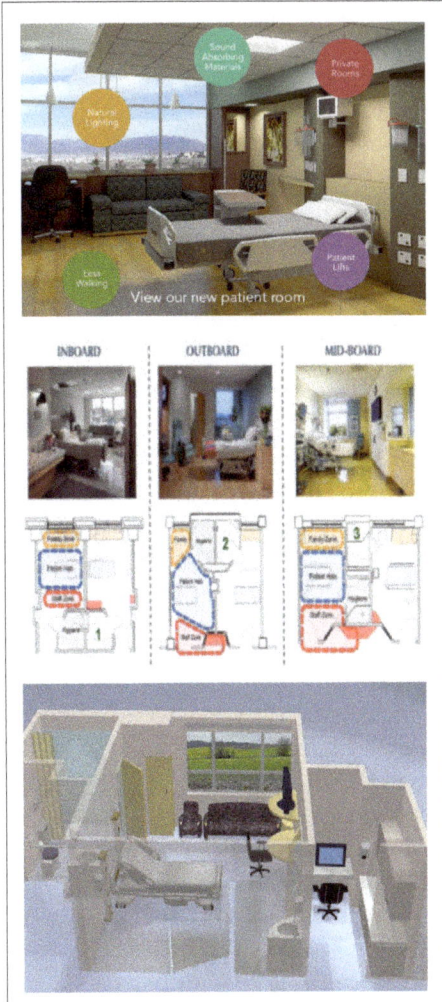

Figure 10. Layout of acute care rooms.

Wellness by design is characterized by: building single-patient rooms; providing adequate space for families to stay overnight in patient rooms; building larger patient bathrooms with double-door access; installing a hand sanitizer at each bedside and in all high patient volume areas to reduce infections; installing ceiling-mounted lifts in the majority of patient rooms to reduce staff back injuries; meeting established noise-level standards throughout the facility; using music as a positive distraction; providing access to natural light in patient and staff areas; using artwork and virtual-reality images; building decentralized nursing stations; including effective way-finding systems.

Sample layouts of inpatient acute care rooms must be able to accommodate the following activities: patient education; nursing out of bed; clock and calendar assisted way-finding; patient information (IT); engaged multi-disciplinary team; comfortable bedside chairs; activity room; family area.

DETAIL DESIGN, FINISHES

The floors, walls and finishes must be able to ensure the following performances: infection control; resilience; pleasing; safe; functional. The following factors should also be borne in mind for the design of the bathroom: location, details, grab rail, door size, accessibility and furniture.

105

Figure 11. Creating private healing spaces.

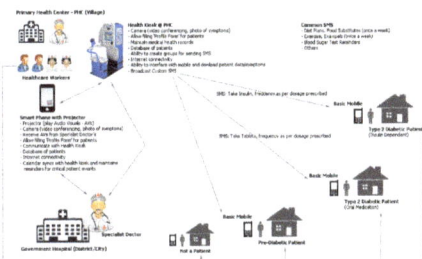

Figure 12. IT enables the use of communication technology to improve care.

106

REFERENCES

Ontario Integrated Client Care Project, September 2011

Ontario's Action Plan for Healthcare, 2012

Ontario's Action Plan for Seniors for a healthy, vibrant and active senior population. 2012- 2036.

Québec's 2012-2017 Action Plan for Seniors. Healthcare facilities in Québec.

Reiling J., Hughes R. G., Murphy M. R. (2008). Chapter 28 The Impact of Facility Design on Patient Safety. In Hughes, R.G. (ed.), Patient Safety and Quality: An Evidence-Based Handbook for Nurses. Rockville (MD): Agency for Healthcare Research and Quality (US).

Toward Patient Centre Care: Digitizing Healthcare Delivery, CMA 5-year strategy for health information technology (HIT) investment Canada. Canadian Medical Association.

Shaping the Future of Continuing Care in Nova Scotia, 2008.

Calculated from data presented in the International Comparisons of Administrative Costs in Health Care, September 1994.

Barker et al. Medication Errors Observed in 36 Health Care Facilities, Arch Intern.

Transforming Aging through Healthier Design (2012). DuPont Healthcare Design Series.

(Fall 2012). Innovation Pilot Study: Acute Care for Elderly (ACE) Unit – Promoting Patient-Centric Care, Health Environments Research and Design Journal HERD.

(March 2012). Acute Care Toolkit-3: Acute medical care for frail people, Royal College of Physicians London UK.

Acute Care of Elderly (ACE), NSW Department of Health, North Sydney, June 2006, www.Health.nsw.gov.au.

(August 5, 2013). HKS Smart Healthcare, HKS Research Team (lean/ nurse station types).

(January 2011). Senior and Health Care System: What Is the Impact of Multiple Chronic Conditions? Canadian Health Information, Institute Canadian, www.chi.ca.

(2009–2016). Health Service Framework for Older People, Australia.

(August 2010). Trends in Service Redesign and New Models of Care, Ministry of Health New Zealand.

Recent Developments
in Health Facility Planning & Design in Australia

Kerr W.[1]

w.kerr@hamessharley.com.au
[1] Adjunct Professor AM, National Director Hames Sharley Architects and Planners, Australia

This presentation provides an overview of the Australian healthcare system and then focus on the arrangements for health facility planning and design in Australia as they pertain to the themes of the seminar.
It provides details of the roles and responsibilities for healthcare provision by the different levels of government in Australia at Federal, State and local levels, and then indicates how this impacts on the provision of healthcare facilities.
This article provides an outline of the arrangements commonly made in Australia for the delivery, operation and maintenance of major health facility projects including the mix of public and private sector roles normally used in these processes. It covers trends in Australia to provide more energy efficient and sustainable buildings and for the built environment to contribute to the promotion of wellness and good health.
The emphasis is on providing an overview of the changes in the Australian healthcare system as the context for the innovations now being observed in the provision of health facilities. The increasing use of public private partnerships is noted as well as the impact of overseas trends on the planning and design of Australian health facilities.

AUSTRALIA AND THE WORLD – AN OVERVIEW

The population of Australia is 22.8 million people. It is a nation of migrants. The first immigrants (our aboriginal residents) arrived 51,000 years ago. The first white settlers arrived in 1788, and then there were subsequent waves of immigration during the 1860s and 1890s due to the Australian gold rushes and in the 1950s with the influx of migrants from war-torn Europe.
The first inhabitants (the Australian Aborigines) today make up 2.4% of the population.
The land mass of Australia covers 7.7 million sq kms (3 million sq miles) resulting in a density of 2.5 persons per sq km.
Australia is the world's 13th largest economy and has the 5th highest per capita income, the 3rd longest female life expectancy and the 4th longest male life expectancy. Australia became a Federation in 1901 and the States retain responsibility for many key services including the provision of healthcare services.

AUSTRALIA HEALTHCARE SYSTEM

Because healthcare is a State's responsibility, all State Governments develop, own, and operate hospitals. The State Governments are responsible for acute, mental and community healthcare services.

There are 9 separate health systems in Australia (6 States and 2 Territories) plus separate healthcare arrangements for Aborigines. Unfortunately our aboriginal population suffers from very poor healthcare outcomes.

There are over 1,326 hospitals (753 public, 280 private, and 293 day-only facilities). Approximately 9.4% of Australia's GPD is spent on healthcare (up from 7.6% in 1975).

The Federal (Commonwealth) Government established a national health insurance system in 1975 and a free Government healthcare system (now called Medicare) in 1984. The Federal Government also reimburses the cost of visiting general medical practitioners and funds a substantial portion of the cost of pharmaceuticals for Australian residents.

HOSPITALS

While hospitals today represent the ultimate sophistication in healthcare delivery, it is important to recognise that prior to the twentieth century, hospitals were normally only utilised by the poor and destitute, or those near death. The wealthy and 'well-off' were treated at home.

With advances in medical technology and treatment techniques in the late nineteenth century, the role (and perceptions) of hospitals changed. As health-

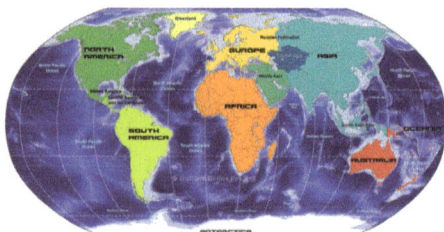

Figure 1.   *Australia and the world.*

Figure 2.   *Fiona Stanley Hospital, Western Australia.*

Figure 3.   *Royal Children's Hospital, Victoria.*

108

care advanced hospitals became a symbol of these medical advances and were utilised by both rich and poor members of the growing Australian population. Salubrity became a priority in hospital design with the role of sunlight and fresh air in the curing of disease having a crucial influence over the design.

HEALTH FACILITY PLANNING AND DESIGN

Because of their responsibility for healthcare, health facility development is also a State duty. Given that Australia is a young country, most hospitals were built after World War II to cope with the influx of postwar migration. Most of these hospitals were built by the Public Works Departments of the State Governments.

However in the 1980-90s, most Public Works Departments outsourced the design work to the private sector, but traditional procurement methods continued to be used until 2000.
During the period 2000-05 a number of State Governments started to use Public

Private Partnerships (PPPs). A number of major PPP projects have now been completed, but because each State utilizes its own processes and procedures, there is very little sharing of information.

As hospital design increased in complexity, each of these separate jurisdictions developed their own standards and regulations for both public and private facilities. It was not until November 2006 that the Australasian Health Facility Guidelines were launched as an attempt at national alignment of the plethora of different standards and guidelines that had evolved since Federation.

During the period 2005-10 the States collaborated with New Zealand to fund the research Centre for Health Assets Australasia. However, unfortunately the funding was terminated in December 2010 and therefore at present there is no national research centre in Australia or formal processes for sharing research information between the project teams located in each State.

109

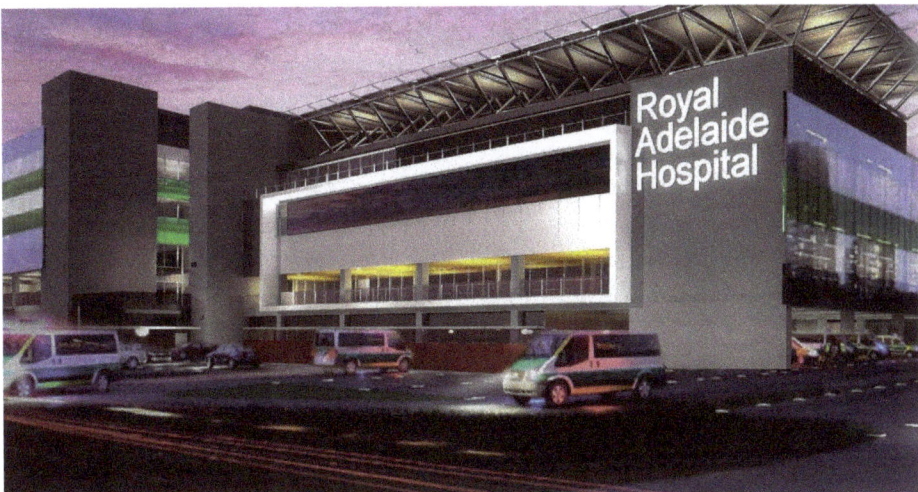

Figure 4. Royal Adelaide Hospital, South Australia.

REBUILDING THE HOSPITALS OF AUSTRALIA

Over the past 15 years there has been a massive program of rebuilding Australia's public and private hospitals. Examples of the projects built during this period include:
- The Royal Children's Hospital in Melbourne, Victoria;
- The Royal Women's Hospital in Melbourne, Victoria;
- The Victorian Comprehensive Cancer Centre in Melbourne;
- Royal North Shore Hospital in Sydney, New South Wales;
- The Royal Adelaide Hospital in Adelaide, South Australia;
- The Gold Coast Hospital in Queensland;
- The Brisbane Children's Hospital in Queensland;
- The Fiona Stanley Hospital in Perth, Western Australia;
- The New Childrens Hospital in Perth, Western Australia.

Many of these projects have made use of the research conducted overseas to provide the foundations for Evidence-Based Design and its application in Australia. Work now needs to be undertaken to evaluate the outcomes achieved by these new facilities to ensure that the outcomes achieved match the expectations of the design teams.

110

Figure 6. Brisbane Children's Hospital, Queensland.

PREPARATIONS FOR THE FUTURE

The lessons learnt from this significant program of rebuilding have highlighted the need for:
- Further research in the field of health facility planning & design;
- Improved coordination between projects and States;
- The need for improved sharing of information;
- The need for a National Centre of Research Excellence;
- The need to establish postgraduate programs in health facility planning and design.

Currently there are no postgraduate programs in health facility design in Australia due to the relatively small population base to support this specialization.

However, to achieve these outcomes we need to ensure that a funding mechanism is established where capital costs are either recompensed as part of the operational budgets or capital works budgets include a "levy" for research and evaluation.

Figure 5. Gold Coast Hospital, Queensland.

DESIGN ISSUES FOR HEALTHCARE BUILDINGS
Session introduction

This session gathers together articles that outline a global vision of hospital design issues in their diverse articulations and connotations. The authors identify the single elements comprising the large and complex topic of hospital design and show the relationships between the various elements at different levels of definition. It is possible see how each element that helps to outline the form of the hospital represents a complex topic in itself: patient rooms, the organization of flows of people and materials, the relationships between the hospital and the city and other facilities dedicated to different levels of care, strategies for the completion of construction works and the management of the building during operation. These elements are observed from the different viewpoints of designers, researchers and professionals engaged in hospital management.

The first core of this complexity is the patient room where it is essential to take into account all aspects that contribute to the well-being of the patient in terms of care, the presence of family and staff efficiency, as well as those related to psychological and physical comfort, natural lighting and views of the outside. The organization of the flow of materials and people is an important aspect for efficiency in the delivery of care. It is also necessary ask what level of flexibility healthcare facilities must have in order to meet the demands of the changing technologies, therapeutic approaches and needs of patients. The originality of these articles is that in gathering and analysing all past and present issues that affect healthcare design, they allow future issues to be accurately outlined.

Looking at the problem from a higher level it is possible see how hospitals have become a point of reference not only for treatment but also for research and education. While the main care activities have been strengthened by placing them alongside the main functions of research and education, many other care activities are not only concentrated in the hospital but are also geographically distributed and are held in external facilities that can provide primary care closest to the daily lives of patients. Healthcare systems have evolved to become complex humanized "landscapes" consisting of a series of facilities that take charge of patients and respond appropriately to different levels of demand for care.

The hospital not only has to deal with the other facilities constituting part of the landscape but has also assumed an essential role in relations with the entire community. The presence of commercial activities or activities related to health promotion within the hospital ensures that the hospital assumes a fundamental role within the functional tissue of the city and in the complex relationship with the infrastructure and the territory.

Comparative Studies of Environment and Hospital Bed Management Between Single-Room Wards and Mixed Multi-Room Wards

Kosuge R.[1]

kosuge-r@kobe-du.ac.jp
[1]Department of Environmental Design, Kobe Design University, Kobe, Japan

This study describes the differences in environment and hospital bed management between single-room wards and mixed multi-room wards on the basis of a before–after comparison in a redesigned hospital in Tochigi prefecture, Japan. The survey took into account patient safety, patient accidents, length of visitor stay, and patient and staff satisfaction. The results indicated that both types of wards showed a tendency to admit patients requiring a high level of nursing care near the staff station. This presentation will provide a closer examination of the effects of single-room wards.

Keywords: *hospital, ward, bed management, patient room*

BACKGROUND AND OBJECTIVES

Background

The Japanese government is currently attempting to separate patients with chronic diseases from acute-care hospitals due to increasing medical expenses and an aging society. In this situation, the proportion of private rooms in a hospital ward is likely to increase in many acute-care hospitals in Japan.

Objectives

This study aimed to compare hospital bed management, patient safety, and length of visitor stay between single-room wards and mixed multi-room wards on the basis of a before–after comparison in a redesigned hospital in Tochigi prefecture, Japan (Figures 1 & 2).

HOSPITAL BED MANAGEMENT

Surveys were conducted for 32 days by nurses both before and after the redesign, and records were kept of each patient's bed location, the extent of nursing required by each patient, and the reasons for each patient bed transfer.

The results demonstrate that both types of wards tend to place patients requiring a high level of nursing care near the staff station (Figure 3).

In the case of mixed multi-room wards, there were many patient bed transfers. The most common reasons for transfer included patient requests for a favorable therapeutic environment, roommate's infection, and terminal phase of disease. The maximum number of bed transfers for a patient was 5 times in 32 days in the mixed multi-room ward. Moreover, the design of a multi-room ward causes a lot of chain-reaction

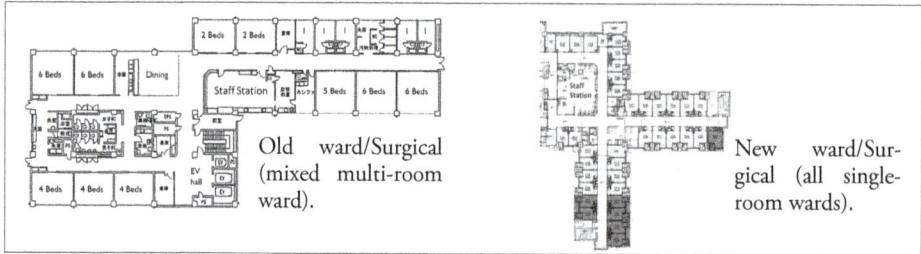

Old ward/Surgical (mixed multi-room ward).

New ward/Surgical (all single-room wards).

transfers (Figure 4). However, in the single-room wards in the Internal Medicine department, these types of bed transfers were not observed.

The study concludes that the number of patient bed transfers is lower in single-room wards than in mixed multi-room wards.

HOSPITAL BED MANAGEMENT

Surveys were conducted for 32 days by nurses both before and after the redesign, and records were kept of each patient's bed location, the extent of nursing required by each patient, and the reasons for each patient bed transfer.

The results demonstrate that both types of wards tend to place patients requiring a high level of nursing care near the staff station (Figure 3).

In the case of mixed multi-room wards, there were many patient bed transfers. The most common reasons for transfer included patient requests for a favorable therapeutic environment, roommate's infection, and terminal phase of disease. The maximum number of bed transfers for a patient was 5 times in 32 days in the mixed multi-room ward. Moreover, the design of a multi-room ward causes a lot of chain-reaction transfers (Figure 4). However, in the single-room wards in the Internal Medicine department, these types of bed transfers were not observed.

The study concludes that the number of patient bed transfers is lower in single-room wards than in mixed multi-room wards.

Japanese Red Cross Ashikaga Hospital, Tochigi, Japan			
Mixed multi-room wards		Single-room wards	
(Before Rebuilding)		(After Rebuilding)	
Total beds	555 beds	Total beds	555 beds
Unit beds	50 beds/unit	Unit beds	35 beds/unit
Average days of hospital stay	Surgical, 17.9 Medical, 28.8	Average days of hospital stay	Surgical, 16.5 Medical, 26.5
Proportion of private rooms	Surgical, 10%, Medical, 18%	Percentage of private rooms	Surgical, 100% Medical, 100%
Japanese Red Cross Ashikaga Hospital, Tochigi, Japan			
Mixed multi-room wards		Single-room wards	
(Before Rebuilding)		(After Rebuilding)	
Total beds	555 beds	Total beds	555 beds
Unit beds	50 beds/unit	Unit beds	35 beds/unit
Average days of hospital stay	Surgical, 17.9 Medical, 28.8	Average days of hospital stay	Surgical, 16.5 Medical, 26.5
Proportion of private rooms	Surgical, 10%, Medical, 18%	Percentage of private rooms	Surgical, 100% Medical, 100%

Figure 1. Case Information.

PATIENT SAFETY

Untoward accidents recorded by nurses both before and after the redesign were compared to check differences in the rate of patient falls.

The number of patient falls increased slightly after redesign in the single-room wards. In a single room patients have their own toilet. This may be the cause of the increase in fall incidents because patients try to visit the toilet by themselves. Encouragement of early rising from patient beds is one of the merits of having a toilet in the room, but it is critical to recognize the increased risks of patient falls and take preventative measures. The floor finishes in single-room wards were renovated from vinyl to carpet so that patients who fell could escape with a minor injury.

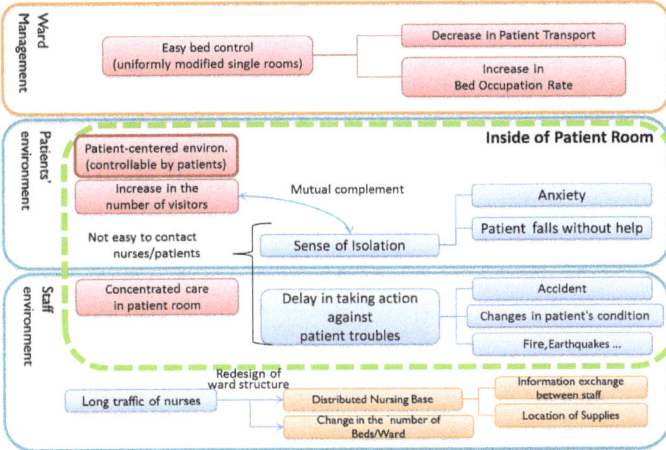

115

Figure 2. Expected changes in hospital wards after renovation of all single-room wards. Source: own elaboration.

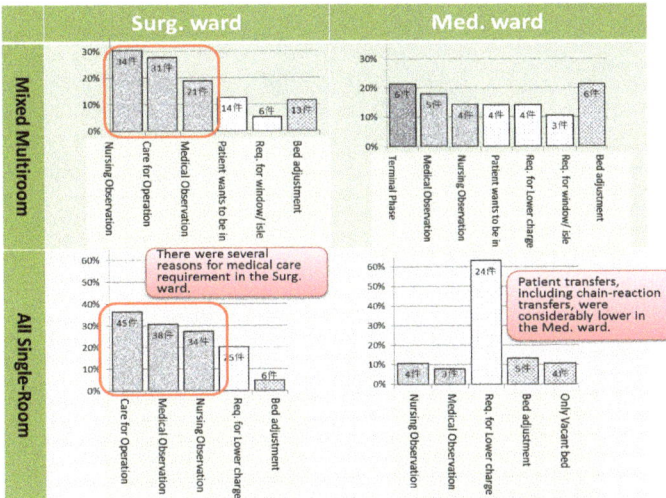

Figure 3. Reasons for patient relocation (multiple answers).

Chain-Reaction of Patient Transfer

Example:
26/4/2011 Surg. ward

The conditions of two terminal patients required that nurses relocate them to rooms near the staff station.

However, bed occupation was near maximum capacity. Therefore, nurses had to relocate other patients who did not need to be moved.

This situation was not rare in this ward; in fact, needless transfers occurred nine times per month during the survey.

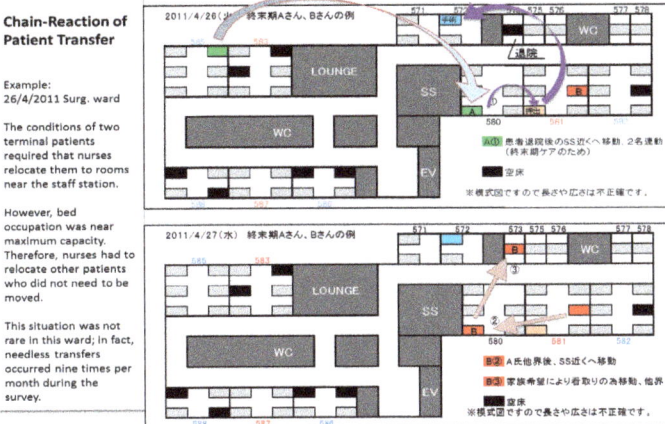

Figure 4. Example of a patient transfer chain reaction in a multi-room ward. Source: own elaboration.

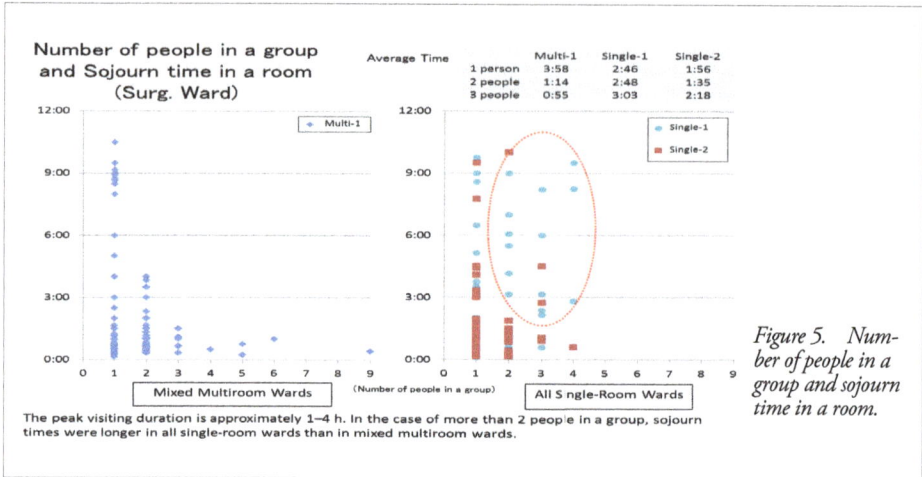

Figure 5. Number of people in a group and sojourn time in a room.

LENGTH OF VISITOR STAY

Visitors' books were used to record visits for a month in both kinds of wards, and it was found that there were two types of visitor groups.

The first can be described as a caretaker for the patient, usually a family member. They came to the patient room early in the morning and spent more than 4 hours at the bedside in both types of wards.

The second type are more transient visitors coming to see the patients recover, usually other family members or friends. These visitors remained at the bedside for approximately 1 hour in the mixed multi-room wards. However, in single-room wards these visitors stayed much longer (Figure 5). If the rooms were designed with spaces for these transient visitors they may linger longer. Social interaction is very important for a patient's recovery.

PATIENT AND STAFF SATISFACTION

The study included a questionnaire survey of patients and staff in the wards. The questionnaire queried the ward environment in terms of recovery and nursing work. Single-room wards were reported to guarantee a restful sleep for patients. Some nurses answered that there was a corresponding decrease in the total amount of hypnotic drugs administered to patients. In addition, the primary reason for nurse satisfaction was the ease of infection control.

CONCLUSIONS

There are still many 4-bed rooms in hospitals in Japan. In this aging society, a lot of portable latrines are used at the bedside with thin curtains.

The surveys in this study revealed that single-bed rooms have many merits. Not all patients like to be assigned to single rooms, but wards exclusively comprised of single rooms may be well suited for current acute hospitals according to the findings of this study.

AKNOWLEDGMENTS

Thanks to the Japanese Red Cross Ashikaga Hospital for its enormous contribution and generous support.

This survey was conducted from March 2011 to December 2011. The work was supported by MEXT KAKENHI Grant-in-Aid no. 50584471.

Balancing Clinical Care Needs with Optimizing the Patient and Family Experience: A Case Study on Interdisciplinary Research and Design Collaboration.

Phillips T.[1], Allison D.[2] and Garvey T.[3]

phillit@algonquincollege.com
[1] Algonquin College School of Media & Design, Professor, Ottawa, Canada
[2] Clemson University Graduate Studies in Architecture + Health, Professor/Director, Clemson, South Carolina, USA
[3] Carleton University School of Industrial Design, Professor/Director, Ottawa, Canada

117

New insights into inpatient hospital room design open up design research potential to address issues around patient, staff and family satisfaction and experience in healthcare settings. With the trend towards mostly private rooms, increasing restrictions on space to accommodate complex levels of care, safety and infection prevention concerns and growing expectations for a health-supportive environment for patients, families and caregivers, a more systematic approach to the design of patient rooms addressing the real context is necessary.

Keywords: *acute care, patient room, patient and family centred, interdisciplinary collaboration, case study.*

This paper shares the methods and results of a recent interdisciplinary design-research study that looks at what elements and features of a patient room address staff and clinical needs while contributing to the patient and family's perception of a supportive healthcare environment. One graduate student on the project focused her thesis research on the perceived patient and family experience in an acute-care patient room. Using a framework addressing the physical, emotional and social implications for the design of patient rooms, the results from an online survey were triangulated with interviews and site observations. Consistent with the literature on patient room environments, noise, lighting and views (of nature) were the top three things that contributed to the perception of a healing environment. However, equipment, furniture and room layout also played a significant role in contributing to both a positive and negative experience for patients and family members.

Findings from this study were condensed into patient and family-centered design criteria based on the functional as well as the potential emotional and social implications of the design of patient room settings.

In response to how these criteria, along with the myriad of complex require-ments for acute-care patient room de-sign, can be better integrated to sup-port patient-and-family-centred care, a case study of a Patient Room Prototype (PRP) project is presented.

118

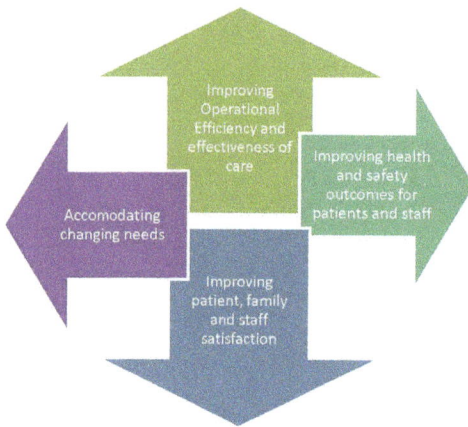

Figure 1. Overlapping/conflicting criteria in pa-tient room design.

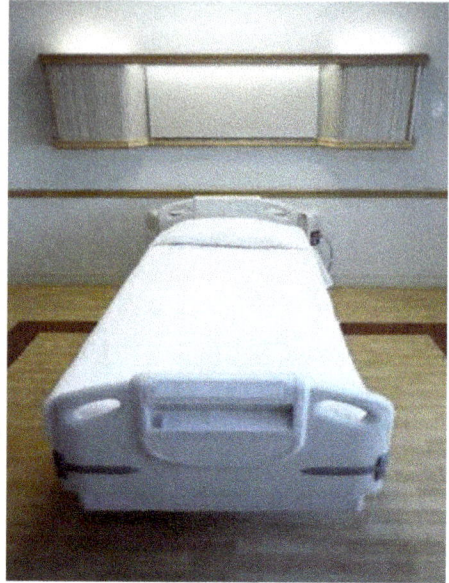

Figure 2. More design research is needed to look at the role of patient room features that address fam-ily caregiver needs and what specific features sig-nificantly contribute to overall family satisfaction in the patient room. Hamilton & McCuskey Shepley, 2010.

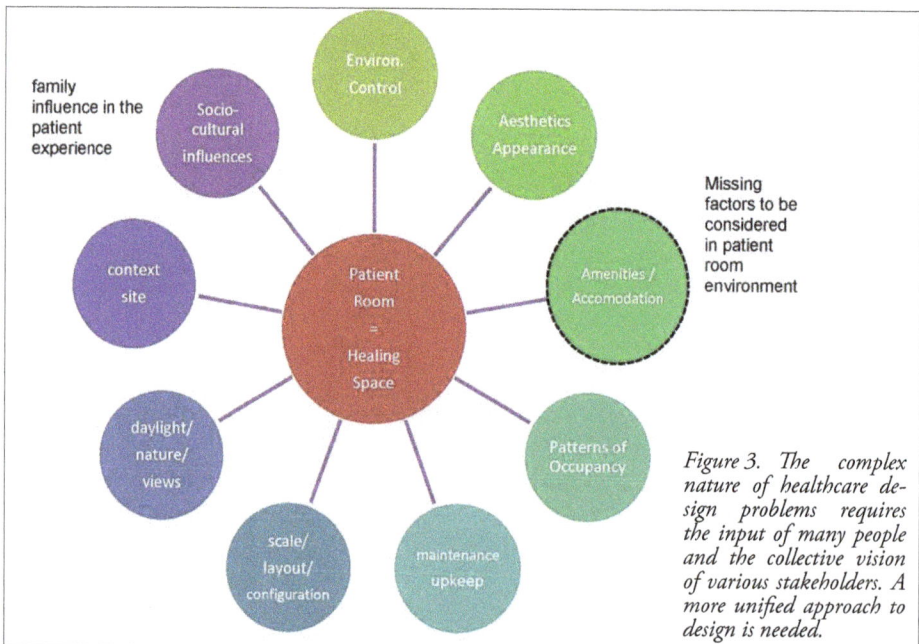

Figure 3. The complex nature of healthcare de-sign problems requires the input of many people and the collective vision of various stakeholders. A more unified approach to design is needed.

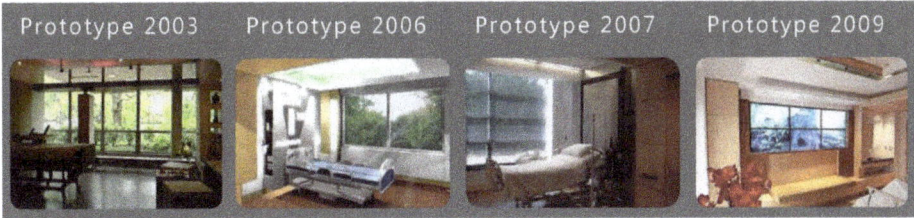

Figure 4. Case Study: Patient Room Prototype Project (PRPP). Interdisciplinary collaboration between Clemson University and Carleton University.

119

Figure 5. Emergent themes: refinement as progress; accommodate rather than integrate technology; push to the point of failure; the value of interdisciplinary design; keeping the user at the centre.

Figure 6. Patients and families as stakeholders.

The case study is an iteration of an on-going collaboration between two universities using a participatory approach to better integrate design and research into the development of new, speculative patient care environments (Battisto & Allison, 2008, Garvey, 2009).

To address the specific concerns of the patient and family experience and accommodation within the patient room environment, the focus of this cycle (PRPv2012) was on the headwall (patient/staff zone) and footwall (family/staff zone). An overview of the project objectives, the Patient Room Prototype process as well as innovative results and lessons learned are discussed.

120

REFERENCES

Battisto, D., & Allison, D. (2008, September). A Patient Room Prototype: Bridging Design and Research. Academy Journal.

Garvey, T. (2009). Looking for the Real World: Balancing Expectations and Inspiration in Design Collaborations. IAS-DR09, (pp. 1-9). Seoul, Korea.

Phillips, T. (2012). Design of Acute Care Patient Rooms for Improved Patient/Family Experience: A Case for Interdisciplinary Collaboration. (Master Thesis), Carleton University, Ottawa, Canada.

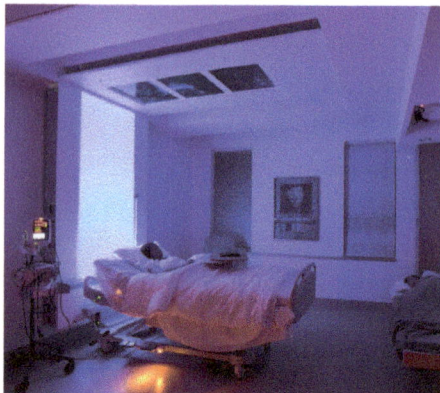

Figure 7. 2012 prototype room.

Design of Intensive Care Unit Windows
for Daylighting and External Views in Desert Climates:
Results of Simulation-Based Research

Sherif A.[1], Sabry H.[2], Elzafarany A.[3], Gadelhak M.[2], Aly M.[1] and Arafa R.[1]

asherif@aucegypt.edu
[1] The American University in Cairo, Cairo, Egypt
[2] Ain-Shams University, Cairo, Egypt
[3] Cairo University, Cairo, Egypt

Access to external views and natural light produce a stress-reducing effect in health-care facilities. They can reduce pain and the length of stay. They provide patients with a sense of time and connection to the environment. Very little research work has addressed satisfaction with daylighting performance and external views in Intensive Care Units in a quantitative way, especially in desert locations.

This paper aims to identify the window sizes (expressed as Window-to-Wall Ratio – WWR) and shading system configurations that could fulfill adequate daylighting requirements, avoid glare and maximize external views.

First of all, daylighting adequacy and avoidance of glare were addressed. In the south orientation, the most promising system was the external solar screen. The second promising case involved the use of three horizontal sun breakers. The triple-glazed clear, low emissivity and argon-filled window also showed acceptable results. For the east orientation the most promising cases appeared when a horizontal sun shading device (45° cut-off sun shading angle) and an external solar screen were used; while none of the glazing systems provided acceptable results. In the north orientation, all tested glazing systems and window configurations were successful. They offered designers a wide range of WWRs to choose from, especially for shading systems.

Secondly, the exposure to external views was analyzed in association with daylighting performance. For windows protected by horizontal sun breakers, the best configuration is a window with a 1:1 Aspect Ratio (AR) and 16% WWR, followed by a window with a 1:2 AR and 24% WWR. The performance of an unprotected window with a light shelf was much lower, where only three configurations resulted in an acceptable performance. These windows had 2:1 and 1:1 ARs with 16% WWR and 2:1 AR with 24% WWR. However, successful cases provided a wider range of acceptable window position options.

Keywords: *daylighting, desert, intensive care unit, window, view*

INTRODUCTION

Most healthcare design guidelines stipulate the existence of windows in hospital Intensive Care Units (ICUs). Access to external views and natural light in healthcare facilities was found to have an important stress-reducing effect, where it can reduce the pain and length of stay in hospital. It also provides patients with a sense of time and connects them to the environment. Careful window design and shading systems for these spaces can help to improve visual comfort and access to external views.

The positive effect of daylighting on hospital users has been addressed in a number of publications. The impact of daylight and window views on patient pain levels, length of stay, staff errors, absenteeism, and vacancy rates were examined in a paper by Shepley, et al. (2012). ICU patients were randomly selected from two ICUs; one was operational until 2007, the second opened in 2007. Comparing light levels, independent of ICU assignment, supported the hypothesis that increased light levels reduce pain perception and length of stay, but the relationship was not statistically significant. However, the research found that high levels of natural light and window views might positively affect staff absenteeism and staff vacancies. Records on patient recovery after cholecystectomy in a suburban Pennsylvania hospital between 1972 and 1981 were examined to determine whether assignment to a room with a window view of a natural setting might have restorative influences. Twenty-three surgical patients assigned to rooms with windows looking out on a natural scene had shorter postoperative hospital stays, received fewer negative evaluative comments in nurses' notes, and took fewer potent analgesics than 23 matched patients in similar rooms with windows facing a brick building wall (Ulrich, 1984).

In another setting, a study by Ozdemir (2010) examined the effect of the window view on the perception of spaciousness, brightness and ultimately on room satisfaction in a campus building for office spaces. The study aimed to assess the openness and naturalness of the window views according to expert reviewers and room occupants. Research results demonstrated that rooms with expanded open window views were perceived to be larger, while rooms on the lower floors were perceived to be darker. Findings also revealed that occupants in offices with more open and natural views rate their room satisfaction more highly.

Very little research work addressed the satisfaction of daylighting performance and external views in Intensive Care Units in a quantitative way. A small number of publications have addressed the utilization of window size and shading systems to control solar penetration, and thus the improvement of daylighting in ICUs located in the desert.

Shaping windows for the provision of acceptable daylighting performance while improving access to external views could prove useful in their utilization as effective means for reaching more sustainable hospital designs, thus helping to improve the delivery of better healthcare facilities.

122

OBJECTIVE

This paper addressed the design of hospital Intensive Care Unit windows to achieve visual comfort and improve access to external views. The aim was to identify the window size and shading system configurations that could fulfill daylighting adequacy, avoidance of glare and maximize external views.

The research approach adopted was divided into two parts:
1. Part One: Analysis of daylighting adequacy and avoidance of glare.
2. Part Two: Analysis of exposure to external views.

PART ONE: ANALYSIS OF DAYLIGHTING ADEQUACY AND AVOIDANCE OF GLARE

Nine glazing and shading designs were simulated for daylighting performance. These were divided into two groups: the first group included "Glazing Systems," while the second included "Shading Systems." These cases were modelled in the south, east and north orientations. They were defined based on the results of previous publications by the authors which examined the daylighting and energy consumption of ICU rooms (Sherif, et al. 2013-a, and Sherif, et al. 2013-b). Table 1 illustrates the shapes of these cases.

• *Glazing Systems:* three types of glazing were selected for the investigations as follows:

o *Case A:* A double-glazed clear window, TR= 75% U= 0.475 W/m² –k

o *Case B:* A triple-glazed clear, low emissivity and argon-filled window TR= 66% U= 0.78 W/m²–k

o *Case C:* A single-glazed, reflective and tinted window TR=25% - U=0.65 W/m²–k

• *Shading Systems:* six shading systems were selected for the investigations as follows:

o *Case D:* A single horizontal sun-breaker. It extends above the window to provide a 30° cut-off sun shading angle (reflectance = 50%).

o *Case E:* A single horizontal sun-breaker. It extends above the window to provide a 45° cut-off sun shading angle (reflectance = 50%).

o *Case F:* Three horizontal sun-breakers. These were spaced to provide a 45° cut-off sun shading angle (reflectance = 50%).

o *Case G:* Four vertical sun breakers. These were spaced at a 45° cut-off sun shading angle (reflectance = 50%).

o *Case H:* An external light shelf located at 2/3 of the window height: (upper surface reflectance = 90%).

o *Case I:* An external perforated solar screen with 1:1 aspect ratio and 90% perforation rate (reflectance = 50%).

123

Table 1: The studied glazing and shading systems.

124

Methodology of Part One

A typical ICU patient space was selected for investigation. Its layout, dimensions and parameters were based on standard ICU space requirements (FGI, 2010). These are illustrated in Figure 1 and Table 2. The space was assumed to be located on the first floor of a hospital building in the outskirts of Cairo, Egypt, which enjoys a year-round desert clear sky. External conditions assumed that no external obstruction was located in front of the window, and the external ground had a reflectance of 20%.

Simulation was conducted using the climatic data of the city of Cairo (30°6'N, 31°24'E, alt. 75 m). The typical meteorological year (TMY3)

weather data of Cairo was used in the simulation. According to Climate and Temperature (2013), Cairo is classified as a subtropical desert/low-latitude arid climate (Köppen-Geiger classification: BWh) that is hot year-round. The annual average temperature is 21.4 °C. The average maximum temperature during the summer months is 35 °C, while the average minimum temperature in the winter months is 9 °C. Annual sunshine averages 3451 hours.

Six window sizes were examined. These had Window-to-Wall Ratios (WWR) equal to 8%, 16%, 24%, 32%, 40% and 48%. Their shapes and locations along the external wall of the ICU space are illustrated in Figure 2.

Figure 1. Floor plan and cross section of the tested ICU space.

Indoor Space / Window Parameters		
Floor level	First Floor (+4.00 m)	
Dimensions (m)	5.75*4.00*3.00	
Internal Surfaces Materials (Reflectance)		
Walls	Ceiling	Floor
50%	80.0%	20.0%
(Medium Coloured Off-White)	(White Coloured)	(Wooden Floor)

Table 2: Parameters of the tested ICU space.

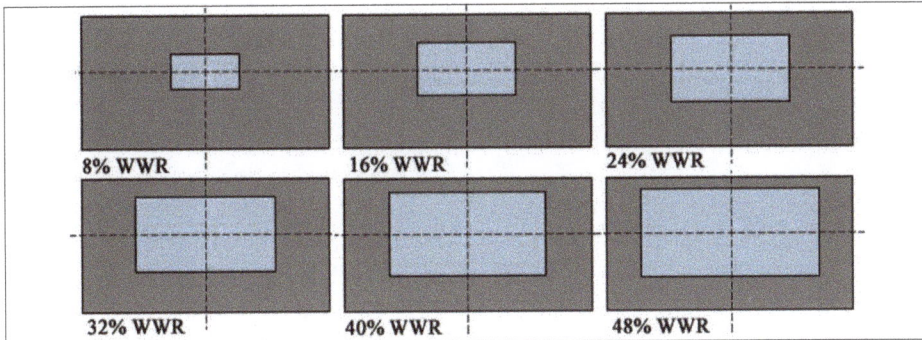

Figure 2. Shapes and positions of the tested windows on the external wall.

Methodology of Daylight Availability Analysis

Experimentation was conducted for year-round performance using the Dynamic Daylight Perf ormance Metrics (DDPM). The DIVA plugin was used to perform the daylight analysis via integration with Radiance and DAYSIM (Reinhart and Wienhold, 2011). DIVA (Design Iterate Validate Adapt) is an environmental analysis plugin for the Rhinoceros 3D Nurbs modelling program (McNeal, 2010). Simulation parameters are presented in Table 3. The occupied time of the simulations was from sunrise to sunset. The sunset and sunrise times were determined for each day using the sunset calculator for the city of Cairo (Time and Date AS, 2012). Simulations were carried out at two reference planes having different Lx threshold levels which meet the IESNA lighting recommendations for Intensive Care Unit spaces (IESNA, 2000). These were 100 Lx on the floor plane (at a 0.05 m height) and 300 Lx on the patient bed plane (at a 0.90 m height). At each reference plane, a measurement was calculated for points spaced using a grid of 0.50 m x 0.50 m intervals. The grid and reference planes were illustrated in Figure 1. Three Daylight Availability evaluation levels were used: "daylit," "partially daylit" and "over lit" areas. The daylit areas are those areas that received sufficient daylight at least half of the year-round occupied time. The partially daylit areas are those areas that did not receive sufficient daylight at least half of the year-round occupied time. The over lit areas are those areas that received an oversupply of daylight, where 10 times the target illuminance was reached for at least 5% of the year-round occupied time (Reinhart & Wienold, 2011). The acceptance criterion adopted in this paper considered the cases where the "daylit" area reached ≥50% of the tested space to have "acceptable" performance. This criterion was to be satisfied at both the floor and the patient bed planes. Cases with larger sizes and wider ranges of accepted WWRs were considered more successful as they provide the designer with more options and better visual access to the outside.

TESIS Inter-University Research Centre "Systems and Technologies for Social and Healthcare Facilities"
University of Florence, Italy

Ambient bounces	Ambient divisions	Ambient sampling	Ambient accuracy	Ambient resolution	Direct threshold
6	1000	20	0.1	300	0

Table 3: Radiance simulation parameters.

Methodology of Glare Probability Analysis

The aim of this stage was to examine patient visual comfort for the cases that achieved acceptable performance in the first stage. Special focus was given to cases that posed a high potential for glare occurrence at the patient bed surface, where the overlit areas were present at ≥ 30% of the patient bed reference plane (1/3 patient bed area). Annual glare predictions were simulated for these cases using Daysim, which employs the Daylight Glare Probability (DGP) metric (Wienold, 2009). DGP represents the probability that a person is disturbed by glare. It is derived from a subjective user evaluation by Wienold and Christoffersen (2006). Annual DGP uses a simplified method that calculates the vertical illuminance at the eye level as a parameter which can affect the brightness of the space. In this method, glare was divided into four categories: intolerable glare (DGP ≥ 45%), disturbing glare (45% > DGP ≥ 40%), perceptible glare (40% >DGP ≥ 35%), and imperceptible glare (DGP < 35%). In this paper, a fish-eye camera was located at the patient eye level (1.20 m above the floor) and facing the window. Acceptance criteria assumed that when the combined values of disturbing and intolerable glare reached ≥ 10% of the year-round simulation occupied time, the patient view was considered to be visually uncomfortable.

Results of Part One

Results of Daylight Availability Analysis

The Daylight Availability results in the south, east and north orientations are presented in Tables 4, 5 and 6. They illustrate the percentage of daylit area relative to the total area of the IUC space for the two measuring reference planes at different WWRs. The cases that achieved the required threshold at both measuring reference planes were identified and highlighted with a light shade in the table.

In the south orientation, one glazing system and three shading systems showed promising results. These are highlighted by a light shade in Table 4.

Window to Wall Ratio	Glazing						Shading											
	Case A Dbl Clear		Case B Triple Argon		Case C Sgl Ref		Case D		Case E		Case F		Case G		Case H		Case I	
	Bed	Floor	Bed	Floor	Bed	Floor	Bed	Floor	Bed	Floor	Bed	Floor	Bed	Floor	Bed	Floor	Bed	Floor
8%	64%	27%	57%	78%	41%	44%	26%	0%	28%	0%	37%	18%	42%	22%	70%	0%	1%	0%
16%	0%	0%	18%	94%	49%	83%	30%	0%	30%	0%	84%	100%	48%	100%	76%	100%	56%	33%
24%			2%	39%	44%	44%	33%	0%	32%	0%	50%	67%	23%	72%	23%	67%	84%	78%
32%	64%	27%	0%	28%	37%	6%	34%	0%	34%	0%	21%	61%	4%	39%	5%	33%	77%	94%
40%	65%	26%	0%	37%	33%	0%	39%	0%	40%	0%	5%	50%	0%	6%	1%	28%	79%	83%
48%	65%	26%	18%	22%	31%	0%	43%	0%	47%	0%	2%	44%	67%	48%	61%	23%	56%	67%

Table 4: Percentage of daylit area relative to the total area on both measuring reference planes in the south orientation.

As for the glazing systems, only the triple clear glazing – low emissivity and argon-filled – type achieved adequacy, at 8% WWR. On the other hand, several shading systems achieved better performance. The most promising one was Case I, where an external solar screen was used to protect the window. This Case provided the designer with large window sizes and a wide range of WWRs to choose from. These ranged from 24% to 48%. In these solutions, the daylit areas reached impressive results, up to 94% of the floor surface area, and higher than the threshold of 50% on the two tested planes. The second promising case was Case F, where three horizontal sun breakers were placed in front of the window. In this case, two WWRs showed promising results. These were WWR 16% and 24%, where the daylit areas ranged from 50% to 100% at the tested planes. Case H, which utilized an external light shelf that prevents solar access while reflecting light deep into the space, provided an acceptable performance at only one WWR (16%).

On the other hand, adequate daylighting was unattainable in Cases E and G where a single horizontal sun breaker and vertical sun breakers were used. The daylight areas on the floor plane were short of reaching the threshold of 50% of the total area in all WWRs. The over-lit areas were dominant in these cases due to excessive solar penetration.

For the east orientation, simulation results were more diversified (Table 5). The daylit area ranged between 0% and 71% at the bed surface area in many WWRs. However, the overlit and partially daylit areas were dominant in all WWRs. Very low unacceptable daylit values (less than 30%) were also observed on the floor and the bed surface especially for the three tested glazing systems and when shading was provided by vertical sun breakers (Case G).

The most promising cases were Cases E and I, where a 45° cut-off sun shading angle and the external solar screen were used. These cases provided the designer with large window sizes having two options for WWRs (16% - 24% and 32% - 40% respectively). In these solutions, the daylit area reached reasonable results, between 50% and 89% of the total floor area. Other WWRs failed to provide acceptable performance, where the daylit area was below the 50% threshold value. The other cases (Cases D, F and H) achieved acceptable performance at 16% WWR.

127

Window to Wall Ratio	Glazing						Shading											
	Case A Dbl Clear		Case B Triple Argon		Case C Sgl Ref		Case D		Case E		Case F		Case G		Case H		Case I	
	Bed	Floor	Bed	Floor	Bed	Floor	Bed	Floor	Bed	Floor	Bed	Floor	Bed	Floor	Bed	Floor	Bed	Floor
8%	25%	6%	48%	0%	0%	27%	39%	17%	29%	17%	5%	0%	24%	6%	33%	0%	0%	0%
16%	44%	0%	31%	6%	0%	43%	62%	50%	71%	89%	62%	50%	42%	22%	62%	50%	23%	0%
24%	21%	0%	8%	0%	0%	19%	44%	11%	59%	61%	48%	33%	30%	0%	32%	39%	48%	0%
32%	14%	0%	3%	0%	0%	13%	22%	6%	35%	17%	26%	33%	9%	0%	3%	0%	66%	50%
40%	9%	0%	1%	0%	0%	3%	14%	0%	17%	6%	10%	0%	3%	0%	2%	0%	56%	72%
48%	4%	0%	0%	0%	0%	4%	10%	0%	12%	0%	3%	0%	0%	0%	0%	0%	27%	39%

Table 5: Percentage of daylit area relative to the total area on both measuring reference planes in the east orientation.

In the north orientation, all cases achieved the required threshold at the two measuring reference planes (Table 6). All tested window configurations were successful in this orientation which receives very few direct sun rays at limited times of the year. All solutions were successful in offering the designer a wide range of WWRs to choose from especially for the shading systems. The only exception was the 8% WWR, where none of the cases were successful.

In contrast to the south and east orientations, Cases D, E and F proved to be more useful in the north orientation. In these cases, the use of horizontal sun breakers, either one or several, provided the widest range of WWRs (from 16% to 48%) and large window sizes. The daylit area reached 100% at WWRs of 32% and 40% at the tested bed surface area, while the daylit area reached 100% at WWRs from 24% to 48% at the tested floor plane in the three Cases D, E and F. Cases G, H and I also provided very good performance, where the range of acceptable WWRs was between 16% and 40% in Cases G and H, and between 32% and 48% in Case I. The daylit area reached 100% in the majority of acceptable cases at the tested floor and bed surface area. The use of external solar screens (Case I) was the least successful among all the alternatives, especially in small WWRs, due to the lim-

ited solar penetration in this orientation. It is worth noting that two cases of glazing systems were acceptable. These were Case A: a double-glazed clear window, and Case B: a triple-glazed clear, low emissivity and argon-filled window. They achieved a 100% daylit area at the tested floor plane at 16% and 24% WWRs.

Results of Glare Probability Analysis

Glare Probability was tested for the cases that provided acceptable Daylight Availability levels while having a high potential for glare occurrence. These were the cases where the overlit area percentage exceeded 30% of the bed surface area. Testing was not conducted for the north orientation cases since this façade does not receive direct solar penetration almost all year round, thus there is very limited possibility of glare occurrence.

In the south orientation, two cases were tested for Glare Probability. These were the cases that provided acceptable Daylight Availability levels while having a high potential for glare occurrence. These were Case F, at a 24% WWR; and Case I, at a 48% WWR. In these cases, the overlit area reached 33% of the bed surface area. The results of the analysis are presented in Figure 3.

Window to Wall Ratio	Glazing						Shading											
	Case A Dbl Clear		Case B Triple Argon		Case C Sgl Ref		Case D		Case E		Case F		Case G		Case H		Case I	
	Bed	Floor	Bed	Floor	Bed	Floor	Bed	Floor	Bed	Floor	Bed	Floor	Bed	Floor	Bed	Floor	Bed	Floor
8%	32%	0%	68%	11%	0%	0%	1%	0%	0%	0%	0%	0%	20%	0%	9%	0%	0%	0%
16%	79%	100%	97%	100%	0%	20%	68%	83%	61%	56%	77%	83%	79%	89%	92%	61%	20%	0%
24%	68%	100%	74%	100%	0%	56%	91%	100%	87%	100%	97%	100%	92%	100%	100%	100%	72%	33%
32%	49%	100%	41%	100%	17%	77%	89%	100%	96%	100%	100%	100%	81%	100%	87%	100%	93%	100%
40%	38%	100%	15%	100%	83%	85%	73%	100%	79%	100%	100%	100%	60%	100%	56%	100%	98%	100%
48%	29%	100%	0%	100%	100%	91%	55%	100%	70%	100%	98%	100%	39%	100%	26%	100%	100%	100%

Table 6: Percentage of daylit area relative to the total area on both measuring reference planes in the north orientation.

128

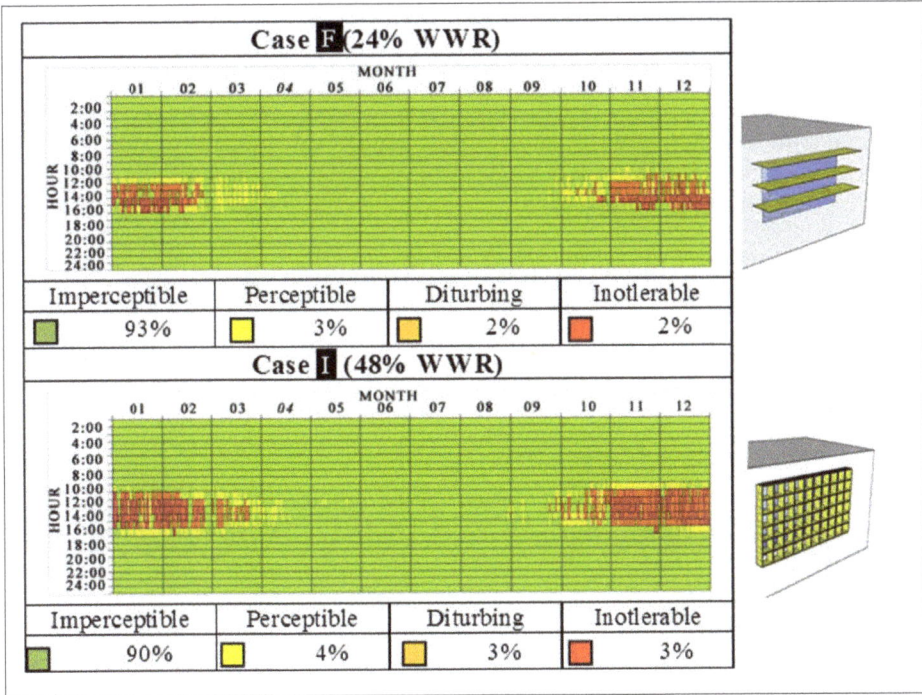

Figure 3. Annual Daylight Glare Probability percentages for cases with an overlit area of more than 30% in the south orientation.

The Annual Daylight Glare Probability (DGP) was acceptable in the two cases. In Case F (at a 24% WWR), the disturbing glare and intolerable glare were only present in 4% of occupied simulation time collectively. The imperceptible glare was 93% of the occupied simulation time. As for Case I (at a 48% WWR), it achieved a slightly lower result. The disturbing glare and intolerable glare were present in only 6% of occupied simulation time collectively. The imperceptible glare reached 90% while the perceptible glare was found to be 4% of the occupied simulation time.

In the east orientation, three of the cases that were accepted for Daylight Availability were identified as having a high potential for glare occurrence and, thus,

were analyzed for DGP (Figure 4). These were the cases where the overlit area percentage exceeded 30% of the bed surface area. These were Cases F and H, at a 16% WWR, and Case I, at a 32% WWR. Figure 4 illustrates the results of the DGP analysis.

Case F (at a 16% WWR) did not succeed in satisfying the required criteria. The disturbing glare and intolerable glare were found at 10% of the occupied simulation time. The imperceptible glare was present 87% of the time, while the perceptible glare was present at only 4%. As for Case H (at a 16% WWR), it achieved a better result. The disturbing glare and intolerable glare were present at only 6% of the occupied simulation time. The imperceptible glare reached

TESIS Inter-University Research Centre "Systems and Technologies for Social and Healthcare Facilities"
University of Florence, Italy

89%, while the perceptible glare was present at only 5% of the time. As for Case I (at a 32% WWR), it achieved a slightly lower result. The disturbing glare and intolerable glare were present at only 8% of the occupied simulation time. The imperceptible glare reached 88%, while the perceptible glare was present at only 4% of the time. However, it was noticed that the disturbing

glare was observed at 8 AM almost all year-round, and at 9 and 10 AM in all seasons, except in the summer. In addition, the intolerable glare was observed almost all year round at the same times. Their effect can be seen in Figure 4. Movable, temporary sun protection systems, such as blinds and curtains, should be used at these specific time periods to totally eliminate glare occurrence.

130

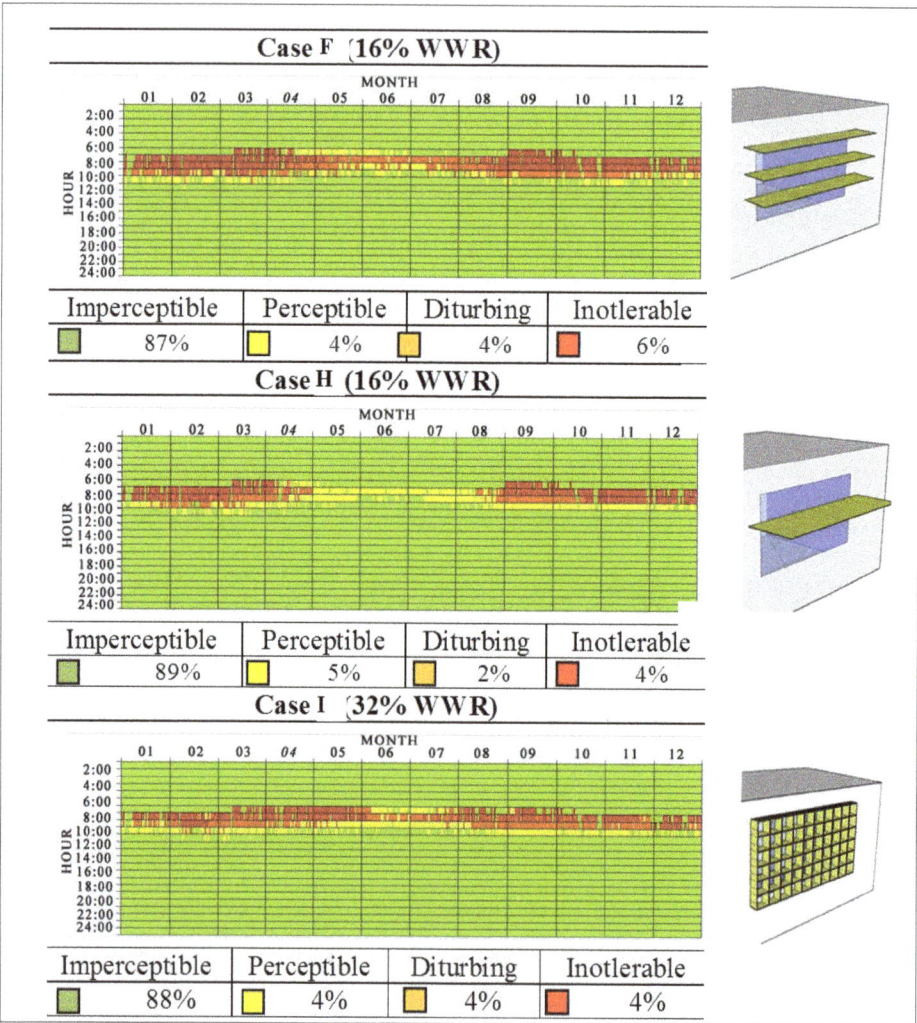

Figure 4. Annual Daylight Glare Probability percentages for Cases with an overlit area of more than 30% in the east orientation.

PART TWO: ANALYSIS OF EXPOSURE TO EXTERNAL VIEWS

In this part, two shading designs were simulated for exposure to external views. These were Cases F and H of part 1 (see Table 1). Their description is as follows:

o *Case F:* Three horizontal sun-breakers. These were spaced in a way that provides a 45° cut-off sun shading angle (reflectance = 50%).

o *Case H:* An external light shelf located at 2/3 of the window height: (upper surface reflectance = 90%).

Methodology of Part Two

A typical ICU patient space was selected for investigation. Its layout, dimensions and parameters were similar to those of the space tested in part 1. Analysis in this part addressed the size, aspect ratio and position of the window. Two window sizes (expressed as Window-to-Wall Ratio - WWR) were used in the analysis. These were 16% and 24% WWRs. Three window Aspect Ratios (AR) were examined. These were 2:1, 1:1, and 1:2 ARs. These are illustrated in Figure 5.

The effect of window position on the exposure to external views was addressed by calculating the amount of external view associated with locating the window in all possible positions on a regular grid drawn on the face of the external wall. The grid size was 0.40 m in the horizontal and vertical directions. The window head was assumed to have a minimum height of 2.10 m, and the window sill reached a maximum of 0.90 m (Figure 6).

131

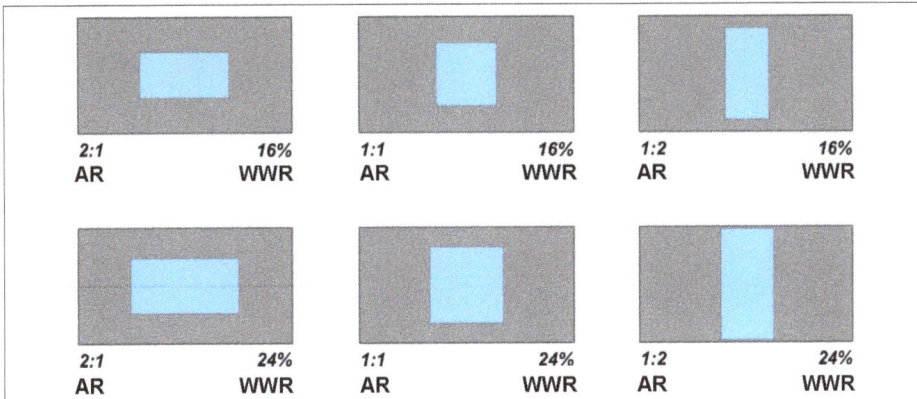

Figure 5. *Size and Aspect Ratio of the tested windows.*

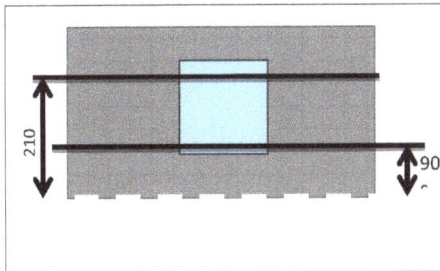

Figure 6. *The minimum window head and maximum window sill levels.*

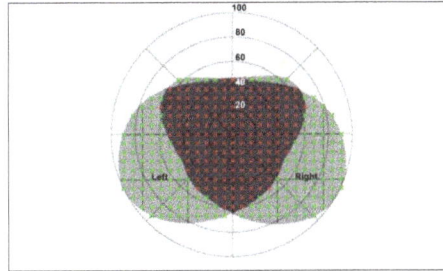

Figure 7. *The cone of vision of a typical patient.*

TESIS Inter-University Research Centre "Systems and Technologies for Social and Healthcare Facilities"
University of Florence, Italy

132

Methodology of View Exposure Analysis

The cone of vision and the rays extending from the patient's eyes were modeled (Figures 7 and 8). The patient was assumed to be reclining in bed, thus the eye level was assumed at 1.20 m from the floor and the centre of vision was assumed to be tilted 30° towards the external wall direction and looking at a 15° angle upward.

The external view was calculated by counting the percentage of rays which passed through the window opening of the tested case, in comparison with the maximum possible number of rays that intersected with the external wall surface.

Methodology of Daylighting/View Exposure Analysis

Daylighting simulation was conducted for each of the possible window positions that were defined above. It was performed with the same methodology adopted in part one of this research. The window positions that resulted in acceptable daylighting performance were identified. These were overlaid with the results of the evaluation of the external view exposure. The number of possible window positions and grid cells that resulted in acceptable daylighting performance while at the same time providing an external view exposure of more than 35% were identified.

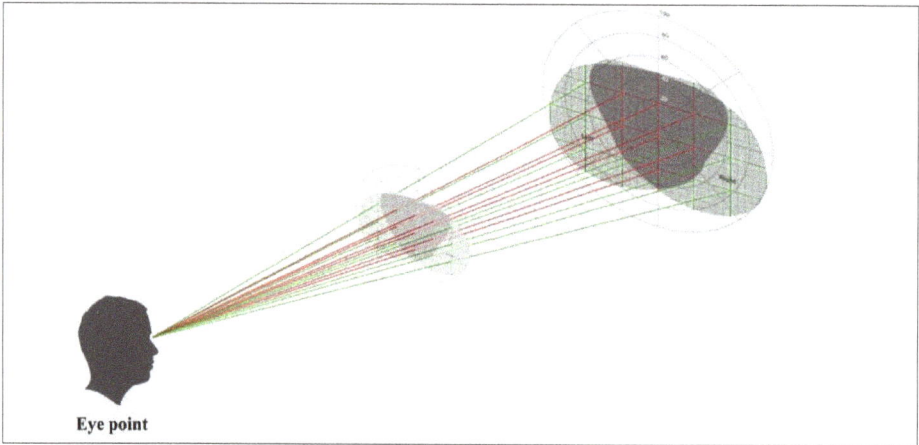

Figure 8. *The cone of vision of a typical patient.*

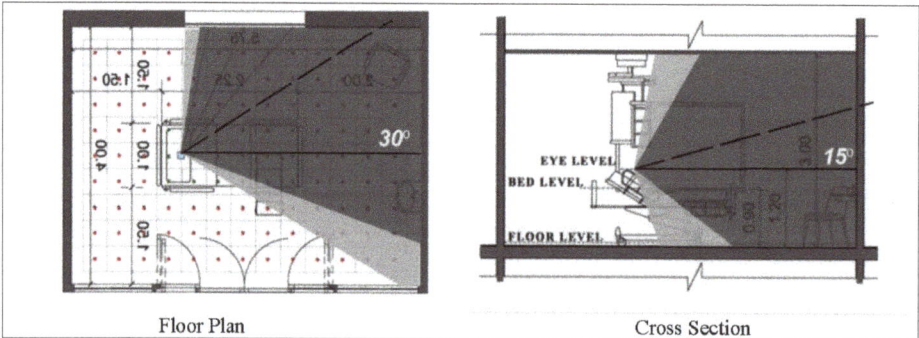

Figure 9. *The view directions of a typical patient.*

Results of Part Two

The results of the external view exposure are illustrated in Figures 10 and 11. These illustrate all the possible positions of the window for each of the tested cases. The degree of external view exposure is demonstrated by colour coding as illustrated in the legend of these Figures.

The view exposure results for Case F, where three horizontal sun breakers were used to protect the window, are illustrated in Figure 10. As expected, the best performance was achieved by the larger window size. Windows having WWR 24% produced an external view exposure reaching 55% of the maximum possible. This was attainable in windows having 1:1 and 1:2 aspect ratios. On the other hand, only one case provided the 55% level of exposure, when smaller windows were used (16% WWR). It was the 1:1 AR window. It was noted that the horizontally aligned windows, having an aspect ratio of 2:1, achieved a lower level of performance in comparison with the other aspect ratios. The maximum level of external view exposure of these windows was only 45%.

The position of the window greatly affected view exposure. Windows located near the centre of the external wall produced higher values in comparison with side windows. Better performance appeared when the windows were located in a central position leaning slightly away from the side of the patient head wall.

The results of view exposure for Case H, where an external light shelf was used with an unprotected window, are illustrated in Figure 11. External view exposure was better in this case. A larger number of options achieved a 55% level of exposure. The three tested cases of windows having a 24% WWR achieved this level at several positions. Also, two of the tested cases of windows having a 16% WWR achieved the same level of performance. These were windows with 1:1 and 1:2 aspect ratios. The only case that did not reach this level of performance was the window with a 2:1 aspect ratio, at a 16% WWR. It achieved a maximum of 45%.

133

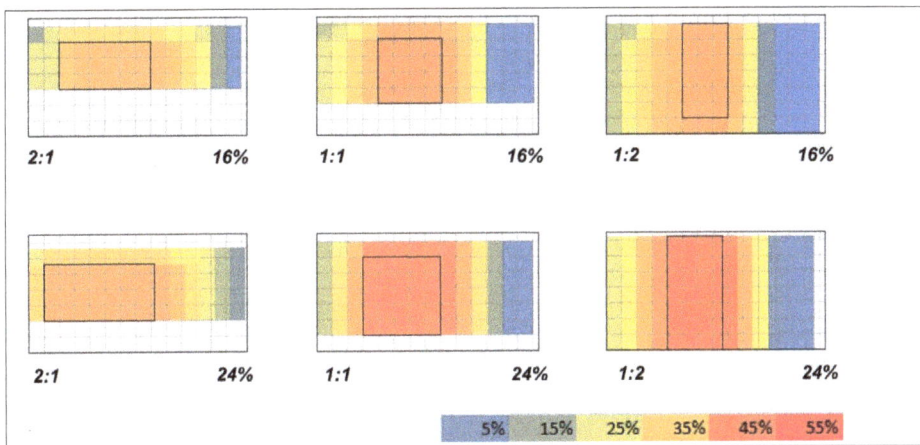

Figure 10. Degree of external view exposure of alternative window positions using horizontal sun breakers (Case F).

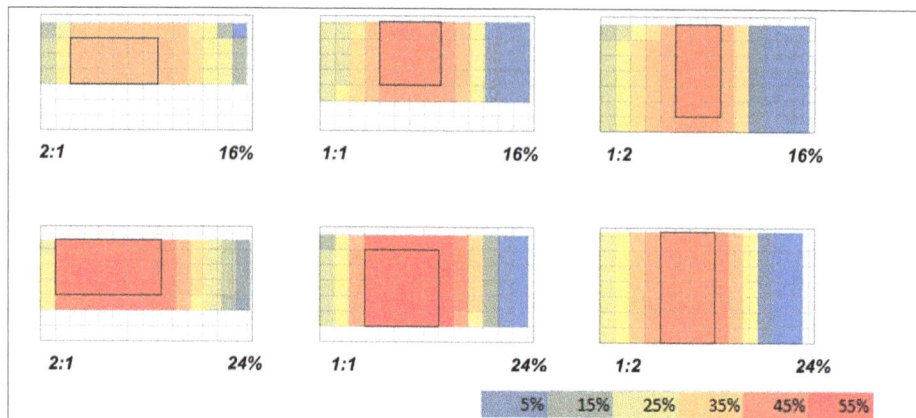

Figure 11.Degree of external view exposure of alternative window positions using a light shelf with an unprotected window (Case H).

Similar to the previous case, the position of the window greatly affected view exposure. Windows located near the centre of the external wall produced higher values in comparison with side windows. Better performance appeared when the windows were located in a central position leaning slightly away from the direction of the patient head wall.

Balance of Daylighting and External View

The above external view results were overlaid with a daylighting analysis of similar cases. The following figures (Figures 12 and 13) illustrate the window positions that provided acceptable daylighting performance. These are highlighted in a light shade in these figures. The darkened slots are those positions that do provide acceptable daylighting performance. Furthermore, the number of acceptable window positions that provided an external view exposure of 35% or more were counted and indicated for each case.

The range of window positions that provided acceptable daylighting performance were identified for Case F (horizontal sun breakers) in Figure 12.

According to the above analysis, the best configuration was a window with a 1:1 Aspect Ratio (AR) and 16% WWR. Its use resulted in 5 acceptable window positions. Second, was a window with a 1:2 AR and 24% WWR. Its use resulted in 3 acceptable window positions. The lowest performance was a window with a 1:2 AR and 16% WWR. Its use did not result in any acceptable window position.

The results of the analysis for the unprotected window assisted by a light shelf (Case H) are illustrated in Figure 13.

According to the above analysis, the performance of Case H was much lower than that of the window protected by sun breakers. Only three configurations resulted in acceptable performance. These were windows with ARs of 2:1 and 1:1 with a 16% WWR and a window with a 2:1 AR and 24% WWR. However, the three successful cases provided a wider range of acceptable window position options to choose from. The smaller windows provided more window position options to choose from. In fact, the 1:1 AR-16% WWR window provided 9 options for the location of the window along the external wall. Also, the 2:1 AR-16% WWR window provided 6 acceptable window positions to choose from.

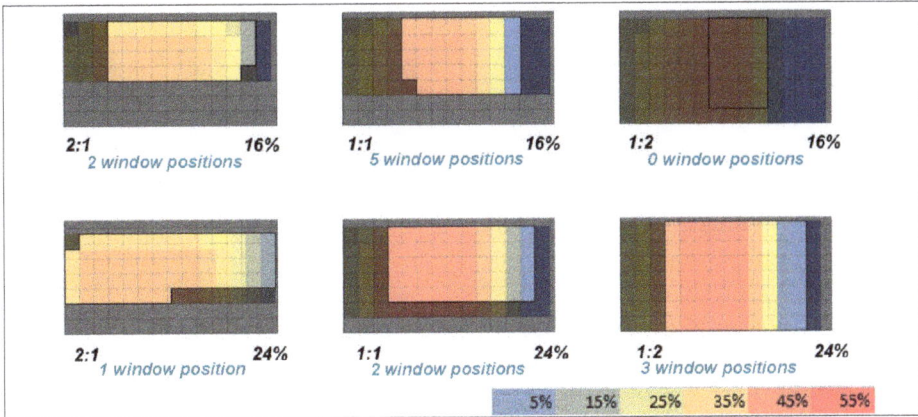

Figure 12. Acceptable window positions when using horizontal sun breakers (Case F).

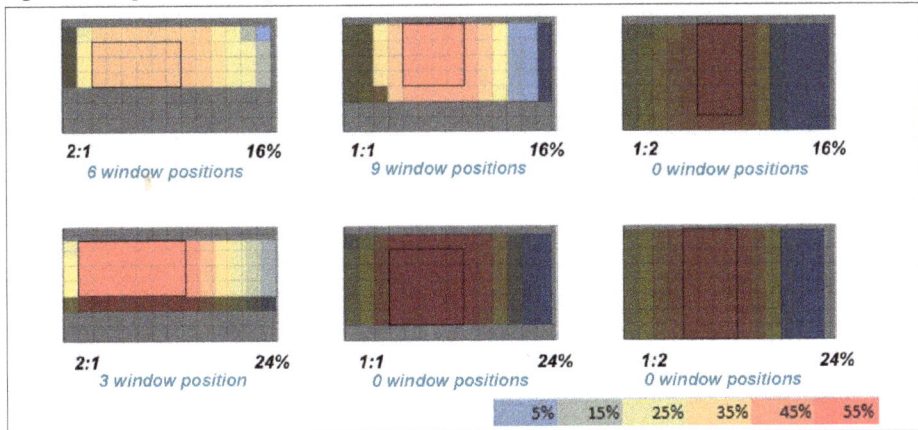

Figure 13. Acceptable window positions when using a light shelf with an unprotected window (Case H).

CONCLUSIONS

This paper addressed the design of hospital Intensive Care Unit windows. The main objectives were the achievement of visual comfort and the improvement of access to external views. The paper aimed to identify the window sizes (expressed as Window-to-Wall Ratio – WWR) and shading system configurations that could fulfill daylighting adequacy, avoidance of glare and maximize the external views.

The first part addressed daylighting adequacy and avoidance of glare. The results of the south orientation demonstrated that the most promising glazing/shading system was the external solar screen, which provided the designer with large window sizes with a wide range of WWRs to choose from. The second promising case was the use of three horizontal sun breakers placed to protect the window. The use of different types of glazing showed limited success where only one glazing type provided acceptable results. This was the triple-glazed clear, low emissivity and argon-filled window. As for the east orientation, simulation results were more diversified. The most promising cases appeared when a horizontal sun shading device (45° cut-off sun shading angle) and an external solar screen were used. None of the tested glazing types provided acceptable results. In the north orientation, all tested window glazing/shading configurations were successful. Since this orientation receives very few direct sun rays at limited times of the year, all solutions were successful in offering the designer a wide range of WWRs to choose from. The shading systems provided a wider range of options in comparison with the tested glazing types.

In the second part of the paper, the exposure to external views was analyzed in association with daylighting performance. For windows protected by horizontal sun breakers, the best configuration was a window with a 1:1 Aspect Ratio (AR) and 16% WWR. Second, was a window with a 1:2 AR and 24% WWR. All other tested configurations resulted in acceptable performance. The only exception was a window with a 1:2 AR and 16% WWR, which did not result in any acceptable window position. The performance of an unprotected window with a light shelf was much lower than that of the window protected by sun breakers. Only three configurations resulted in acceptable performance. These were windows with ARs of 2:1 and 1:1 and 16% WWR and window with a 2:1 AR and 24% WWR. However, the successful cases provided a wider range of acceptable window position options to choose from.

REFERENCES

Facilities Guidelines Institute (FGI), American Institute of Architects (AIA) (2006). *Guidelines for Design and Construction of Health Care Facilities*. The American Institute of Architects Press, Washington DC, USA.

IESNA, Rea M. S. (ed.) (2000). *IESNA Lighting Handbook References and Application*. 9th ed., Illuminating Engineering Society of North America, USA.

Ozdemir A. (2010). Effect of Window Views' Openness and Naturalness on the Perception of Rooms' Spaciousness and Brightness: A Visual Preference Study. *Scientific Research and Essays,* Vol. 5(16), 2275-2287.

Reinhart, C. F. and Wienold, J. (2011). The daylighting dashboard – A simulation-based design analysis for daylit spaces. *Building and Environment*, 46, 386-396.

Shepley, M. M., et al. (2012). The impact of daylight and views on ICU patients and staff. *Health Environments Research & Design Journal* (HERD), 5(2), 46-60.

Sherif, A., et al. (2013-a). Energy simulation as a tool for selecting window and shading configuration in extreme desert environment – Case Study: Intensive Care Unit in Aswan. *Proc. of the Sustainable Building Conf. (SB 2013)*, Cairo, Egypt.

Sherif, A., et al. (2013-b). Daylighting simulation as means for configuring hospital intensive care unit windows under the desert clear skies. *Proc. of the Building Simulation Conf. (BS 2013)* August 25-28, 2013, Chambery, France.

Ulrich R. (1984). View through a window may influence recovery from surgery. *Science*, 27, Vol. 224 no. 4647, 420-421.

Wienold, J. (2009). Dynamic daylight glare evaluation. *Proc. of Buildings Simulation 2009*, 944-951.

Wienold, J., and Christoffersen, J. (2006). Evaluation methods and development of a new glare prediction model for daylight environments with the use of CCD cameras. *Energy and buildings*, 38(7), 743-757.

State-of-the-Art Hospital Segregation of Flows

Carrie C.[1]

ccarrie@keppiedesign.co.uk
[1] B. Arch, Bsc. Hons, RIBA, FRIAS, Healthcare Director of Keppie Design, United Kingdom

137

The clear and unambiguous separation of the three principle movement streams (patient/visitor/facilities management) is essential for any hospital to function efficiently. Combined with this is the aspiration to address the site-wide movement of people and vehicles to, from and through the hospital environs. This allows the hospital to establish better coherence and an improved identity. Keeping visitors, deliveries and blue-light traffic separate from each other is a priority.

INTRODUCTION

Modern, large-scale hospitals are essentially small urban communities. They are constantly accessible and are active during the daytime and quieter at night. The best hospital design understands and embraces this morphology; it can make specific reference to the importance of public 'streets and squares' as a means of imposing order and identification. The success of a large development is to have the significant pedestrian and vehicular flows work seamlessly together.

The clear and unambiguous separation of the three principle movement streams (patient/visitor/facilities management) is essential for any hospital to function efficiently. Combined with this is the aspiration to address the site-wide movement of people and vehicles to, from and through the hospital environs. This allows the hospital to establish better coherence and an improved identity. Keeping visitors, deliveries and blue-light traffic separate from each other is a priority.

SEGREGATION OF FLOWS, THE HISTORICAL CONTEXT

The National Health Service in the United Kingdom has been in existence for over 60 years and Keppie Architects have been designing healthcare facilities for over 150 years. Hospital design 30 years ago still focused on altering Florence Nightingale-designed wards built at the turn of the 19th century. Although patients rarely look back on these wards with fondness some nursing staff still hold the aspects of good patient observation in high regard.

Incredibly these wards are still in use in some parts of England and they demonstrate all the aspects we are trying to design out in new hospitals in favour of:

– Privacy and dignity, assisted by single bedroom wards;
– Evidence-based design principles of the modern healing environment: maximising day lighting, outlook and the interior design of the surroundings.
– Segregation of flows that are best not mixed in order to control infection, privacy and dignity;
– Designing a deinstitutionalised hospital.

PRIVATE FINANCE INITIATIVE AND PUBLIC PRIVATE PARTNERSHIPS PFI/PPP

In 1995 the architecture firm commenced designing and advising the PFI/PPP new UK hospitals programme. These projects have been a mixed success. The government set a challenge to use the PFI/PPP programme as a platform for innovation. The architects assumed this meant the design of innovative patient environments. The first innovation awards were held two years after starting the process and the government award for innovation went to.....an innovative model of financial funding!
The competitive environment of PFI/

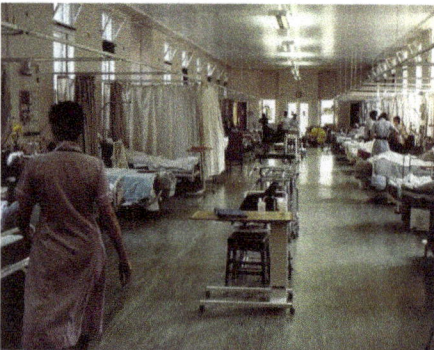

138

Figure 1.   Nightingale Wards: then and now.

Figure 2.   Queens Park Hospital, Blackburn.

Figure 3.   Tameside Hospital, Manchester.

Figure 4.   Queens Hospital, Birmingham.

Figure 5.   Hairmyres Hospital, Glasgow.

PPP set architects thinking about what edge could be brought to the design; metaphors for airports and hotels were widely presented. The architects at Keppie quickly realised that patients were more reassured by a non-institutional environment so a well-designed clinical but sympathetic environment was considered. Although perhaps under stressful conditions, they were after all going to hospital and not a hotel. This rethinking of hospital design led to the realisation that there had to be increased attention to the control of infection, and patient privacy and dignity. The practice of mixing patients with hotel services and patient flows did not meet these criteria and the opportunity was taken at the Royal Infirmary of Edinburgh to create new levels of segregation.

139

Figure 6.   Royal Victoria Hospital, Newcastle.

Figure 7.   St Helens Hospital.

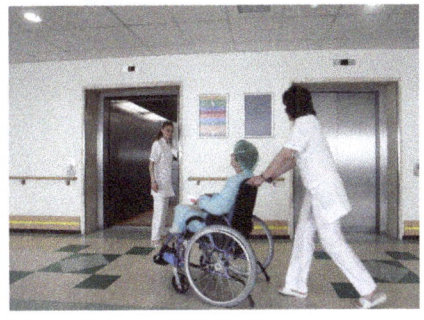

Figure 8.   Pedestrian and vehicular flows.

THE ROYAL INFIRMARY OF EDINBURGH AND UNIVERSITY OF EDINBURGH MEDICAL SCHOOL

Design commenced on the Royal Infirmary of Edinburgh and University of Edinburgh Medical School fifteen years ago. When it opened in 2003 it was the UK's leading design both in healthcare planning by specialist grouping and in segregating visitors, facilities management (FM) and patient flows though dedicated pathways and lifts served by a 250 metre long underground tunnel system utilising electric tugs to distribute supplies and waste.

A lot of lessons were learned from this project, not least about human behaviour; for example it was only logical to staff that if a visitor lift was nearer to the X-ray department that they would use the lift to transfer a patient in a wheelchair.

ROYAL FORTH VALLEY HOSPITAL

The core of this paper is centred around the design of the Royal Forth Valley Hospital serving central Scotland, but ends with some ongoing development concepts for the Forth Valley.

When commencing the design of the Royal Forth Valley Hospital the lessons learnt from the Royal Infirmary of Edinburgh were incorporated into the new design and it is considered an example of the state-of-the-art segregation of flows for a hospital complex.

The segregation of flows in a campus design can be more challenging than in a tower and podium design. The tower and podium solution is not favoured in the UK principally due to the cost and fire escape issues, although inner city designs are dictated by available site size.

Segregation of External Flows

The hospital is accessed from a roundabout with the exception of blue-light traffic which gains access from a dedicated entrance. The Council Town Planners stipulated that a single access/egress point be utilised; however, the original hospital entrance is maintained for emergency use in case the main entrance becomes blocked.

On entering the hospital grounds traffic is segregated as soon as practical using a zoning strategy. This avoids any unnecessary mixing of heavy and light traffic further within the site.

Accessible Public Transport

In line with the Scottish Government and NHS Policy, all hospital users will be encouraged to use public transport. A shuttle bus has been provided from the local train station. Buses and taxis arriving at the hospital are guided towards the Public Transport Interchange which is located to the front of the main entrance. There is direct and safe access from this point to the acute adult hospital and to the Women and Children's Hospital. The buses then travel round the perimeter loop road with stops for the staff and Mental Health entrances.

Blue Light

There is a dedicated Blue-Light traffic road that provides access/egress from Stirling Road directly to A&E and the Women and Children's entrances. This separation of blue-light traffic minimises any risk of disruption to this vital route and also satisfies the turnaround targets of the Scottish Ambulance Service.

Figure 9. The Royal Infirmary of Edinburgh and University of Edinburgh Medical School.

141

Cars

Visitor and outpatient cars have the option of dropping off patients at the main, Women & Children's, A&E, Mental Health, and Day Hospital entrances. Direct access from the drop-off points to the main car park is provided. There is also a dedicated staff car park. All parking areas have been reviewed for "secure by design" criteria.

Pedestrians

Careful consideration has been given to those arriving at the site on foot. Dedicated footpaths lead pedestrians to all entrances. A segregated footpath parallel to the perimeter road allows for exercise and access to the adjacent parkland.

Service Traffic

On reaching the internal roundabout, service vehicles are directed away from other site traffic to either the clean/goods in service yard or the energy centre/dirty goods out yard.

Appropriate Entrances

Part of the design strategy for the hospital is to provide simple, intuitive way-finding, with as many destination points as possible adjacent to the entrances. Arriving at a hospital for an appointment or to see a relative can be a stressful time. People do not necessarily behave in a predictable manner or think clearly. It is important to segregate incompatible activities that could lead to accidents. At

142

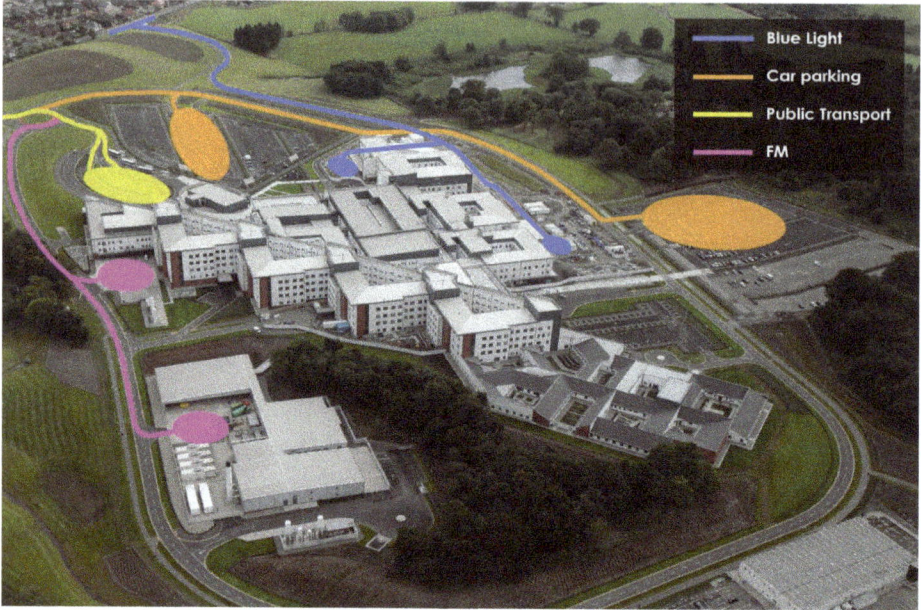

Figure 10. Royal Forth Valley Hospital – segregation of external flows.

Forth Valley there is a single point of entry to the site and upon entry the flows are segregated for service vehicles, visitors/outpatients, staff and blue-light traffic.

FORTH VALLEY INTERNAL FLOWS

Moving to the internal design, the images illustrate the principal zoning of the hospital. Forth Valley is unique in how the design handles the visitors and facilities management, leaving a very private environment for clinical movements.

In a similar concept to the external entrances, the whole hospital philosophy with regard to internal circulation is to bring the hospital users into and out of each department as simply and in as short a route as possible while segregating activities that are inappropriate to mix.

Figure 11. Royal Forth Valley Hospital.

The movement of patients within the hospital is segregated from visitor flows and there are separate patient, visitor and FM lifts to ensure that patient dignity is maintained at all times. A by-product of this segregation is improved safety and security which occurs with the restricted access arrangements. There is no requirement for patients or members of the public to access any of the FM areas at department or ward level, nor will they be able to access the basement FM corridors.

Underlying principles

Wards are paired to allow the sharing of FM and visitor entrances, which are located at alternate hubs.

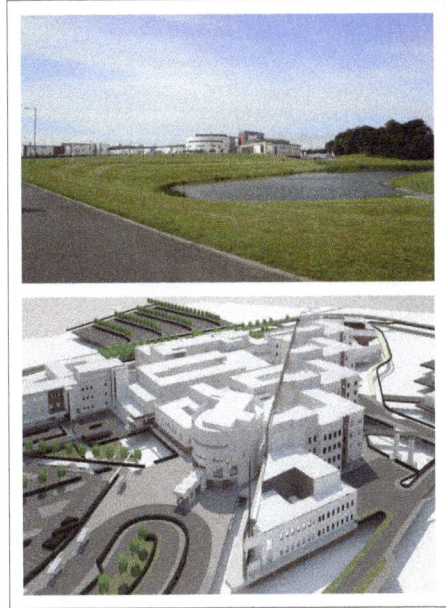

Figure 12. Royal Forth Valley Hospital.

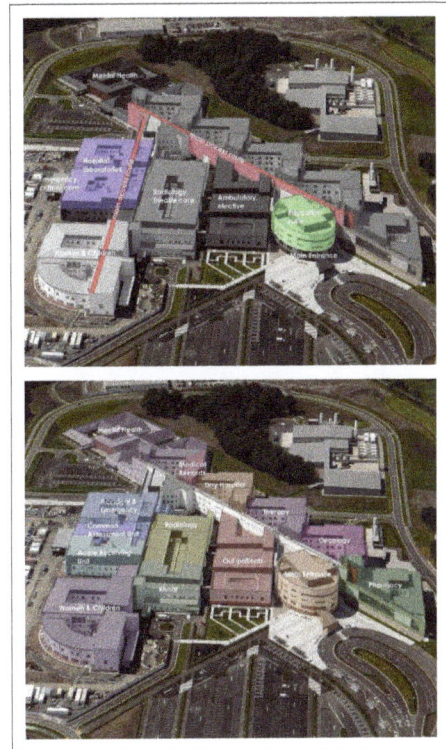

143

Figure 13. Principal zoning of the hospital.

Visitor access to wards is gained vertically where visitors arrive at the ward entrance.

Patients are moved to treatment and diagnostic accommodation from the first floor and above by dedicated corridors and lifts, which cannot be accessed by the public or FM services.

FM access is via the basement corridor system and then vertically into each department.

The segregation of flows and resilience of delivery at Forth Valley is achieved through 9 FM lifts, 6 visitor lifts and 6 patient lifts.

Visitors to Adult Inpatients

From the main entrance and contiguous atrium, visitors are directed to one of two "addresses" where they will access dedicated visitor lifts which arrive at their destination ward. This is similar to finding an address or flat number in a town street. Alternatively, stairs are available adjacent to the hub lift lobbies.

Outpatients

As the diagram in Figure 15 illustrates, the atrium space behind the main en-

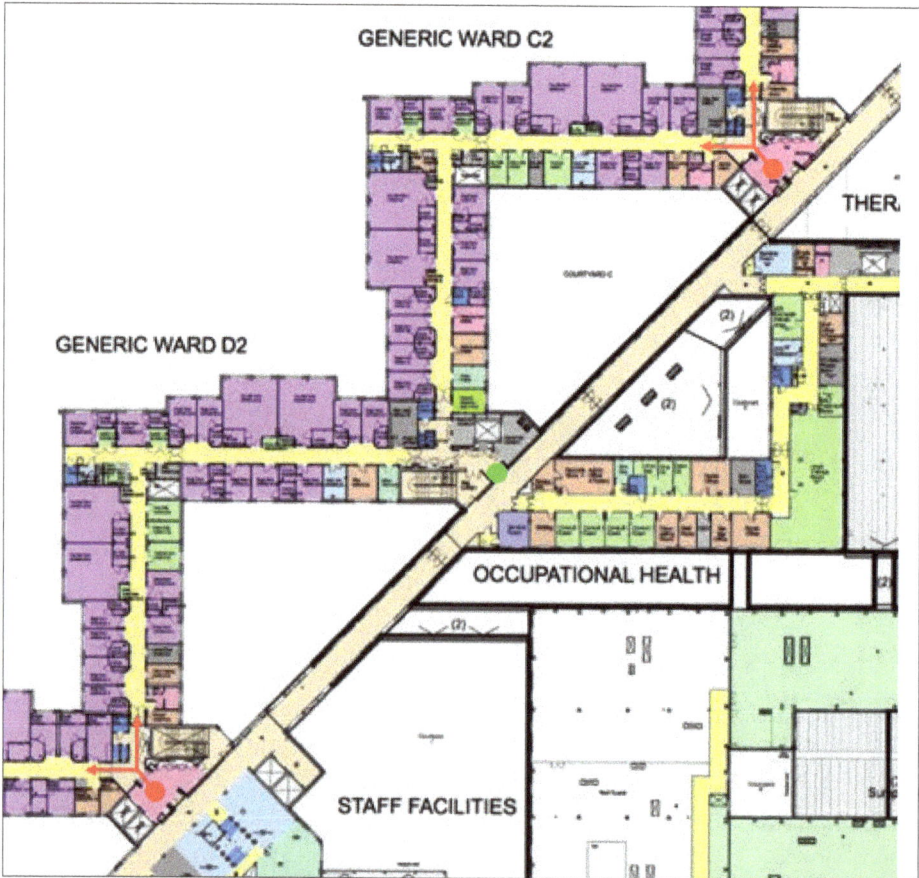

Figure 14. Generic wards.

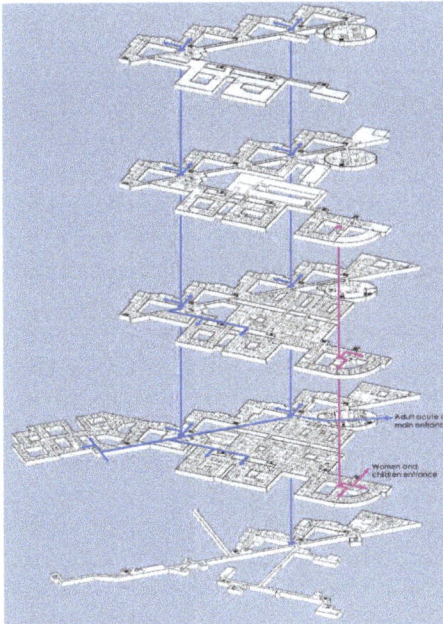

Figure 15. Outpatients.

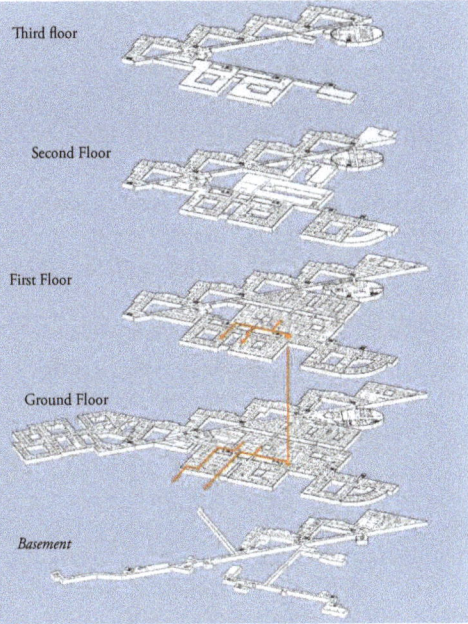

Figure 16. Accident & Emergency flows.

145

trance drum, on the ground floor, gives direct access to the majority of outpatient departments including the following:
– Main outpatients clinics;
– Therapy departments;
– Oncology;
– Day Hospital;
– Pharmacy.
This strategy minimises way-finding challenges, associated signage and allows the monitoring of activity within the atrium from the outpatient reception.

Ambulatory Care

Patients accessing Ambulatory Care for day procedures use lifts in the main entrance that take the patients and carers to the front door of the department, again minimising the stress of way-finding in an unusual environment.

Paediatric Patient Movement

Paediatric care at Forth Valley is integrated into the overall hospital and located on the top floor of the Women and Children's Hospital. Children have clear and direct routes through the hospital, either through A&E or the Women and Children's entrance, which are also linked to radiology, theatres and paediatric inpatient wards.

Accident & Emergency Flows

As shown in the diagram in Figure 16, A&E is located on the ground floor of the hospital and is contiguous with Radiology and the Assessment wards. Theatres, Critical Care and Coronary Care are located on the first floor level, directly above. These vertically adjacent departments are linked by bed lifts central to the emergency complex. The patient circulation routes are again segregated from the public.

Operating Theatre Flows

The diagram in Figure 17 illustrates the complex flows to and from the Operating Theatre suite. The suite is made up of 24 theatres, and four entrance/exits are provided to maintain segregation whilst also allowing flexibility in the conjoined theatre suites and common staff/supplier area.

Facilities Management

A visit to the George Pompidou Hospital in Paris convinced the architects that the future lies in robotic materials handling. With rising labour costs and an aging

population leading to labour shortages this makes sense. Other benefits are that the remaining hotel services staff can be trained to interface more with patients thereby allowing more time for nursing staff to attend to more skilled activities. At Forth Valley the unique design for hotel services includes dirty and clean sides to the FM hubs, i.e. the future waste and dirty/clean linen chutes.

As illustrated in the diagrams, the movement of goods within Forth Valley occurs within a dedicated network of underground tunnels and FM lifts.

The work is carried out principally by precision robotics. This was the first use of such robotics in a UK hospital.

The robotics system transports clean goods through the basement tunnel network to the appropriate FM lift and then transfers them to the clean side of

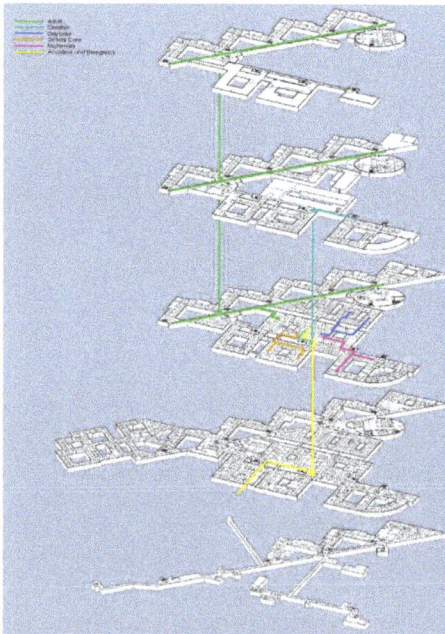

Figure 17. Operating Theatre flows

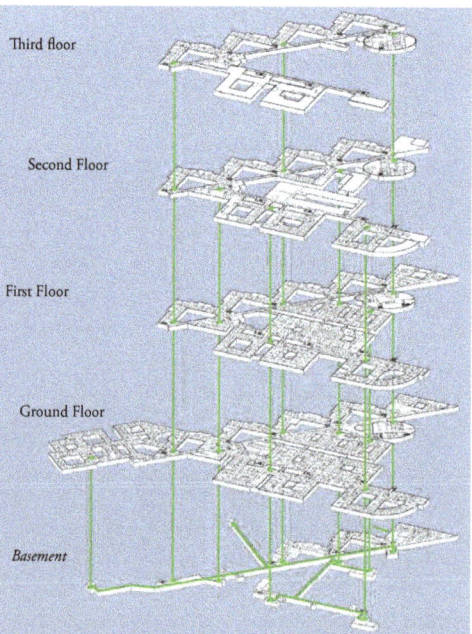

Figure 18. Facilities Management flows.

the FM hub. Refer to the diagram of such hubs.

Waste is mainly removed throughout the night by the robots which access the waste disposal rooms directly from the FM hubs.

The intention of this design is to completely segregate clinical waste bins from non-FM staff. Each morning the lifts are cleaned prior to breakfast deliveries.

Soiled linen and household waste are placed into separate gravity-fed disposal chutes and transported to basement holds where robots move the waste bins to the dedicated waste and soiled linen holding area in the external waste compound.

This segregation of visitor and FM flows leads to extremely quiet upper floor clinical corridors allowing the calm transfer

of patients in trolleys or wheelchairs with privacy and dignity. Similarly clinical staff are able to move in a safe and dedicated environment encouraging clinical interaction.

The aim thus far was to demonstrate the innovation of the Forth Valley segregation of flows. As with earlier hospitals, there are lessons to be learned and continuing improvements to consider.

The majority of new hospitals can be simplified, as shown in the Conventional Modern Hospital Section above: the wards are located above the private treatment and diagnostic facilities, which in turn are above the public and ambulatory care areas, which in their turn are above the clinical and non-clinical support areas.

Akershus Hospital has an additional service level below.

147

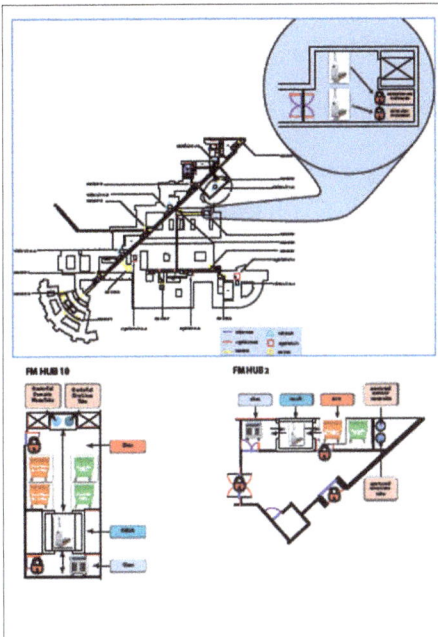

Figure 19. Facilities Management hubs.

Figure 20. Robotic handling in basement.

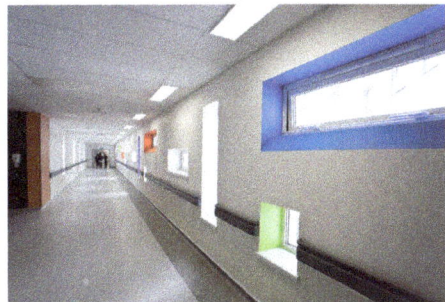

Figure 21. Calm environment of clinical corridors.

TESIS Inter-University Research Centre "Systems and Technologies for Social and Healthcare Facilities" University of Florence, Italy

AKERSHUS HOSPITAL

Akershus Hospital in Norway utilises robotic movement at the clinical and non-clinical support level leaving a lower sublevel for the large-diameter pneumatic tube distribution of clinical waste and dirty linen, again building on the segregation of the movement of clean and dirty materials.

148

DUMFRIES AND GALLOWAY ROYAL INFIRMARY

Visitor and patient environments can be improved by creating larger landscaped spaces with visitors and staff arriving at waiting areas that overlook the countryside.

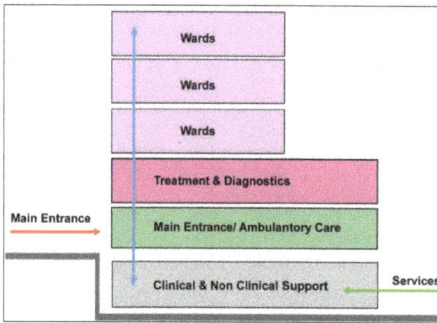

Figure 22. Conventional modern hospital section.

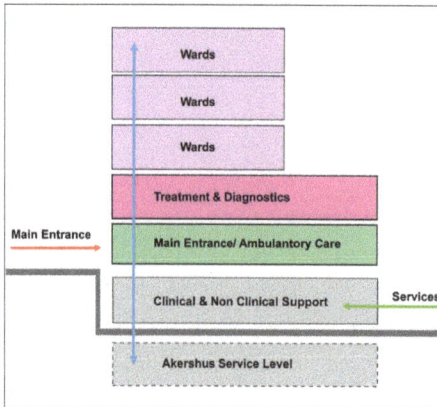

Figure 23. Akerhsus Oslo hospital section.

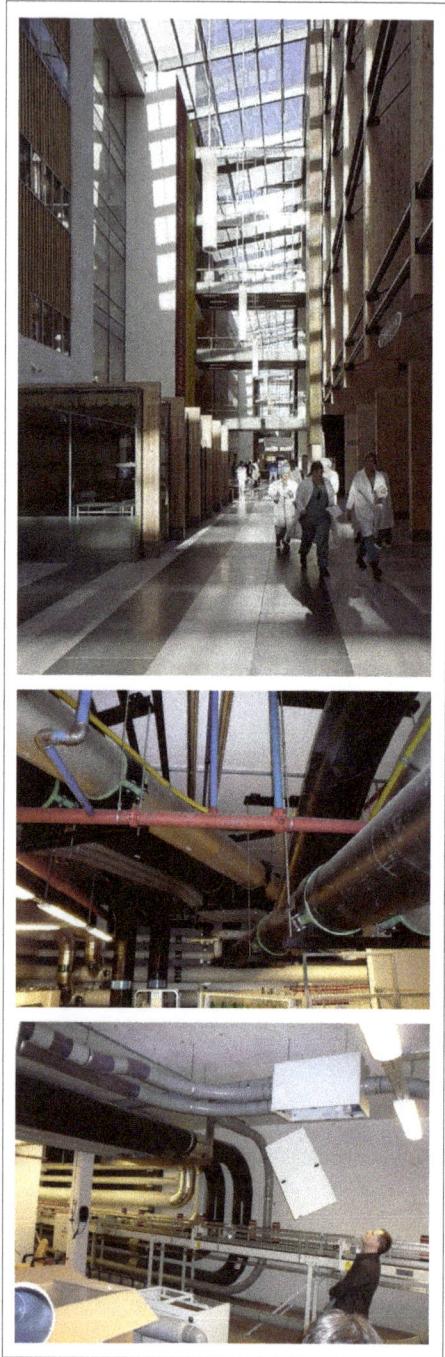

Figure 24. Akershus Hospital, Oslo Architect, C.F. Møller.

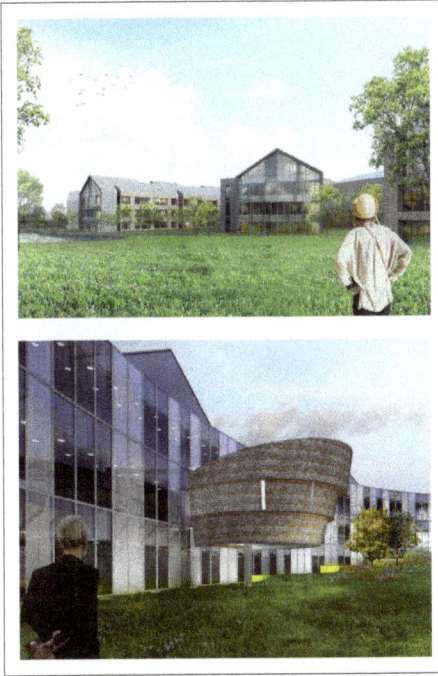

Figure 25. Dumfries and Galloway Royal Infirmary: enhancing the integration of the building with the countryside.

Figure 26. DGRI, aerial view.

This project in Southern Scotland raised some challenges around the segregation of flows and led to some changes to the absolute segregation of patient flows. The new hospital affords magnificent views of the countryside from the majority of patient areas and has more of a campus feel than most new hospitals. To safeguard the view from the wards and to allow access to the gardens while responding to the sloping site, all service activity has been taken away from the wards. This compromises the absolute segregation of flows but presents significant hospital setting opportunities as can be seen from the comparative sections.

149

Another conscious decision was to create a calming arrival atmosphere for the visitors. Unlike at Forth Valley where visitors are held in a windowless hall, visitors arriving at Dumfries will find a landscaped parkland in a calming interior environment.

Absolute segregation from visitors and hotel services has however been maintained for patients being taken to and from theatre when they feel at their most vulnerable.

SHENZHEN TEACHING HOSPITAL, CHINA

These segregation of flows principles can be applied to larger hospitals, such as this large tertiary hospital in Shenzhen where again separately designed patient, visitor and hotel service routes have been created. This is similar to a lot of inner city and Canadian projects where the majority of servicing and parking happens in the lower levels below the hospital.

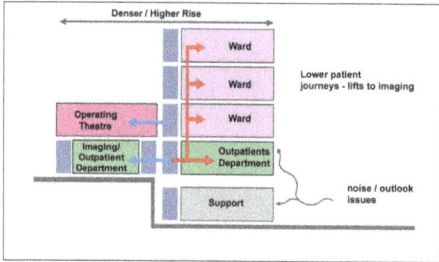

Figure 27. Forth Valley comparison.

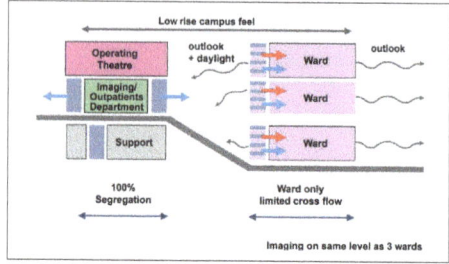

Figure 28. New DGRI comparison.

150

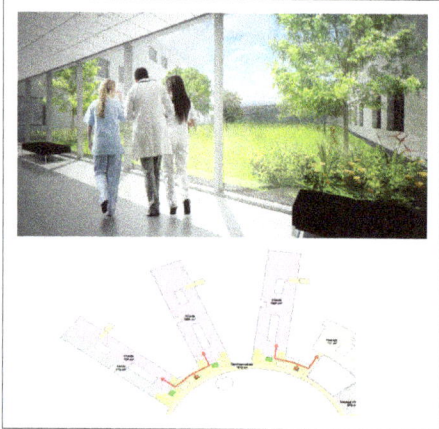

Figure 29. DGRI: views of the countryside from corridors.

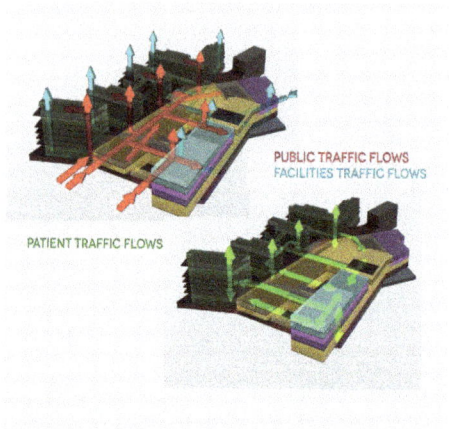

Figure 30. Shenzhen Teaching Hospital, traffic flows.

Figure 31. STH, China.

Saudi Experiment in International Design Locally Implemented Case Study: Medical Cities Project

Zeyad Al Swaidan[1]

zeyad@swaidan.net
[1]Dr., CEO of Medical Cities Projects, Ministry of Health, Kingdom of Saudi Arabia, Chairman of Saudi HealthCareArchitects (SHCA), Saudi UMRAN Society, KSA

Forty years ago healthcare services were regarded as one of the most important priorities in The Kingdom of Saudi Arabia (KSA) in order to provide the best healthcare to its citizens and residents. Although the Ministry of Health (MoH) faced some obstacles such as the geographically large area of KSA, which accounts for 2,149,690 sq km with a total population of 28,376.355 (2011 Health Statistics Year Book), it has made extensive efforts to provide the best healthcare services. Moreover, it ranks prominently for healthcare practices both regionally and internationally. These efforts have enabled healthcare services to reach their current status as the compatibility of the healthcare system with the geographical and population distribution, and the statistical indicators for all patients and diseases in different areas, have contributed to the development of the MoH's strategy for the coming decade through the verification of current and future needs. This paper aims to highlight the system of healthcare in KSA and the level of services provided, and evaluate the healthcare services over the last decade.

Keywords: healthcare, medical cities, saudi arabia

BRIEF INTRODUCTION: KINGDOM OF SAUDI ARABIA (KSA)

Recently, the Kingdom of Saudi Arabia has taken the lead among Arabic and Islamic countries in providing healthcare services to its citizens through the construction of healthcare buildings and medical cities throughout the Kingdom that take into consideration the latest international standards, with modifications to suit the Islamic and Arabic culture.

Kingdom of Saudi Arabia (KSA)

Area: 2,150,000 square kilometers (830,000 square miles), about one-fourth of the size of the United States. Location: Located in the southwest corner of Asia.

Saudi Arabia is an Arab Islamic country, its language is Arabic, and its capital city is Riyadh. The government in Saudi Arabia is a monarchy.

KSA (Economy)

Saudi Arabia is among the twenty largest economies in the world, and ranked first in the Middle East and North Africa.

Saudi Arabia is the largest free economic market in the Middle East, with 25% of the total Arab GDP. It also has the largest oil reserves in the world (25%).

152

Indicators & Statistics

Figure 1 explains population growth in Saudi Arabia since 2002, to 2011, and expected growth by 2020.

Figure 2 explains total beds number in Saudi Arabian hospitals over 18 years.

Figure 3 explains the bed number percentage for every 10,000 persons since 2002, to 2011, and the expected percentage in 2020.

Figure 4 explains the Ministry of Health Budget ratio from 2006 to 2011.

Figure 5 explains healthcare levels in Saudi Arabia.

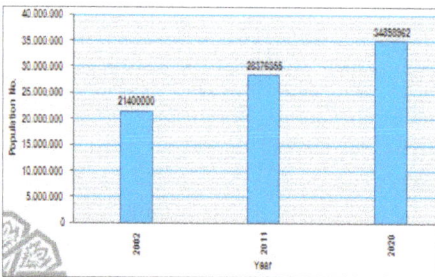

Figure 2. Bed nos. (2002 - 2011 - 2020).

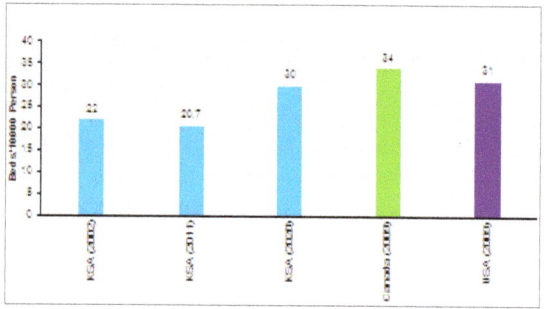

Figure 3. Bed nos./10,000 persons (2002 - 2011 - 2020).

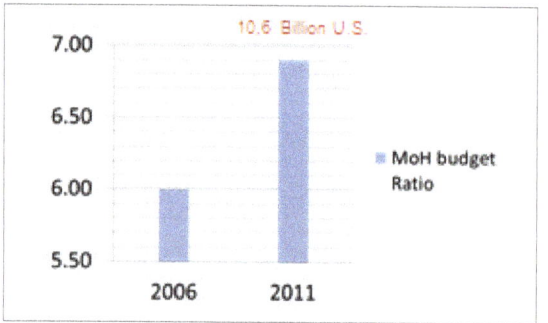

Figure 4. MoH (Ministry of Health) budget ratio.

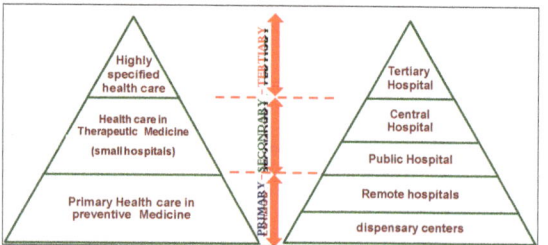

Figure 1. Population estimates (2002 - 2011 - 2020).

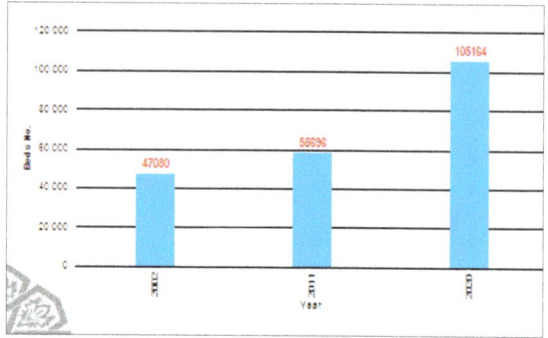

Figure 5. Healthcare in KSA.

QUICK OVERVIEW OF MEDICAL CITIES

Five medical cities will be constructed in KSA, decentralizing medical services:
– KAMC (King Abdullah Medical City) to serve the western region with a capacity of 1000 beds;
– KKMC (King Khalid Medical City) to serve the eastern region with a capacity of 1500 beds;
– KFMC (King Faisal Medical City) to serve the southern region with a capacity of 1350 beds;
– PMMC (Prince Mohamed Medical City) to serve the northern region with a capacity of 1000 beds;
– KFMC (King Fahad Medical City) to serve the central region and KSMC (King Saud Medical City) in Riyadh.

153

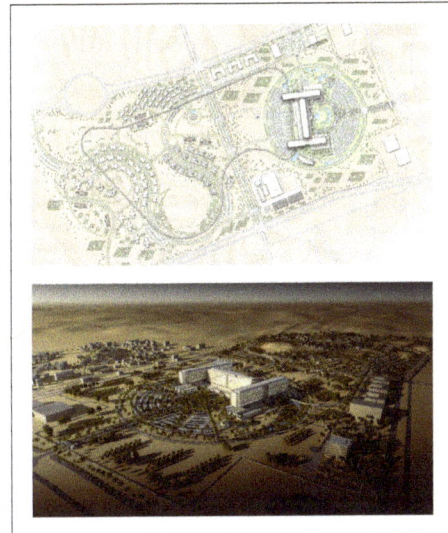

Figure 7. King Faisal Medical City.

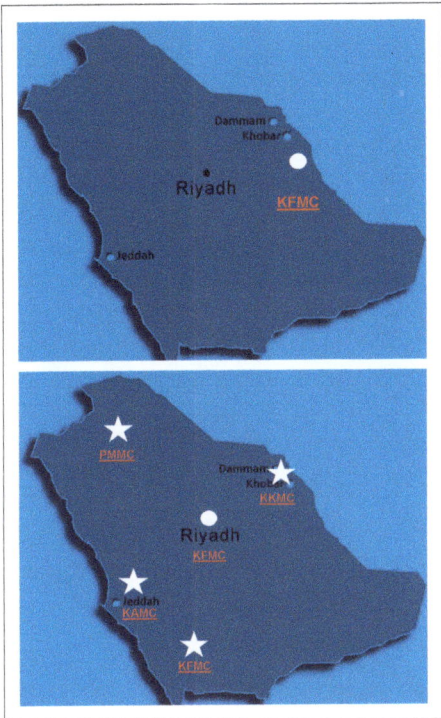

Figure 6. Current healthcare map and future healthcare map.

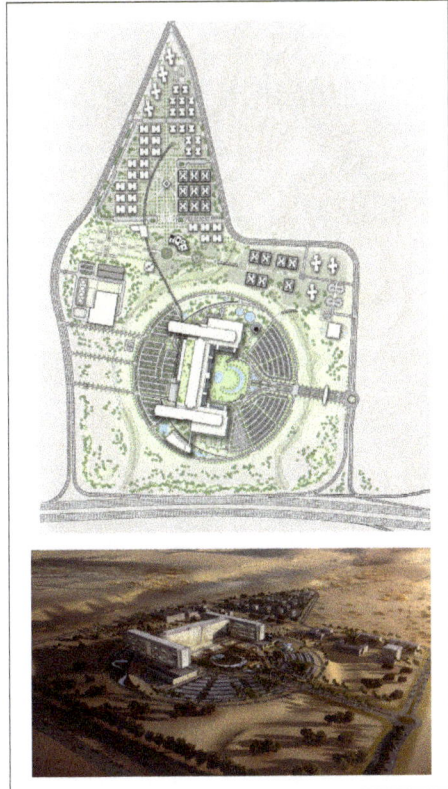

Figure 8. Prince Mohamed Medical City.

154

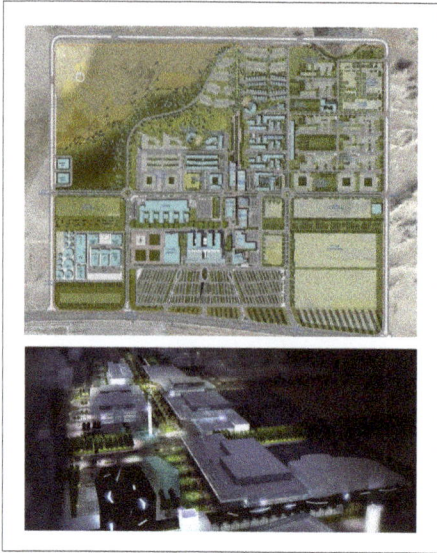

Figure 9. King Abdullah Medical City.

Figure 10. King Fahad Medical City.

WHAT DISTINGUISHES HEALTHCARE BUILDINGS IN KSA FROM THEIR COUNTERPARTS IN WESTERN COUNTRIES

The design of healthcare buildings in Arab countries differs from that of their counterparts in Western countries due to the provision of prayer halls and ensuring the separation of men and women. This concerns many spaces such as waiting areas, examination rooms, and preparation rooms (pre-surgeries). Sealed rooms for scrubbing up can be used alternately by men and women. Clinical spaces should be large enough to accommodate the family. Afterlife preparation and the morgue are designed with cultural dignity to reflect regional and religious values.

Integration between local and international design includes the following environmental factors: furniture arrangement; building environment; building layout; ergonomics; air quality; noise control; way-finding; access to nature and light; flooring materials; standards and codes; privacy; prayer halls; separation between men and women; culture; morgue.

Figure 11. King Khalid Medical City.

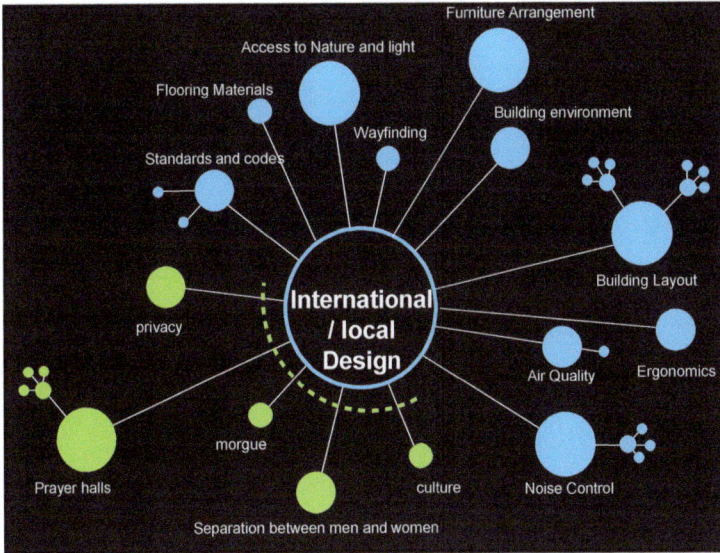

Figure 12. Environmental factors.

A few of the 12 factors of the healing environment are: way-finding – which provides an intuitive understanding of the building and how to navigate it; access to light and nature – which decreases heart rate and respiration and reduces the amount of pain medication required; noise control – which reduces the negative stressors on patients and staff; ergonomics – which makes staff more efficient and reduces injuries.

Islamic and Arabic Culture

The Islamic and Arabic culture is reflected in the design by placing touches and accents of Islamic and Arabic culture, such as wooden decorations, artifacts, and Quran verses, at the entrances and waiting areas.

Geometricy key features include: natural geometric lines that define the building and its façade; a deep understanding of defined squares and eight-sided stars.

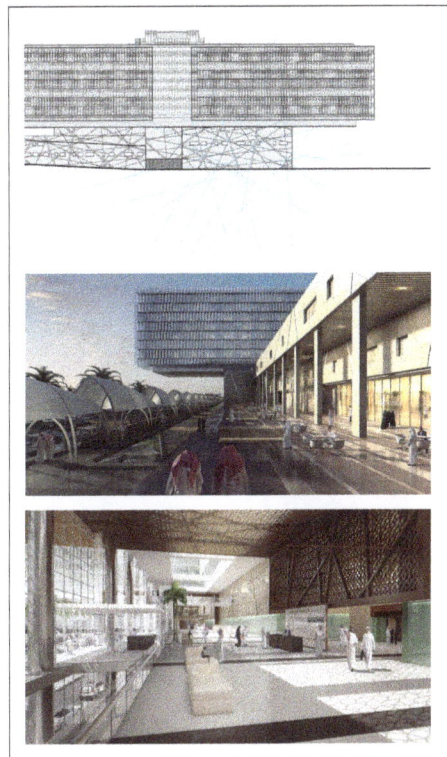

Figure 13. King Faisal Medical City, KFMC, and Prince Mohamed Medical City, PMMC.

156

Figure 14. King Khalid Medical City, KKMC.

ENVIRONMENTS

Typical environments include:

Prayer halls: serving the medical and residential buildings, with others located inside the hospital, take into consideration the Qiblah direction.

Prayer rooms: there are ample prayer rooms for both staff and visitors throughout the facility. All can accommodate the ritual timings of the five daily prayers that are prescribed for Muslims.

Clinics: increasing clinical spaces for families takes into consideration the close family and social relationships that characterize Islamic countries.

Waiting areas for visitors, patients, and medical crews: specifying separate waiting areas for men and women achieves privacy.

Figure 15. King Abdullah Medical City, KAMC.

Figure 16. Prayer halls – KKMC: adding prayer halls to the site plan to serve the medical and residential buildings.

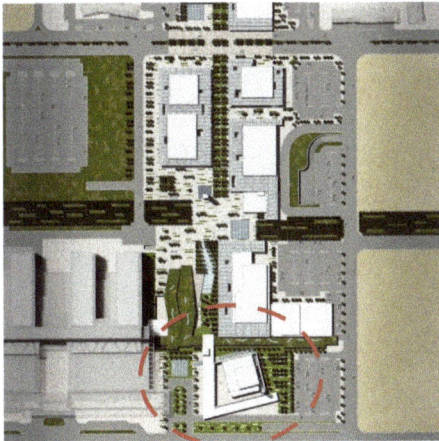

Figure 17. Prayer halls – King Abdullah Medical City, KAMC.

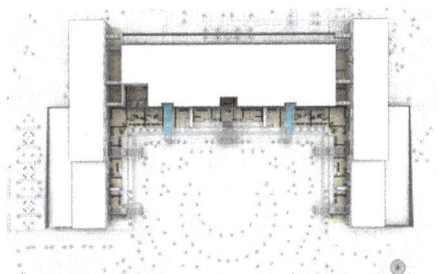

Figure 18. Prayer halls: near the waiting area, centrally located, gender separated.

Inpatient floor: the key features are the tea room; decentralized waiting area; segregated waiting area; promoting family involvement and improving outcomes.

Rehabilitation: specifying separate areas for men and women achieves privacy.

Operating theatre: the scrub zone needs to allow for the segregation of male and female surgeons as they prepare for surgery.

157

Morgue: even in the afterlife the bodies of the different sexes are segregated; preparing and washing are done by same-sex staff; the body is then prepared for wrapping; the family can collect the body with dignity using a private carport for transport.

Inpatient rooms: most of the inpatient rooms in Islamic and Arabic countries are inboard to provide the maximum level of privacy for patients, especially when their condition is stable. Inpatient rooms could have alternative layouts (Figure 24). Islamic and Arabic countries prefer the use of inboard layouts to achieve the highest level of privacy for patients.

Acute-Care patient room: panels closed –, medical gasses are hidden behind a panel thus, further reducing the institutional look of the room; panels open –, when the panels are open, the medical gasses are easily accessible.

Figure 19. These prayer and ablution rooms allow visitors the opportunity to ritually cleanse, worship and connect with their community.

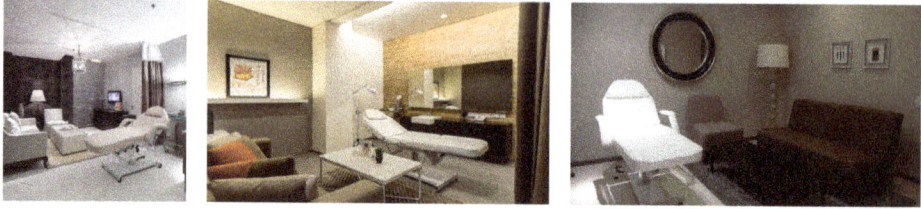

Figure 20. Clinics.

158

Figure 21. Inpatient floor.

Figure 22. King Abdullah Medical City, KAMC – rehabilitation building.

CONCLUSIONS

An evaluation of the "Saudi Experiment in International Design Locally Implemented" has been provided as well as an overview of what distinguishes healthcare buildings in KSA from their counterparts in Western countries, namely prayer halls, separation between men and women, and reflecting the Islamic and Arabic culture in the design.

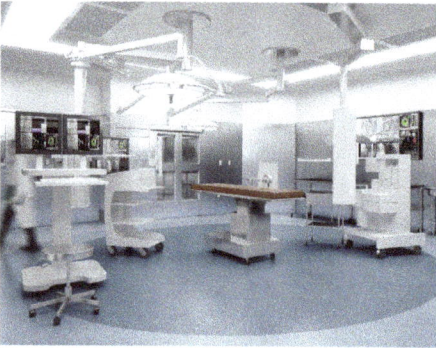

Figure 23. Operating theatre.

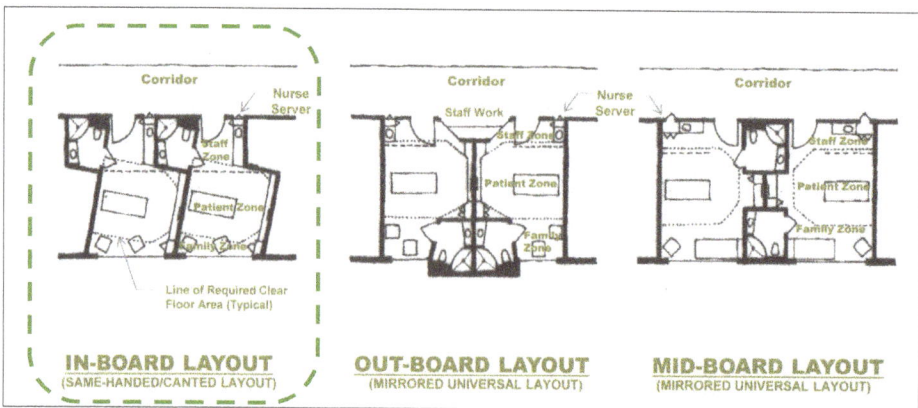

Figure 24. Alternative layouts for inpatient rooms.

Transformative Design:
Hospitals that Enable Lean Process Improvement

Kowalsky B.[1]

barry.kowalsky@stantec.com
[1]Stantec Architecture, Canada

The healthcare system is adopting major changes in its structure, function, and flow. The role of preventative medicine is now at the forefront of healthcare. Technology helps link various subspecialties allowing better communication between physicians and other clinicians. Efforts must be made in order to be efficient and eliminate waste in the healthcare system. Hospital architects and planners play a key role in providing an appropriate environment for a lean system that will minimize capital and operating costs and support optimal patient outcomes. We believe the patient journey not the distinct clinical subspecialties must guide the design and planning. The concept of transformative design provides a new outlook and a new attitude towards the way the design process should flow.

DON'T RULE OUT LEAN RENOVATIONS

That the lean design improvement process gaining popularity in healthcare facilities has limited applications in renovation projects is a misconception.
While the phenomenon of using lean design as a tool to improve patient care and efficiency in new hospitals has gained in popularity—for example, its use at the new Moose Jaw Union Hospital—there is a perception that unless a complete rebuild of the space is planned, lean design has limited application in renovation projects. This need not be the case. The challenge for healthcare planners and designers, along with their clients, is to evaluate how existing hospital space can be modified to better support significant, sustainable improvements to the seven flows of medicine (patients, clinicians, medication, supplies, equipment, information and reengineering) and determine whether the cost is justified.

LEAN-BASED DESIGN

Simply put, lean process improvement in hospitals provides a better patient experience by increasing efficiency while benefiting hospitals by eliminating waste. For designers, lean processes have a significant influence on types of spaces, their functional relationships and organization, and even on the quantity of space required to deliver equivalent levels of service.

Lean-based design uses the following ideas to generate space that supports process improvement: Capitalize on the hospital's existing commitment

160

to lean process improvement by integrating staff responsible for organizational process improvement into the facility planning teams. This will help embed the concept of continuous improvement into the structure of the planning and design process. Establish aggressive project objectives that capture the organization's goal of improved quality and increased efficiency, such as lowering operational costs per discharge and reducing adverse events and readmissions. Assess which operational strategies will best enable achieving project objectives. This needs to be done before design starts, as these are the real drivers of design.

These strategies may include changing supply management procedures and implementing new information and communications technology to reduce staff time and space needs. Evaluate which design strategies best support the operational strategies given the constraints of the existing physical space and the budget available. Considerations should include: To what degree can room sizes be standardized and enlarged to meet the new needs of multi-disciplinary care teams given the existing structural system? How can the point of care distribution of clean supplies be accommodated without extensive structural or code-related renovations?

The list goes on and is very specific to each situation. Remember that one of the principles of lean is collaboration, real and meaningful collaboration between the design team and the client—especially the front line staff.

$1.1 billion or 1,485 beds

Approximate annual cost of preventable adverse events in Canada

Figure 1. Annual cost of preventable adverse events in Canada.

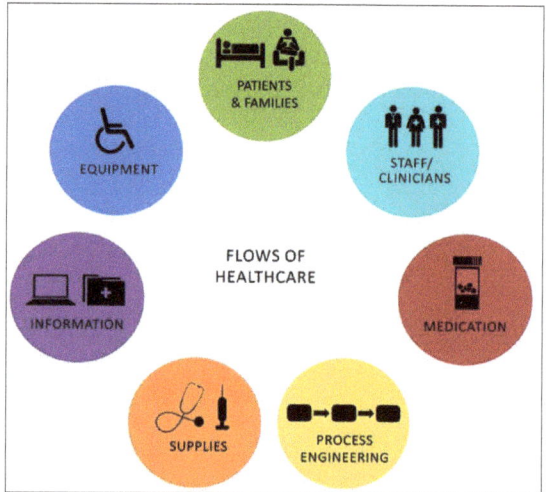

Figure 2. Work flow analyses for the prevention of adverse events.

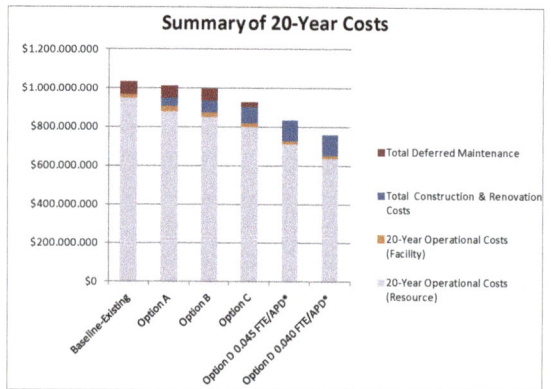

Figure 3. Current state: not addressing the real costs.

CREATE A MASTER PLAN

There are always simple changes that will yield substantial process improvement with little capital investment; however, investing in lean-based design in an existing facility will take time, as it is unlikely all of the funding to take maximum advantage of the lean potential of the space is available.

A long-term master plan that identifies priority areas can help any organization achieve its long-term process improvement goals and objectives. A case in point: interventional procedures are usually done in multiple locations throughout a hospital based on the clinical specialties. If you look at this from a patient flow perspective, interventional procedures share common staff and equipment for patient preparation and recovery as well as equipment cleaning and sterilization.

Rather than establishing multiple locations that inhibit standardization of care and support processes, consolidating the common resources for interventional procedures improves access to qualified staff, improves equipment utilization, better enables standards of care, and speeds patient throughput. Achieving this in an existing hospital has challenges, but by applying this approach consistently, as funds become available, the development of an interventional procedures platform can be achieved.

161

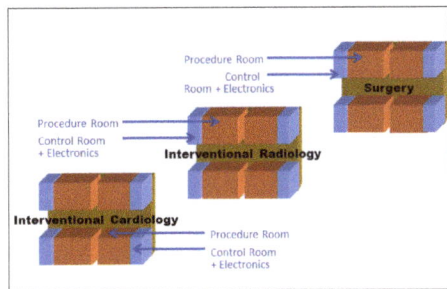

Figure 5. Flexible planning modules.

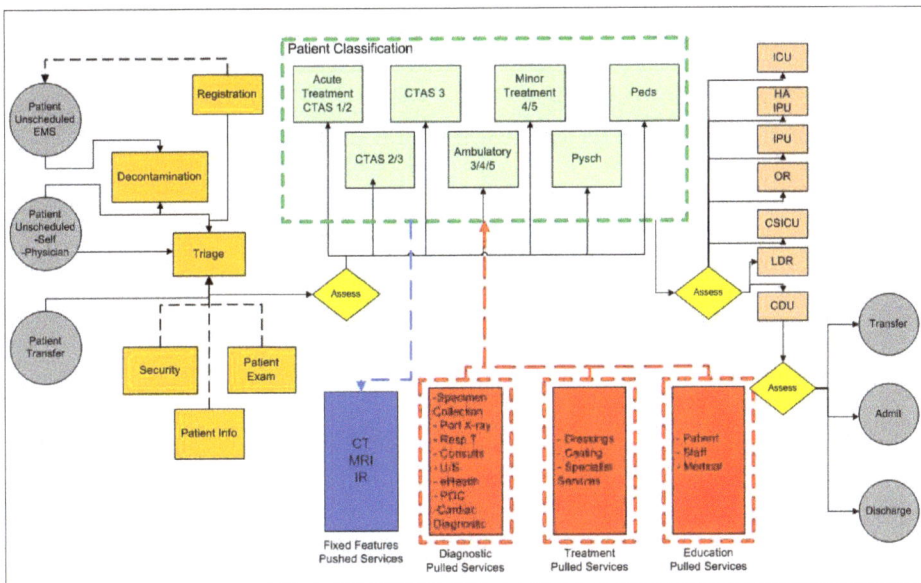

Figure 4. Royal Columbian Hospital patient flow assessment: future state – ER.

CONCLUSIONS

Regardless of the level of renovation being planned, the lean spatial strategies identified in this article can be applied to varying degrees. This can result in significant improvements to operational processes, both clinical and support. Accomplishing this requires a planning process that actively engages clinical and non-clinical staff to achieve long-term solutions that ultimately improve working conditions and patient care.

162

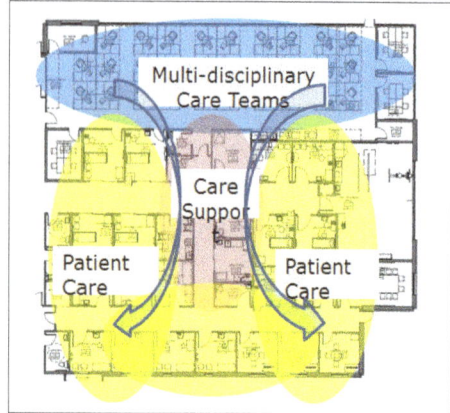

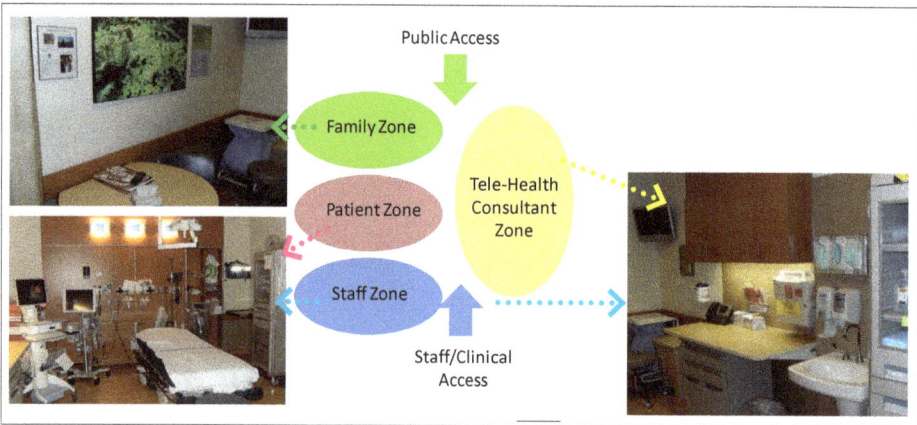

Figure 6.   *Key design concepts in the functional distribution of spaces: collaborative, flexible, universal.*

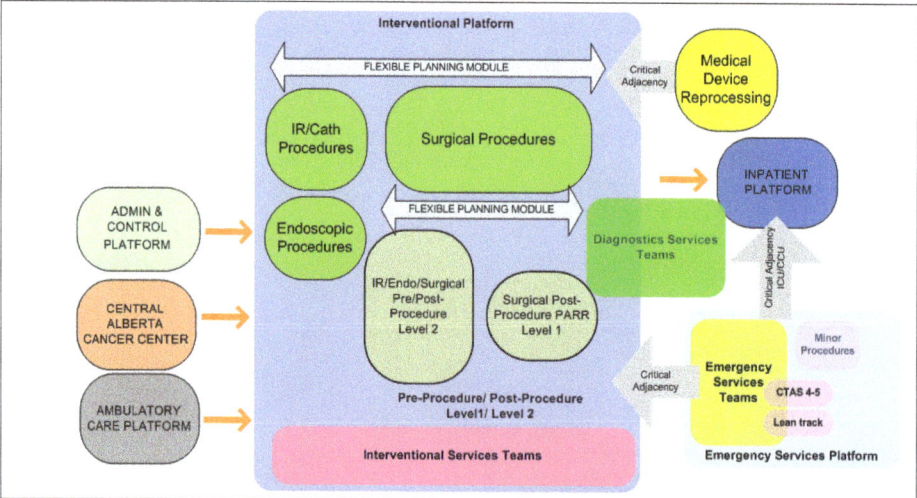

Figure 7.   *Key design concepts: care platforms.*

Current Issues & Trends in the Design of Healthcare Facilities & Construction in India

Chandrashekhar R.[1]

chandrashekhar_54@yahoo.co.in
[1] Dr., Chief Architect, Ministry of Health, Government of India

163

Good architecture is much more encompassing than its outward appearance. It is the result of a team effort yielding good building design through a process of good design and problem solving, to create a well-designed, therapeutic and diagnostic environment that supports a robust, cost-efficient and comfortable environment for patients, faculties and all others.

In accordance with the Government of India, the present focus is on strengthening primary and secondary healthcare services in the country as a priority, particularly by using technology to bridge the gap. The question is who will drive the change? How much money are we spending as a percentage of the GDP allocation? Is the money being spent, and beyond that is it being utilized or not?

INTRODUCTION

In view of the federal nature of the Constitution, areas of operation have been divided between the Union Government and State Governments. Health is a State subject, the Union Ministry of Health & Family Welfare is instrumental and responsible for implementing various programmes on a national scale in the areas of health and family welfare, the prevention and control of major communicable diseases and the promotion of traditional and indigenous systems of medicines. The Ministry also assists states in preventing and controlling the spread of seasonal disease outbreaks and epidemics through technical assistance.

Expenditure is incurred by the Ministry of Health & Family Welfare either directly under Central Schemes or by way of grants–in–aids to autonomous/statutory bodies and NGOs. The Ministry is implementing several World Bank assisted programmes for the control of AIDS, malaria, and tuberculosis in designated areas. The Ministry of Health & Family Welfare comprises the following four departments, each of which is headed by a Secretary to the Government of India, they are: Department of Health & Family Welfare; Department of AYUSH; Department of Health Research; Department of AIDS Control. The Directorate General of Health Services (DGHS) is an attached office

TESIS

of the Department of Health & Family Welfare and has subordinate offices spread all over the country. The DGHS renders technical advice on all medical and public health matters and is involved in implementing various health schemes.

NATIONAL HEALTH PROFILE

164

The population density of India in 2011 was 382 per sq km while the urban population was 31.60% of the total population. Urban migration over the last decade has resulted in the rapid growth of urban slums. The age distribution of the population showed 31.4% in the 0-14 age group and only 7.4% in the 60+ age group.

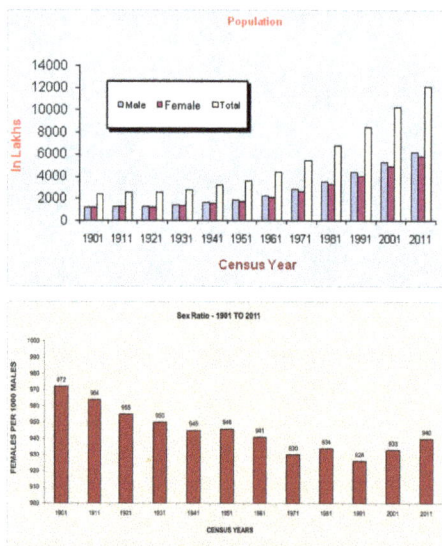

Figure 1. Population and sex ratio. Source: Registrar General of India.

The Infant Mortality Rate has declined considerably (i.e. 47 per 1000 live births in 2010), however rural (51) & urban (31) differentials are still high.

Figure 2. Birth rate, death rate and natural growth rate.

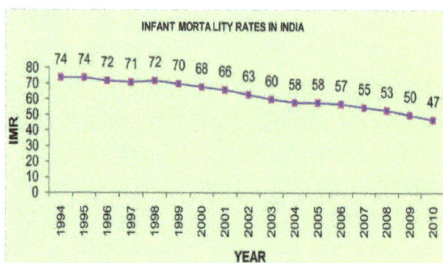

Figure 3. Infant mortality rates in India.

Rural Health Infrastructure

The rural health infrastructre of a Sub-Centre (SC) incorporates the following: Primary Health Centre (PHC); Community Health Centre (CHC); Sub-Divisional /Sub-District and District Hospitals;we have Indian Public Health Standards (IPHS) for Infrastructure, equipment. and drugs for the above mentioned facilities supported by Mobile Medical Units/Health Camps; the National Health Portal (NHP) gives all related information about Healthcare facilities; under NHM (National Health Mission) we have the National Rural Health Mission (NRHM) and the National Urban Health Mission (NUHM).

Medical Education Infrastructures

The country has 335 medical colleges, 291 colleges for BDS courses, and 140 colleges conduct MDS courses. Total admissions amounted to 39,474 (in 318 medical colleges) and 23,800 for BDS during 2011-12.

There were 2028 institutions for General Nurse Midwives with admission capacities totalling 80,332, and 608 colleges for Pharmacy (Diploma) with an intake capacity of 36,115 as of March 31, 2010.

The country has 11,993 hospitals with 7,84,940 beds. Of these, 7,347 hospitals with 1,60,862 beds are in rural areas, and 4,146 hospitals with 6,18,664 beds are in urban areas.

There were 1,48,124 Sub Centres, 23,887 Primary Health Centres, and 4,809 Community Health Centres in India as of March 2011.

The number of medical care facilities under AYUSH according to management status, i.e. dispensaries and hospitals, amounted to 24,280 & 3,193 respectively as of April 2011.

The total number of licensed Blood Banks in the country as of July 2011 was 2,517.

"Good Architecture is much more encompassing than its outward appearance."

It is the result of a team effort yielding good building design through a process of problem solving and innovative thinking to create a well-designed therapeutic and diagnostic environment that supports the efficient delivery of healthcare services, and a robust, cost-efficient, friendly and comfortable environment for patients, faculties and others.

In the 12th Five-Year plan, the Government of India's focus is on strengthening: Primary Healthcare; Secondary Healthcare; upgrading 642 District Hospitals; new medical colleges; upgrading some District Hospitals to medical colleges based on land availability; upgrading 39 existing medical colleges adding Super Speciality Beds resulting in an increase in PGSeats; setting up 2 more AIIMS-like institutions; one national & eight regional Institutes of Paramedics; National Mental Health Programme: Burns Unit pilot programme in states; Regional Cancer Centres; medical education reform envisaged.

165

Initiatives in the IT Sector

"Delivering healthcare without using information technology is like driving a car without a dashboard and steering wheel. Neither can you make out what's happening, nor can you maneuver the vehicle to avoid mishap." R. P. Gupta, international healthcare expert.

Hospital Projects are generally Green Field Projects or Brown Field Projects, which operate with following models.

BACKGROUND OF EXISTING MODELS

Model 1

Preparation of the Detail Project Report (DPR); supported by Project Management Consultant during execution; Project Monitoring Unit as a monitoring regulatory body; 6 new AIIMS-like institutes; 1000 beds each (1.4 million sq ft); approx. 150 million USD were spent in this model.

Model 2

EPC (Engineering Procurement Construction); also known as DESIGN & BUILD; Regulated by the Project Monitoring Unit.

PREPARATION OF THE DPR

The Detail project report describes a series of aspects that can be summarized as follows: project background; constraints/limitations; all detail working/tender drawings, PERT chart: architectural, structural, plumbing & drainage, HVAC, electrical, fire fighting, waste management, medical gases, landscaping, signage, interior design, furniture /furnishings, bulk services, HIS, IT services; detailed estimate of project; list of medical equipment & specifications; manpower requirement; running, maintenance & operation costs; budgetary projections.

The Design Team is comprised of:
1. Hospital Consultant – conducts a market survey and produces a financial feasibility report to establish the intended role of the proposed healthcare facility in the region it is to serve.
2. Consulting Architect – offers specialized healthcare programming and design services, as well as conceptual planning and schematic layouts for individual hospital projects.
3. Local Architect – responsible for obtaining all the requisite permits / No Objection Certificates (NOCs) from the regulatory authorities concerned.
4. Structural Consultant/MEP (Mechanical, Electrical, Plumbing) Consultants – Structural and MEP Consultants are engineers.
5. Construction Manager – performs a variety of functions, such as managing general conditions on-site, including start-up and overall supervision. Towards the end of construction, the construction manager is responsible for drawing up a certificate of substantial completion.

6. Landscape Architect – responsible for the design of outdoor areas around the hospital or the spaces in between buildings on a campus.
7. Interior Design Consultant/Graphic Designer – designs furniture/furnishing/signage systems.
8. Bio-Medical Engineer/Medical Equipment Consultant – involved in the layout design, specifications, procurement and installation of medical equipment.

The DPR Evaluation Checklist analyses the following points: architectural and civil; electrical; HVAC; medical equipment/medical gases; public health engineering; electronic services of the project, from which the Tender Packages and Time Schedule are derived.

Brownfield Projects

A business model that utilizes existing infrastructure, local resources, trains local manpower, corrects deficiencies and overrides constraints by constantly innovating. Referred to as a "Light Asset Model" of expansion which can be replicated fast and has a low gestation period. "A retrofit model of expansion which optimizes on all available resources in the vicinity yet manages to create its own brand identity." This model can be used in existing hospitals or other existing buildings. The approach to this type of project involves improvements to or the upgrading of: infrastructure; medical equipment; human resources; bulk services. The following images show two significant examples of redevelopment: Lady Hardinge Medical College LHMC (Figures 5-7) and Safdarjung Hospital (Figures 8-9).

166

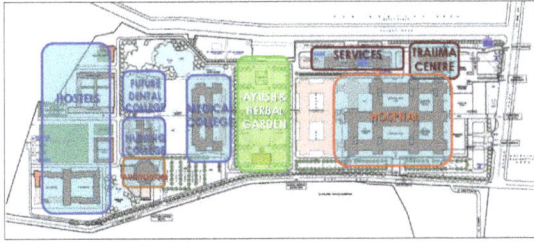

Figure 4. *Master plan layout (zoning & future blocks).*

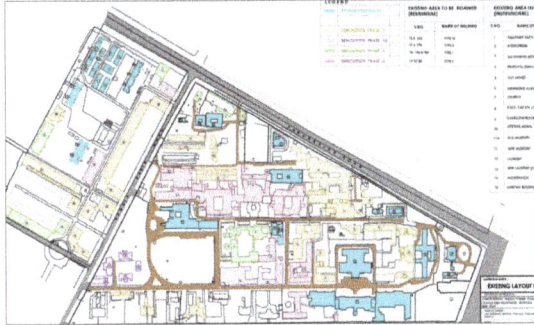

Figure 5. *Existing layout plan of LHMC.*

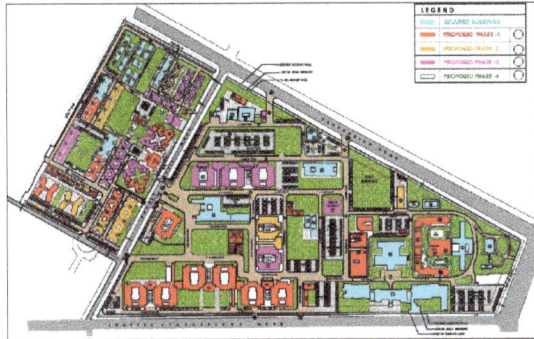

Figure 6. *Master plan for revised proposal.*

Figure 7. *Street view from Shahid Bhagat Singh Marg and view of IPD block.*

Figure 8. *Existing layout of Safdarjung Hospital.*

167

Figure 9. *Redevelopment of the Safdarjung Hospital Campus.*

EPC OR DESIGN BUILD MODEL

JIPMER Hospital – Phase I, Puducherry

The project scope covers: super speciality block 2,51220 sq ft; trauma care centre 38990 sq ft; Regional Cancer Centre 37890 sq ft; Nursing College 38650 sq ft; Nurses Hostel 41640 sq ft; Patient Day Care Shelter 14290 sq ft; service buildings 18240 sq ft.

The hospital site is located in Puducherry on an area of 195 acres and the following data describes the project: client: Ministry of Health & Family Welfare, Government of India, New Delhi; consultant: HLL Lifecare Ltd; end user: Jipmer Hospital, Puducherry; scope of work: Design & Build; agency: L&T; built-up area: 437000 sq ft; no. of beds: 550; structure: G+4 storied structure; cost of project: 30 million USD; du-

168

ration of 24 months; completed in 22 months; 12 well-equipped operating theatres; 5 minor OTs; 58 ICU beds; 10 renal dialysis beds; 2 cath labs; state-of-the-art nursing college with residential facilities; intake of 75-100 students/year for B.Sc. Nursing (4 Years); oncology block upgradable to a Regional Cancer Centre with 65 beds and 8 ICUs with a linear accelerator, brachytherapy, and other equipment.

Figure 10. JIPMER Hospital Design & Build Experience, master plan.

Figure 11. JIPMER Hospital.

Figure 12. Super specialty block, JIPMER – Phase I, Puducherry.

Figure 13. JIPMER Hospital.

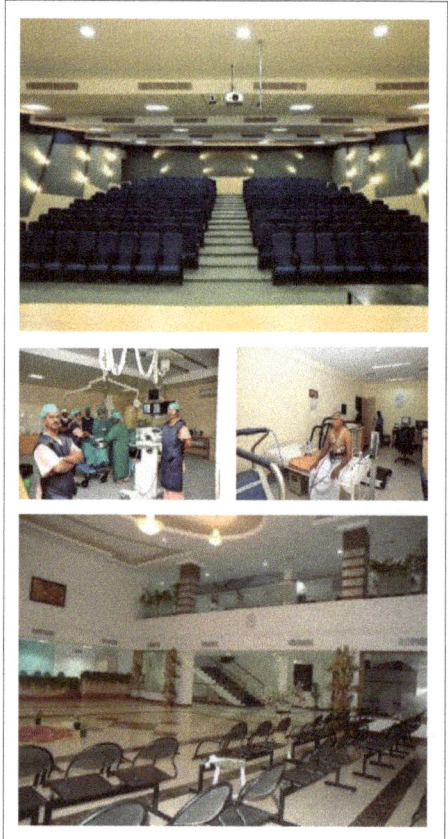

Figure 14. Super specialty block, JIPMER Hospital.

Figure 15. Nursing college, JIPMER Hospital.

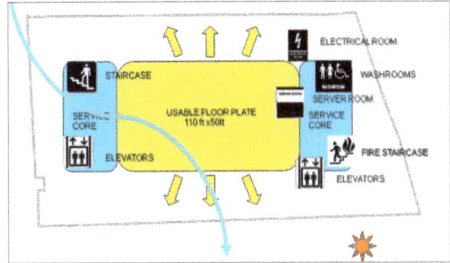

Figure 17. Rehab centre, functional program.

169

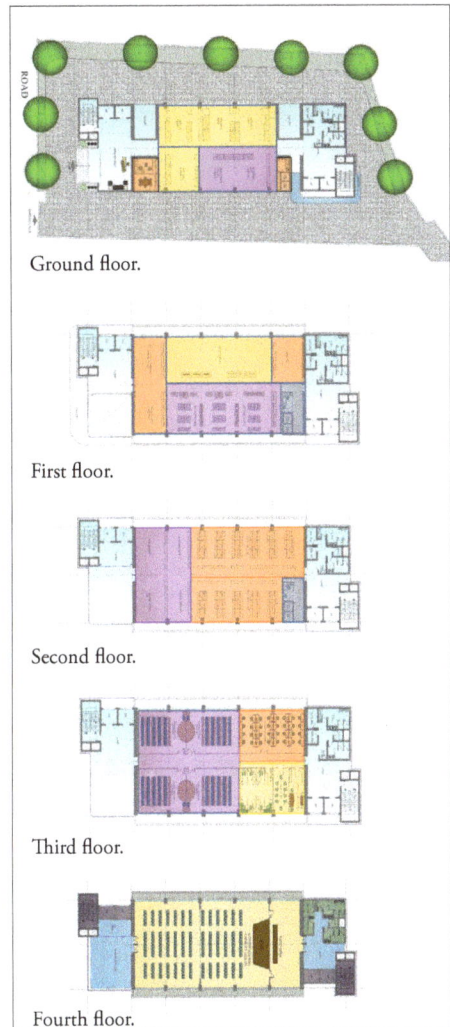

Figure 16. Oncology block.

Ground floor.

First floor.

Second floor.

Third floor.

Fourth floor.

Figure 18. Rehab centre.

Smaller Size Project for a Rehab Centre: All India Institute of Physical Medicine and Rehabilitation

The different functions within the building are distributed as follows in a column-free structure:

Ground Floor. Orthotic workshop consisting of: inspection & quality control; packaging & delivery; workshop manager cabin; store manager cabin; small meeting room; dumbwaiter.

First Floor. The workshop consists of: prosthetics; carpentry; vocational training; leather lining; ankle/footing; floor manager's cabin; dumbwaiter.

170

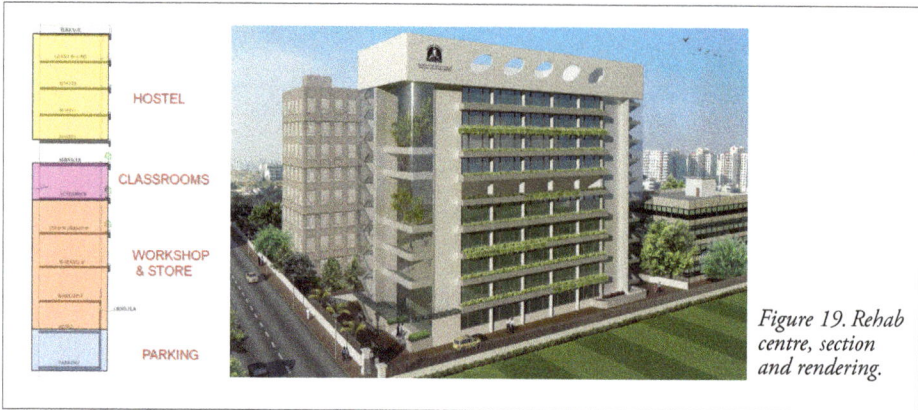

Figure 19. Rehab
centre, section
and rendering.

Second Floor. The students' workshop consists of: orthotics lab; prosthetics lab; machine shop; mobility devices; biomechanics lab; floor manager's cabin; dumbwaiter.

Third Floor. This floor consists of: 4 classrooms; computer training; girls' common room; faculty room; conference room.

6th & 7th Floors. These floors consist of: rooms for UG students; 18 rooms; each shared by 3 students; total of 54 beds per floor; communal bathrooms/toilets; utility area.

Dr RML Hospital (Pre-Engineered Structure)

Dr RML Hospital is a 300-bed emergency block co vering 80,000 sq ft, in New Delhi. The project used the pre-engineered structure methodology. In order to apply this methodology the essence was time management which was achieved by identifying: activity; activity sequence; co-ordination chart; on-site works; off-site works; administrative works; technical approvals.

Figure 20. Dr RML Hospital, New Delhi, floor plan.

Figure 21. Dr RML Hospital, New Delhi, rendering.

Figure 22. Foundations, site levelling, and activity sequence.

171

Figure 23. Stiffeners, fire protection paint, hollow concrete partition walls, and Modifoam external wall.

Figure 24. Medical gas pipe, drywall partition, and façade.

Figure 25. Pre-engineered building built in 48 hrs in Mohali.

WORKING WITH A DESIGN AND BUILD MODEL. IS THIS THE FUTURE OF THE INDUSTRY?

Sustainable Design

An environmentally friendly & green hospital incorporates the following: use of non-conventional energy; waste management; excellent features that result in environmental protection, water conservation/harvesting, energy efficiency; use of eco-friendly, recycled products; building management systems to monitor and control; barrier-free environment; healing architecture.

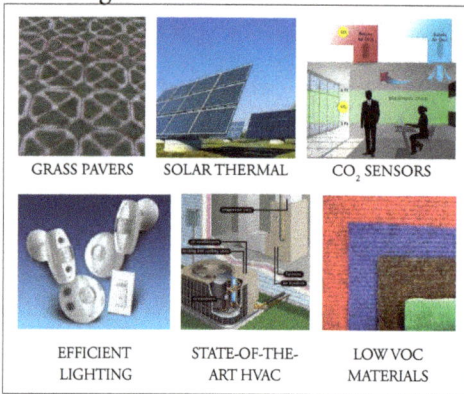

GRASS PAVERS   SOLAR THERMAL   CO$_2$ SENSORS

EFFICIENT   STATE-OF-THE-   LOW VOC
LIGHTING   ART HVAC   MATERIALS

Figure 26. Environmentally friendly & green hospital.

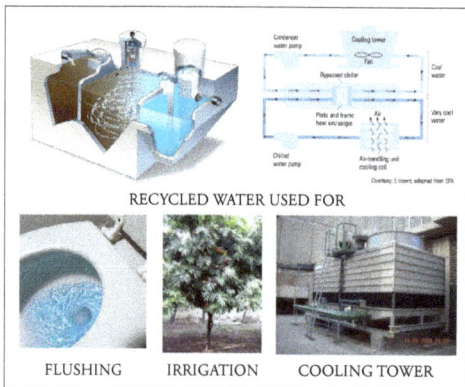

RECYCLED WATER USED FOR

FLUSHING   IRRIGATION   COOLING TOWER

Figure 27. Sewage treatment plant treats 100% waste water.

Figure 28. Government Medical College, Salem.

Figure 29. Leed Gold Certified.

The Mandatory Requirement

– Focus on compliance with the 2007 Energy Conservation Building Code;
– 3 star GRIHA (Green Rating of Integrated Habitat Assessment).

Five areas in which hospitals will have to take action, according to the JCA report, are: economic viability; adoption of technology; patient-centered care; staffing; hospital design.

Economically, hospitals will be expected to increase efficiency and reduce costs, among other things. Technologically, hospitals will have to make changes that can reduce the workload and that are also easy to integrate.

Changes in the Ontario Healthcare Landscape:
A View from a Province in Canada

Lo V. [1], Harvey C. [2]

vivianlo@sympatico.ca, cliff.harvey@nygh.on.ca
[1]Hon.B.Sc. (Toxicology), M.Arch., MRAIC, IDC, Healthcare Design Specialist, LINE Architect Inc., Toronto, Canada
[2]FRAIC, OAA, Vice President, Planning, Facilities and Support Services, North York General Hospital, Toronto, Canada

173

In the past, one's personal journey through the healthcare landscape in Ontario was rather monolithic. It was flat like the prairies until you needed care, and then it was off to the hospital that appeared on the landscape as overwhelming as the Rocky Mountains. Except, you can hire a guide to take you through the mountains, whereas in a hospital you are often handed a referral slip and told to be there at a particular time, end of story. Over time, as the specialities of healthcare expanded, they continued to be housed in the same hospital building regardless of the patient acuity. The mountain got bigger and less easy to navigate. In Ontario, a public healthcare system, the hospital became a system in itself and with over 220 hospitals serving over 13 million people; Ontario became a system of systems, and an unaffordable system at that.

The nature of economic forces, like many natural forces, started to erode the monolithic healthcare landscape into a diverse and more natural setting. This setting is based on a system approach to delivering care. The healthcare landscape is expanding to not only deliver general primary, ambulatory, acute, and post-acute care services, but also to develop a wide range of support focused on patient-centred care. The boundary of healthcare facilities becomes blurred. The building types range from a distinct structure at a noticeable location to the penetration of an indefinite number of mid-scale to small commercial units into the community. The terms doctor and patient are also being reconsidered. Alternatives ranging from "healthcare provider" and "client" to "healthcare professional" and "customer" have been suggested to replace the traditional labels. This new landscape is crystallized in the Ontario Action Plan for Health, with a transformation agenda to create a sustainable patient-centred healthcare system. To do this, the patient journey has to be simplified whenever possible to make it a quality-based experience. The mountainous hospital must be reduced to create easy and accessible foothills for ambulatory care, closer to home and more affordable to construct and operate. On the other side of the mountain similarly, there should be post-acute facilities to care for those that cannot be cared for in their homes; again more quality-based experiences. Finally, for those who must transverse through the mountain of healthcare, our traditional hospitals, the patient should be armed with navigators and the clinicians with care pathways wherever they can, to facilitate the quality passage through this difficult time.

Keywords: *healthcare, design, facilities, ontario, canada*

SEISMIC SHIFTS

Healthcare is changing and evolving fast. The landscape in Ontario, a member of the British Commonwealth, slowly developed a mix of profit and non-profit institutions from the early settlers through to the 1950s. Then in the 1950s, following the lead of other industrialized nations, Ontario introduced a public healthcare system. Almost overnight, Ontario with the help of the Federal government, started building a new landscape of public hospitals. Originally they were primarily acute care facilities, but as the specialization and development of medicine allowed for specialization – new models of care were introduced. Today we have primary care, ambulatory care, post-acute care, long-term care, home care and mental health care.

Through the growth of this period, hospitals grew to take in these different types of care, often under one roof. Hospitals became healthcare institutions; they increasingly became the centres from which all kinds of healthcare services are delivered. Then starting in the 1980s new building forms to deliver healthcare started to enter the landscape, and the hospital as the institution started to be eroded. This also corresponded to a slowdown in the building activities for the Ontario healthcare system. It represented a pause for the system as it tried to redefine itself. It is the "whole of the hospital's functioning, the whole of healthcare" that concern us rather than that fraction which "hospitals" have customarily been assigned to deliver.[1]

All these not only indicate the effectiveness of specialization in the development of medicine, but also the success the system was having in the healing process. However, healthcare costs continued to rise. New building types were sought after to correspond to the new models of care (Fig. 1).

_____

1. Sloane, D. C. and Sloane, B. C. (2003). *Medicine Moves to the Mall.* Baltimore: Johns Hopkins University Press, 3.

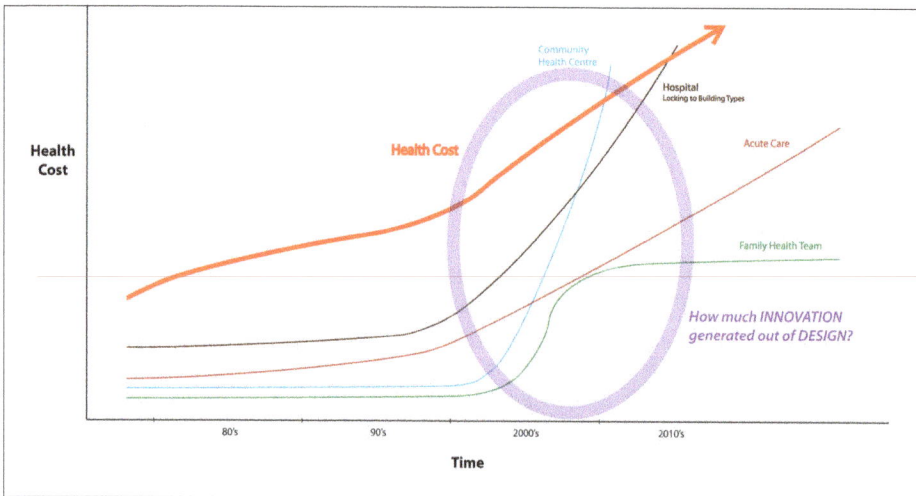

Figure 1.   Healthcare cost vs time. © Illustration by Clifford Harvey and Vivian Lo, Toronto, Canada. 2014.

174

The challenge for architects, then, lies not only in designing innovative and sustainable healthcare spaces, but also in establishing historical and architectural perspectives that promote broader urban and cultural values.[2] Such a challenge requires transformation in the agenda, which takes innovative processes and makes them sustainable.

Other new agendas also influenced the development of healthcare architecture. The effective use of resources helps promote the sustainability of the healthcare system and can be achieved through energy conservation and planning for future flexibility to accommodate changes in the provision of care and/or program expansion. Sustainability considers not only the direct capital projects in the built environment, but also indirectly the on-going services delivered in these buildings (i.e. total cost of operation). After all, as Verderber indicates, the first and foremost priority must continue to remain clear: to promote and advance the health and well-being of all individuals and populations everywhere in an ecologically responsible manner.[3]

Healthcare is part of a whole world that is moving at a faster pace. Different characteristics of healthcare buildings reflect historical changes in hospital design. Moreover, due to the changing demographics of the patients a hospital serves, the ongoing advances in biotechnology and information technology, the restructuring of healthcare funding,

and the growing role of the patient as a partner in healthcare[4], individual departments in a hospital may be closed or have to be merged with other hospitals. The characteristics of healthcare buildings play a role in shaping perceptions of healing, healthcare practice, and sickness itself.

SHIFT IN HOSPITAL DESIGN AT A GLANCE

In the nineteenth century, hospitals were institutions categorized as civic or public enterprises and their designs were used to mirror their moral mission.[5] Sloane et al. pointed out that later by the early twentieth century, the modern hospital's façade was used to symbolize society's faith in science and the hospital's mission as a functional place for healing. With the advance development of communication technology, people nowadays stay in touch by fax, e-mail, pager, video conference, and cellular phone.[6]

The relationship between doctor and patient – the most important element in healthcare – is then less permanent. Patients may change from one doctor to another.[7]

Increasingly, hospitals and allied healthcare facilities share society's drive for convenience and service, diminishing the boundaries between the "moral" model of medicine and customer service.[8]

---

2 Adams, A. and Theodore, D. (Mar 2002). Medicine by Design. *Canadian Architect*. v.47, n.3: 14.

3 Verderber, S. (2010). *Innovations in Healthcare Architecture*. New York; London: Routledge, 4.

4 http://www.uhn.ca/uhn/background/?nav=5;5 (as of Feb 24, 2006).

5 Sloane, D. C. and Sloane, B. C. (2003). *Medicine Moves to the Mall*. Baltimore: Johns Hopkins University Press, p. 6.

6 Sloane, D. C. and Sloane, B. C. *op.cit.*, p. 4.

7 *Ibidem*.

8 Sloane, D. C. and Sloane, B. C. *op.cit.*, p. 7.

Moreover, rather than using the word "system" or "institution" to define the hospital environment, the word "landscape" is used instead. This implies a place where medicine is practiced, but not focused on its organizational or economic structure.[9] Sloane et al. cites the cultural geographer Paul Groth's definition of "cultural landscape studies" as that of studying "the history of how people have used everyday space – buildings, rooms, streets, fields, or yards – to establish their identity, articulate their social relations, and derive cultural meaning." In other words, such places may include corporate campuses and even garages – as long as they are spaces where the people involved interact as well as play out their lives.[10]

Healthcare landscapes change due to a number of reasons. New anti-inflammatory drugs, anesthetics, pain medications, and antibiotics combine to make inpatient stays shorter or even unnecessary. Diseases such as pneumonia that in the recent past incapacitated people for weeks are typically handled on an outpatient basis. Even complex healthcare treatments are happening faster, with fewer days in the hospital.[11] For instance, the treatment of cancer patients changes drastically. Patients who needed to receive chemotherapy had to stay in hospital for days in the past. Besides, a significant number of patients also suffered from the adverse effects of the treatment. As a result oncology clinics were always fully packed with patients who needed to receive treatments for the side effects. Nowadays, however, with

the advancement of healthcare research and biotechnology, powerful drugs that suppress the adverse effects caused by chemotherapy are usually added to the chemotherapy treatments and are given to patients at the same time. Thus, the patients not only suffer less, but also their stay in hospital is largely shortened from a few days to a few hours. The physical size of such oncology clinics is then reduced.

Hospital planners typically point to the increase in day surgery as a justification for new construction. In general, hospitals are less residential than ever before: very few people who go to hospital even stay overnight, as opposed to the past century, around the 1950s, when not just patients but nurses, interns and other personnel lived at the hospital.[12]

The care journey, which used to be a simple linear process with hospitals as almost the only choice, has currently been evolved into a complex path with multiple options; various types of healthcare facilities deliver different levels of care services.

CHANGES IN HOSPITAL DESIGN – TORONTO, ONTARIO

The hospital is the locus of natural processes like childbirth; it is the place where death can be made easier – for patient and family – by removing terminal cases from the family situation. An active healthy man may come in for a thorough check-up combined with a few days of rest. (It has all the service operations of a hotel.) As a public insti-

9 Sloane, D. C. and Sloane, B. C. op. cit., p. 5.
10 Ibidem.
11 Sloane, D. C. and Sloane, B. C. op. cit., p. 4.

12 Adams, A. and Theodore, D. (Mar 2002) Medicine by Design. Canadian Architect. v.47, n.3: 15.

tution and a monument to civic pride or parsimony, it is a budgeting and development problem for officialdom or civic leaders. More and more, the hospital becomes an institution for training at all levels – technicians, nurses, doctors, scientists. Frequently it is also a research institution.[13] The complex thus contains within itself many things. It retains the character of a charity hospice, the first refuge of those in desperate straits – though an emergency is more often likely to be mental or social rather than physical.[14]

The essence of the modern hospital – its pride and its success – is the workshop where a sophisticated assemblage of specialists, working as a team, can apply skills and techniques in successful interventions. It is no longer the workshop of the individual doctor. This is where the modern hospital has departed from the past.[15]

In Ontario, the early policies of the Ministry of Health and Long-term Care (MOHLTC) focused on two extreme scales of healthcare services provided by hospitals (centre excellence) and primary care (home care). At the same time, with the emergence of the necessary intermediate scale of community-based healthcare support such as hospices, walk-in clinics, and urgent care centres, and a growing emphasis on primary and home care, the building type itself – the modern university-affiliated general hospital with a three-part mandate for

research, teaching, and patient care – is mutating.[16]

Many of the healthcare services provided in Ontario are publicly funded, which includes fees for family doctors and healthcare specialists, as well as most basic and emergency healthcare services, including surgeries and hospital stays.[17]

In addition, MOHLTC is responsible for establishing the overall strategic direction and provincial priorities for the health system. The provincial government also develops legislation, regulations, standards, policies and directives to support those strategic directions.

During the 1990s at least twelve Canadian cities saw the closure of major hospital buildings. These robust structures were declared obsolete due to a lack of patients or because of advances in medicine, underlined by institutional mergers and changes in the delivery of healthcare.[18] In the last decade, administrative mergers and financial restructuring in Canada's healthcare system have dramatically reshaped our building stock. Together, there is also a demand from patients, governments and healthcare personnel for new, state-of-the-art facilities. Indeed, Adams et al. states that since the establishment of the Health Care Restructuring Commission in 1996, Ontario boasts that it initially poured $1.9 billion into the expansion and modernization of sixty-four hospital

177

13 Rosenfield, I. (1969) *Hospital Architecture and Beyond*. New York: Van Nostrand Reinhold company.
14 *Ibidem*.
15 *Ibidem*.

16 Adams, A. and Theodore, D. *op. cit.*, p.15.
17 http://www.health.gov.on.ca/en/common/system/default.aspx#1
18 Adams, A. (Jun 2004). Reviving the Dead: Art and the Twentieth-century Hospital. *Fuse Magazine*. v.27, n.2, 18.

sites.[19] From then on, we continuously saw the building of "landmark-like" hospital complexes in the city, where the complexes may house more than one hospital, like the University Health Network on University Avenue which consists of Toronto General, Toronto Western, and Princess Margaret Hospital. Moreover, within the structure, certain departments of a particular hospital may merge with other departments of another hospital – some portions of the Department of Oncology of the Princess Margaret Hospital, for instance, are merged with those of the Sunnybrook and Women's College Health Sciences Centre on Bayview Avenue. The healthcare landscape in Ontario has changed drastically since 2000 and this active blooming of healthcare infrastructure involving over 120 capital projects has now cost the provincial government over ten billion dollars. Such changes fade the boundaries of individual hospitals indicating their disintegration but, at the same time, the integration and penetration of individual departments or affiliated clinics into the community.

Known as healthcare centres rather than hospitals, these "mega-institutions" draw on postmodern architectural principles such as contextual sensitivity (fitting into the neighbourhood) and historicism (drawing on past architectural styles) to diminish their real scale and often the hard edge of healthcare technology.[20] The emergence of "mega-institutions", also identified as design excellence – hospital, education, and research all located in one institution, was clearly seen during the millennium when the

Government of Ontario brought up the "SuperBuild" initiative. This billion-dollar government investment was designed to modernize and improve Ontario's healthcare facilities across the province, which included building new hospitals, as well as upgrading and renewing old ones.

In fact, hospitals become commercial nowadays. Running as if they were commercial companies, hospitals are restructured in such a way that their presidents now name themselves CEOs instead. Hospitals also have well-developed plans to promote themselves not only for their healthcare technologies and research advancements among others in the industry, but also to include the excellent client services and community outreach programs they provide as "the selling point". One of the obvious reasons behind this promotion strategy is to help fundraising for the hospitals.

Hospitals have now changed and rapidly evolved. They were passively waiting for patients to visit them in the past; now they are actively reaching out to maintain "good client relationships" partly due to their purpose of securing a portion of the funding through donation from the community. A significant number of the donors or sponsors are once their patients (client) or family members of patients.

Additionally, hospitals recognize that good design attracts patients. Arcidi quotes Arneill's observation that hospitals promote responsive service as earnestly as their more commercial counterparts.[21] These healthcare centres also

19 Adams, A. and Theodore, D. *op. cit.*, p. 14.
20 Adams, A. *op.cit.*, p.18.
21 Arcidi, P. (Mar 1992). P/A Inquiry: Hospitals

presume, and even encourage, visitors and staff to arrive by car, as they are typically surrounded by a sea of parking, like a suburban mall.[22] Arcidi believes that this is because people are being accustomed to the conveniences of fast food and shopping malls, therefore they also expect amenities in hospitals: easy parking, attractive reception areas, good views from the patient care rooms, and nursing units where the staff are visibly present.[23]

Thus, hospitals are being redesigned to make them more accessible and familiar. Shopping malls and hotels are not the only models from which designers have adapted characteristics to alter the relationship of the patient to the hospital's physical spaces. The introduction of atriums in hospitals has become a popular design decision in recent decades. The home is also an important source. The location of care from the hospital is thus shifted to the hotel and the burden of care from the system is then transferred to the patient's family.[24] Besides, the growth of the population needing long-term care has led to assisted living facilities and other types of care for elderly persons, along with significant changes in skilled nursing.[25] Such changes in healthcare practices have forced architects and hospital managers to search for models in places where people feel comfortable and where they can easily familiarize themselves.

Ontario, as of April 2013, has 157 public, private, and specialty psychiatric hospital corporations with 239 sites. There are 146 public hospital corporations which operate on 224 sites, including geriatric care, complex continuing care, rehabilitation, and children's hospitals, such as Baycrest Centre for Geriatric Care, Bridgepoint Active Healthcare, Toronto Rehabilitation Institute, and The Hospital for Sick Children respectively.

Seven but one private hospitals funded by the Ministry of Health and Long-Term Care provide healthcare services at seven sites, and four specialty psychiatric hospitals function at eight sites.[26]

The characteristics of healthcare buildings play a role in shaping perceptions of healing, healthcare practice, and sickness itself. Adams et al. indicates that such "patient-centred care," whereby healthcare treatment is brought to patients rather than patients to treatment, is hailed as a more dignified, humane, and efficient mode of medicine. She further indicates that these changes are a striking part of the new $128 million Clinical Services Building at the Toronto General Hospital site of the University Health Network, designed by HOK/Urbana during the millennium.[27]

Despite the widespread public interest in healthcare, Adams indicates that hospital design gets little mainstream coverage. One problem is that healthcare professionals and hospital administrators are encouraged to think of hospitals

Made Simple. *Progressive Architecture*. v.73, n.3, 93.
22 Adams, A. *op. cit.*, p.18.
23 Arcidi, P. *op. cit.*, p. 93.
24 Sloane, D. C. and Sloane, B. C. *op. cit.*, p. 5.
25 Verderber, S. and Fine, D. J. (2000). *Healthcare Architecture in an Era of Radical Transformation.* New Haven: Yale University Press, 225.

26 http://www.health.gov.on.ca/en/common/system/services/hosp/faq.aspx
27 Adams, A. and Theodore, D. *op. cit.*, p. 15.

TESIS Inter-University Research Centre "Systems and Technologies for Social and Healthcare Facilities" University of Florence, Italy

180

Figure 2. Hospitals distribution in the City of Toronto. © Illustration by Vivian Lo, Toronto, Canada. 2014.

not as buildings but as technologies.[28] In fact, as Adams et al. further quotes, American historians Stephen Verderber and David J. Fine argue, in their book Healthcare Architecture in an Era of Radical Transformation (Yale University Press, 2000), true innovation in healthcare architecture is usually the result not of technological progress but rather of non-specialists tackling hospital design for the first time.[29]

Arcidi asserts that we go to the hospital in the hope that technology will vanquish disease.[30] Hospitals in turn become healthcare machineries to treat disease. The major trend in the design of healthcare facilities nowadays thus reflects not only people's diverse needs and related demographics, but also con-

siders both patients' emotional as well as physiological needs, for example it takes into account varies issues concerning the spatial relationship of different programs, barrier-free design, accessibility and flexibility design, and natural lighting etc., which all integrally contribute to patients' healing processes.

Arcidi highlights that the hospital architect's task can be twofold: to synthesize program, structure, and services into a smoothly functioning hospital; and also to mold an environment that appears to be simpler than it actually is. He further quotes Sontag's explanation of "de-amplifying" the illness.[31] In a sense, hospital architects are doing the same – they make the whole look like less than the sum of its parts.

28 Adams, A. and Theodore, D. *op. cit.*, p. 14.
29 *Ibidem.*
30 Arcidi, P. *op. cit.*, p. 86.

31 *Ibidem.*

EMERGENCE OF NEW TYPES OF COMMUNITY-BASED HEALTHCARE SERVICES

On the other hand, a network of healthcare facilities has been introduced within the city fabric in Ontario since 2005 – Family Health Teams (FHT) is one of the examples. FHTs provide the necessary intermediate scale of healthcare support to fill in the gap created by the two extreme scales of healthcare services provided by hospitals (centre excellence) and home delivery (home care). However, the emergency rooms in hospitals are always overloaded by non-emergency cases. The number of healthcare professionals is insufficient. Healthcare professionals are always on demand and people's lifestyles have changed. Physicians tend not to work overnight and not to accept an unlimited number of patients due to additional liability and fixed wages.

An aging population leads to higher demand in healthcare and at the same time increased healthcare costs. Toronto has over 15% of the Canadian population and many people have no family physicians. The transitional types of healthcare services are jumping across boundaries[32], however, concurrently, they are helping to reduce the overload of non-life threatening cases in emergency departments and shorten waiting times in hospitals, as well as provide patients with faster and better access to healthcare professionals. While some of these decade-old mid-scale community-based healthcare facilities are stand-alone buildings, a significant number of them come to embody the integration of patient-centred care hubs with urban architecture such as retail outlets, community centres, and residences. Such changes in healthcare landscapes have become more and more obvious in recent years.

Hundreds of FHT clinics are distributed across the province to provide patient-centred primary healthcare services for more than three million Ontarians. Each Family Health Team has a core group of healthcare professionals including doctors, nurse practitioners and nurses, and may also employ dieticians, social workers, pharmacists, or other healthcare professionals to meet the needs of their patients. Each team is set up based on local health and community needs, and focuses on chronic disease management, disease prevention, health promotion, as well as providing healthcare specialist referrals, healthcare checks and routine screening tests for cancer etc.[33] FHTs work with other healthcare organizations, such as public health units (PHU) and Community Care Access Centres (CCAC) to ensure patients receive high quality care. The Public Health Unit (PHU) helps support health communities by providing health promotion information and disease prevention programs, such as information on immunization, food safety, and services on sexually transmitted infections (STIs).[34] Each PHU has a healthcare officer and qualified staff to promote community health. They inform the public about healthy lifestyles, sexual health education in preventing STIs/AIDS, vaccinations, addictions, healthy growth

181

32 Verderber, S. (2010). *Innovations in Healthcare Architecture*. New York; London: Routledge, 4.

33 http://www.health.gov.on.ca/en/public/programs/hco/options.aspx
34 *Ibidem.*

and development including parenting education, health education for all age groups and selected screening services. PHU also offers a free dental program to eligible children under 17 years old.[35] Community Care Access Centres help provide healthcare support to patients who need care at home, at school, and in the community. There are fourteen CCACs in Ontario.[36] CCACs are the local organizations established by the provincial government to provide access to government-funded home and community services and long-term care homes. CCACs also identify patients' healthcare needs and explore the services that will best suit those needs.[37]

The Family Health Team is a diverse healthcare team that provides ongoing care to their roster of patients and promotes healthy living.[38] FHTs take part in solving the ineffectiveness of the current health system due to the lack of interaction between healthcare professionals concerning the secure sharing of patients' electronic healthcare records with other health professionals. Moreover, many FHT clinics have extended evening and weekend hours for urgent healthcare problems (similar to outpatient clinics in hospitals) including the Family Health Team Telephone Health Advisory Service, which is an after-hours service providing access to a registered nurse. Patients are also able to book same or next-day appointments. When patient waiting time is minimized, patients' illnesses can then be treated faster which helps prevent serious complications arising which lead to higher levels of care due to delayed treatment. FHTs are the front line of healthcare in Ontario, providing advice and guidance to people on living healthier to avoid illness. They also act as navigators of the healthcare system when their patients require specialized care.

There are also other types of healthcare facilities. Community Health Centres (CHC) are non-profit organizations that provide non-emergency healthcare and health promotion programs to individuals, families, community groups, new immigrants, and those who are not covered by the provincial government health insurance plan (OHIP), such as people who are facing homelessness and poverty. Each CHC is unique and is a health centre established and governed by a community-elected board of directors.[39] CHCs provide and offer clinical care from doctors, nurse practitioners, nurses, dieticians, social workers, and other healthcare providers within one facility. The healthcare services delivered in this type of facility are specific to the needs based on the demographics in the community. CHCs offer culturally-adapted programs for the needs and preferences of the communities they serve including delivering healthcare services in many different languages.[40]

Urgent Care Centres (UCC) provide treatment for illnesses and injuries that are urgent but not life threatening. Patients will

35 Ibidem.
36 http://www.health.gov.on.ca/en/common/system/services/default.aspx
37 http://www.health.gov.on.ca/en/common/system/default.aspx#4
38 http://www.health.gov.on.ca/en/public/programs/hco/options.aspx

39 http://www.health.gov.on.ca/en/common/system/services/default.aspx
40 http://www.health.gov.on.ca/en/public/programs/hco/options.aspx

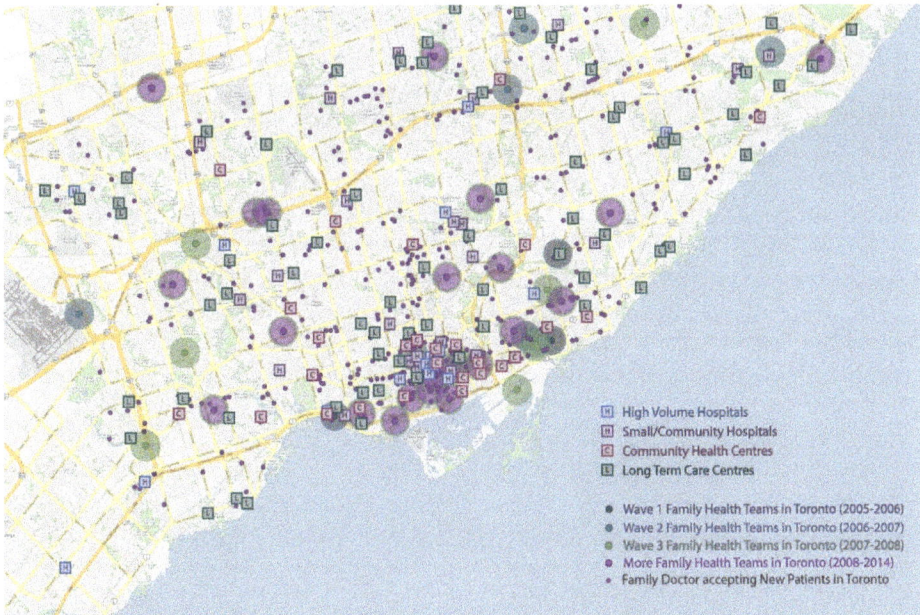

Figure 3. Healthcare landscape in the City of Toronto. © Illustration by Vivian Lo, Toronto, Canada. 2014.

be diagnosed and treated for most injuries and illnesses by emergency trained doctors and other healthcare professionals. Some UCCs may offer follow-up appointments.[41]

Walk-in or after hours clinics provide healthcare services in non-emergency situations. This type of facility offers people convenient access to healthcare advice, assessment and treatment for minor illnesses and injuries such as cuts and bruises, burns and strains, fractures, emergency contraception and advice, stomach upsets, minor infections, and skin complaints. Patients will be seen by an experienced nurse or doctor, often without an appointment.[42]

Nurse practitioners in Nurse Practitioner-Led Clinics collaborate with an inter-professional team of healthcare providers and

41 *Ibidem.*
42 *Ibidem.*

support staff, which may include registered nurses, registered practical nurses, collaborating family physicians, registered dieticians, pharmacists and social workers.[43] Nurse Practitioner-Led Clinics provide ongoing care, promote disease prevention and healthy living.[44] A nurse practitioner (NP) is like an advanced nurse. NPs can assess and treat basic illnesses and injuries, order lab tests, X-rays and other diagnostic tests.[45] NPs are also found in Family Health Teams and other types of clinics. These clinics can serve as an alternative to a traditional doctor's office or walk-in clinic.

All this administrative and financial restructuring in Ontario's healthcare system has dramatically reshaped the

43 http://www.health.gov.on.ca/en/common/system/services/default.aspx
44 http://www.health.gov.on.ca/en/public/programs/hco/options.aspx
45 http://www.health.gov.on.ca/en/common/system/default.aspx#2

TESIS Inter-University Research Centre "Systems and Technologies for Social and Healthcare Facilities"
University of Florence, Italy

TESIS

province's healthcare landscape. Such changes in the healthcare landscape also reflect a worldwide trend in the context of global climate change, the planet's diminishing natural resources, and the spiralling cost of operating healthcare facilities to achieve and maintain high quality care for diverse patient populations in carbon neutral care settings.[46]

HOME CARE SERVICES

Aside from healthcare services provided by centres of excellence, Ontarians can also receive healthcare services through home delivery (home care). There are circumstances, such as illnesses, injuries, and old age, when people need extra help and support to maintain their health and to keep living safely and independently at home. The government provides funds for many home care services. Moreover, there are government agencies and non-profit organizations in the community that offer additional support to these types of services.[47] Thus, many people who choose to stay in their own homes are able to arrange a mix of home care services funded in different ways.

Some home delivery healthcare services, which include visiting health professional services, are provided to people after their stay in hospital while some are given to individuals who need personal care and support to perform daily living and routine household activities. There are also community support services that offer meal delivery, transportation, caregivers' assistance, and adult day programs.[48]

46 Verderber, S. *op. cit.*, p. 20.

47 http://www.health.gov.on.ca/en/common/system/default.aspx#4.

48 *Ibidem*.

CONCLUSIONS

The seismic shifts in the Ontario healthcare system may appear to have quietened down for now. However, with the emergence in the past few years of Health System Finding Reforms (HSFR) based on Quality Based Procedures and Health Based Allocation Models, we may be seeing another shift towards the patient experience. If this is the case, the hospital and system will be rewarded for addressing how easy and safe it is to navigate the patient on their journey through the healthcare landscape of Ontario; a challenge and a goal for all architects.

ACKNOWLEDGEMENTS

The authors wish to thank the Ontario Ministry of Health and Long-Term Care and many healthcare providers, professionals, researchers, and stakeholders in different disciplines who provided valuable information.

REFERENCES

Adams, A. (Jun 2004). Reviving the Dead: Art and the Twentieth-century Hospital. *Fuse Magazine*. v.27, n.2: 16- 23.

Adams, A, and Theodore, D. (Mar 2002). Medicine by Design. *Canadian Architect*. v.47, n.3: 14-15.

Arcidi, P. (Mar 1992) P/A Inquiry: Hospitals Made Simple. *Progressive Architecture*. v.73, n.3, 86-95.

184

Donnelly, E. (May-Jun 2004). Go with the flow [chatham-kent health alliance]. *Canadian Interiors*. v.41 n.3: 56-57.

Donnelly, E. (Nov.-Dec. 2003). Wellness by design [Clinical Services Building, Toronto]. *Canadian Interiors*. v.40, n.6: 40-42.

Kamiker, B., Izumi, K. and Angus, D. L. (Mar 1958). Some elements of hospital design. *Royal Architectural Institute of Canada. Journal*. v.35: 93-100.

Lasker, D. (Mar-Apr 2000). Humanizing the hospital. *Canadian Interiors*. 37: 40-44.

Lobsinger, M. L. (Apr. 1993). Animation for Sick Kids. *Canadian Architect*. v.38., n.4: 16-21.

McLaughlin, H. (Mar 1970). Keys to long-lasting hospital design are operating efficiency, ability to expand. *Modern Hospital*, v.114: 82-86.

Rosenfield, I. (1971). *Hospital Architecture Integrated Components*. New York: Van Nostrand Reinhold Company.

Rosenfield, I. (1969). H*ospital Architecture and Beyond*. New York: Van Nostrand Reinhold Company.

Rosenfield, I. (1960). *Hospital Architecture Integrated Design*. New York: Reinhold Publishing Corporation.

Sloane, D. C. and Sloane, B. C. (2003). Medicine *Moves to the Mall*. Baltimore: Johns Hopkins University Press.

Sontag, S. (1989). *Illness as Metaphor and AIDS and its Metaphors*. New York: Doubleday.

Toronto Zeidler Roberts Partnership/ Architects (Dec. 1986). Award of Excellence: The Hospital for Sick Children, *Canadian Architect*. v.31, n.12: 20-23.

Verderber, S. (2010). *Innovations in Healthcare Architecture*. New York; London:Routledge.

Verderber, S. and Fine, D. J. (2000). *Healthcare Architecture in an Era of Radical Transformation*. New Haven: Yale University Press.

Warson, A. (Oct. 1998). Zeidler Roberts Partnership: Canada's Friendly Giant. *World Architecture*. n.70: 72-79.

Wheeler, E. T. (1964). *Hospital Design and Function*. New York: McGraw-Hill.

Wheeler, E. T. (Oct 1963). Method of evaluating an existing hospital building. *Royal Architectural Institute of Canada*. v.40: 51-57.

Yee, R. (Oct 1994). Health Care's Hostage. *Contract Design*. v.36, n.10.

WEBSITES

AIA Guidelines for Design and Construction of Health Care Facilities
http://www.aia.org

Canadian Association of Emergency Physicians
http://www.caep.ca

Canadian Healthcare Technology
http:// www.canhealth.com

185

186

Canadian Institute for Health Information
http:// www.cihi.ca
Reports: Geographic Distribution of Physicians in Canada: Beyond How Many and Where; Healthcare in Canada; Health Reports – How Healthy are Canadians? Annual Report 2006; Hospital Report: Acute Care 2005; Hospital Trends in Canada – Results of a Project to Create a Historical Series of Statistical and Financial Data for Canadian Hospitals Over Twenty-Seven Years; Housing and Population Health; Social Determinants of Health in Canada Nov 2005; The Evolving Role of Canada's Family Physicians 1992 – 2001.

Centre for Healthcare Architecture & Design
http://195.92.246.148/nhsestates/chad/ chad_content/home/home.asp

City of Toronto
http:// www.toronto.ca

Green Guide for Health Care
http://www.gghc.org

Hospitals for a Healthy Environment
http://www.h2e-online.org

Hospital News
http://www.hospitalnews.com
Infrastructure Ontario
http://www.infrastructureontario.ca/en/ index.asp

Markham Stouffville Hospital
http://www.msh.on.ca

Ministry of Community and Social Services
http://www.cfcs.gov.on.ca

Ministry of Health and Long-Term Care
http://www.health.gov.on.ca

Newsroom Ontario's Official News Source
http://news.ontario.ca/

Ontario Hospital Association
http://www.oha.com

Ontario Medical Association
http://www.oma.org

Parkdale Community Health Centre
http://www.parkdalehealth.ca

Sherbourne Health Centre
http://www.sherbourne.on.ca

Statistics Canada
http://www.statcan.ca
http://www.statcan.ca/english/freepub/82-221-XIE/2006001/regions.htm

The Centre for Healthcare Design
http://www.healthdesign.org

Toronto Grace Hospital
http://www.torontograce.org

Transit Toronto
http://transit.toronto.on.ca/subway/5109. shtml

University Health Network
http://www.uhn.ca

Flexibility and Future Proofing Healthcare Buildings
A Structured and Strategic Approach

Carthey J.[1]

jcarthey@gmail.com
[1] B. Arch., MPM, EDAC, FRAIA, AFCHSM, Chair of the Australian Health Design Council, Senior Health Designer - Thinc Health, Sydney, NSW, Australia

Change is constant – and clearly not a new phenomenon. Healthcare buildings have coped with change for a long time – and longer than most of us would believe. Major healthcare buildings usually represent a significant investment in urban infrastructure, and in addition they are often well loved by their communities. Rather than demolishing buildings that still have useable life left in them, many adaptation and modification strategies to cope with newer demands have been adopted over time. Yet, although often claimed as "successful," which of these strategies have actually worked? Have we ever tested or evaluated these strategies and what can we learn for future projects?

It is rare these days to review either a client brief or a discussion regarding a completed healthcare project without noticing two things: firstly the brief usually requires, and secondly, the architect/design team usually claims that the health building is "future proofed," and that it is highly flexible and adaptable to cope with future demands.

Every health project will need to respond to changes in demographics, service delivery models, new technologies, workforce issues, and political and funding environments, and in fact this is no different to any other sector of the economy. In addition, an increasing focus on environmental sustainability including energy use and carbon reduction measures is now also required. So how should we assess and balance these requirements in developing the future-proofing strategies for a healthcare project?

We propose a matrix, developed from evidence-based research, as a framework for defining, categorizing and testing the flexibility and future proofing of health buildings. This assists in testing strategies which may justify the additional financial investment often required to future proof health facilities.

INTRODUCTION

How should we define "flexibility and future proofing" so that we can evaluate them in the design of healthcare buildings, and then long after the buildings have been commissioned and adapted throughout their useful lifespan? What can we learn about designing health-care buildings today so they are flexible and future proofed? What evidence is there for identifying successful strategies to achieve this, and what should be avoided?

Research undertaken in 2009 for Health Infrastructure NSW by the former University of New South Wales (UNSW) Centre for Health Assets Australasia

(CHAA) found that longer term flexibility for health buildings is assisted by "a generous site area, lower rise hospital buildings along a horizontal circulation spine ("hospital street"), surplus building services capacity facilitating easy expansion/alteration, and a consistent workable planning grid supporting a range of standardized room sizes." The research study outcomes included the development of a matrix for assessing the flexibility and adaptability of healthcare buildings, with a view to building an evidence base for successful and unsuccessful approaches to future proofing these buildings (Carthey et al, 2009).

Initially focusing on literature from a range of national and international sources, the research looked for:

– definitions of "flexibility" and related terms including "adaptability" and "convertibility" so that meaningful comparisons could be made between projects and outcomes discussed;

– a range of contexts and reasons for "flexible" design in order to understand the major drivers for future proofing healthcare facilities;

– national and international case studies (19 in total were found) that discussed real-life approaches to flexibility and, where identifiable, the success or otherwise of each approach.

A second study in early 2010 for the same client reviewed several Australian hospitals in terms of their ability to flex and adapt over time and compared these strategies to those set out by the matrix developed in the first study. From this exercise in review and comparison, conclusions were drawn regarding successful approaches to future proofing healthcare buildings. In addition, and perhaps not surprisingly, it also raised further ques-

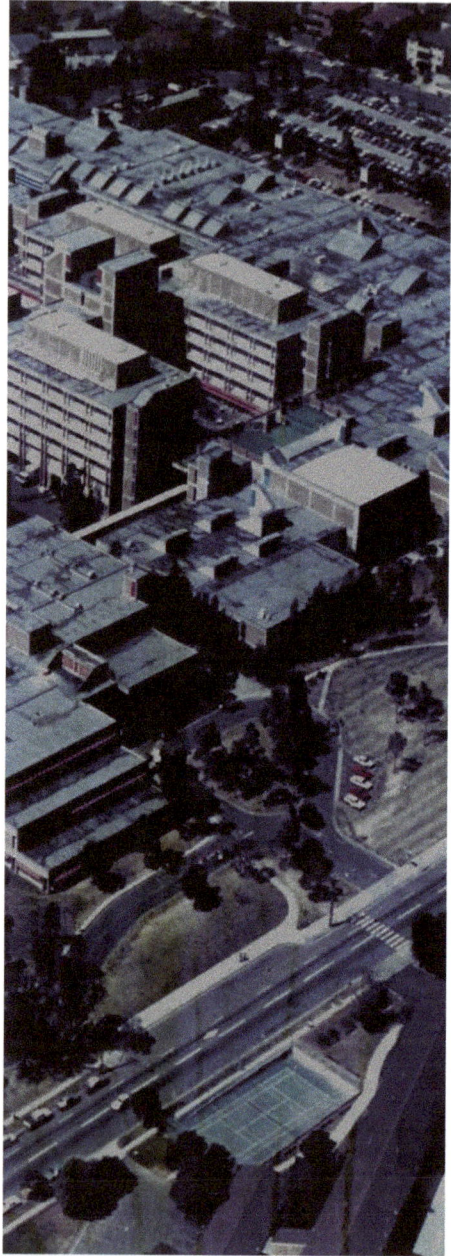

Figure 1. Case studies derived from recommendations from stage one (2009): large NSW urban hospitals – Westmead, Blacktown, Mt Druitt, POW, RNSH "brown building"; up to 35 years old; undergone at least one major refurbishment since opening. Westmead Hospital Campus.

188

tions that could be answered by additional research in the future.

Unfortunately, at the end of 2010, CHAA had its research funding withdrawn by Health Infrastructure NSW, and as a result UNSW ceased its significant contribution to the funding of the research centre and its research team dispersed. Thus, the baton must now pass to other researchers so they can take these studies further in order to continue to improve the performance of all Australian healthcare facilities.

This paper discusses definitions of flexibility and future proofing identified by the CHAA research so that comparisons between projects can be made. It looks at how these relate to various timeframes and also how they respond to the different agendas of those owning, operating and working within Australian healthcare facilities. The main strategies adopted are outlined, especially those that have proved successful in Australian and international facilities.

DEFINING "FLEXIBILITY": BEYOND THE BUZZWORD

"Flexibility" is a broadly applied term that can be used to describe many aspects of a healthcare facility and for these reasons it is useful to look more closely at the various uses of the word. "Flexible" is used to describe a range of outcomes – from the need to accommodate flexible staffing requirements (or workforce shortages) via a short-term building solution through to the need to accommodate future growth or contraction, renovations or refurbishment to meet future healthcare delivery needs. For example, "flexibility" may be required to respond to changing service

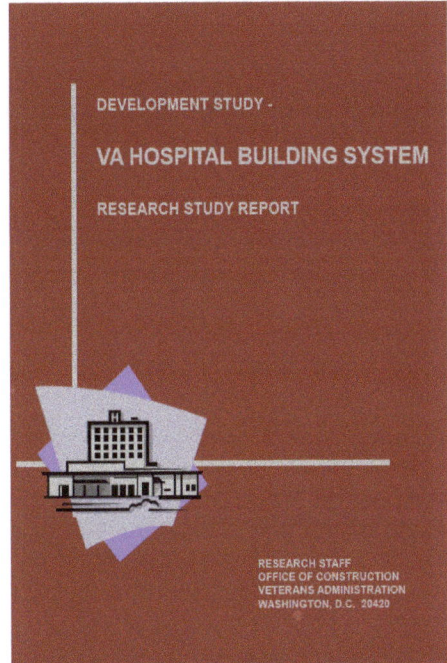

189

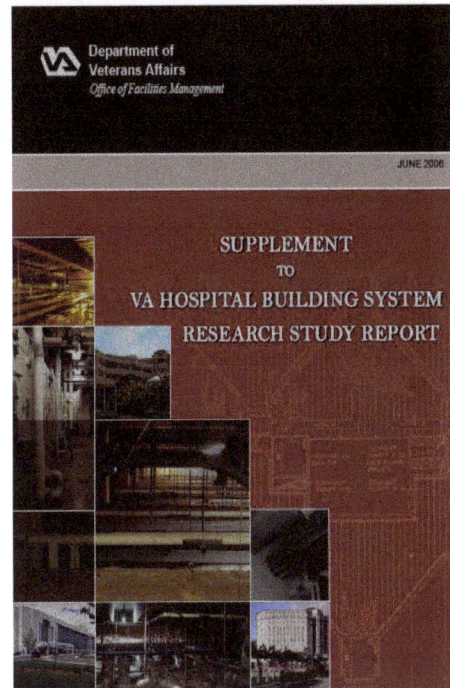

Figure 2.   Veterans Affairs, Hospital Building System.

190

delivery needs, or to support the introduction of new forms of technology, or even the changing demographics of the health service catchment area. Each of these demands requires one or more changes in the operation of the facility. Yet, without exception, all will be supported by a physical building solution that, by its very nature, is much slower to change than the constant operational challenges placed upon it.

Therefore, it could be suggested that "flexibility" is not a physical attribute as such, but rather a performance indicator for a building over time. It is also a form of "insurance policy" whereby additional expenditure may be incurred today to ensure that a building can respond without significant reconfiguration, expense or downtime, to a range of changes required in the future.

FUTURE PROOFING AS "INVESTMENT"

As an investment and insurance against an uncertain future, future proofing appears sensible. Yet it also begs the question as to how we know when we have done enough and that the expense is justified over the lifecycle of the healthcare building. Too much may be extravagant and unlikely to be used; too little may also be unwise as it may push significant expense and other resources onto future generations. Ultimately, like most insurance policies, how much one spends depends entirely on the assessment of the risk faced.

Ideally, assessment of this risk also depends on the extent and quality of available research into what, how and why things may change plus a rating of the likelihood of each of these occurrences. Finally, responding to the risk associated with spending/not spending on future proofing definitely depends on the appetite for risk of those charged with delivering healthcare and procuring healthcare buildings, and how they prioritize future proofing in the context of the limited available capital funding that seems endemic to most health systems.

In the Australian health system risks include the electorate's response to increased expenditure on healthcare buildings in order to avoid transferring the burden of significant expense to future generations – both in terms of money and environmental sustainability.

EXAMPLES FROM OTHER HEALTH SYSTEMS

It should be noted that the future proofing issues faced by Australian hospitals are certainly not unique to that system and have been addressed internationally for quite some time. Examples include: the Veterans Affairs (VA) Health System in the US; historic examples in the UK such as the Harness, Best Buy and Nucleus Hospitals, and more recently the NHS Health Guidelines; Dutch hospitals such as the Martini Hospital at Groningen and various Scandinavian hospitals including St Olav's in Trondheim, Aarhus and Rikeshospitalet in Oslo, and the INO Bern Hospital in Switzerland.

Again, it was the CHAA's mission to learn from these various examples for use in Australia, and this was started in the research it undertook. The cessation of funding for CHAA means that this mission has now been passed to others – to undertake research, and to compile and disseminate the findings to the Australian healthcare facility design community.

FLEXIBILITY ASSESSMENT MATRIX

The various drivers for flexibility and future proofing are summarized in the matrix below which sets them out on two axes – a micro to macro (time-based) focus on one axis, and a managerial-operational-physical focus on the other.

There are clearly overlaps between the various categories, yet each is drawn from one or more real-life project examples that illustrate a response to each driver and also suggests the success of each response over time.

STRATEGIES FOR ACHIEVING FLEXIBILITY AND FUTURE PROOFING – AN OVERVIEW

Possible approaches to achieving flexibility and adaptability in healthcare buildings are discussed in more detail below and range from room fit outs through to building planning and site planning. Each reflects one or more of the matrix classifications in Table 1.

Acuity-Adaptable and Universal Rooms

An acuity-adaptable patient room is designed to a standardised layout and is fit-

Focus	Managerial considerations	Functional requirement	Building system
Micro	***Operational*** Easy to reconfigure, low impact on time and cost (e.g. furniture and interior spaces)	***Adaptability*** Ability to adapt to operational changes e.g. workplace practices	Tertiary 5-10 years lifespan, no structural implications e.g. furniture
	Tactical Involves commitment of capital expenditure; changes not easy to undo (e.g. design of operating theatres)	***Convertibility*** Ability to convert rooms to different functions	***Secondary*** 15-50 years lifespan, e.g. walls and ceilings
Macro	***Strategic*** Substantial increase in the lifetime of the infrastructure (e.g. long term expansion plans)	***Expandability*** Ability to expand the building envelope and specific hospital function	***Primary*** 50-100 years lifespan, e.g. building shell
Source	(de Neufville, Lee, & Scholtes, 2008)	(Pati, et al., 2008)	(Kendall, 2005)

Table 1.   Definitions of flexibility and associated concepts.

TESIS Inter-University Research Centre "Systems and Technologies for Social and Healthcare Facilities" University of Florence, Italy

ted with a full range of equipment and medication to cater for the majority of required treatments and procedures. In Australia the Australasian Health Facility Guidelines (AusHFG) recommend 15 sq m for single rooms (exclusive of the floor area for ensuite bathrooms) in most inpatient units and these would not accommodate an acuity-adaptable care model (AHIA & UNSW, 2009).

Provision of Surplus Capacity

Surplus capacity may be provided in areas that use high levels of technology especially for electrical and ICT components. This would cater for rapid advances in technology which usually require more power and data capability.

Modular Layout

A modular layout has a uniform grid and a core distribution system which may then be subdivided when the need arises, resulting in spaces that are "fit for purpose" for a specific function whilst also allowing the space to morph to suit different activities and service conditions (Diamond, 2006). At St Olav's Hospital in Trondheim, Norway, all rooms in the inpatient wards were designed to a standardised module that would enable 2 bedrooms to become offices in the future (Valen & Larssen, 2006).

In NSW, the Health Infrastructure modular building system has attempted to impose a modular approach to the design of NSW healthcare buildings by defining a preferred building grid size (8.4 m x 8.4 m), and locating plant space at the end of building wings so as not to compromise the internal use of space.

Interstitial Floors

Another method of ensuring future flexibility is through the use of interstitial floors which are inserted between each primary floor to free them from the demands associated with upgrading or servicing structural, mechanical and electrical plant or other building elements thus enabling more flexible floor plans. They were pioneered in the McMaster Health Sciences Centre in Ontario, Canada, by Eberhard Zeidler (The American Institute of Architects, 2005; Verderber & Fine, 2000).

They are also used at St Olav's Hospital in Trondheim, which has interstitial floors above the operation suites and image diagnostic area (Valen & Larssen, 2006). St Vincent's Hospital in Darlinghurst, NSW, Australia, utilises fully accessible interstitial spaces thus allowing for universal wall-less cabling and servicing (Farrelly, 2002).

Zoning and Decentralisation

The zoning and decentralisation of functions can improve the flexibility and efficiency of facility operations.
One approach is to adopt a "vertically stratified" building system, whereby each specific floor or level accommodates a specific function such as a diagnostic and technology zone, an inpatient or nursing zone, or the public and administrative zone.

The vertical circulation e.g. lifts and stairs, and other service amenities are provided in a central location on each floor (Nitch, 2006). This approach was adopted at St Olav's Hospital in Norway.

192

Open-Ended Corridors

Corridors are designed to be open-ended where there is the potential to expand the building in that direction (Westlake Jr, 1995). The use of open-ended corridors was successfully used in Addenbrooke's Hospital in Cambridge, UK, built over 80 years ago, to permit future extensions to departments with the least possible disruption to the hospital service (de Neufville, et al., 2008).

In the 1970s, an early pioneer of this concept in the Australian setting was Westmead Hospital, Sydney, as discussed by Neild (2008). More recently, built in 1983, the use of open-ended corridors at St Vincent's Hospital in Sydney, Australia, not only allows for future expansion but also invites light into the building and enables views of the street and surrounding areas (Farrelly, 2002).

Discrete Building Systems

At the McMasters Health Science Centre, in conjunction with "interstitialism," the building structure was separated into "permanent" and "non-permanent" elements (Verderber & Fine, 2000), with the permanent building shell containing electrical and mechanical services offering a "plug and play" approach from departmental to room level (Scalise, et al., 2004). At the 50,000 sq m INO building at Insel Hospital in Bern, Switzerland, the building structure was classified into: primary (building shell – intended to last for 50-100 years); secondary (walls and ceilings with a life of 15-50 years); and tertiary (furniture and fit out replaced every 5-10 years) systems. These three systems were treated autonomously, to the extent that they were designed by different ar-chitects and built using separate procurement contracts (Kendall, 2005).

Soft Spaces and Hot Spots

Inherent to this approach is the "plug and play" system for building services, whereby services are confined to the perimeter or central locations of the building envelope and not built into internal walls in such a way that they are then difficult to move or alter in the future.

As permanent "core" programs or departments are difficult to relocate, areas of unassigned or "soft" spaces are deliberately placed adjacent to the facility "hot spots." For example, examination or diagnostic and treatment areas ("hot spots") could be located adjacent to patient waiting rooms and other ("soft" or more flexible-use) spaces.

Site Masterplanning

Empty Chair

The masterplanning of Martini Teaching Hospital in Groningen, Netherlands, is a good example of the "empty chair" approach to site planning. This is based on the principle of defining four quadrants of the site to be used sequentially for facility development – renewal, replacement or conversion for other purposes. One quadrant of the building site is always left vacant so that as the building ages and repairs, or extensions or renovations become needed, they can occur in the vacant quadrant. The "empty chair" approach requires a master plan that looks forward for up to 50 years, with renewal occurring sequentially around the quadrants in turn until the facility is either completely renewed or subsumed for another purpose such as offices or housing.

193

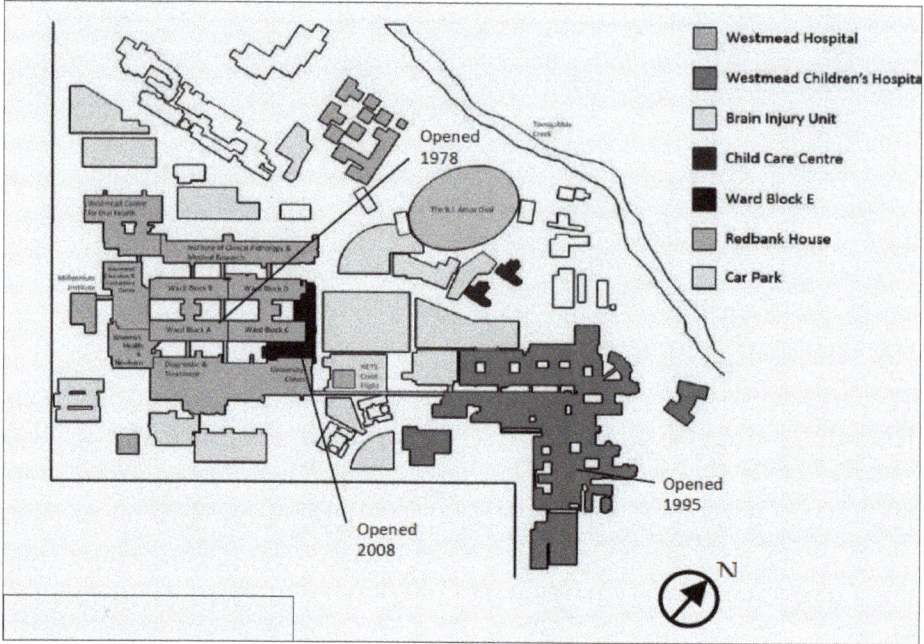

Figure 3. Westmead Hospital Campus.

194

Site Conversion

When a hospital building finally reaches the end of its useful lifecycle, it may be more appropriate for the whole facility to be converted to another use such as commercial office space or an apartment building. However this will only be feasible if the initial design of the building allows for this change to occur. For example, the Martini Teaching Hospital in Groningen, Netherlands, used a 16 m x 60 m plan in conjunction with carefully located building services and circulation pathways, which can easily be adapted for other uses, e.g. office or apartment blocks. Demonstrating such a possibility in reality, the old site of Addenbrooke's Hospital in Cambridge, UK, was converted in the early 1990s to the newly founded Business School of Cambridge University (de Neufville, et al., 2008).

LAND PURCHASING OPTION AND "HOSPITAL ON-DEMAND"

Dutch studies suggest that as little as 50% of the traditional floor area of a hospital needs to be accommodated in the main building with the rest located in ancillary buildings around the "Core Hospital" (Bjørberg & Verweij, 2009).

Considering the increasing trend towards home-delivered care, the hospital of the future may consist of a main hospital with other surrounding buildings on an as-needed, or on-demand basis in order to cope with fluctuations in care delivery models, patient numbers and consequent demands for space (Diamond, 2006; Worthington, 2008).

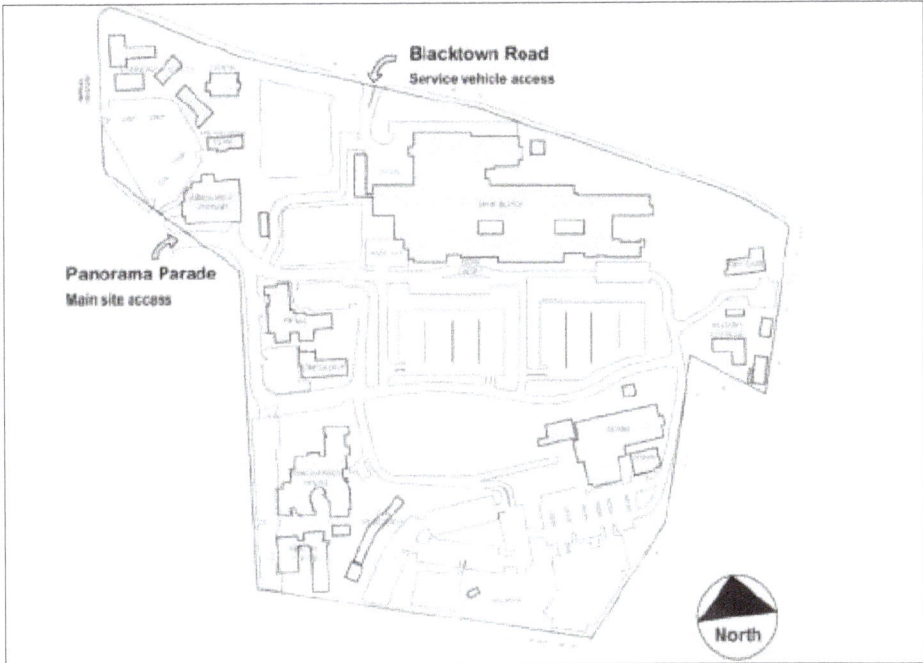

Figure 4. Blacktown - site plan.

195

Figure 5. Blacktown – site development.

TESIS Inter-University Research Centre "Systems and Technologies for Social and Healthcare Facilities"
University of Florence, Italy

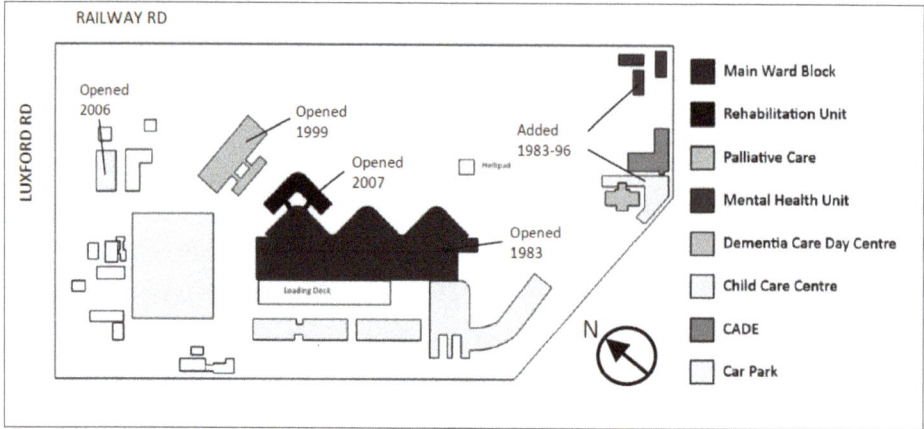

RAILWAY RD

LUXFORD RD

Opened 2006

Opened 1999

Opened 2007

Opened 1983

Added 1983-96

Loading Deck

Heliped

N

- Main Ward Block
- Rehabilitation Unit
- Palliative Care
- Mental Health Unit
- Dementia Care Day Centre
- Child Care Centre
- CADE
- Car Park

Figure 6. Mount Druitt Hospital.

196

CONCLUSIONS

Approaches to the future proofing and flexibility of healthcare buildings are many and varied. Decisions on which should be adopted must be made for every project. These will ultimately be guided by the client's specific acceptance of an amount that will cover "reasonable" expenditure for future proofing – as a form of insurance to guarantee a longer life for the building being constructed.

The acceptance of such an amount should be derived from evidence-based research into what actually prolongs the life of a healthcare building, and driven from a stance of protecting the community's built assets against premature obsolescence. This looks after the interests of the community today, while also safeguarding the needs of the community of the future. In addition, it protects the environment against the unnecessary consumption of resources, and in doing so preserves a significant investment in urban infrastructure for the use of future generations.

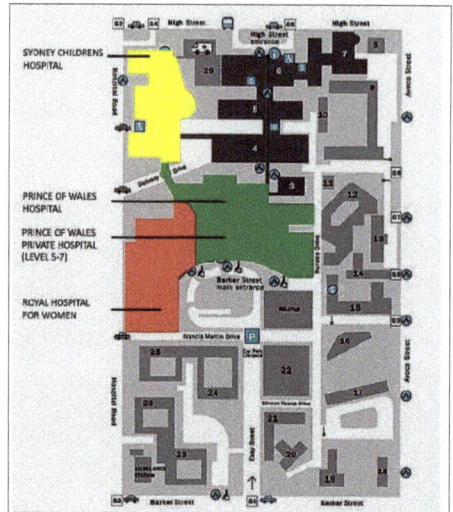

Figure 7. Prince of Wales Private Hospital, Randwick, New South Wales, Australia.

Figure 8. The Royal North Shore Hospital RNSH of Sidney.

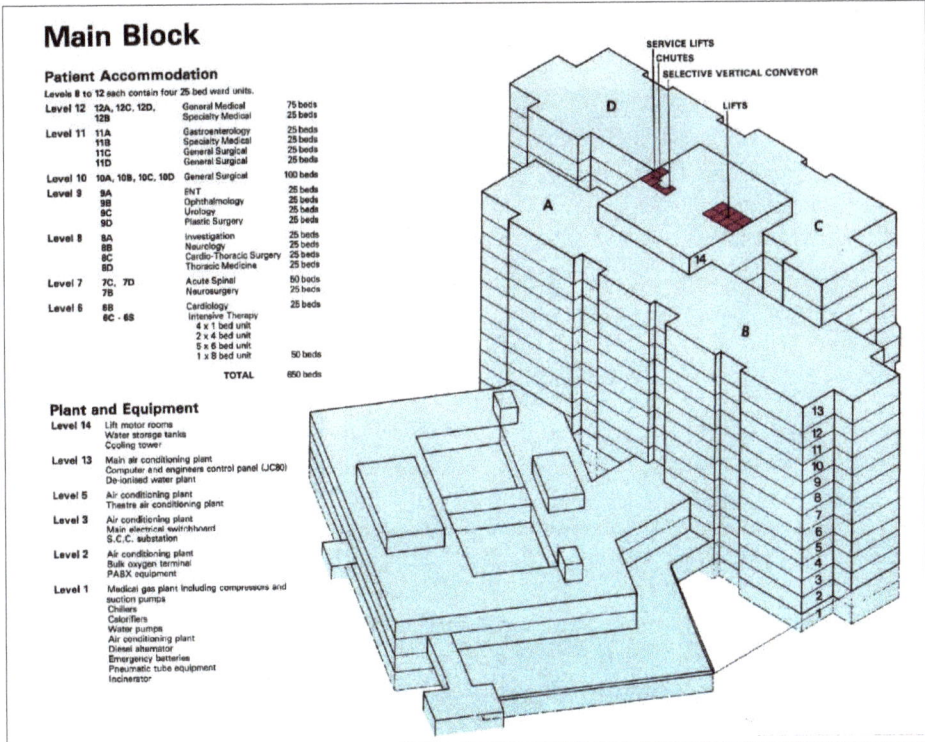

Figure 9. RNSH 'brown building'.

197

Farrelly, E. (2002). Taming St Vincent's. *Architecture Australia,* 91(4), 58-63.

Kendall, S. (2005). Managing Change: the application of Open Building in the INO Bern Hospital. Design & Health World Congress Retrieved September 29, 2009, from http://www.designandhealth.com/Media-Publishing/Papers.aspx

Neild, L. (2008). Changing hospital design in Australia. In S. Prasad (Ed.), *Changing Hospital Architecture.* London: RIBA Enterprises Ltd, 223-250.

Nitch, M. P. (2006). The architecture of enabling technology in the critical care setting: The role of architecture in addressing the health care - technology paradox, Master of Architecture, Clemson University South Carolina. ABI database.

Pati, D., Harvey, T., & Cason, C. (2008). Inpatient Unit Flexibility: Design Characteristics of a Successful Flexible Unit. *Environment and Behavior,* 40(2), 205-232.

Valen, M. S., & Larssen, A.-K. (2006). Adaptability of Hospitals: Capability of Handling Physical Changes. Paper presented at the Trondheim International Symposium: Changing User Demands on Buildings – Needs for Lifecycle Planning and Management, Trondheim.

Scalise, D., Thrall, T. H., Haugh, R., & Runy, L. A. (2004). The Patient Room. *Hospitals and Health Networks,* 78(5), 34-38.

The American Institute of Architects. (2005). Planning for Change: Hospital Design Theories in Practice Retrieved September 29, 2009, from http://info.aia.org/nwsltr_print.cfm?pagename=aah_jrnl_20051019_change

Valen, M. S., & Larssen, A.-K. (2006). Adaptability of Hospitals: Capability of Handling Physical Changes. Paper presented at the Trondheim International Symposium: Changing User Demands on Buildings - Needs for Lifecycle Planning and Management, Trondheim.

Verderber, S., & Fine, D. J. (2000). *Healthcare Architecture in an Era of Radical Transformation.* New Haven: Yale University.

Worthington, J. (2008). Managing hospital change: lessons from workplace design. In S. Prasad (Ed.), *Changing Hospital Architecture.* London: RIBA Enterprises Ltd, 49-63.

Westlake Jr, P. (1995). Safe for Future Use? Stages in Master Planning, Programming, and Architectural Design. *Journal of Ambulatory Care Management,* 18(4), 58-68.

The Temporal Dynamic in the Planning of Health Facilities

Bögedam de Debuchy, A. M. C.[1], Debuchy, A. M.[2]

ArqSalud@fadu.uba.ar
[1]Director: Prof. Cons. Arch. CIRFS FADU UBA, Argentina
[2]Senior Researcher: Dr. Arch. CIRFS FADU UBA, Argentina

199

The objective of this presentation is to acknowledge the chronological dynamics involved in the planning of health facilities. If we look back at the last fifty years, we can see there has been a theoretical leap from the quantitative to the qualitative, which is at the same time concurrent with the development in global health planning processes.

While in the 1960s healthcare planning was designed to be efficient and was assigned to specific segments of the population, this concept later evolved to identify the health situations of people and their surroundings, based on the unique ways in which people interact with their physical and social environments.

This presentation has two thematic axes, "The Methodology of Health Facility Planning" and "The Characterization of the Health Facility," which will be addressed by looking at some projects developed by CIRFS, the Research Center of Health Facility Planning, Faculty of Architecture, Design and Urban Planning, of the University of Buenos Aires, CIRFS / FADU / UBA Argentina.

First Thematic Axis: The Methodology of Health Facility Planning

The Methodology of Health Facility Planning is analysed through geographic scenarios where this methodology is applied, and through Guidelines for the Development of Health Facilities.

Geographic Scenarios

The geographic scenarios are separated into two levels: the Macrosystem level, where the health services network defines the role of each healthcare facility integrated into that network, and the Microsystem level, the level of the Health Unit.

At the Macrosystem Level

Examples: Greater Buenos Aires

1983-1986/1987-1990. Project for the Reformulation of Health Care and Health Facilities, in the Municipalities of Vicente Lopez and San Fernando.

Figure 1 of the Municipality of Vicente Lopez shows a geographical area with a "vulnerable" population, and highlights the design of the Health Networks: Education – Promotion of Health; Mental and Social. There was also participation from Social Resources: Development Society, Kindergarten and Caritas Centres.

Figure 2-4 of the Municipality of San Fernando highlights the spatial location of some variables of the Social and Physical Environment: population density, natural environment variables, and the Homogeneous Areas of Living Conditions – geographical areas with different and particular social and environmental conditions.

City of Buenos Aires

1989-2000/2001-2003 Project for the Assessment of Health Facilities and the Environmental Impact on the City of Buenos Aires, which also identifies the characterization of the social and physical environment.

The Social Environment highlights the spacialization of demographic variables: population, population growth rate, birth and death rates, whereas the Physical Environment highlights the environmental characterization of the built environment. All this information combined allows us to acknowledge and design the Homogeneous Areas of Living Conditions.

The Macrosystem level approach evolved to the notion of sets in order to acknowledge not only differences in age, gender, living conditions and habits, but also differences in spacialization for the Social and Physical Environment variables.

The multi-causal and multi-sectorial interaction of these variables defines the Homogenous Areas of Living Conditions, which point out and identify

200

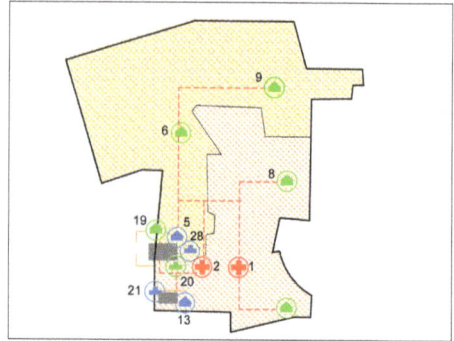

Figure 1. Macrosystem level, Municipality of Vicente López, health networks.

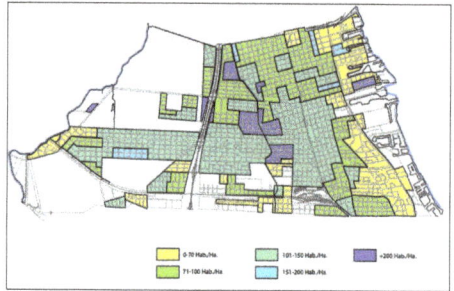

Figure 2. Macrosystem level, Municipality of San Fernando, population density.

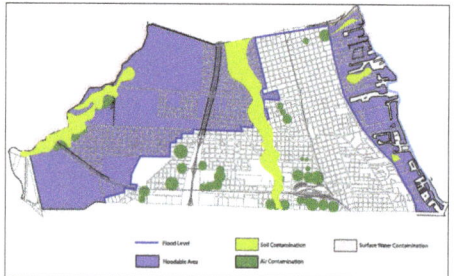

Figure 3. Macrosystem level, Municipality of San Fernando, variable spacialization - natural environment.

Figure 4. Macrosystem level, Municipality of San Fernando, definition of homogeneous areas of living conditions.

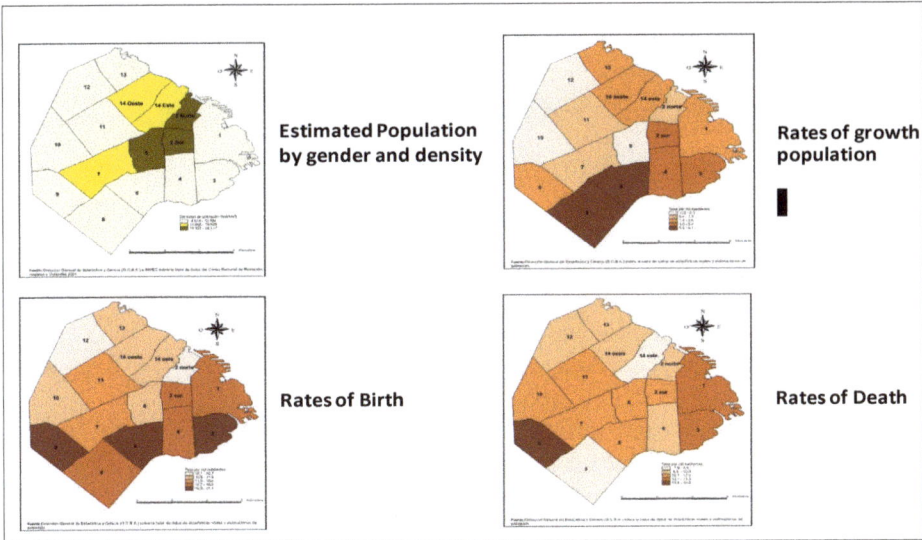

201

Figure 5. *Spacialization of demographic variables, City of Buenos Aires.*

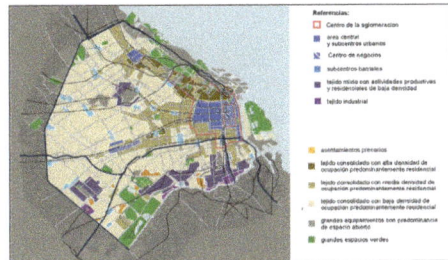

the health situation of the people and their surroundings.

Finally, the design of the Health Networks with the participation of Health Resources, involving non-traditional resources from the everyday habitat, should be acknowledged.

Figure 6. *City of Buenos Aires, physical environment - environmental characterization - built environment.*

At the Microsystem Level

The Microsystem level focused on the Health Unit.

2002-2006 The project Master Plan for Jose de San Martin University Hospital, City of Buenos Aires, Argentina, was presented at the 23rd Seminar of the Public Health Group of the International Union of Architects in San Francisco, US, 2003, with the title "Centralization versus Decentralization."

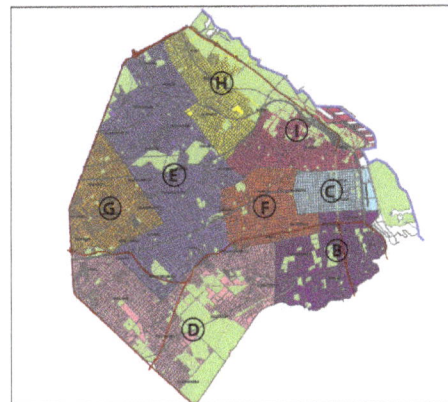

Figure 7. *City of Buenos Aires, definition of homegeneous areas of living conditions.*

Figure 8 shows an aerial view of the hospital and its effect on the urban plot. The hospital covers an area of 135,000 sq m, developed over eighteen levels.

The methodology applied by CIRFS was the Interaction of Models, and it started with the interaction of two models: the Observed Model and the Proposed Model.

202

The Observed Model is defined based on a survey of the various services in order to recognize the use of space, production, type of organization and future trends. These plans are characterized by the "Functional Units" and "Supportive Areas" of the services.

Functional Units: where the main activity of the service is conducted, and where the production balances are made (e.g. inpatient rooms, consulting rooms for outpatient care, and operating rooms for surgical treatments). Supportive Areas: where the activities supporting and complementing the main activities take place. This analysis allows us to detect situations that may be problematic in terms of location, interrelations, proximity, etc.

The challenge in this project was how to create Centres of Care, Education, Research and Management with the restriction of the services located at different levels. This problem was resolved through a core organization where the relationships and links with the services could be real-contiguous (immediate) or virtual-distant (mediate), always with the support of certain centralized services, such as Ambulatory Care, Emergency Care and Diagnostic & Treatment Services.

Figure 8. University Hospital "José de San Martín," City of Buenos Aires.

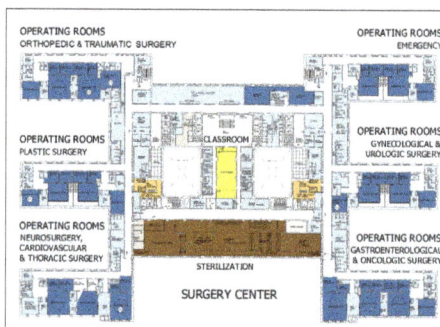

Figure 9. University Hospital "José de San Martín," City of Buenos Aires, characterization of the services in functional units and supportive areas.

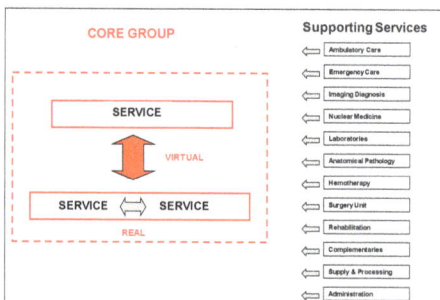

Figure 10. University Hospital "José de San Martín," City of Buenos Aires, conception of the Centre of Care, Education, Research and Management.

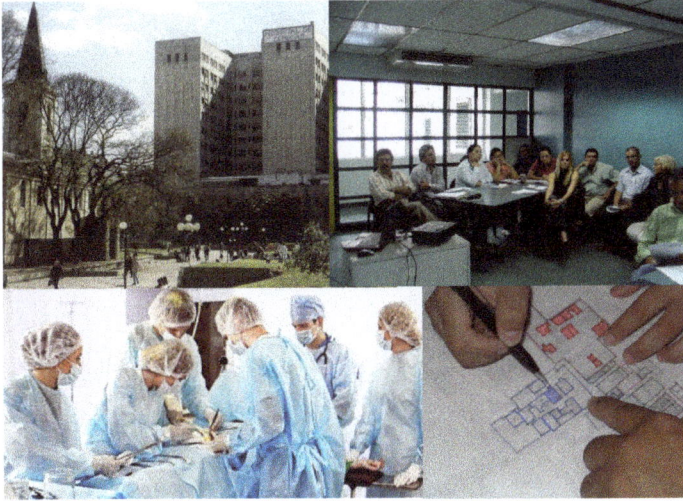

Figure 11. The University Hospital "Jose de San Martin", City of Buenos Aries and the design of Master Plans and Centers of Excellence in Care, Teaching, Research and Management.

The presentation concluded that "Centralization versus Decentralization" must be interpreted without conflict but rather as complementary actions of decentralization with the centralization of selected services.

The Microsystem level approach has also evolved in recent years, and an important aspect to highlight is the joint work of the management team at the Health Unit (doctors, nurses and technicians) together with those responsible for the Health Facilities project. The importance of the definition of the Functional Program, which precedes the Program of Architecture, Equipment, Engineering and Maintenance, should also be highlighted.

Another important evolution in the Microsystem level was the conformation of "space systems,"spatial-functional, circulation, engineering and structural subsystems, centralization and decentralization strategies, and the design of Master Plans and Centres of Excellence in Care, Teaching, Research and Management.

Guidelines
Elaboration of the Guidelines

1986-1990 Guidelines for the Development of Health Facilities.
Successive applications and evaluations of the CIRFS planning methodology generated a great amount of knowledge and experience, published in 1990 as Guidelines for the Development of Health Facilities. This publication was sponsored by the Pan-American Health Organization (PAHO) and the World Health Organization (WHO).
The Guidelines were coordinated by CIRFS, and jointly developed by three other Latin American Centres.

The Center of Biomedical Engineering, State University of Campinas (UNICAMP) San Paolo - Brazil, the National Hospital Fund (FNH), the Ministry of Health in Bogota, Colombia, and the Development and Technological Applications Center (CEDAT), Ministry of Health, Mexico.

Figure 12. 1986 – 1990, "Guidelines for the Development of Health Facilities," Technical Cooperation Project PAHO / WHO.

204

Below are the twenty-three guidelines created by CIRFS / FADU / UBA:
- Guideline G1. Organization for the Formulation of the Health Facility Development Process
- Guideline G2. Analysis and Characterization of the Population's Health Needs
- Guideline G3. Analysis and Characterization of Technological Networks of Health Facilities
- Guideline G4. Technology Network Administration, with an emphasis on Local Health Systems
- Guideline G5. Health Facility Functional Programming
- Guideline G6. Development of the Architecture Program
- Guideline G7. Development of the Installations-Engineering Program
- Guideline G8. Development of the Equipment Program
- Guideline G9. Development of the Conservation Program
- Guideline G10. Development of the Economic-Financial Program
- Guideline G11. Development of the Master Program
- Guideline G12. Development of the Architecture-Engineering Project
- Guideline G13. Development of the Equipment Project
- Guideline G14. Development of the Operation Project
- Guideline G15. Development of the Conservation and Maintenance Engineering Project
- Guideline G16. Criteria for the Procurement of Architecture and Engineering Studies and Works
- Guideline G17. Criteria for Equipment Purchase and Procurement
- Guideline G18. Execution and Oversight of Architecture and Engineering Works
- Guideline G19. Equipment Assembly, Installation and Oversight
- Guideline G20. Health Facility Commissioning
- Guideline G21. Execution and Management of Conservation and Maintenance Engineering
- Guideline G22. Evaluation of the Operating Health Facility
   o Guideline G22-1. Health Facility Evaluation at National-Regional Network Level
   o Guideline G22-2. Health Facility Evaluation at Network Level
   o Guideline G22-3. Health Facility Evaluation at Health Unit Level
- Guideline 23. Plant Operation Costs Control

In the development of these guidelines, the conceptual framework of CIRFS was adopted for the Health Facilities Planning process. The guidelines can therefore be used at different stages of the process.

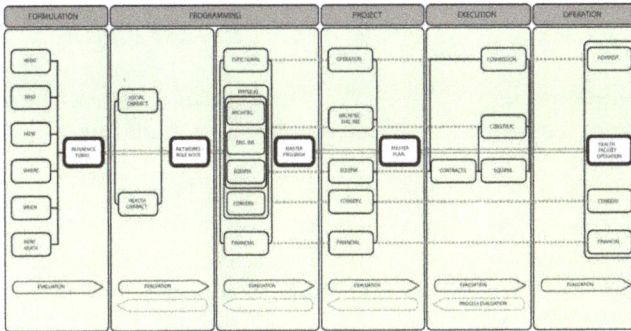

Figure 13. Guidelines for the Development of Health Facilities, health facilities planning process.

205

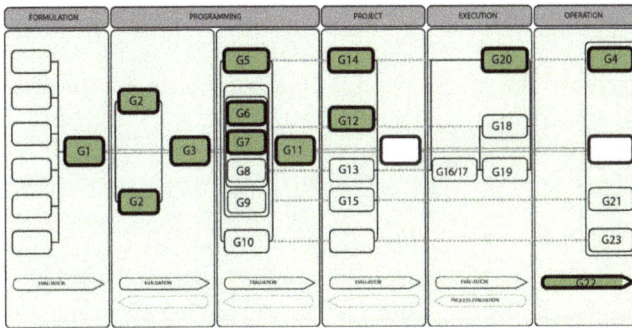

Figure 14. Guidelines for the Development of Health Facilities, guidelines for different stages of the process.

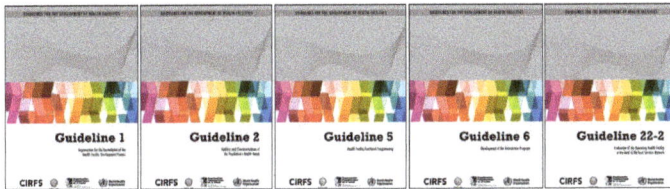

Figure 15. 2010 Technical Cooperation Project WHO - PAHO/WHO "Update of the Guidelines for Development of Health Facilities.

2010 Updated Guidelines

The Update of the Guidelines for the Development of Health Facilities project was developed by CIRFS in 2010 and sponsored by PAHO and WHO. This update was based on the incorporation of new trends into health facility planning, with new study cases, the use of IT and translation into Spanish and English.

The process began with the five most representative and in-demand guidelines:
– Guideline G1: Organization for the Formulation of the Health Facility Planning Process.
– Guideline G2: Analysis and Characterization of the Population's Health Needs
– Guideline G5: Health Facility Functional Programming
– Guideline G6: Development of the Architecture Program
– Guideline G22-2: Health Facility Evaluation at Network Level

The equipment guideline was later developed through the Process of Health Facility Planning: Interaction Architecture / Equipment-Space / Object project.

TESIS Inter-University Research Centre "Systems and Technologies for Social and Healthcare Facilities" University of Florence, Italy

SECOND THEMATIC AXIS: HEALTH FACILITY
CHARACTERIZATION METHODOLOGY

This methodology was studied through
the "Technical Records" and the "Approach" to the characterization of the
Health Facility.

Technical Records

206

Elaboration of the Technical Records

1983-1986 Models of Planning at Microsystem level - Health Unit.
1987-1990 Technical Records about
Health Facilities-Space, Equipment
and Engineering, according to Services for the First Level of Health Care.

The Technical Records were published by PAHO / WHO, the Kel-
logg Foundation and CIRFS / FADU
/ UBA. They comprise six volumes,
fifteen hundred pages and are divided
into three chapters: Operational Technology - Health Facility Typologies,
Equipment System and Engineering
System.

Elaboration of Ambulatory Surgery and Ambulatory Care Research Projects

1995-1997 Development and Evaluation
of Models of Planning Ambulatory Surgery.
1998-2000 Models of Planning Ambulatory Surgery.
2011-2013 Characterization of Health Facilities for the Development of Ambulatory
Care, which resulted in the Technical Records for Ambulatory Care.
CIRFS has identified thirty-one Health
Facility typologies. One example is the
Operating Room typology where two tables (Figures 17) were incorporated to fit
the dimensional image of the typology: one
table includes tasks, patients and staff, and
environmental conditions, and the other
table includes the equipment and installations.
CIRFS began the research projects by developing models with IT support and the
evaluation and application of these models in different hospitals. As a result of this
research, a technological transference tool
was developed and structured along the
lines of the 1990 Technical Records.

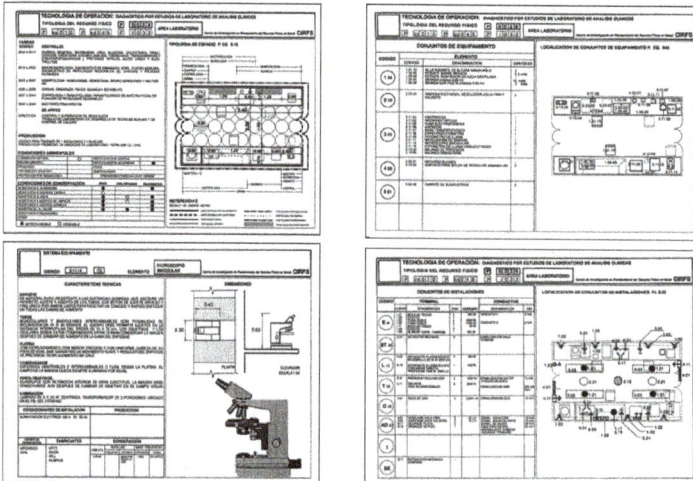

Figure 16. Technical Records 1990.

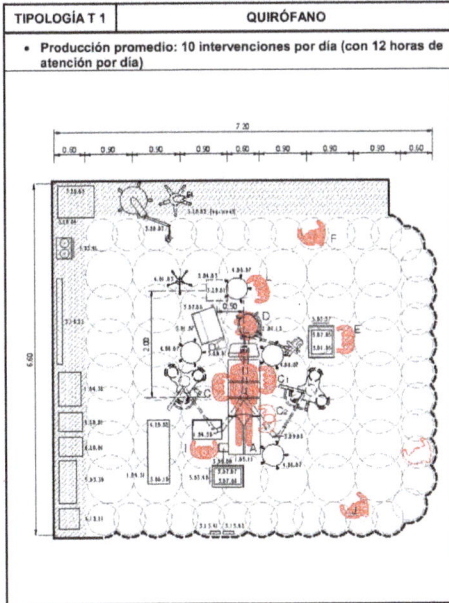

Figure 17. Technical Records 2000, ambulatory surgery.

207

Approach / Focus

Humanization

2006-2009 Environment and Humanization, Conditions of the Space in the Development of Health Facilities research project.

The Project was presented at the 28th Seminar of the Public Health Group of the International Union of Architects in Florence, Italy, in 2008.

The research focused on the humanization of spaces for inpatient care. In this case the analysis was restricted to the patient's room.
The project highlighted the criteria for patient-centered healthcare, researching the Health Facility conditions.

Based on this analysis, CIRFS identified four sets of environmental conditions:

1. Environmental factors that stimulate the senses;
2. Optimization of operational aspects;
3. Patient well-being;
4. Published standards and guidelines.

The first set of conditions comprises the variables of colours, lighting, sounds, odors and textures; the second set of variables includes accessibility, orientation, proportions and distribution of the equipment; and the third set of variables comprises the incorporation of nature, art, music and comfort.

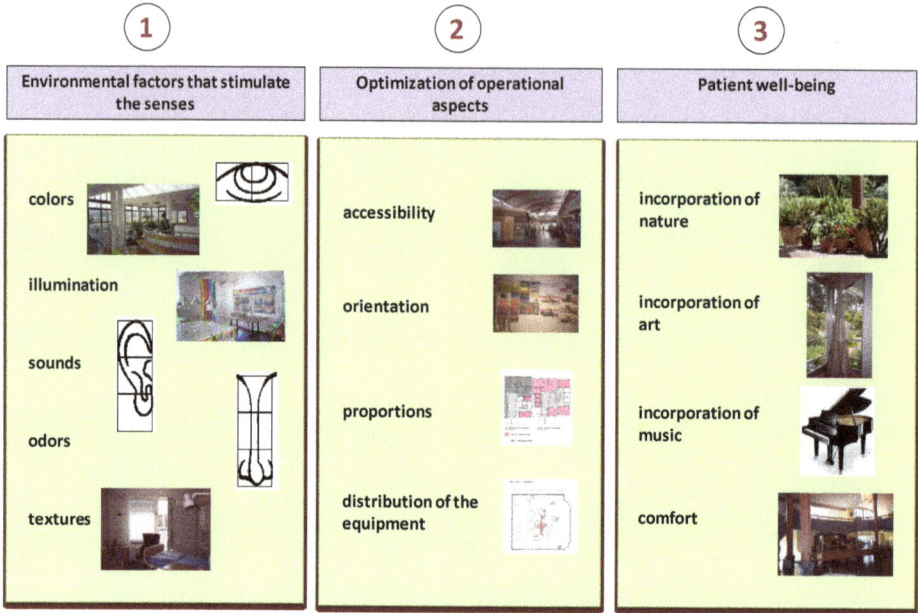

Figure 18. Variables of the first set of conditions for humanization.

Quality Assurance

2011-2014 The Health Facilities Quality Assurance research project aims to introduce physical resources as a condition to support and achieve quality.

The objectives of this research are to develop, implement and evaluate the indicators of Health Facilities Quality Assurance in healthcare facilities. The work involved the participation of students from the Specialization Career in Health Facility Planning course, run by CIRFS at FADU / UBA since 1980, and with the collaboration of IUHRP – Institute of Urban Health Research and Practice, at the Bouvé College of Health Sciences, Northeastern University, Boston, USA.

Figure 19. Observed model, Municipal Hospital Dr. Teodoro Alvarez, City of Buenos Aires, Argentina.

Figure 20. "Entre Familia" Residential Program, BPHC Boston Public Health Commission, Boston Massachusetts, US.

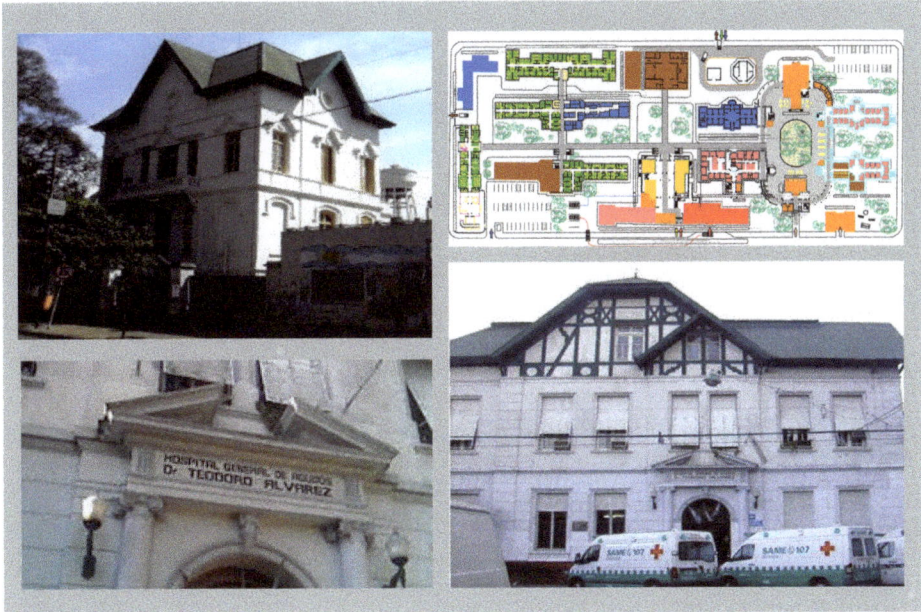

Figure 21. Master Plan Municipal Hospital Dr. Teodoro Alvarez (2012), City of Buenos Aires, Argentina.

209

In this case the "Interaction of Models" methodology is based on the design of three models: Reference, Observed, and Normalized Model.

The Reference Model was developed by analysing the influence of the latest innovations on variables that promote quality and that could be applicable for healthcare facilities. To do this, national and international organizations were selected, and the most significant documents produced by these organizations were studied:

– Research Center on Health Facility Planning (CIRFS): Health Care Facility Planning Process;
– National Program for Quality Assurance (PNGC): Organization and Operation Guidelines;

– American Institute of Architects (AIA): Guidelines for Design and Construction of Healthcare Facilities;
– Kaiser Permanente (KP): Eco – Toolkit: Environmentally Responsible Design and Construction Practices;
– International Standard Organization (ISO): Quality Management Systems
– Guidelines for Performance Improvements – ISO 9004:2000;
– Joint Commission International (JCI): Joint Commission Accreditation Standards;
– Technical Institute for Health Facilities Accreditation (ITAES): Curso 2010 de Formación para Evaluadores en Acreditación;
– International Society for Quality Healthcare (ISQUA): International Principles for Health Care Standards.

CONCLUSIONS

As a result of this analysis, the following variables can be acknowledged: Interdisciplinary process, continuous improvement of healthcare quality, functionality, sustainability, security, flexibility, accessibility, humanization – privacy, conservation and development of quality standards and indicators for healthcare.

Two Observed Models were selected: the Dr. Teodoro Alvarez Municipal Hospital in Buenos Aires, and Entre Familia, a Residential Treatment Program for substance abusing women sponsored and directed by the Boston Public Health Commission in Boston, Massachusetts, US.

The master plan proposed for the Dr. Teodoro Alvarez Hospital (2012) acknowledges the incorporation of some of the quality variables. The humanization variable should be emphasized for the value it places on gardens and large windows that promote natural lighting.

There is an evolving trend, from the quantitative to the qualitative, in the planning and characterization of healthcare facilities.

The importance of the development of Guidelines and Technical Records as a technological transference tool and as an instrumental support for teaching should be highlighted.

Finally, from an architectural point of view, the permanent search for humanization and quality assurance, both in healthcare as well in healthcare facility planning should be emphasized.

This is why we should say "get better" with the understanding that this "better" must be qualified by aiming to attain better quality health facilties.

REFERENCES

American National Standard Institute (ANSI) (2009). *Accessible and Usable Buildings and Facilities A117.1.* International Code Council, Washington DC, USA.

Facilities Guidelines Institute (FGI), American Institute of Architects (AIA) (2006). *Guidelines for Design and Construction of Health Care Facilities.* The American Institute of Architects Press, Washington DC, USA.

Frampton, S., Guastello, S., Brady, C., Hale, M., Horowitz, S., Bennett Smith, S. and Stone, S. (2008). *Patient Centered Care, Improvement Guide.* Planetree and Picker Insititute, USA.

Joint Commission on Accreditation of Healthcare Organizations (JCAHO) (2014). *Accreditation Standards Books.* Joint Commission Resources, Inc. (JCR), Oakbrook Terrace, Illinois, USA.

International Society for Quality in Health Care (ISQua) (2000). *Principios de la ISQua, Alpha Agenda,* Vol. 1, May, No. 2.

Health Services and Promotion Branch (1978-1981). *Evaluation and Space Programming Methodologies series.* Minister of Health and Welfare, Health Facilities Design Division, Ottawa, Canada.

Lemus, J. D. (2001). *Salud Pública. Marco Conceptual e Instrumentos Operativos.* C.I.D.E.S., Buenos Aires, Argentina.

National Facilities Services (2002). *Eco-Toolkit. Environmentally Responsible Design and Construction Practices.* Kaiser Foundation Health Plan, Oakland CA, USA.

Ministerio de Obras Públicas, Transporte y Medio Ambiente, Subsecretaría de Estado para las Políticas del Agua y del Medio Ambiente (1995). *Guías Metodológicas para la Elaboración de Estudios de Impacto Ambiental.* Tomos I a IV, España.

Ministerio de Salud de la Nacion, Programa Nacional de Garantia de Calidad de la Atención Medica. *Directrices de Servicios de Salud, Habilitación Categorizante de Establecimientos, Herramienta para la Mejora Asistencial, Seguridad de los pacientes.*

Organización Panamericana de la Salud (OPS), Organización Mundial de la Salud (OMS) (1984). Usos y Perspectivas de la Epidemiología, *Boletín Epidemiológico*, 5 (1): 1-4.

Organización Panamericana de la Salud (OPS), Organización Mundial de la Salud (OMS) (September, 1999). Resúmenes Metodológicos en Epidemiología: Análisis de la Situación de Salud (ASIS). *Boletín Epidemiológico*, Vol. 22, No. 3, 1-3, Washington DC, USA.

Organización Panamericana de la Salud (OPS), Organización Mundial de la Salud (OMS) (June 5, 2000). Reporte Comprensivo de Siete Investigaciones de Situación de Salud a Nivel Local según Condiciones de Vida con Enfoque de Género realizadas en Centroamérica Período (1994-1995). *Serie Género y Salud Pública OPS*, San José, Costa Rica.

Organización Panamericana de la Salud (OPS), Organización Mundial de la Salud (OMS) (2004). *Guía para la Reducción de la Vulnerabilidad en el Diseño de Nuevos Establecimientos de Salud.*

Organización Panamericana de la Salud, Organización Mundial de la Salud (OMS) (2008). *Clasificación Estadística Internacional de Enfermedades y Problemas Relacionados con la Salud (CIE-10).*

Organización Mundial de la Salud (OPS) (2008). *Informe sobre la Salud en el Mundo 2008. La Atención Primaria de Salud, más necesaria que nunca.*

Organización Panamericana de la Salud (OPS), Organización Mundial de la Salud (OMS) (2008). *Índice de Seguridad Hospitalaria, Guía del Evaluador de Hospitales Seguros.*

Organización Panamericana de la Salud (OPS), Organización Mundial de la Salud (OMS) (2009). *Situación de salud en las Américas: Indicadores básicos.*

Organización Panamericana de la Salud (OPS), Organización Mundial de la Salud (OMS) (2010). *Hospitales Seguros frente a Desastres, Guía para la Evaluación de Establecimientos de Salud de Mediana y Baja Complejidad.*

Páez, L. R., Villalobos, E. M. (2000). El Costo y la Efectividad de las Inter-

211

TESIS Inter-University Research Centre "Systems and Technologies for Social and Healthcare Facilities"
University of Florence, Italy

TESIS

venciones en Salud: Estrategia Metodológica para Mejorar la Definición, Asignación, Distribución y el Uso de los Recursos en Salud. *CEPAR, Quito,* Ecuador.

Research Center for Health Facility Planning (CIRFS), Faculty of Architecture, Design and Urbanism (FADU), University of Buenos Aires (UBA) (1990, update 2010). *Guidelines for the Development of Health Facilities.* Pan American Health Organization (PAHO), Word Health Organization (WHO), Washington DC, USA.

Robles, S. C. (1994). *Desarrollos Metodológicos en el Análisis de Situación de Salud según Condiciones de Vida.* OPS, Washington DC, USA.

Sociedad Argentina para la Calidad en Atención de la Salud Sacas (2012). *Programa de Indicadores de Calidad de Atención Médica PICAM. Manual de Indicadores de Calidad 2ª. Versión.* Buenos Aires, Argentina.

The Center for Health Design (1996). *An investigation to Determine Whether the Built Environment Affects Patients' Medical Outcomes.* Progress Report. California, USA.

Verderber, S. (2002). Report on Global Hospitals in the Year 2050. Global University Programme in Healthcare Architecture (GUPHA), Japanese Government Ministry of Health Report, Tokyo.

World Bank (1990). Environmental Assessment Sourcebook. Technical Paper, Number 154, Environment Department, WB, I, II and III, Washington DC, USA.

World Bank (2001). Priorities in Health (English) - Las Prioridades en la Salud (Spanish). Publications, Report 36460, Enero.

212

Hospital Reuse in a Heritage Context: Principles of Integration with the Urban and Social City Cores

Del Nord R.[1]

romano.delnord@unifi.it
[1]Professor, University of Florence, Director of TESIS Inter-University Research Centre, Director of CSPE Professional Office, Italy

213

The presentation will describe the reuse of the Parini Hospital, a 20th century Modernist building that needed to be restored and expanded to become a state of the art healthcare centre. The regeneration of old hospital buildings can no longer be confined to the hospital precinct but must involve larger scale urban connections. The study aimed to understand: the critical points of the urban network, possible synergies between the urban and the service system, and how to create integration between public, social and hospital functions. The study highlighted a strategy based on the reuse of the existing building for polyclinics and day services while high-technologies will be hosted in the new addition.

HOSPITAL REUSE IN A HERITAGE CONTEXT

This presentation deals with the topical issue of hospital updating in historical areas. A condition that sparks off a whole set of multi-disciplinary connections and strategic decisions that affect the healthcare, social and urban systems. More and more frequently, in Europe and in Italy in particular, hospitals located in historic centres are perceived as no longer adequate to provide the services that people expect today.

The problem of 'if' and 'how' to update, is often addressed through a feasibility study that evaluates whether it is more appropriate to build a new hospital to "delocalize" out of the city centre or to "extend, adapt & reuse" the existing hospital with permanence in the urban context.

PLANNING OPTIONS

It is not always easy to assess whether it is appropriate to retain the existing hospital within the urban context and therefore adapt and often improve the existing facilities.

They are often monumental buildings or more recent facilities with a strong architectural identity dating back to early Modernism ... or whether it is the case to delocalize the functions outside the urban area for easier accessibility, cheaper building costs and quicker buildability.

Once the way forward has been established, planning options address the implementation strategies.

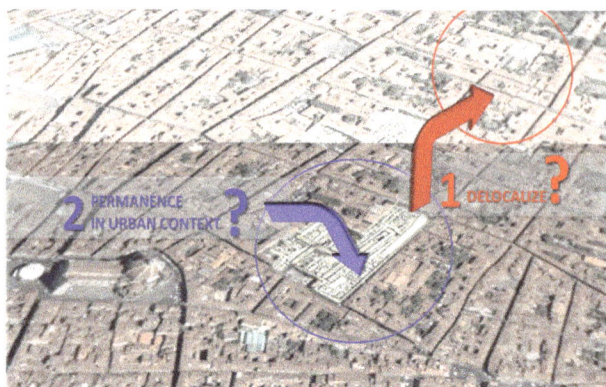

Figure 1. The two options in the case of the renewal of hospitals located in historic centres: permanence in the urban context or delocalize.

The choice to keep a hospital in its original location implies two different expansion strategies:

1. the first one is *densifying* the existing area with new infill that integrates the old buildings with the new ones. A good example is the hospital of Gentofte in Denmark.

2. the second choice addresses the same issue with a rather different approach. New independent facilities are *built ex novo* nearby to the hospital precinct. A symbolic example is the case of the Hospital de la Santa Creu in Barcelona.

The choice to delocalize the functions outside the urban area implies moving the entire structure into larger and infrastructured areas, such as in Deventer Hospital in Holland.

OPTION 1

More and more advanced assessment methodologies are used to compare the advantages and disadvantages (pros & cons) of the two alternatives. The many parameters of "value analysis" procedures that favour permanence in the urban context include:

1. Integration of the healthcare facility with social and public centres;

2. Sharing facilities with the community;

3. Facilitated accessibility;

4. Regeneration of urban areas through hospital refurbishment programs;

5. Revitalization of monumental buildings.

The decision of permanence in the urban context brings many community benefits (as an extension of the Patient-Centred Approach), which include the following:

1. Easy accessibility (pedestrian), zero-mile accessibility;

2. Opportunity to regenerate historic centres;

3. Reinterpretation of the hospital as a social, commercial and cultural environment, as well as a place for care;

4. Enhancement of confidentiality in the relationship between the patient and the hospital (psychological affectivity with places);

5. Cultural sustainability as defined by UNESCO.

Benefit 1: Integration with Social and Public Centres

The new healthcare system will be functionally linked with other facilities and social services available in the urban context.

Benefit 2: Sharing Facilities with the Community

The hospital hosts socio-cultural spaces and community activities such as: exhibition spaces, museums, artistic and cultural initiatives.

Benefit 3: Facilitated Accessibility

The Hospital is easily accessible through short distance footpaths or cycle paths, facilitating access for the disabled and vulnerable road users.

Benefit 4: Regeneration of Urban Areas

Hospital reorganization becomes an opportunity to redevelop some areas of the city for the benefit of the whole community.

Benefit 5: Revitalization of Monumental Buildings

Often hospital refurbishment is also an opportunity to enhance historical monuments and give them a new lease of life.

PARINI HOSPITAL – CASE STUDY

This scenario of decision-making assessments represents the framework of the "case study" of the presentation, in which the final decision was based on an evaluation process that involved extensive participation and even a "referendum" extended to all local citizens. The pivotal problem underlying the final decision concerned the way such large-scale expansion would have affected the city of Aosta and, above all, its hospital services network.

The Mauriziano Hospital is a 1940s building representing mainstream modern Italian architecture. It was built in the same location as the demolished 18th century hospital. So, both from an architectural and urban point of view, the hospital is charged with historical references and connections.

The Parini Hospital today is nestled in the city and surrounded by the public parking and modern road system. The hospital is the centre of the mobility network both at the scale of the local and regional road system. It is also strongly integrated in the urban core as a landmark for the community.

215

Figure 2. Mauriziano Hospital. North side: the building complex surrounded by the park and the road system leading to the historic centre. Eastern façade facing the historic square and green land.

Figure 3. The Parini Hospital today.

216

The local urban context consists of pedestrian routes that cut through the city and connect to the hospital as a major civic landmark. The proximity of the hospital to other facilities within the city helps to create a network of services. (How to organize or re-organize the 'network' of care is an extremely important issue that affects the quality of care as well as the way facilities are designed and managed).

Over the years, the hospital has grown with uncontrolled expansions but without a proper planning vision. This situation has caused at least 4 kinds of problems: it has cluttered the hospital area, changed the original architectural image of the hospital, limited pedestrian accessibility to the hospital precinct, and limited its social appeal.

Hospital – City – Context

The hospital is axially placed along the historical road (Figure 6, green line). Parking spaces are placed along the regional road network. The hospital is the centre point of a hierarchy of routes: pedestrian, mechanized, fast flowing, and is fully integrated with local services, mobility and transport.

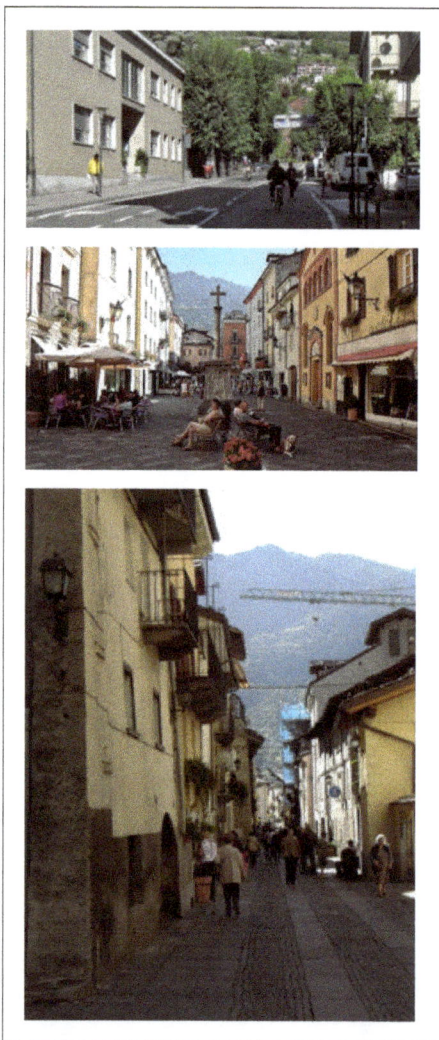

Figure 4. Pedestrian routes cut through the city and connect to the hospital as a major civic landmark.

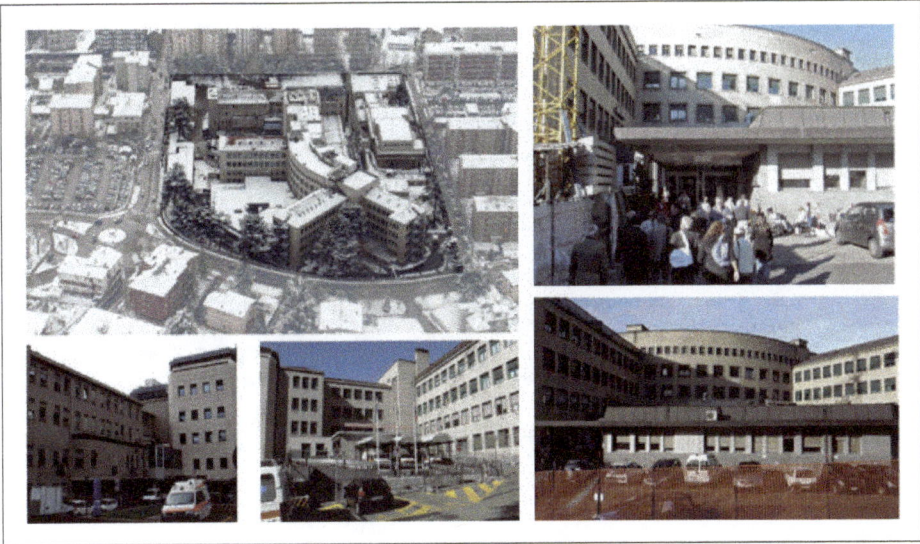

Figure 5. *Parini Hospital and the «uncontrolled» expansions over time: the unclear emergency entrance (two images bottom left) and the cluttered extended entrance (two images bottom right).*

217

Figure 6. *Urban identity and connections.*

TESIS Inter-University Research Centre "Systems and Technologies for Social and Healthcare Facilities" University of Florence, Italy

218

Figure 7. Aosta Valley – the hospital location.

The hospital's connections with the mobility system allows the hospital complex to connect with the rest of the city thereby facilitating access for the community. The mountain landscape in the background (Mont Blanc) places the hospital in a setting of natural beauty.

The characteristics of the area, the existing urban typologies and neighbouring functions generate input for the reorganization of the new hospital complex: the civic square and the City Hall; the city in winter, the historic city core; the urban pedestrian paths; places for daily activities.

THE MASTERPLAN DEFINED BY THE CLIENT AND THE CLIENT REQUIREMENTS AT TENDER STAGE

The client's masterplan included: an extensive renovation of the existing Mauriziano hospital, a new extension for the critical and emergency department, and a car park underneath the new hospital.

The integration of the old with the new blocked the north-south road link. The masterplan did not take into account that the proposed reorganization implied a critical extensive refurbishment of the old Mauriziano Hospital and, above all, closing the historical axis of viale Ginevra thereby disrupting the existing road system.

THE PROPOSED PROJECT PRINCIPLES

The new design concept reorganized the master plan into a three hub layout divided by the intensity of care.

The three hubs house: high intensity, low intensity and the Mother and Child centre. An important consequence of this arrangement is that it allows Viale Ginevra to be kept open, restating the hospital as a pivotal urban and social node. The new systems have different types of access to the hospital. The "hospital street" acts as the main circulation axis which produces different flows of users (Figure 9). The old Mauriziano Hopital works as

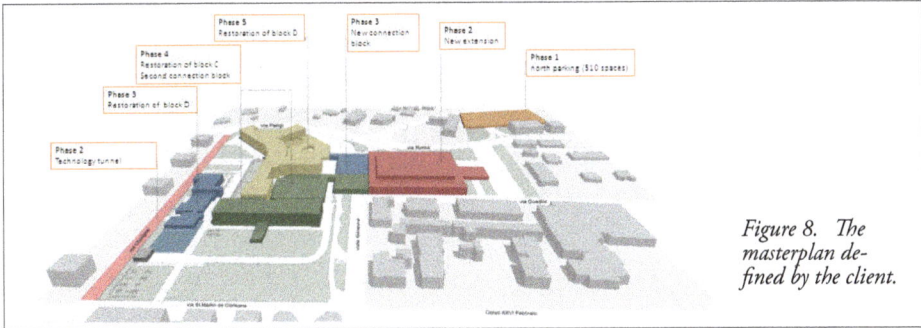

Figure 8. The masterplan defined by the client.

219

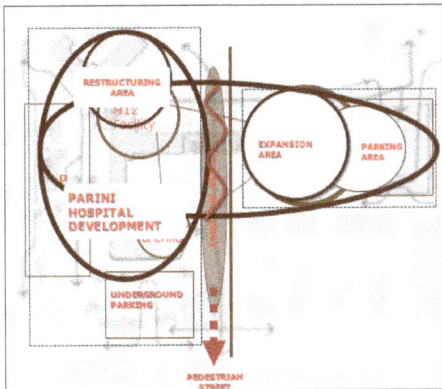

Figure 9. New healthcare services criteria.

Figure 10. General plan.

Figure 11. General axonometric projection.

12H-Hospital with a day hospital, clinics, and support services. The new Parini Hospital operates as the 24H-Hospital. The city services are brought inside the hospital through the definition of the "hospital street." The services inside the Hospital Street are the same as the ones along the historical city avenues: shops, cafeteria, and pharmacist. The new axis is conceived as an urban thoroughfare with activities and services for the community.

Figure 12. The south pedestrian and driveway link, pedestrian friendly access and smooth transit flow (public – private).

Figure 13. The north pedestrian and driveway link, and integrated green space to enhance and humanize arrivals and regenerate the urban and civic contest.

Figure 14. The reopened thoroughfare and the connecting bridge between the old and the new.

220

Figure 15. The new 24h hospital.

Figure 16. The hospital as a beacon at night.

Figure 17. The sustainable atrium overlooking and integrating the landscape.

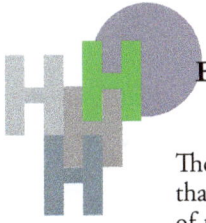

Session introduction

The articles in this section describe the design experiences and research that have been implemented in a number of actions to improve the quality of the care environment. The interventions described in some significant projects have been adapted to specific design features and require long and detailed experience in this particular area of design. Care facilities should have qualitative features that help ensure patients have a comfortable stay in the facility and at the same time there should be pleasant environments for personnel involved in charitable activities. In this sense, the following are essential: the presence of natural light, attention to the orientation of the views of the outside, streamlining the functional organization of environments, the presence of gardens and green spaces, and the use of colors, materials and furniture which can make the hospital seem like a familiar and more homely environment. The efficiency of the emergency environments can be improved through the use of special tools that allow the streamlined use of the rooms. At the same time it is equally important for the environments to be designed so as to improve the welfare of workers who work under particular stress conditions.

Green design is an essential step for improving the quality of the environment as it allows designers to create relaxing spaces for personnel which can also be observed and enjoyed by hospitalized patients. Engineers and researchers working in this field aim to find the best possible design solutions taking into account the viewpoints of the users. User participation is required in the design of green spaces surrounding hospitals. In this particular context, the design is achieved through interdisciplinary collaboration between architects, landscape architects and artists. In the specific case of the design quality of social and healthcare environments dedicated to care the concept of sustainable design is key and complementary.

Since the framework for the design of healthcare environments must take into account an articulated series of issues, it is clear that the training experiences related to healthcare planning and design are extremely complex as they aim to educate and sediment in students a comprehensive previous experience and also make students aware of the need for a multidisciplinary and collaborative approach to the subject.

In this scenario it is necessary to understand which factors help to increase the wellbeing of people and to create environments for the promotion of health in which patients experience the disease under the best possible conditions. Professionals involved in healthcare design should be capable of understanding patients' experiences so they can suggest, to physicians and professionals involved in care activities, which environmental characteristics can make a positive contribution during the course of treatment.

221

Designed to Thrive
Creating Salutogenic Environments

Farrow T. [1]

tyef@farrowpartnership.com
[1] B Arch, M Arch UD, LEED AP, FRAIC, AIBC, SAA, OAA, NSAA, NLAA, Assoc. AIA

223

Designers have an opportunity to dramatically improve health and prosperity in future so-cieties that will thrive, rather than merely cope with medical costs. As outspoken advocates for salutogenic (health-causing) design, they can raise public expectations for the built environment. This transformation begins by understanding the roots of historically low standards for design quality. In order to take a leadership role in this movement, designers must engage - rather than attempt to "educate" - the public.

Keywords: *salutogenesis, health, design, urbanism, architecture*

1. THE QUEST TO CHANGE EXPECTATIONS FOR THE BUILT ENVIRONMENT

In order to reduce the burden of health-care costs on society, there must be global awareness of how the built environment affects our state of mind and sense of well-being. Specifically, what elements cause health and what elements cause dis-ease?
How will places of dis-ease become unacceptable?

Similar to health-awareness campaigns in the past that succeeded in reducing rates of smoking, there can be a global movement to reduce the prevalence of boring, dangerous, and energy-draining places. Similar to the evolution of attitudes toward smoking on airplanes, public awareness of health attributes in our built environment can change dramatically in less than a generation.
This movement depends on more knowledgeable critics who can analyse elements that contribute to healthy and unhealthy places. The quest to change what people expect from their built environment begins with simple questions such as: How does this space make you feel? What changes to the space would make you feel better? Every scale and type of project—from stairways to office buildings to parks and hospitals—can be assessed in terms of the continuum of health to dis-ease. For example, consider the potential for designing more light-filled and attractive stairways to invite use, in contrast to exit stairs that are dull and often difficult to find.

224

Figure 1. How will this environment become unacceptable?

SEEING HEALTH AS MORE THAN THE ABSENCE OF DISEASE

Our culture has developed an imbalanced focus on illness while neglecting studies of what causes health. For example, we have a commonly-used term that refers to the origins of disease: pathogenic. A corresponding term that refers to the origins of health is relatively unknown: salutogenic.

Medical sociologist Aaron Antonovsky coined the term salutogenesis, a concept which reframes health as a positive force rather than the absence of deficiencies. Salutogenesis is derived from salus, a Latin word meaning health, and the Greek word genesis, meaning origin. Antonovsky saw a continuum from health to dis-ease, rather than a state of either wellness or illness.

Figure 2. Richard Jackson quote.

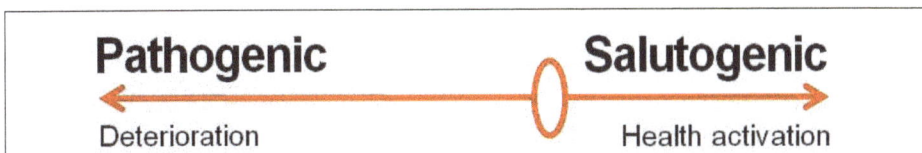

Figure 3. Pathogenic-salutogenic illustration.

ENTERING THE 3RD ERA OF PUBLIC HEALTH

The history of public health can be seen as consisting of three eras. Until the mid-20th century, public health was focused on combating communicable diseases. The second era has focused on curbing chronic, non-communicable disease (mid-20th century until today).

In the past, anyone who avoided disease was considered healthy. Today health is recognized as much more than a neutral state of being free of illness. The 3rd era of public health can be seen as that of salutogenesis or optimum health activation. This shift will require a salutogenic orientation rather than a pathogenic perspective, as depicted by this chart:

The focus of Antonovsky's research was: why do some people remain healthy while others become ill?
He developed a framework for analysis which he termed a "Sense of Coherence" (SOC) regarding life and its challenges. Three essential factors contributed to SOC: comprehensibility, manageability, and meaningfulness. These factors contribute to each individual's capacity to make sense of his or her world.

The need to see a bigger picture of health and the environment comes at a time when the very meaning of health is changing. As we enter the 3rd era of public health at the start of the 21st century, people are living longer and have greater expectations than to merely avoid ill

225

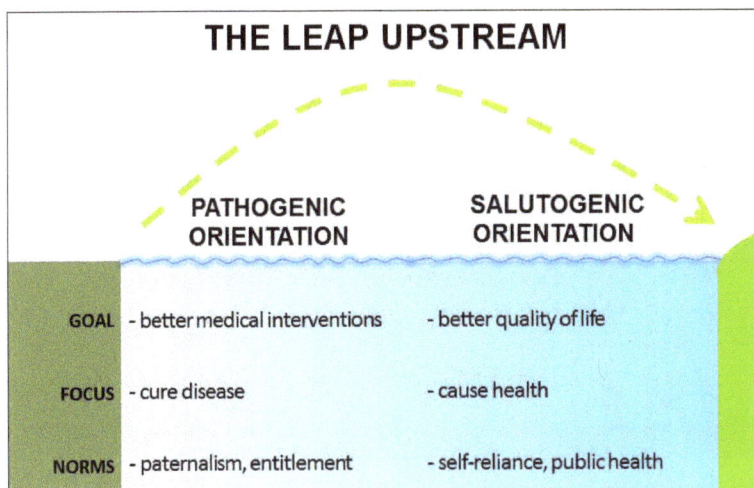

Figure 4. Leap Upstream.

health. There is a growing desire to live lives to their full potential, that is, to thrive rather than merely survive.

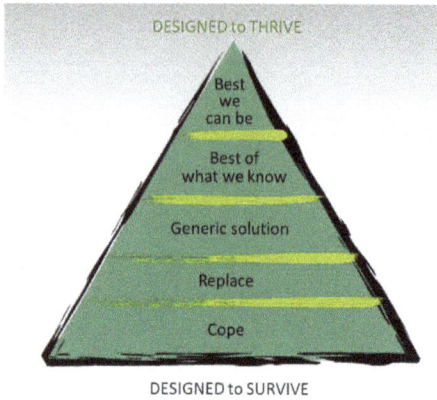

Figure 5. Aspirations chart.

ONE FUNDAMENTAL QUESTION CAN INSTIGATE CHANGE

Research by the psychologist Daniel Kahneman has highlighted a human tendency to make decisions based on emotions which are subsequently rationalized. It is therefore vital to fuel an emotion-based demand for higher expectations through personal engagement by asking: How healthy is this place?

Consider that the public has become accustomed to assessing and rating every detail of hotels and restaurants. Likewise, rating the built environment can become routine.

FIVE VITAL ELEMENTS THAT HELP THE PUBLIC SEE HOW PLACES MAKE THEM FEEL

Nature: design that is inspired by the natural world;
Authenticity: design that draws on meaningful local influences;
Variety: design that promotes a range of experiences and a sense of discovery;
Vitality: regenerative space that facilitates the flow of people and ideas;
Legacy: design that makes a lasting contribution to health.

Comparatively little is known about what causes health compared to our knowledge of what causes disease. In a brain-powered, post-industrial economy, a more balanced picture of health is beginning to emerge. This growing interest in the quality of our built environment may create an escape route from pathology-centric spiraling medical costs.

Figure 6. How healthy is this place?

226

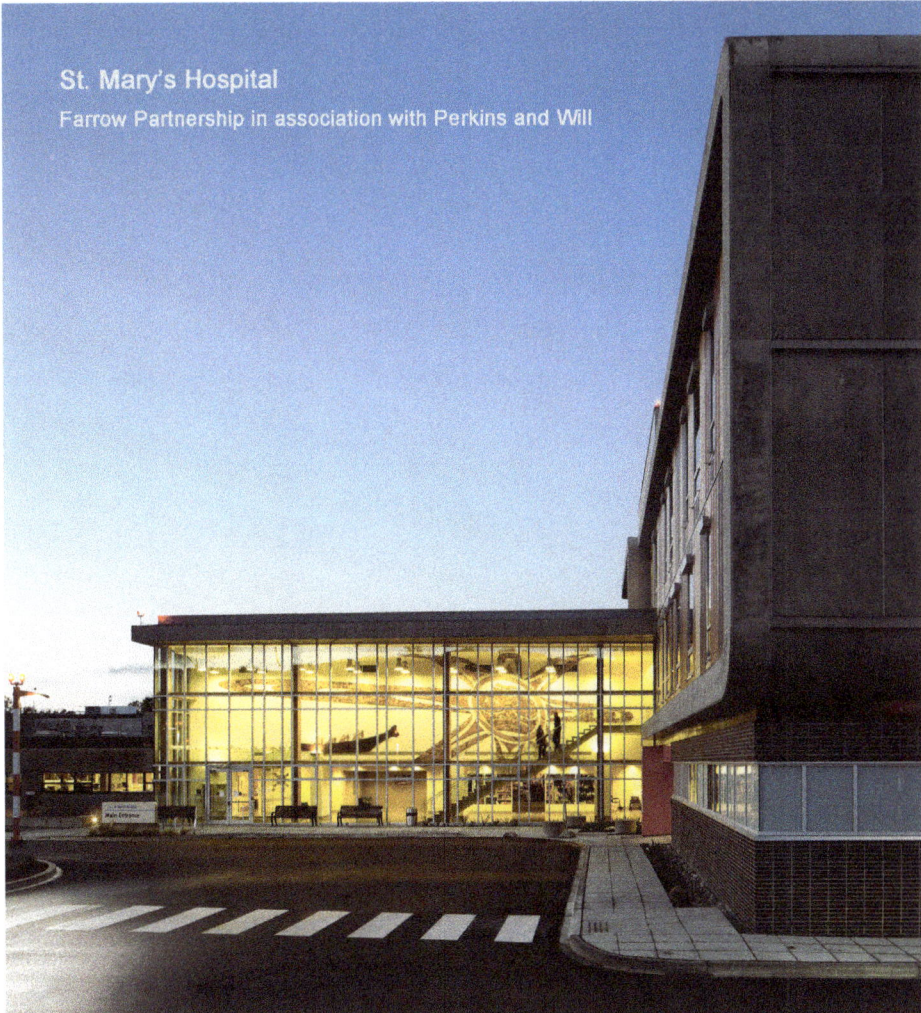

St. Mary's Hospital
Farrow Partnership in association with Perkins and Will

227

Figure 7. The design of St Mary's Hospital draws on a rich First Nations' heritage, a prime example of authenticity and legacy.

Discussions about architecture and urban design are typically limited to issues of style and personal likes or dislikes. In order to increase the demand for health-causing design, the public must begin to assess the potential of every building, every public space and every home. This awareness campaign could make dreary design and merely functional places unacceptable.

Instead, people would expect optimistic design that encourages social interaction, instills pride in community identity, strengthens connections to nature, reinforces cultural meaning and creates a positive legacy.

TESIS Inter-University Research Centre "Systems and Technologies for Social and Healthcare Facilities"
University of Florence, Italy

228

Figure 8. Credit Valley Hospital, Farrow Partnership.

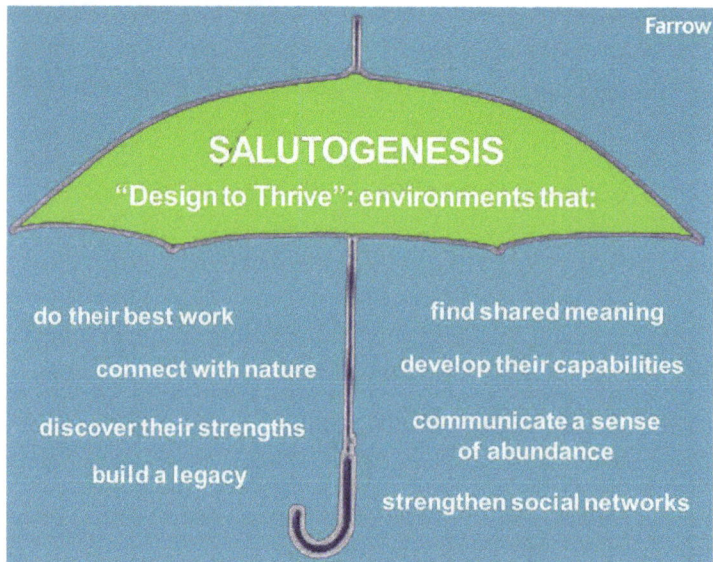

Figure 9. Chart: salutogenic environments.

Healing Gardens and Landscapes: From Big Ideas to Eye Sparkling Detail

Burt V.[1]

virginia@visionscapes.ca
[1] OALA, RLA, ASLA, Principal of Visionscapes Landscape Architects, Inc., Canada

229

The use of a case study revealed many opportunities for creating meaningful space, how healing gardens really work and how they become an intrinsic part of the supportive care offered at a healthcare facility. It demonstrated the use of collaborative techniques and answered the question "what makes a healing garden, a healing garden?", unpacking it through a journey of exploration, discovery and dreaming, with photographic examples of conceptual through to built work. As part of a particular project example, the four elements of nature were included in the design. Landscape architects affect people's experiences as they move through spaces - ideally this experience is a positive one of magic and wonder.

Keywords: *healthcare design, architectural design, landscape architecture, lighting, urban design*

DESCRIPTION OF THE PROJECT

The case study revealed many opportunities for creating meaningful spaces, how healing gardens work, and how they become an intrinsic part of the supportive care offered at a healthcare facility. "What makes a healing garden, a healing garden?" was answered and unpacked through a journey of exploration, discovery and dreaming, with photographic examples of conceptual through to built work. Collaborative sessions with cancer survivors, staff and caregivers provided the input for the process of master planning a facility.

As the macro plan evolved, the criteria, requirements for obtaining permits and working drawings on a micro-scale were presented. As the project moved into the implementation phase, the details and means needed to address the multiple challenges of creating a garden were discussed, for instance contractor and administrative needs, the garden's opening, managing donor expectations, maintenance and long-term goals. This award winning project evidences innovative techniques and results. Techniques such as sacred geometry and sfumato were used, and meaningful meetings were held with both clients and patients.

TESIS Inter-University Research Centre "Systems and Technologies for Social and Healthcare Facilities"
University of Florence, Italy

TESIS

Figure 1. University Hospitals Case Medical Center in Cleveland, Ohio, United States. Site plan.

230

Figure 2. University Hospitals Case Medical Center, landscape master plan.

The role of sustainability initiatives was discussed in the context of LEED accreditation. As part of the project, the four elements of nature were included in the design. Incorporating the mission of the facility, this example tied programming to the design of these elements while taking people thorough various Rogerian therapy techniques. The incorporation of artists' works and collaboration with the landscape enabled the architects to link back to the overall intent of the project. Detailed soul-filled works of art were integrated into the healing garden creating meaning for anyone who visits. Landscape architects affect people's experiences as they move through spaces - ideally this experience is a positive one of magic and wonder. Come prepared to be inspired.

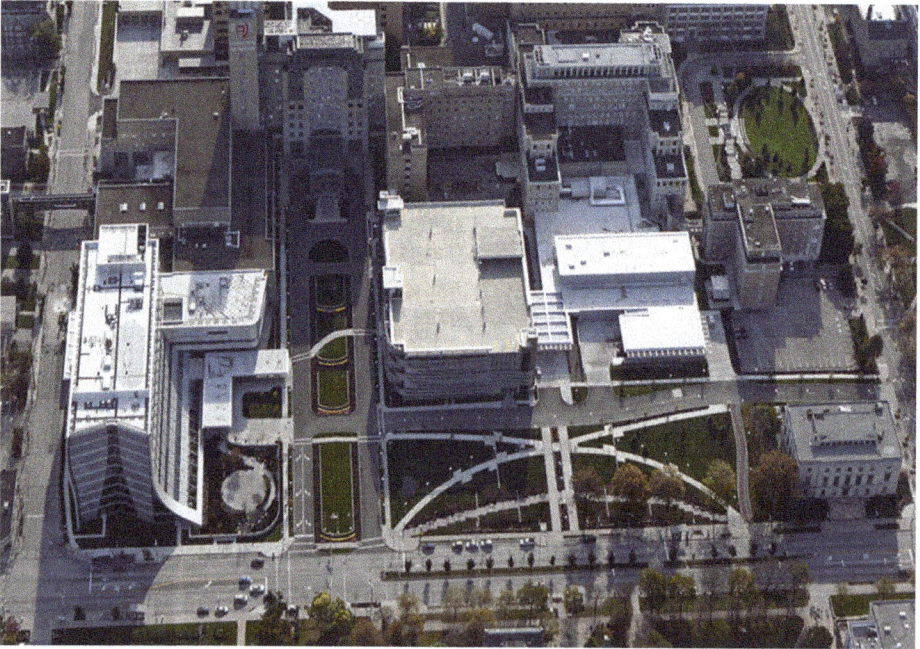

Figure 3. University Hospitals Case Medical Center.

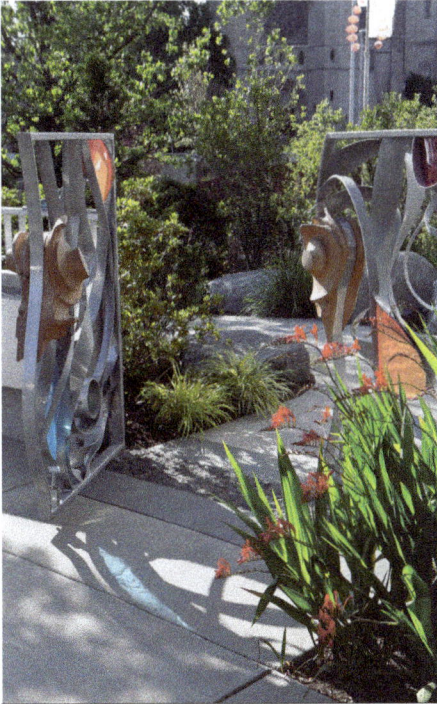

LEARNING OUTCOMES

1. Development of the "BIG idea" in detail through collaborative design with artists, other professionals and user groups.

2. Developing an understanding of navigating with multiple client group agendas: hospital administration, medical staff, donors.

3. Applying lessons learned with an understanding of built work.

231

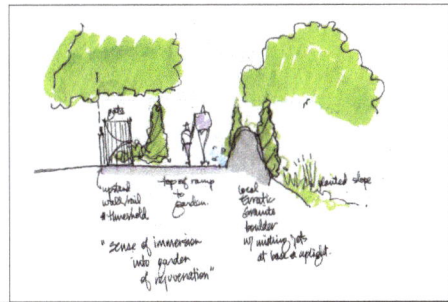

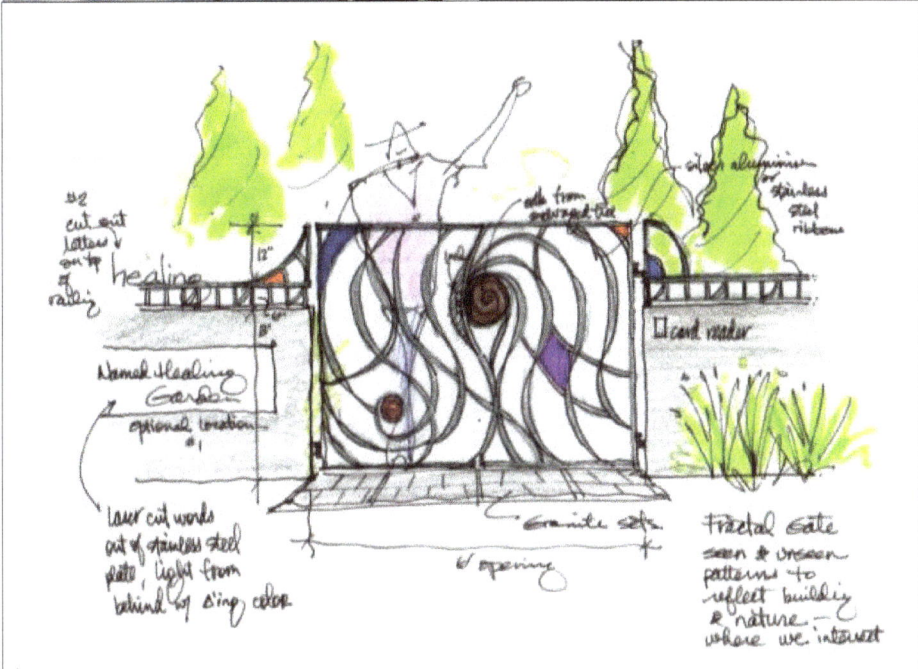

Figure 4. Healing garden – gate.

TYPES OF PROFESSIONALS TARGETED

Administrators, Vice-Presidents, Directors, Architects, Corporate Executives, Doctors, Nurses, Clinicians, Executive Level Management: CEO, COO, CFO, Owners, Healthcare Executives, Landscape Architects, Lighting Designers.

232

Figure 5. Healing garden – labyrinth.

The New Nanaimo ED
Designated to Be an "Environment That Staff Would Want to Come to on Their Day Off"

Pradinuk R.[1], Fox S.[2], Raber B.[3]

ray.pradinuk@stantec.com
[1]Architect AIBC, LEED® AP, Stantec Architecture Ltd.
[2]MSN, RN, Manager Emergency Services, Vancouver Island Health Authority
[3]Architect AIBC, Stantec Architecture Ltd.

233

Sparked by the challenge to create an "environment that staff would want to come to on their day off," the new Nanaimo Regional General Hospital (NRGH) Emergency Department and Psychiatric Emergency Services in Nanaimo, BC, Canada, may be the first in the world to include nature imbued courtyards within actual patient treatment zones. The most important considerations informing the design were improved patient flow, functionality, privacy/confidentiality, safety, and an abundance of natural daylight. This presentation will also address the question of how it has actually turned out and what the "evidence" really shows.

ARCHITECTURE AS LIFE SUPPORT

If one were to try to write an important book about how people should design hospitals for other people to use, it would be good to have a really nice place to write it in because writing is hard work, and it can be stressful or even depressing. Whenever the going got tough, one could watch the people coming and going from the park or the shops under the arcade, watch the rain falling, admire the effects of changing light on the building façades, or, in the case of full-blown writers block, watch the leaves changing colour.

WHAT WOULD A HOSPITAL DESIGNED AS A NATURE INSTRUMENT BE LIKE?

For so long we've thought of a hospital, most buildings for that matter, as hermetically sealed boxes that we can't imagine them as nature instruments.

The beauty of the world and our happiness within it are intertwined – as patients, caregivers or designers. How about this? Lets say that any building, much less a hospital, that doesn't provide a life-world connection for the vast majority of its inhabitants for the majority of their day, gets an 'F'.

234

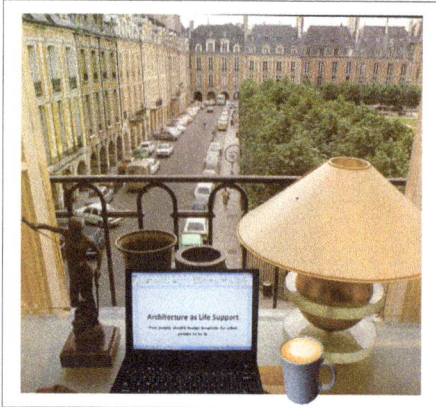

Figure 1. A nice view to inspire the writer of the book "Architecture as Life Support".

A recent visit was made to Basel Rehab hospital. Its architects, Herzog de Meuron, were Pritzker Prize winners. After meeting with clinicians, first-time healthcare architects Herzog & de Meuron prescribed "daylight, nature and space" – space to make it easier for the mostly wheelchair-confined patients to move around, and daylight and nature for their wellbeing. The five smaller within-care-area courtyards – outlined in blue in the plan, Figure 2 – imbue each care area with daylight and nature.

When the proposal for the design of a new ED for Nanaimo Regional General Hospital was accepted, a 'visioning session' was organized. The yellow rectangle shows the new ED in the master plan the architects were given to work with (Figure 4). Just like adding a big blob of clay to a sculpture, the new ED addition was to be globed-on to the existing hospital.

So when the first plans were sketched out, the memory of the beauty of those small courtyards at Basel Rehab was just

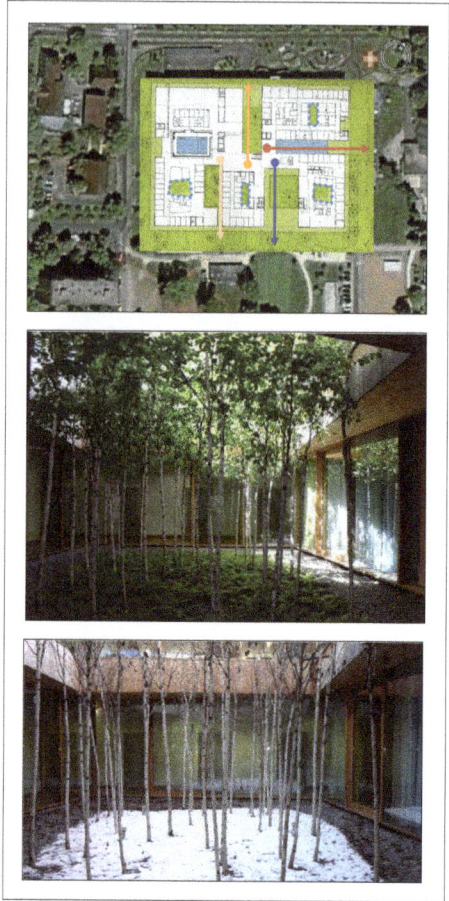

Figure 2.   Rehab, designed by Herzog & de Meuron.

Figure 3.   The concept of the small courtyards at Basel Rehab was incorporated in the new project.

Figure 4. Nanaimo Regional General Hospital, Nanaimo, BC.

Figure 5. Two sketch-up views of an urgent/emergent care pod.

235

enough to prevent the architects filling in the space between the charting stations in the urgent/emergent care pods at Nanaimo's new ED with clean and soiled equipment rooms. Instead a green courtyard was scribbled in for discussion. The architects decided to see where the idea would go.

These two sketch-up views of an urgent/emergent care pod were prepared for the first user-group meetings (Figure 5). They show the clinician's view from one of the charting stations on the left and a patient's view from one of the treatment spaces on the right. It took the users about two minutes to say they wanted the courtyards. When the cost/benefit of the courtyards was being reviewed, the ED doctors would later on in the process write a letter to VIHA saying that they would not accept a plan without them.

Figure 6. Image of the urgent/emergent care pod built in the new Nanaimo ED.

Figure 7. Acoustic wallboard and wood ceilings, radiant heating and cooling panels.

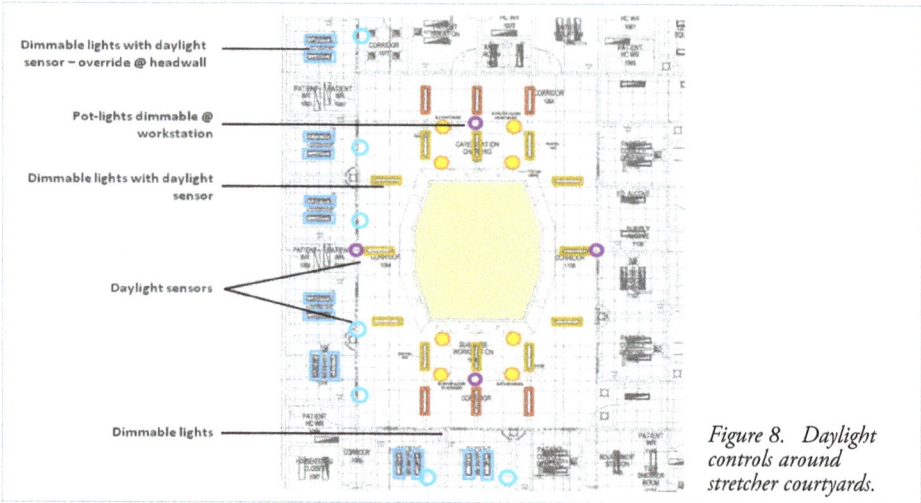

Dimmable lights with daylight sensor – override @ headwall

Pot-lights dimmable @ workstation

Dimmable lights with daylight sensor

Daylight sensors

Dimmable lights

Figure 8. Daylight controls around stretcher courtyards.

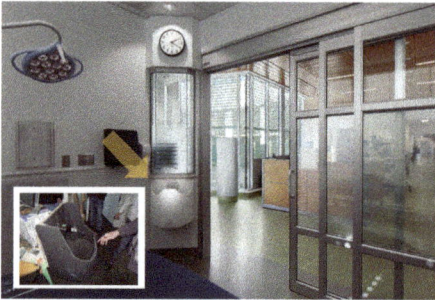

Figure 9. Hand wash: custom hand-wash sinks.

Figure 10. Plan.

NATURE

In time, the little trees at the bottom of the courtyards will become big trees, diffusing daylight and providing a nature view for the staff working and the patients in care around them. Lanarc, the landscape architects, put a section of a 'nurse log' from the forest at the bottom of one of the courtyards. The log provides life support for countless species.

Figure 11. Nature in the courtyards.

AMBULATORY

This is the ambulatory or streaming courtyard. 80% of the patients who come to the ED are treated in this area, which is right beside the triage/registration desk. The patients cycle, sometimes several times, between the waiting areas – either the red or the blue – and the exam or treatment rooms. The care station overlooks the courtyard as well. Phlebotomy and the X-ray room are close at hand. Making the layout efficient for care is another – if slightly lesser – form of life support for clinicians.

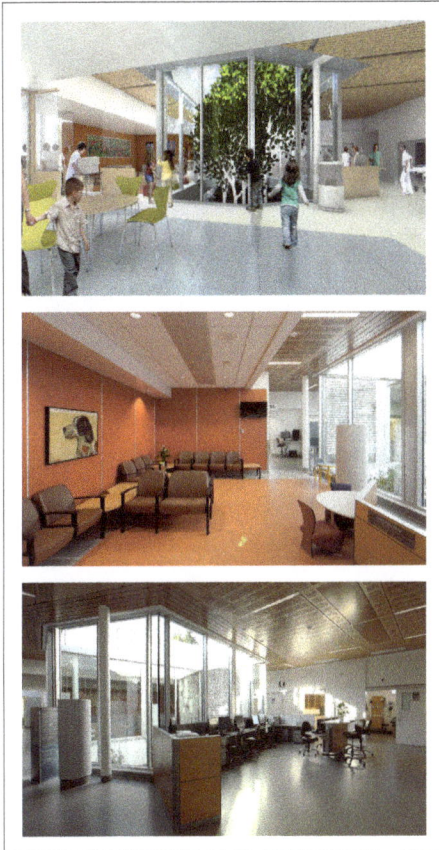

Figure 13. Ergonomic triage desk.

237

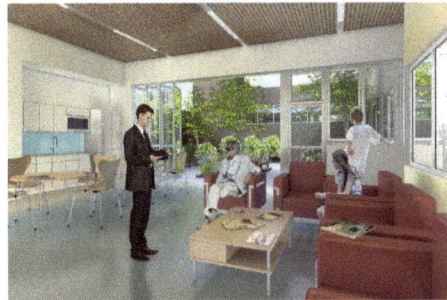

Figure 14. Psychiatric emergency services zone.

Figure 15. Psychiatric emergency treatment courtyard.

Figure 12. Ambulatory.

This is the psychiatric emergency treatment courtyard (Figure 15). In good weather it acts as an extension of the large patient treatment lounge by sliding open a glass panel wall. The wall was open most of the month of October and into November apparently. This picture was taken before the courtyard furniture had arrived. The users and project manager were incredibly dedicated to this project and its innovations are a direct result of their engagement.

TESIS Inter-University Research Centre "Systems and Technologies for Social and Healthcare Facilities"
University of Florence, Italy

TESIS

238

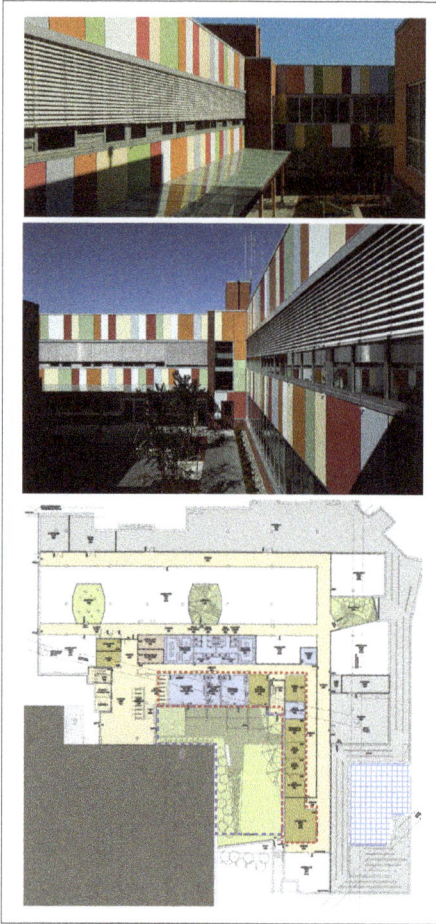

Figure 16. The L-shaped staff courtyard.

Figure 16 shows the L-shaped staff court-yard that opens off the lower level clinician offices, lounges and education spaces. More offices and the corridor that connects the ED to the rest of the hospital overlook it from the second floor. You can see the exterior solar shades deployed in the two top photos. The staff courtyard is situated in the space between the old hospital and the addition that would not have been there if the ED had been slapped onto the old hospital like wet clay.

The Nanaimo ED was budgeted at the high end of the market and bid at the low end of the market. So, thanks to the global financial crisis, it was on-budget. It has everything that is normally found in a modern ED, and in addition it has things that modern EDs do not have: lots of daylight, e-glass sliding doors in urgent/emergent care, perforated wood ceilings around the courtyards, lighting controls, automatic exterior solar shading that allows the displacement ventilation system to work, a thermal labyrinth and super quiet air handling units. Architects would rather not wait for the next GFC to get a chance to design life supporting healthcare buildings.

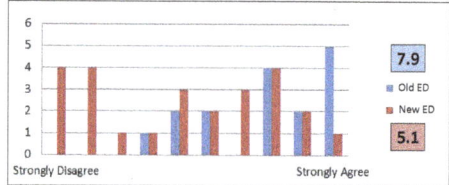

Figure 17. POE: The layout generates many opportunities for face-to-face communication between caregivers.

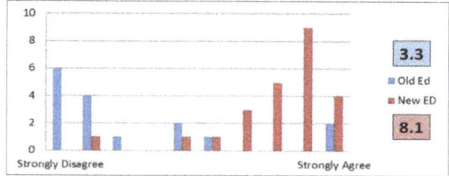

Figure 18. POE: The interior is very comfortable most of the time.

VISION

The NRGH Emergency Department is an open door to wellness and care: a place that cares for its community and a place where people want to work. The staff believes in, and honours the following values: empathy, respect, advocacy, excellence, enthusiasm, communication collaboration, initiative, integrity, leadership, diversity, and timeliness.

The Care Environment in Emergency Departments with Growing Requirements

Eggen H.[1]

h.eggen@ittenbrechbuehl.ch
[1] M.Sc. ETH SIA, Senior Partner, Itten + Brechbühl AG, Bern Switzerland

In Switzerland many of the very small hospitals have closed down in order to provide better healthcare services in fewer but larger units. Reaching the emergency department of the nearest hospital by helicopter is no longer a problem. The planning challenge of the continuous pursuit of better health, better healthcare and lower price per capita cost is a contradiction.
The design of a flexible layout for a continuously growing number of emergency cases, providing better services and almost more privacy for each patient is the present challenge for hospital architects. Are there any planning standards or new planning tools?

INTRODUCTION

Children and adults alike can become fascinated by ambulance or helicopter transportation in emergency situations, where everything is moving and changing. This aspect of change is also relevant for the whole healthcare system.

WHAT IS CHANGING IN THE SWISS HEALTHCARE SYSTEM?

Compared with Canada, Switzerland is a tiny country – only 450 x 220 km with 8 million inhabitants. The red dots indicate the healthcare facilities (Figure 1). As things stand, many of the very small hospitals have had to be closed or downgraded in order to provide better healthcare services in a smaller number of larger units.

The original Swiss population is not growing in number, but it is gradually becoming older and as a result emergency cases are becoming more complex. There are also more and more immigrants who get involved in accidents in our technical world. Both effects are the source of a growing number of emergency cases.

This paper will explain new emergency departments in a comparative study of a medium-sized regional centre and a large emergency department at the university hospital in the main city. The study starts with the medium-sized unit.

THE MEDIUM-SIZE REGIONAL CENTRE

The planning process with a local architect apparently took many years precisely because the number of emergency patients was growing at a rate of 3-5%

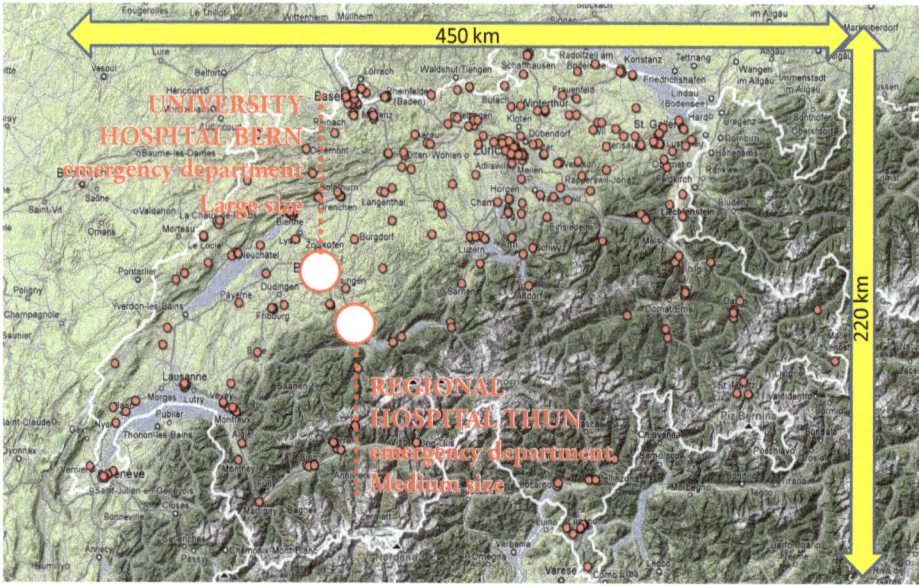

Figure 1. Switzerland's healthcare system.

per year and therefore the project had to be adapted again and again. One day the desperate hospital manager asked for the project to be finished disregarding all those questions, and for the new emergency unit to be built and ready for operation within half a year.

To achieve this, a new volume 3 times as big as originally planned was introduced to fill the gap on the site on several levels, placing the emergency department on the ground floor and leaving the other levels empty. During construction the existing facility was connected to the X-ray department, surgical units and the intensive care unit which had to continue to operate normally. It became obvious that this hospital had further requirements, not only concerning the emergency department but also the surgical department which intended to use the left over area. There were even more requests from third parties.

The foregoing provides a brief history of the project.

Figure 2. Regional Emergency Department, hospital in Thun, before construction.

Figure 3. Regional Emergency Department, hospital in Thun, construction completed.

THE FUNCTIONING OF AN EMERGENCY DEPARTMENT

The following explains how the medium-sized emergency department functions in relation to the adjacent OP department located on the same level, as a horizontal concept.

A distinction is made between minor and major cases. Patients with minor problems arrive at the main gate, sometimes just walking in by themselves. They can be treated in one of the two cubicles near the main entrance.

Major cases normally arrive by ambulance, or by helicopter landing on top of the hospital roof. There are 19 individual treatment rooms for these patients.

Figure 6 shows a view of the nursing centre for the major cases.

The planning challenge for the architects was to support the quality of the services with a flexible layout providing even more privacy by using single cubicles only.

In real life-saving situations patients are delivered directly to the shock room, which is the best equipped therapy room with a direct link to an adjacent CT scanner. Figure 7 shows a view of the shock room. There are two, more specialised X-ray machines available next door. Clearly offices and staff rooms are also available. Rooms for minor surgery

241

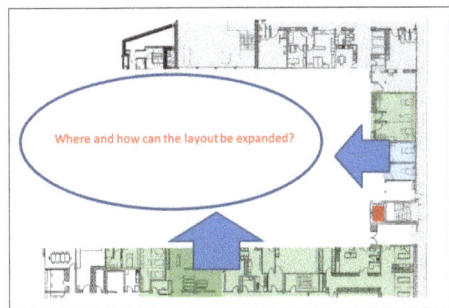

Where and how can the layout be expanded?

Figure 4. Design issues relating to the new requirements.

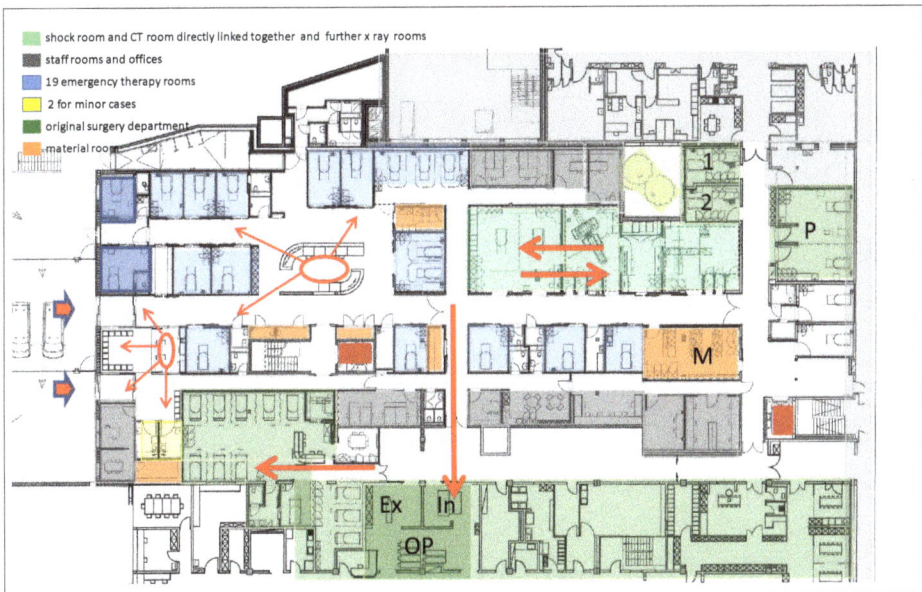

shock room and CT room directly linked together and further x ray rooms
staff rooms and offices
19 emergency therapy rooms
2 for minor cases
original surgery department
material room

Figure 5. The functioning of an emergency department.

TESIS Inter-University Research Centre "Systems and Technologies for Social and Healthcare Facilities" University of Florence, Italy

include the plaster room and additional treatment areas with the corresponding material rooms.

The emergency department must, however, also be ready for the major cases, and it was therefore placed directly adjacent to the surgery department. The procedure for such a patient is as follows: patients received in the shock room who have been moved over to the CT scanner and back can immediately be taken to the operating theatre. Once the surgery is over they are taken to the waking-up zone which has been extended, but it is still connected to the original surgery department.

All together, a horizontal concept with the shortest possible walking distances can help to reduce the number of staff required, which can be seen in the comparison at the end.

242

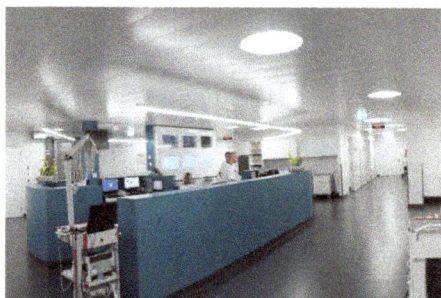

Figure 6. The nursing centre.

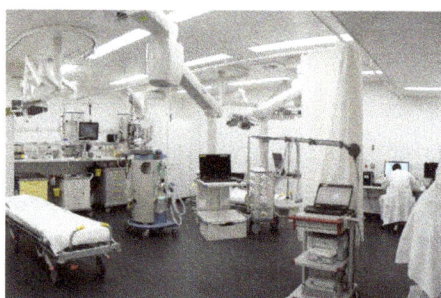

Figure 7. Shock room.

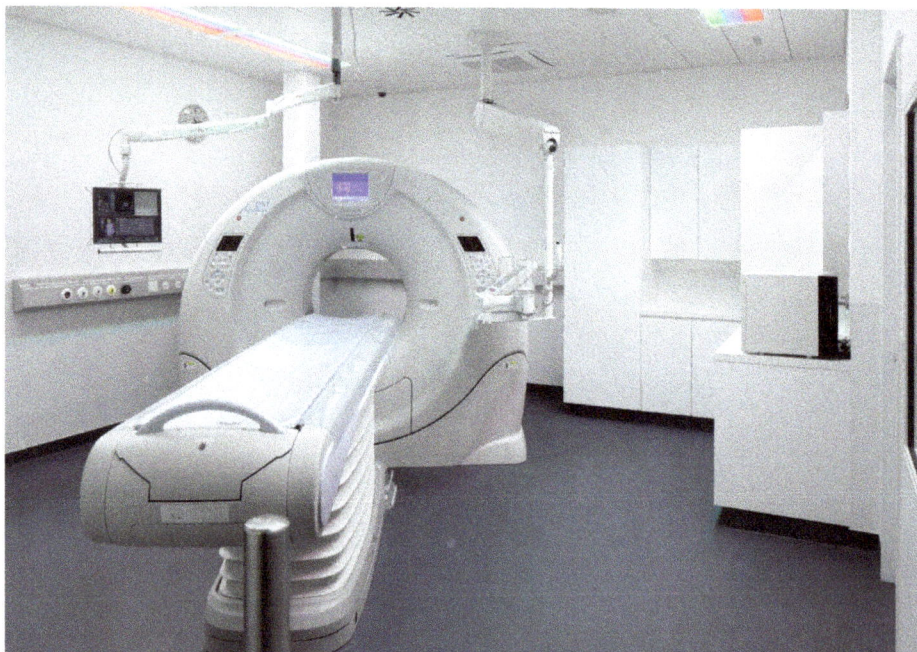

Figure 8. The CT scanner is directly adjacent to the shock room.

A FIRST COMPARISON

In order to produce a comparison between this regional emergency centre and the university emergency department it is useful to examine the layouts of both facilities at the same scale.

– The regional centre in Thun covers 1747 m2 for 23,000 patients/year.
– The university hospital in Bern covers 3600 m2 for 35,000 patients/year.
The second example, however, has completely different dimensions in terms of emergency cases and medical technical capacities.

243

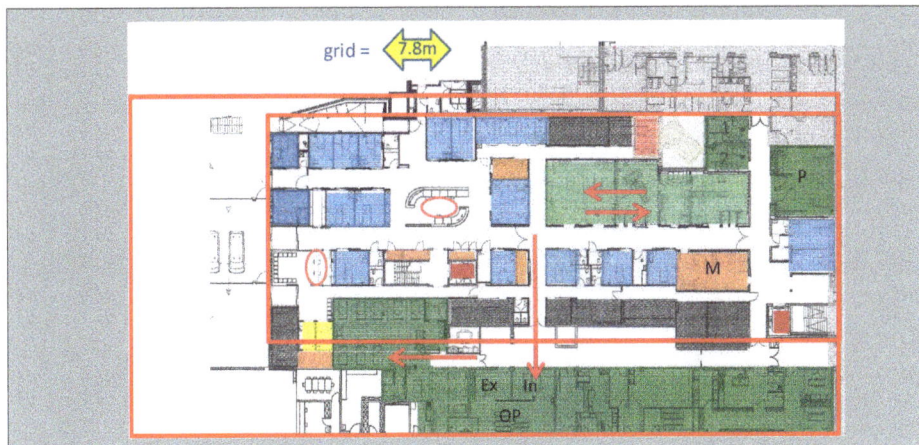

Figure 9. Regional Emergency Department, hospital in Thun.

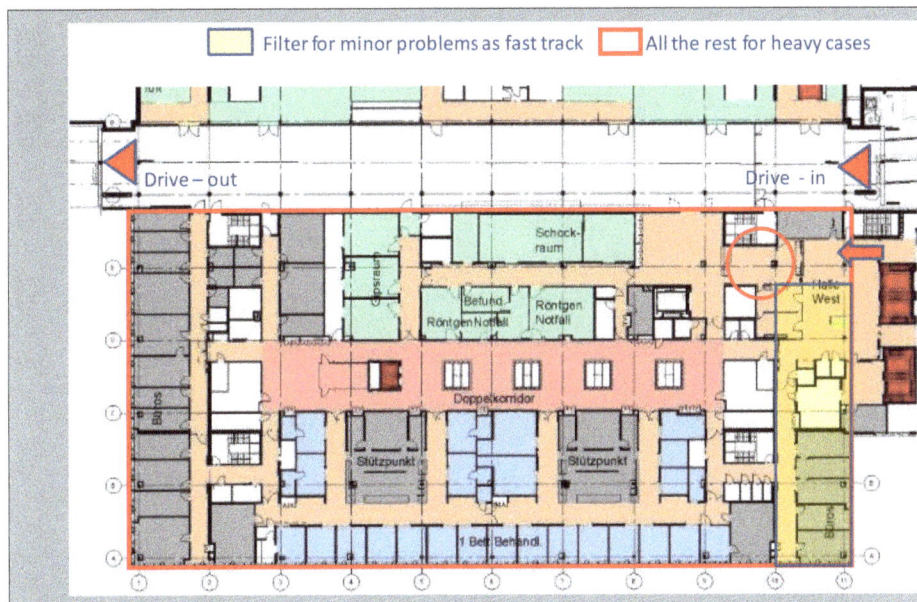

Figure 10. University Emergency Department, INO Bern.

TESIS Inter-University Research Centre "Systems and Technologies for Social and Healthcare Facilities"
University of Florence, Italy

TESIS

THE LARGE EMERGENCY DEPARTMENT OF THE UNIVERSITY HOSPITAL

The completely flexible emergency department of the University Hospital in Bern is built on a structural grid of 8.4 by 8.4 m; it was put into operation in 2012.

The ambulances drive in from one side of the building and leave from the other side. In the large unit it is especially important to make a clear distinction between the minor and major cases.

The "fast track" for patients with minor problems is accessed through the right-hand entrance. All the major cases re-quiring more complex procedures enter through a separate door. They are all controlled by the same check point.

Figure 11 gives an overall impression of the whole treatment building of the University Hospital put into operation in 2012; it shows the very first idea produced for this huge treatment block before the competition.

The cross section of the final project shows the drive-in drive-out tunnel for the ambulances with:
– the adjacent emergency department;
– the surgery department above;
– the intensive care unit even one floor above;
– the X-ray department below.

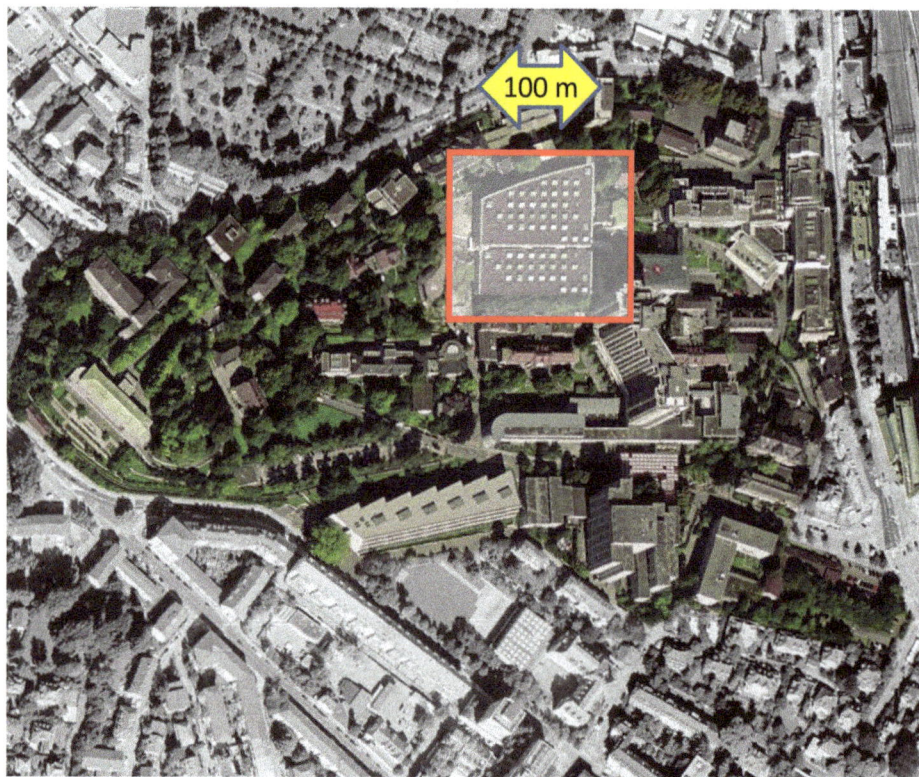

Figure 11. University emergency Department, INO Bern.

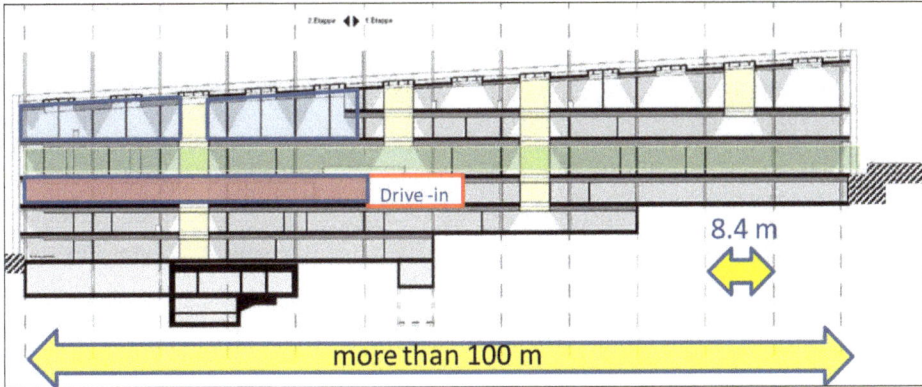

Figure 12. Emergency unit with the OP as a vertical concept, INO Bern.

245

All these departments are on separate levels but close to many other treatment areas, including the laboratory. This is a vertical concept.

Returning to the layout, patients in real life-saving situations are delivered directly to the shock rooms.

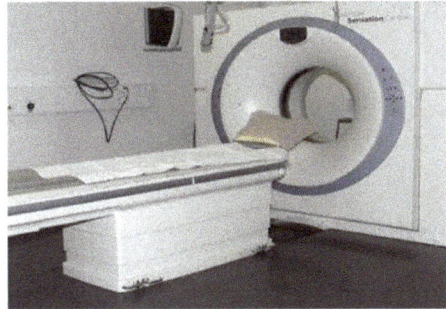

Figure 13. Emergency CT scanner, INO Bern.

There are also a number of adjacent X-ray facilities right in the heart of the emergency department, which are accessible at any time and even include two CT scanners. A new piece of equipment imported from South Africa is also worth noting. With a Lodox machine (developed for diamond quarries), a full body scan can be made within 2-3 minutes with an absolute minimum of X-ray exposure.

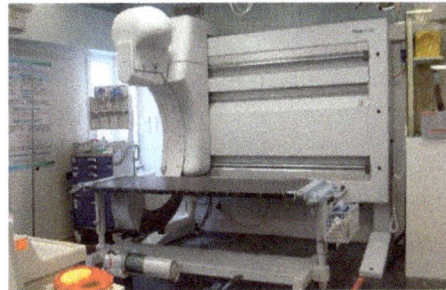

Figure 14. Lodox, INO Bern.

In other major cases, emergency patients are delivered to one of the 40 emergency treatment rooms. For this number of rooms, two separate nursing stations with ancillary rooms are required in order to reduce staff walking distances. Figure 15 shows one of the single treatment rooms.

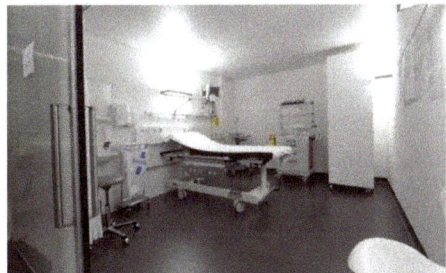

Figure 15. Therapy room, INO Bern.

Number of cases (Consultation)	NR of patients /year / day		facilities Number of treatment rooms		investment Number	total area m2	area/room average m2		staff		cost/year Nr of staff
Regional Hospital Thun											
"2011" old	17'800	49			11	600	54				
"2013" new	23'000	63			21	1747	83				11
University Hospital Bern											
"2011" old	31'107	85			25	1680	67				
"2012" new	35'000	96			40	3600	90				100

Figure 16. Comparison of emergency departments.

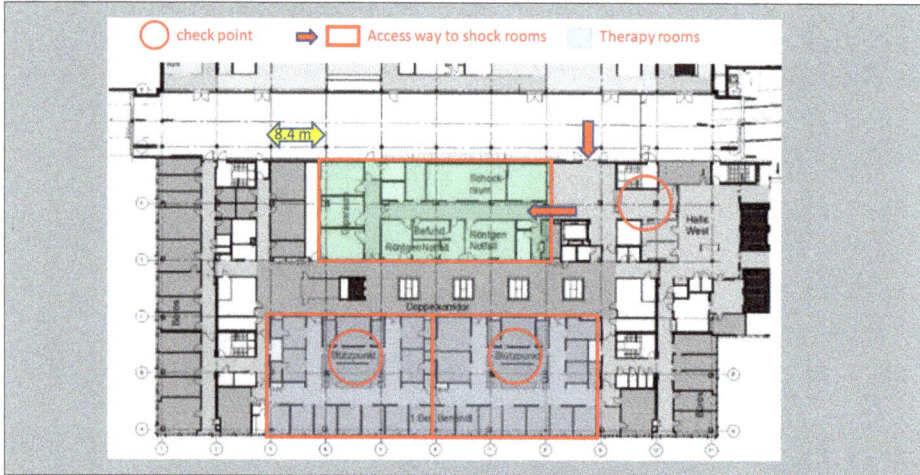

Figure 17. University Emergency Department, INO Bern: check point, access route to shock rooms, treatment rooms.

COMPARISON

The comparison of the two completely different emergency units shows that there is not such a big difference between the numbers of consultations per year, 23,000 versus 35,000. The number of treatment rooms, 21 versus 40, results in a difference in the floor area ratio of 1:2. The all-decisive criteria of quality in an emergency centre, however, is determined by the qualifications of the staff. That the difference of 1 to 10 would be so significant was surprising, and the impact on the operational costs can be imagined.

The next question is therefore: are there any new planning tools that take into consideration the realistic flow of emergency patients and can prove the precise number and qualifications of the staff required?

NEW PLANNING TOOL

Such planning tools have been developed, as we shall see without going into details. Figure 18 shows the same layout of the University Hospital in Bern, however presented in a more schematic way indicating the access from the ambulances and the entrance for patients arriving on foot through the "fast track" route.

It is important to use actual data. In order to obtain this basic data, during one complete year the total number of patients and their medical cases were recorded minute by minute, including the staff involved; this was done for each room. This is the realistic basis from which the computer programme can se-

lect any of the days at random in order to produce a simulation of the patient flow and the staff required. The situation is of course different every day. This example represents a moment during the middle of the night. There is only one patient and one doctor in the triage room. Nobody is in the 3 shock rooms or the corresponding X-ray rooms etc.

WHAT IS A NORMAL SITUATION?

247

The vertical bar of this graph (Figure 19) indicates the number of patients and the horizontal bar indicates the days with 24 hours for each cycle. 50 patients present at one specific time can still represent a normal situation as indicated by the red line. If, however, more patients were to

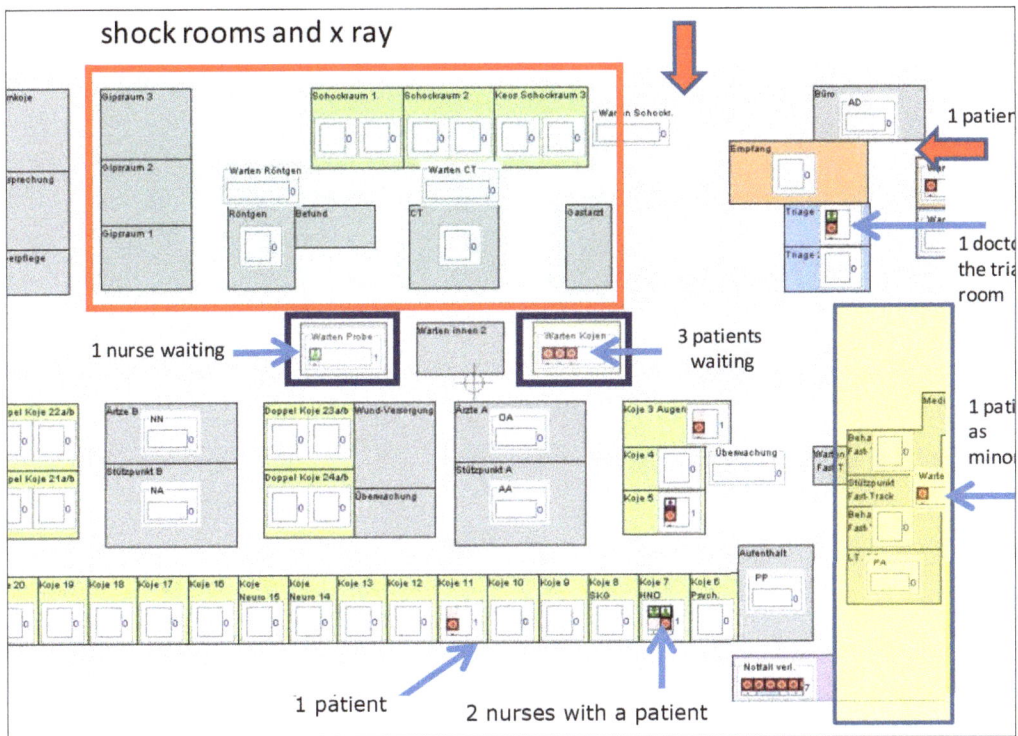

Figure 18. Actual moment in the middle of the night.

TESIS Inter-University Research Centre "Systems and Technologies for Social and Healthcare Facilities"
University of Florence, Italy

arrive, as indicated by the blue line, the waiting time would increase. An acceptable waiting time has to be defined. The university hospital has set a target of 5 minutes as an international standard.

VIDEO

The result for a specific question can be shown in a slow motion video, as well as in fast motion video presenting one complete week condensed into 1 minute.

One of the case studies assumes a situation where all the other hospitals in the city of Bern have closed down their services for patients with eye problems, and asks: What would happen at the University Hospital if approximately 4000 more patients with eye problems showed up? How many more staff would be needed and with which qualifications? The result is that one more nurse would be needed and for only half the time.

SUMMARY

To summarize, there is an enormous difference between the University Hospital and the Regional Centre, but in each unit the maximum effort is made to provide the best service. The criteria for architects are:

– The number of patients per day or per year;
– The number of treatment rooms;
– Fast track separation for minor cases;
– Maximum privacy and minimum waiting times;
– Many more further criteria.

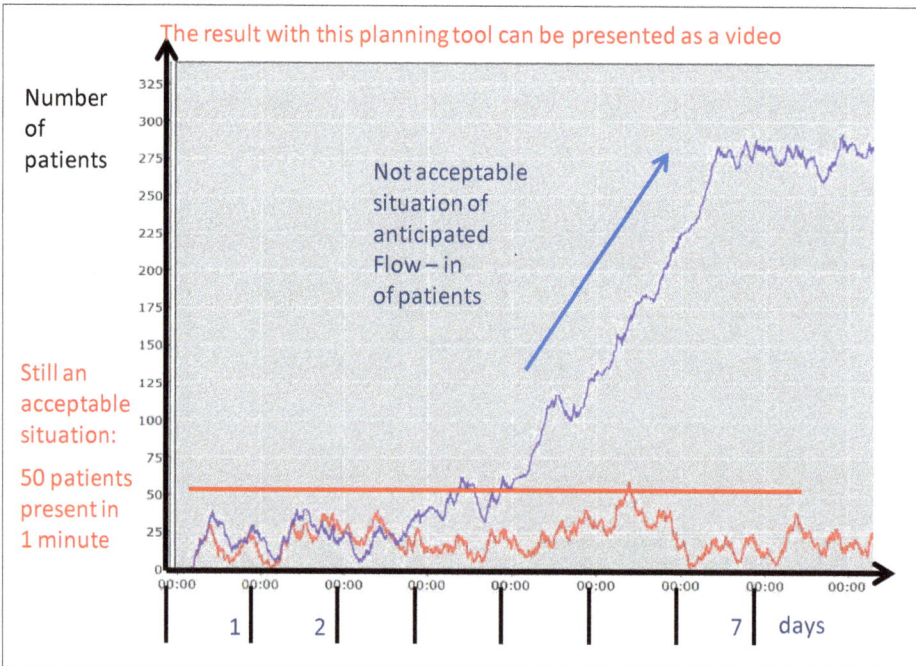

Figure 19. The vertical bar of the graph shows the number of patients and the horizontal bar shows the days with 24 hours for each cycle.

Vasconi Architects – A French Experience in Healthcare Design

Schinko T.[1]

schinko@claude-vasconi.fr
[1] Vasconi Associes Architectes, France

249

Vasconi Associates has over 30 years experience in healthcare design. A critical review of some recent projects, such as the New Civic Hospital Strasburg, the Civic Hospital in Valence, the Research Centre Neurospin C.E.A., and the New Hospital Princess Grace in Monaco, may help to find better ways of achieving an integrative design process for today's healthcare environments.

INTRODUCTION

The French healthcare system is recognized worldwide for its excellence and it was ranked 1st in the World Health Organization Report in 2000. No one was more surprised about this ranking than the French medical community itself, as numerous reports since 1987 had reported the alarming situation of the clinical system, culminating in an ambitious reform plan Hôpital 2007. The French Public (non-profit) Healthcare system manages more than 1000 healthcare institutions with over 300,000 beds and employs more than 750,000 people. These public hospitals mobilize more than 40% of the expenses of healthcare insurance. The private sector provides more than 170,000 beds with around 800 hospitals.

The management of public hospitals is organized by a multitude of councils: within the hospital compound we find the administrative council, the hospital director and the Commission Medical d'Etablissement (CME) – a council integrating the diverse chef de services. These councils and decision-makers come under the administrative supervision of national public authorities which interfere in practically every level of decision-making down to the appointment of medical physicians. These include the central administration, the Regional Hospital Agencies (ARH) and the Prefects, assisted by DRASS (Directions régionales de l'action sanitaire) and DDASS (Direction Départementale de l'Action Sanitaire). DHOS (Direction de l'Hospitalisation et de l'Organisation des Soins) oversees the recruitment and turnover of more than 32,000 medical physicians.

This organization partially explains why it takes nearly two years to recruit a medical physician for a hospital. The lack of clear leadership due to the split authority is one of the main reasons the hospital system has been slow to adapt to a fast changing healthcare environment.

The new demands for patient associations to actively participate in the system is certainly not helping to simplify the decision-making process as more and more people without specific knowledge want to be involved.

Another problem of the healthcare system was the accumulated deficits, which made it difficult for hospitals to acquire heavy medical equipment, such as MRI devices, so France found itself way behind countries like the United States and Germany. Another aspect is the obsolescence of building complexes with 85% of the buildings being more than 20 years old and 60% of the greater public hospitals (CHU) facing a refusal to exploit up to 25-75% of their floor spaces.

THE *HÔPITAL 2007* AND *HÔPITAL 2012* PLANS

In this situation the *Hôpital 2007* plan and the later version *Hôpital 2012* relaunched investments of over 25.5 billion euros in the building infrastructure.

The new activity-based pricing system *Tarification a l'activité* (T2A) requires hospitals to be aware of their expenses for treatments and to master and optimize their costs. The modernized governance of hospitals gives more authority to the directors and promotes cooperation between all institutions in order to provide the best services for patients.

New design, build and maintain concepts were legally explored in order to launch public-private partnership models as experienced with success in other European countries such as the United Kingdom.

The success of this program not only depends on the investment side, but also on the quality of the new hospitals, which should allow flexible use of the space so that services can easily be extended, shifted or reorganized. Nowadays the adaptability of a hospital is a crucial criteria for its success. The older monoblock structures of the 1970s are no longer suited to a quick changing environment able to deal with internal reorganizations and regular extensions, and where more and more medical and technical services have to be organized on the same level.

MONOSPACE – THE NEW TYPE OF NEO-MODERN HOSPITALS

A radical answer to the search for efficiency and adaptability is the idea of the "monospace" as developed by Brunet et Saunier Architecture. One of the most radical illustrations of this hospital monospace is their latest project in Marne la Vallée.

This huge 200 m x 100 m slab has 3 levels covering 72,000 sq m, with 600 wards based on a flexible homogeneous grid measuring 7.20 m x 7.20 m x 4.20 m allowing infinite combinations of how the different services are organized. "A chessboard of solids and voids in a perfect equilibrium," as the architects say. The building perfectly illustrates the merging of spaces related to the wards and the technical platform within a homogeneous monospace. All circulation areas have the same width and their ceiling heights vary from 2.70 m to 2.40 m. The fine equilibrium of voids within this slab provides sufficient daylight to 80% of the rooms. Of course a traditional façade composition is not compatible

Figure 1. Hospital in Marne La Vallée, Jossigny, by Brunet et Saunier Architecture.

251

with this idea of a neo-modern hospital, or as the architects state, "However, a kind of aesthetic must be provided and we have to deal with aging and pollution, as a hospital whose image is tarnished can lose its clients."

CLAUDE VASCONI – AN ARCHITECTURAL PRACTICE IN HEALTHCARE DESIGN

Claude Vasconi, the founder of Vasconi Architectes, over the years and through his architectural practice, developed some major convictions on the role a hospital should have in society today. As Claude saw architects as generalists, his firm was not specialized and architects got involved in all kinds of projects. Every hospital project is first treated as an architectural project. Therefore all projects are integrated into their greater urban context. Hospitals as public buildings can help to animate and structure their urban environment. A process-driven design approach should of course focus on the best functional layout and dimensions, but besides all technical constraints it should first of all consider the welcoming experience for patients and users by providing views, daylight and comfort. Another concern is to look for quality materials, reduce maintenance costs and achieve savings in energy consumption so

that the saved money can be spent on treatments. The most important lesson of the practice is still, however, that you cannot design a good hospital without involving and respecting the medical staff. By selecting three major projects of this firm from the last 3 decades the aim is to illustrate a French experience in hospital design.

These hospitals were the result of a close collaboration between the architects and the clients. All projects were the result of an exhaustive analysis of the processes and the integration of user needs in the layout. The initial program was only the point of departure of a journey to explore the real needs of the clients and how they can be translated into architecture. All three examples represent the very personal approach of the architectural firm based on the very beliefs of its founder Claude Vasconi.

Figure 2. Paul Brousse Hospital: French President François Mitterrand, Professor Bismuth and Claude Vasconi.

THE PAUL BROUSSE HOSPITAL IN VILLEJUIF, PARIS

Professor Bismuth is perhaps one of the most respected pioneers and experts in the hepatobiliary field and was the founder of the first French hepatic transplantation program with more than 2500 transplantations performed to date. With his charismatic personality and humanistic beliefs he was able to achieve an ambitious program within a very restricted and regulated public hospital environment. His hospital was one of the first to be partially financed by private funds, to integrate facilities and laboratories for INSERM research programs and to provide the facilities necessary for teaching and instructing young medical staff. Vasconi's winning project matched the ambitions of a new hospital design and it convinced the jury by concentrating the program into a 6-storey building, thereby freeing half the site for future extensions. In close coordination with Professor Bismuth, the project and the program were defined in accordance with his favorite quote: "If the quality of treatment remains the priority of caregivers, placing the patient in a welcoming and secure environment becomes a second priority. The quality of the welcome is the first stage of the treatment." Through a symphony of granite stone, aluminium and glass, this building, with its technical precision, reflects the high-end surgery practiced inside. The patient enters a generously glazed reception level providing views over a green park. The attenuated dark granite stones on the floor and the dark aluminium cladding create a serene atmosphere. Visitors enter through the alfresco ambiance of an Italian restaurant on the right-hand side and find a nicely integrated reception area on the left-hand side. The waiting area is situated in a day-lit gallery with green planter boxes.

Figure 3. View of main entrance: consultation rooms and operating theatres on the east side and hospital rooms on the west side, in accordance with the design principle for this hospital.

There is no suggestion of a hospital within these spaces, and as patients have to visit the facility on a regular basis this ambiance contributes to the general appreciation of the building by its users. While the ground floor houses the consultation rooms and day clinic, the basement provides space for the research laboratories. The first floor integrates the technical platform with 5 operating theatres and houses the intensive care unit and reanimation area. The second floor provides facilities for students such as the auditorium and meeting rooms and gives access to the viewing domes above the operating theatres, allowing students and surgeons to participate in the operations. The third and fourth levels provide space for the 72 wards, while the rooftop is used as a terrace with stunning views over the surrounding hospital grounds and represents surfaces for future extensions.

252

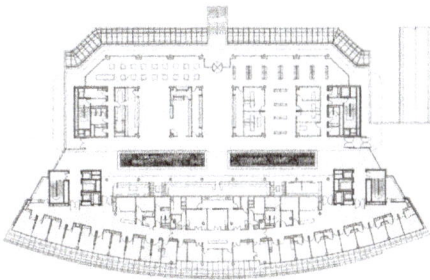

Figure 4. Ground floor plan: consultation rooms, restaurant and reception area.

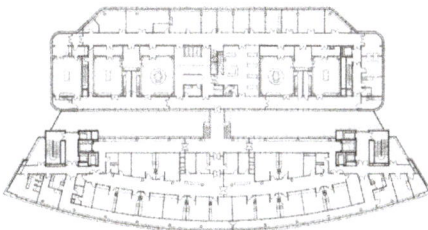

Figure 5. First floor: operating theatres and intensive care. Domes above the operating theatres allow trainee surgeons to observe operations.

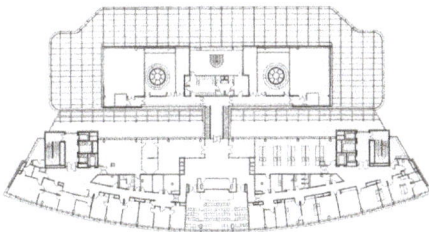

Figure 6. Second floor: pedagogical area with auditorium.

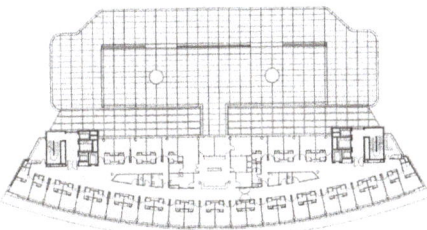

Figure 7. Third and fourth floors: the hospital rooms are centered around the nursing station.

NEW CIVIL HOSPITAL OF STRASBOURG

In the heart of the old city is a compound so vast that it has become a sort of city within the city, a preserved enclosure which constitutes a sort of museum of hospital architecture from the 15th century to the present day. In 1993 the firm won a competition for the new cardiopulmonary hospital to be built in the middle of this unique architectural heritage, and it would mark the hospital's transition into the 21st century. Experience had already been gained on how to create a hospital facility while minimizing its footprint. This way the hospital project only occupied a part of the site and left space for a future extension. On a vast rectangular area, bordered to the south by a magnificent tree-lined avenue which already existed, the structure rises four stories above the ground floor and is completed by a recessed fifth floor. This top floor, greatly set back, is reserved for the doctors' offices, administration and library. Flanked by a belvedere terrace, it offers a superb panoramic view over the old city with its gorgeous cathedral.

253

Figure 8. New Civil Hospital, Strasburg.

254

Profiting from the available space, an additional architectural contest was launched in 1995 for an extension and once again Vasconi's team were able to convince the jury with a compact and efficient design approach. Finally the hospital decided to ask the firm to merge the two buildings into a single project which was presented in 1999. The result is a densely compact building or, as Claude Vasconi said, "It was a question of gaining space, of playing on solids and voids, of light."

Figure 9. Master plan illustrating the fusion of the two stages into a single project.

Another charismatic personality influenced this design process with radical new ideas about how new technologies could be integrated into this hospital. Professor Jacques Marescaux founded IRCAD (Research Institute for Digestive Cancer) in 1994 with the objective to create less invasive surgery. In 2001 he succeeded with the Lindberg project: the first transatlantic long distance surgical operation performed by a robot. It involved a surgical team in New York operating on a patient in an operating theatre in Strasbourg using a Da-Vinci robot. Since 2004, the Anubis project has developed instruments and methods of performing transluminal surgery through natural orifices, exploring this way to minimize post-surgical trauma for patients.

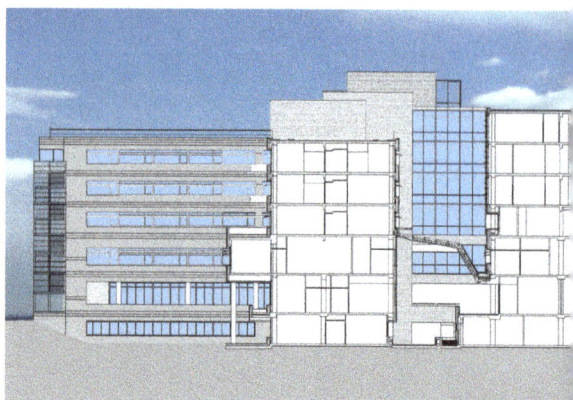

Figure 11. Section through the cardiopulmonary unit and the second stage with the general hospital.

Naturally, knowledge of these new, confident and successful modern technologies pushed the team to achieve an efficient layout while integrating the latest technologies: a "health machine," clearly marked by corridors, self-contained units, easily recognizable functions and carefully established hierarchical relations.

A large public gallery separates the aluminum-clad technical platform with operating theatres from the wards and interconnects all levels by panoramic elevators.

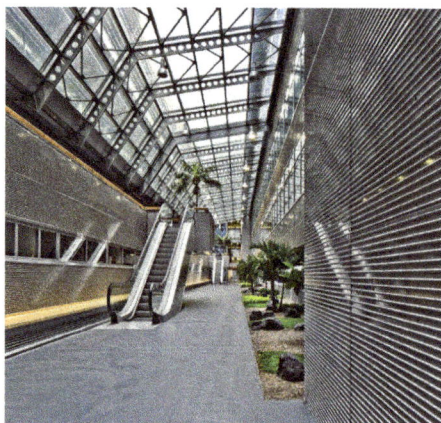

Figure 10. The five-level complex of the cardiopulmonary wing is constructed out of two buildings connected together by a central glass hallway allowing natural light to flood into the various interiors.

255

The basement houses the more logistical areas. Driven by a client pushing to integrate the newest technologies, the brief looked for an automated guided vehicles (AGV) system; it was one of the first to operate in France and is now standard in all major French hospitals. This level also houses the robotized pharmacy and the central sterilization unit. For treatment, the northern part houses the dialysis centre and the southern building houses the consultation level linked by several escalators to the light-flooded public gallery.

The ground floor hallway, entered from the east side, holds all the public facilities such as the waiting room, bank, cafeteria, florist, children's play area, press area, prayer hall and information desk, which transform it into a genuine public space with green linear gardens to provide a calm and relaxing atmosphere. The day-lit gallery enhances orientation and concentrates the essential horizontal and vertical circulation areas. The emergency station is located on the northwestern side, closely connected to the large imagery facilities. A nuclear medicine facility is situated next to the imagery facilities in the very centre of the building. Consultations are held in

the southern L-shaped buildings profiting from a view over the sunken gardens.

The first floor level is dominated by the medico-technical platform with 18 operating theatres dimensioned to integrate the latest imagery technologies and fit for robotized interventions. An ambulatory block, reanimation and intensive care units are situated around the central operating theatre block. On both sides of the operating theatres additional space is kept free for extensions to the technical platform.

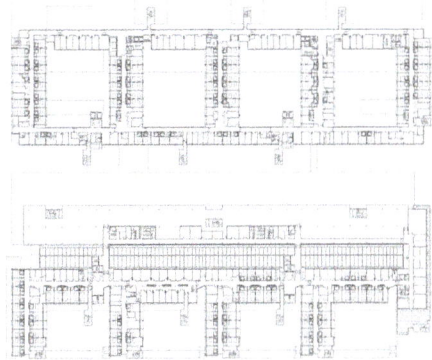

Figure 12. Levels 2 to 4 housing the wards in units of 24 rooms.

TESIS Inter-University Research Centre "Systems and Technologies for Social and Healthcare Facilities" University of Florence, Italy

TESIS

The upper floor has a total of 720 beds in flexible L-shaped units of 24 rooms.

Within the jumbled puzzle that makes up the Strasbourg hospital complex, the new hospital stands out as a piece of urban architecture – an orthogonal building wedged onto its plan with a 200 m long façade. While the hallways are generously glazed, the main construction of the wards facing south is clad in grey-bluish granite stone to interact with the old medical pavilions, preserving that reassuring sense of time.

The suspended surgery block on the west side, totally clad in aluminum, adopts a more industrial look, exalting the high-tech facilities of the new complex in contrast with the existing buildings.

Figure 13. View from the east above the main entrance on the technical platform of the first floor integrating laboratories and the operating block.

The building structure has been conceived to convey utmost simplicity in a context of seismic-proof structures. The only expressive steel structure is the cantilevered helicopter landing platform.

The hospital was inaugurated in 2009 by the French president after 6 years of construction. Together with the George Pompidou Hospital in Paris it was one of the biggest modern French hospitals and covers the greater regional area for acute cardiovascular treatments also requested by Germany and Switzerland.

THE PRINCESS GRACE HOSPITAL EXPERIENCE

The competition for the new Princess Grace Hospital was organized in two stages, and launched in 2006. The first stage involved the initial selection of five teams and then a further selection of two finalist projects. After an exhaustive second revision stage, the project was attributed to the Vasconi team in 2008.

In 2007 Claude Vasconi was diagnosed with cancer followed by surgical treatment. Some months later the cancer had spread to other organs. A race against time started as Claude Vasconi wanted the project to be irreversibly designed and adopted by the Monaco government.

With full sensitivity towards his projects and architectural creations he decided to keep his health condition confidential, wishing to keep his promise to bring this last and most important project of his career to construction.

Vasconi's design focuses on two key features: the quality of patient services in terms of accommodation, comfort and the efficiency of medical care, and how the project fits into the Monaco landscape. The building looks like a precious glass wave set dominantly into the rocky hills of Monaco. The uniqueness of the Monaco landscape and the difficulties posed by the small amount of buildable land available informed the design, which delicately breaks the huge volume of 90,000 sq m into two distinct elements: the glass wave volume of the wards levitating above an open belvedere and the solid block below with green planted façades integrated with the medical logistics parts. The hospital is built above the Avenue Pasteur and therefore had to integrate this main access road into the design.

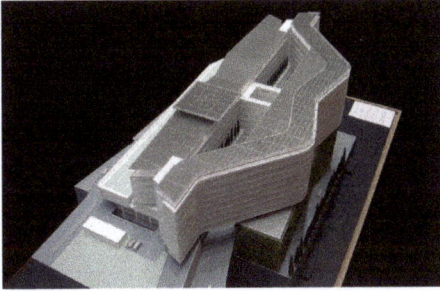

Figure 14. Model view from the west of the wave of the wards, backed by administration and the operating platform.

The compact design of a vertically organized healthcare facility aimed to liberate space for future extensions and additional programs for the hospital. The design was ambitious as it tried to integrate the best of the modern technologies in order to become an international showcase for healthcare design. The new facility integrates the maternity and psychiatric units, thereby freeing up space in the west wing occupied by the existing maternity and psychiatry buildings. This newly created free space could be used for a future extension of the hospital or handed over for the ambitious development of three mixed-use towers.

Figure 15. Master plan showing the hospital project, the future extensions on the newly freed-up area on the western border and the possible extension for integrated laboratories next to the belvedere on the southwestern side.

The strong demand for a healthcare facility of this size for research laboratories could be satisfied by an extension on the western wing of the logistics building. This way the program could be enriched with a complementary 5,200 sq m extension offering enough space for an integrated research laboratory and an additional teaching facility with classrooms and an auditorium. The program could thus be completed and the hospital could provide state-of-the-art services to the greater community.

While the glazed curve of the wards faces south and seems to gently embrace the bay of Monaco, the technical platform with the operating blocks faces the northern hillside, thus providing the best light conditions for these more technical rooms.

Figure 16. Section of the hospital indicating the canyon created by the Avenue Pasteur separating the wards from the administration building, which, in the lower levels, also integrates the technical operating platforms of the ambulatory and regular operating blocks.

For seismic reasons, the whole hospital is built on buffers as a "box-in-a-box" solution. This provides the best protection for the entire hospital facilities in the event of an earthquake.

The design also had to correspond to high sustainability standards, integrate renewable energies and minimize its environmental impact. The aim was to achieve a "factor 4": the hospital should use 4 times less energy than the existing hospital, i.e. an average of 100 KWh/m2a.

257

This could be achieved by cogeneration with biofuel, a cooling system based on a seawater exchanger and extensive use of photovoltaic and solar heat pipes. The cogeneration would deliver electrical energy and steam. The steam would be used for the laundry and sterilization units and provide the required temperatures for hot tap water and the heating circuit via heat exchanger. The wards and offices would be cooled and heated by reversible cooling ceilings in combination with minimal hygienic ventilation with heat recovery. By adopting this new energy concept, the project could considerably reduce the space for technical rooms by 50% as there was no need for cooling towers and the air treatment units could be considerably reduced. This meant the rooftop could be used as a roof terrace accessible to visitors and provide space for additional extensions of the wards or offices.

Right under the terrace, the eighth floor provides space for the "check-up level". This specific floor is designed for private clients, such as managers and celebrities, to follow medical treatments or analyses while having access to all the amenities of a high-end business hotel. This floor produces additional income for the hospital and provides access to expensive cutting-edge treatment and check-up facilities for the wider community.

The initial brief dimensioned the single-patient rooms within 18 sq m. After long discussions the client was convinced that with today's constraints of bigger beds, improved accessibility for the handicapped and obese people, and growing interventions and treatments in the patient-room, 22 sq m rooms were justified. All patient rooms have a sea view and a 1.5 m deep loggia that protects the rooms from direct southern sunlight with series of pivotable glass louvers. The rooms have a clear width of 3.42 m. There are two units per floor with 24 beds and a centralized nursing station. All staff offices, meeting and rest rooms have daylight and outside views.

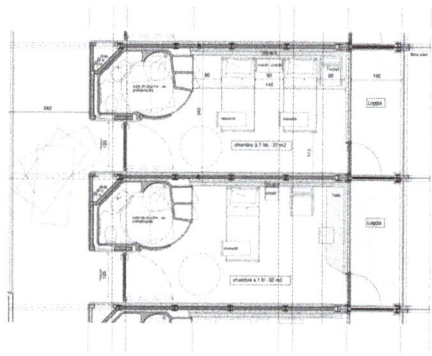

Figure 18. The patient room design was Claude Vasconi's greatest concern, as he himself followed harsh medical treatment as a patient and tried to integrate as much of the patient's vision as possible into the design process.

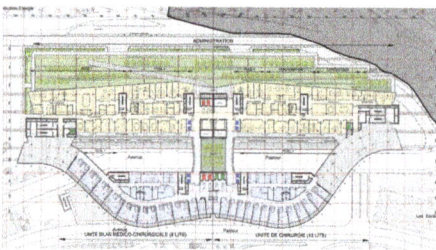

Figure 17. Level 8: "Check-up Level" with lateral free space for possible extensions.

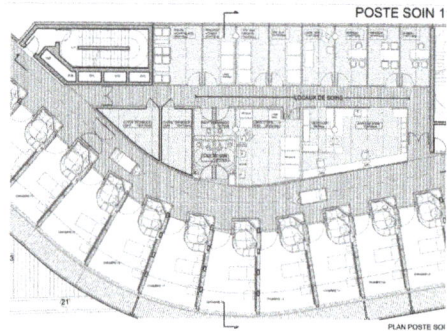

Figure 19. The patient rooms are arranged around a central nursing station.

The seventh floor has regular patient room units on the southern side which are linked via central bridged cores to the northern medical offices, with terraces as break out areas for the medical staff. The seventh and fifth floors house wards and the psychiatry hospital on the northern side with an access to the roof garden above the technical platform providing stunning views of the botanical garden.

On the third floor are the main operating block and the maternity unit with its consultation rooms, next to the dedicated obstetrics block.

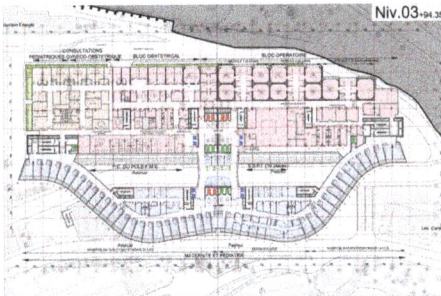

Figure 20. Level 3 with typical wards facing the seaside and the technical operating platform with the maternity unit to the north, linked together by a bridge.

The operating wing with 10 hybrid operating theatres includes two robotized operating theatres. The obstetrics block has an independent operating theatre and is directly connected to the main operating unit. The operating theatres were deeply influenced by Marescaux recommendations and aim for the highest technical standards. Claude, due to his own experience, wanted to soften the cold technological appearance and pushed the design team to fight the feeling of being in an enclosed space. The situation of the operating wing facing the northern hillside with the garden

made it possible to integrate huge panoramic windows offering natural daylight and views to the outside. This way the central anesthesia preparation area offers a panoramic view over the botanical garden and floods the circulation area between the operating theatres with daylight.

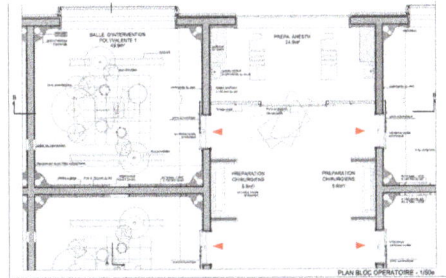

Figure 21. Level 3: operating room detail with panoramic windows and central anesthesia preparation area.

Most of the operating theatres also have panoramic windows that can be shaded if necessary. This way the operating block should create a calm and serene atmosphere. Patients awake from general anesthetic in a room with a nice relationship to the outside.

The second floor houses the surgical day hospital and a cardiology unit in the ward building and the ambulatory operating block with an annexed endoscopy unit, sharing the wake-up room.

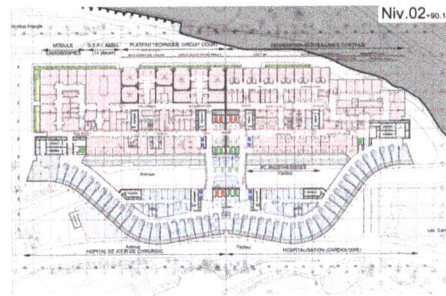

Figure 22. Level 2: ambulatory operating block with endoscopy unit and connected surgical day clinic.

259

The ambulatory block has 3 operating theatres similar to the operating theatres of the main block and two bigger operating theatres for interventional cardiology and radiology.

The first floor is dedicated to consultation services, connected via escalators to the longitudinal gallery that interconnects all access cores. The waiting areas are situated on a planted balcony overlooking the hallway and offer views over the bay of Monaco.

260

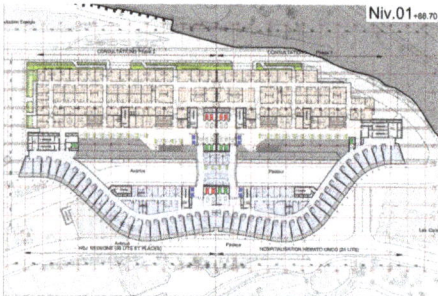

Figure 23. Consultations on Level-1 organized along the daylight-flooded visitor gallery.

The front building is home to a medical day hospital and the oncology unit. The consultation areas are organized around shared medical secretary spaces and provide flexible consultation rooms that can be freely attributed. Besides some equipped consultation rooms, such as those used for ophthalmological checkups, this allows greater flexibility and a better workflow for the consultation areas. The individual medical offices are situated on the seventh floor.

The ground floor is the main access floor; it integrates all kinds of public facilities and connects with the fully glazed and widely open belvedere, a space with restaurants and cafeterias offering stunning seaside views. This very animated and public space also integrates the central information, reception and admissions desk.

Figure 24. View into the visitor gallery linking the first floor consultation level with the interventional imagery level in basement level B-1. Emergency admissions are situated behind the gallery and directly accessible for ambulances from behind.

Accessible from the northern side road, the recessed area under the technical platform houses the emergency units integrating separated psychiatric and paediatric emergency admissions. The emergency unit houses a satellite of the imagery and radiology department for emergency use.

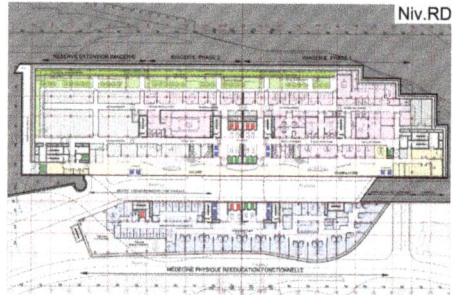

Figure 25. Basement B-1: interventional imagery/radiology.

Escalators in the main gallery provide access to the lower gallery level where outpatients can wait in the day-lit area of the glazed and slightly curved waiting areas, enjoying views of the outside. A long and deep sunken garden offers a nice view and provides enough daylight for the offices of the imagery and radiology departments in the basement level. In the west wing an open space is kept free allowing future extensions of the department. The green-planted basement building facing the seafront houses a two-level functional re-education and rehabilitation centre; it has 20 wards and therapy rooms, and on the level below a double-height gymnasium and balneotherapy facilities with huge panoramic windows overlooking the sea.

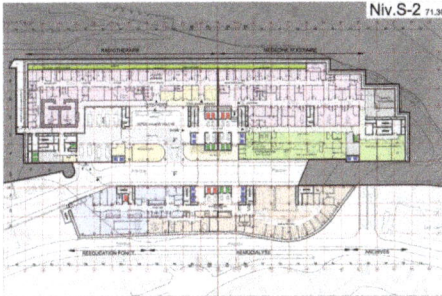

Figure 26. Basement B-2: nuclear medicine and radiotherapy with bunkers are accessible from the ambulance drop-off area. In the front building hemodialysis and balneotherapy profit from huge bay windows overlooking the sea.

On the B-2 level a hemodialysis department offers 24 therapy places and provides dedicated parking access from the level below. Separated by Avenue Pasteur, the building behind has a drop-off area for ambulances and taxis right in front of the radiotherapy facility with two bunkers and the nuclear medicine unit. A linear sunken garden on the north side provides daylight and views for the offices and waiting areas of these services. The sterilization unit along Avenue Pasteur also profits from daylight.

Level B-3 provides access to public parking, the dedicated hemodialysis drop-off area, and houses the cyclotron connected to the nuclear medicine department above accessible for outside facilities via the parking area and from the helicopter platform. The car park itself has 1100 parking spots on five levels, while

261

Figure 27. View of the belvedere level separating the wards from the logistical areas below. An animated space with cafés and restaurants.

the front building provides the logistical space for the internal laboratories, the robotized pharmacy and the robotized laundry, the central kitchen, facilities for the medical staff and the central stock area. All logistical parts are connected with an automated guided vehicle system with stations for every significant logistical facility and connected with specific elevators in the central core area.

262

CONCLUSIONS

Throughout the whole design development of his last and perhaps best project, Claude Vasconi was undergoing heavy surgical treatment and chemotherapy. It was his wish to see this hospital being built, as he gave his word to the visionary prime minister of Monaco. With remarkable charisma and all his energy he pushed this project for four years and dedicated his last days to making this dream come true. Unfortunately the time was not right for this hospital, as medical care has still not found its place as a real public building in our society. Hospitals are still too often considered to be infrastructural projects and clients rarely realize the changes in healthcare that can turn hospitals into public places where the community increasingly attempts to actively participate in order to develop better healthcare and better treatments by encouraging open debates in open public buildings.

In a world of growing chronic diseases, longer life expectations and incredible technological progress in medical treatments, the idea of the hospital as a place to keep illnesses away from the community has undergone a radical change.

Figure 28. Project of Princess Grace Hospital.

As of today, we are still quite far from Vasconi's vision of building the ideal hospital concept where patients can experience hospitality the same way they would upon entering a hotel.

Claude Vasconi passed away on December 8, 2009, followed three months later by his great supporter the Prime Minister of Monaco. In June 2010 the government of Monaco decided to abandon the project based on the economic situation.

Vasconi Architects by Thomas Schinko was founded in 2010 and took the initiative to continue to travel the given road towards new hospitals in numerous competitions. This approach sees the architecture firm actively involved in various projects for innovative hospital designs full of passion and dedication.

Drafting Meets Doctoring
An Architect's View of Health Design as Resident Physician

Anderson DC. [1]

dochitect@gmail.com
[1] Dr., Columbia University Medical Center/Department of Medicine, Resident Physician,
New York City, USA

The architect Louis Kahn said that "once challenged, the architect will find completely new shapes and means to produce the hospital, but he cannot know what the doctor knows." (Twombley, 1964, 184) Imagine the lessons learned if the architect could know what the doctor knows. Take an inside look at the hospital environment through the eyes of a dochitect, a hybrid professional in medicine and architecture. See health design from the perspective of an architect pursuing internal medicine residency training at a large New York City teaching hospital. A design journal was kept throughout the dochitect's medical internship to record functional annotations for each subspecialty space and their relation to form the urban hospital. Join the dochitect through core rotations including the medical intensive care unit, emergency department, cardiac care unit, outpatient clinics, infectious diseases, general medicine, and geriatrics. Case studies highlighting the importance of space design are presented. Design anecdotes and functional analysis of hospital departments emphasize the practical importance of design qualities that impact the work environment for staff and the healing environment for patients and families. The dochitect's practical knowledge of environmental design qualities promotes health and well-being within the hospital environment. The clinicians will find the design perspectives useful in providing insight into their daily workspace, empowering them to return to their facilities and promote changes or become involved in renovation or new construction projects; the designers will benefit from the medical perspective and the lessons learned from an architect working within various clinical environments. Personal anecdotes from patient case studies allow for a behind-the-scenes look and a practical understanding of the use of hospital space. The architect can know what the doctor knows.

Keywords: *hospital design, medical training, healing environment*

WHAT THE DOCTOR KNOWS

"Once challenged, the architect will find completely new shapes and means to produce the hospital, but he cannot know what the doctor knows." – Louis Kahn, architect, excerpt from his 1964 lecture 'Medicine in the Year 2000' (Twombley, 1964, 184). As a self-labeled *dochitect*[TM] I propose to bridge the gap between architecture and medicine through the field of healthcare design. Throughout

TESIS Inter-University Research Centre "Systems and Technologies for Social and Healthcare Facilities"
University of Florence, Italy

TESIS

264

my medical school years and now during my residency training I maintain two notebooks in my white coat pocket; one for the medical facts, a common finding amongst trainees, and the other for design notes and sketches. Through the following commentaries, I provide observations from these notes – the perspective of an architect now working as a resident physician.

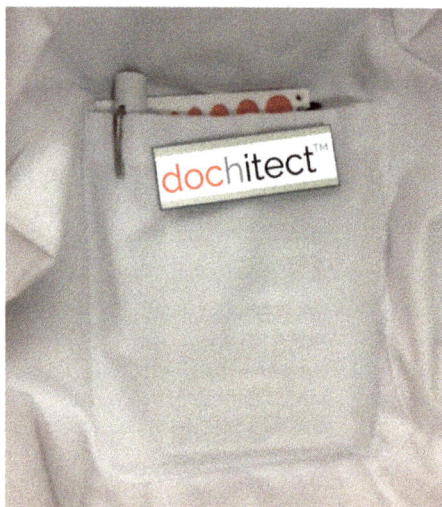

Figure 1. Dochitect™ as a hybrid model meant to bridge the gap between medicine and architecture. Photo: Diana Anderson.

The House Officer

When medical students in the United States and Canada graduate from a 4-year Doctor of Medicine program and earn their MD degree (after having completed an initial undergraduate degree), they go on to enter a medical residency for a minimum of three years, depending on their specialty of choice. At this level we are called Residents, our expertise designated by our Post Graduate Year of training (ie: PGY1, PGY2, and so on). The PGY1 year is also known as the infamous intern year, a tumultuous and dramatic time

which has been portrayed through multiple medical television dramas. We are also known as the "house staff" or "house officers", based on the original model where residents, initially male only, were forbidden from marrying during this period of training, most moving into the hospital and even having mail forwarded. They lived within the hospital in order to fulfill the duties of being "on-call" up to every second night for immediate availability for patient care. Today work hours have changed dramatically with restrictions on the number of on-call shifts and total hours per week an intern or resident can work. Life outside the hospital is emphasized and encouraged, but residency remains an intense physical and psychological period in the life of a doctor in-training, within both the hospital and ambulatory care settings. House officers remain at the forefront of care delivery and the use of healthcare space.

Internists have the advantage of working in many areas of the hospital campus while also interacting with the other medical specialties. A resident training in internal medicine gains a general understanding of adult medicine, not unlike an architect gaining a general understanding of all the aspects of the building process. Many trained internists choose to later pursue additional specialty training known as Fellowship, in an area of choice such as cardiology, gastroenterology, critical care medicine, etc. Paediatrics, psychiatry, neurology, anesthesiology and the surgical specialties including obstetrics and urology, are all separate residencies. However, as internists we often require expertise from these other fields with many acting as consultants to our patient cases.

Design as Treatment

During my first week of intern year I encountered a patient who would solidify for me the importance of design intervention. In my current hospital our critical care unit is racetrack in design, with one side of its patient rooms without windows. This anecdote centres around Ms. T, an 81-year-old woman with dementia. Although we administered fluids and pain medications, her heart rate continued to be elevated for a prolonged period of time. She had been in one of the windowless rooms for several days at which point it was suggested we move her to the other side of the unit, with views overlooking the river. Although there were a few looks of doubt between team members when this was formally mentioned on rounds, she was transferred that afternoon. I recall looking into her room later that day and seeing the distinct light of a summer sunset streaming through her window, noting that her cardiac monitor had stopped its incessant beeping as her heart rate normalized and she appeared calmer. We will never know the exact mechanism for this physiological change given that she was receiving numerous treatments in addition to the room change, but I believe the sunlight and river views had an impact. Although only a medical anecdote, these eventually lead to confirmation studies and change follows. This situation may not apply directly to institutions where private rooms are becoming the industry standard, but many existing facilities maintain shared rooms and may lack windows. This example is encouraging, not only incentivizing the day-lit hospital, but realizing the culture shift of the medical team in accepting the importance of environmental factors as part of the medical plan.

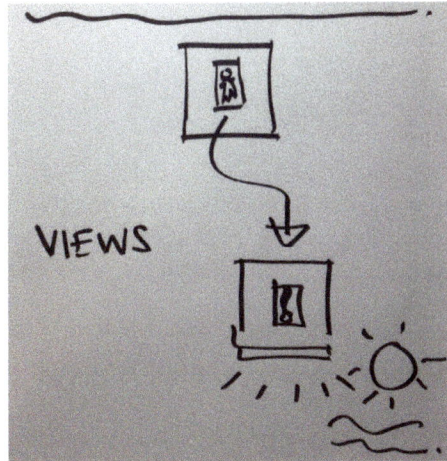

Figure 2. Schematic example of moving a patient to a room with a window and subsequent physiological changes observed. Sketch: Diana Anderson.

265

The Rotating Curriculum

The process of medical training is a time during which residents work day and night within the hospital, acting at the forefront of patient care and use of the built environment. Join me in my experiences as I rotate through the core medical specialties located within a tertiary academic healthcare campus, including the Coronary Care Unit (CCU), the Medical Intensive Care Unit (MICU), outpatient clinics, the Emergency Department (ED), and inpatient wards. The following commentaries explore the healthcare environment and provide readers with an understanding of working in the hospital with multidisciplinary staff, patients and families. Read case reports of patients who have been affected by design, the impact of design on my learning and practice as an intern, and gain an understanding of the structure of a typical work day (or night) for house staff. New work hour restrictions for training programs across the US (also being adopted by Canada) will also be explored, and the impact this has on staff workflow, medical practices and patient care.

Portraying stories of medical training and practice to those who are not clinicians, but who are involved in healthcare design and facility operation, promotes an increased understanding of clinical systems within the high-performance team approach to design. With medical experience enhanced by design perspective, perhaps the architect can know and share what the doctor knows.

NIGHT FLOAT

At night, the hospital environment changes. During the day there is a constant flutter of activity, noise levels are high and support staff are everywhere. At night an eerie silence blankets the building with a skeleton crew of staff wandering the halls until morning. No doctor can work constantly, so cross-coverage is essential. Night float is the product of reforms in medical education, limiting the number of hours that doctors in training, notably interns and residents, can work. Teaching hospitals have had to arrange more cross-coverage when the primary resident is off duty. The position of a resident who works the night shift, usually for a few weeks, was created. This allows other residents to sleep, but also promotes frequent patient handoffs, which can result in the transfer of inadequate information.

Limiting trainee work hours gained awareness with the death of a woman named Libby Zion at the emergency room of New York Hospital, after an intern and resident treating her responded slowly when she reacted adversely to a drug they gave her. Medical educators asked whether the young doctors had been more rested, would they have saved her. A special commission in 1987 proposed a number of changes in residency training in New York State. Residents were prohibited from working more than 24 hours at a time or more than 80 hours per week, averaged over four weeks. They got one day off a week. After much debate, 2003 saw similar changes throughout US residency programs (Lerner, 2009).

Demise of the Call Room?

It is interesting to consider this change in hours on our work culture and use of space. Recently in my hospital we developed a plan to renovate our resident lounge and provide a separate space for our white coats and personal belongings. A representative group from our administration came to assess the space and our proposed plans. They liked it, they said, but recommended we turn one of our neighboring overnight on-call rooms into our coat room – "with the new work hour restrictions, residents shouldn't need sleeping quarters anymore," one of the administrators remarked. If one has ever worked two weeks of night float in a row with shifts starting at 9 pm and ending approximately 12 hours later, they will endorse that a place to rest is still required. Ask any resident and they will tell you that working a 12-hour night shift is not the same as a 12-hour day shift. Especially with our constant switch back and forth between the day and night schedules which can cause extreme fatigue and destroy our circadian rhythms. Research into the new work hour system is underway with preliminary results suggesting interns and residents are no more rested and may even be more fatigued with this model, although it is still too early to know. With this conversion to the shift work model, I wonder whether on-call rooms will remain part of department programs or will we need to develop innovative spaces for short naps and additional forms of rest and rejuvenation?

Figure 3. Example of an overnight on-call room for resident physicians to rest if the opportunity arises. Photo: Diana Anderson.

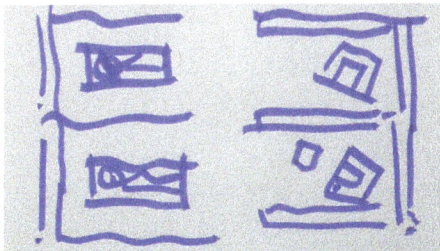

Figure 4. Schematic idea of the traditional physician on-call room with a bed (left); the design possibility for new, smaller spaces for shorter periods of rest using recliners or chairs (right). Sketch: Diana Anderson.

Night float raises a question about work limits for interns: Is it better to be cared for by a tired resident who knows the patient or a rested resident who does not? Many hospitals continue to rely on interns signing out verbally to each other, often at busy and noisy nurse stations, potentially inviting error.

The Bed Check

On night float we typically wake patients throughout our shift to perform necessary "bed checks" as signed out for us to do by the primary team. I carry paper lists of patients in the back pocket of my scrubs with varying instructions; "Lung check for Mr. R once overnight" my sheet will say. So, I enter the room at a point when I have a moment, usually in the deep hours of the night and turn on a light, waking Mr. R and placing my stethoscope on his lung fields to listen for any abnormal sounds. In my hospital many rooms are shared and as I reach for a light switch in the pitch black I often illuminate the whole room, waking my patient and their neighbour.

My sign-out sheet will often have written the dreaded "NTD" or "nothing to do", which is almost never true. On my last intern night float shift I went to see an elderly patient. He did not wake easily for me and could not tell me the year or his name. This was apparently not his baseline function, which I would know as the primary team but I was just the covering doctor. I proceeded to work him up for "altered mental status" taking time to rule out serious events – ordering a chest X-ray and blood work to rule out infection, assessing oxygen status and cardiac function to rule out a heart attack or stroke. Everything returned normal. The next day I learned that he had exhibited the same behavior two nights prior which I was not told. The diagnosis of exclusion was "sundowning", a psychological phenomenon associated with increased confusion and restlessness in patients with some form of dementia, occurring in the evening or while the sun is setting. The next morning the patient was sitting up in bed answer-

267

ing questions appropriately, unaware of overnight events. This case serves to illustrate the environmental night-time effect on patients and the perspective clinicians have at the time, the priority to rule out urgent and emergent issues while working with minimal information.

Arrest, STAT!

268

In addition to our admission and cross coverage duties, the night internal medicine residents form the "code team", the first responders to any cardiac or respiratory arrest called on the overhead loudspeakers. This yields a heightened sensitivity to sounds, almost like symptoms seen in post-traumatic stress disorder, as our hearts quicken and we begin to sweat at any overhead noise, always prepared to stop and run with the call of "Arrest, STAT!" Sometimes we run up or down numerous flights of stairs, or across the connector bridge to neighboring buildings on campus. When considering the hospital layout, wayfinding should be a forefront strategy in the overall design. Periodic views to the exterior, especially at the ends of long corridors, are important features in promoting orientation for both visitors and patients, and serve as a moment of respite for staff or as cues that we are running in the correct direction if going to an arrest. Interestingly, less than ten percent of wayfinding is associated with signage, while the remainder is attributed to architectural layout and building design. In addition to wayfinding, the hospital corridor has additional design potential as many clinical activities and social interactions occur here. At night these corridors can be our running track and wayfinding becomes even more important without the cue of daylight.

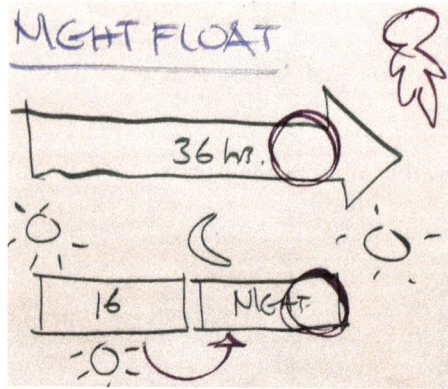

Figure 5. Is it better to be cared for by a tired resident who knows the patient or a rested resident who does not? Sketch: Diana Anderson.

The practice of medicine is changing with the new work hour restrictions. A doctor in training benefits from seeing a patient's illness through its course, in order to understand the dynamics of disease. However, frequent handoffs are now a reality and medical teams and institutions are still figuring out the best system to avoid errors and maximize learning. The way we use the hospital space will likely change with this new model, and may require novel planned spaces designated for handoffs to take place, areas for short rest breaks and ways of bed-checking patients without excessive noise and light during the night float hours.

Figure 6. At night the hospital atmosphere changes and night float residents arrive to take over from the day shift. Photo: Diana Anderson.

Figure 7. Frequent handoffs between clinical staff are now becoming the standard of care, and spaces designed for the accurate exchange of medical information are necessary. Sketch: Diana Anderson.

INTO THE TRENCHES

As incoming residents we are often told by seasoned clinicians that the training period of residency is akin to going to battle. We put on our uniform (in this case our scrubs) and go "into the trenches" (ie: the medical inpatient floors), told not to look back and focus on one task: surviving the training. It is a brutal period complete with sleep deprivation, physical demand, emotional stress and the need to confront human suffering and death on a daily basis. Many ask how we can work such long hours without breaks, but in truth with so much work and little access to natural light our sense of time becomes lost. Major activities on the floors are being on-call and performing bedside procedures.

The On-Call Shift

As an internal medicine intern, the bulk of our year is spent on the medicine inpatient floors. When we say we are "on-call" many outside of medicine consider this to mean we are home awaiting a call

from the hospital. This is not the case, except for "home call" which occurs later in the course of training, and in fact the call shifts are the most intense times. We are "in-house" or in the hospital for these shifts, occurring every third to fourth day of a monthly rotation. They involve a 16 hour shift for interns, but up to 24 hours for higher years in some settings with few, if any, breaks. During these shifts we take care of our list of patients already admitted but we also admit new patients to our service and often cross-cover patients from other teams if they have the day or night off. New admissions generally require leaving our existing patients upstairs on the floors and taking the often long trip to the Emergency Department (ED) to meet our new patients. We must interview and examine new patients, prepare for their admission by researching their case, place orders in the computer, run tests and determine a diagnosis to initiate treatment. This takes time and we have multiple new cases per shift. All the while our pager goes off for ongoing issues for patients upstairs and on-call becomes an exercise in multitasking while learning to triage given minimal information through a text page.

Because we admit several patients over the course of a shift and beds are not always available immediately, we care for patients who may be in the ED for some time. We make the trip back and forth between the ED and the floors numerous times per shift in order to eyeball our new patients and ensure they are not "looking more sick", as the clinical gestalt of recognizing a decline is what we are trying to master as junior doctors.

269

Call days are some of the more challenging times and require residents to travel to many parts of the hospital, including the ED, the laboratory, the blood bank and the imaging suites. Healthcare architects would no doubt benefit from shadowing clinicians or residents during a call shift in order to maximize these departmental adjacencies and the need to shorten certain walking distances.

270

Bedside Procedures

Working in the trenches often means the need to perform bedside procedures. In the realm of internal medicine, these generally involve removing fluid from a particular body cavity in order to provide symptomatic relief for the patient in addition to serving as a diagnostic tool by sending fluid to the laboratory for analysis. With our understanding of infection control, procedures are now taught using sterile techniques, but we frequently lack a surface to gown, glove and set up

in the necessary fashion and then easily access our tray of supplies. We frequently reach for the patient's bedside table, the only mobile and flexible surface we have, also used for patient belongings and food. Because of this lack of space, we generally tell the patient that we will use them as a surface once we have draped their body with a sterile cover. I have never found this to be ideal as patients can move suddenly thus tipping over supply trays and risking needle stick injuries for staff. The ideal room would provide a ledge, portable surface or even convertible nightstand that might provide some additional space. Proper overhead lighting within the room is essential, especially during the night when you cannot reply on daylight for added visibility. Patient rooms already provide a wall-mounted sharps container, although procedures are generally done from either side of the patient, yielding the need to walk around the room to dispose of dirty equipment, where an additional container would be helpful.

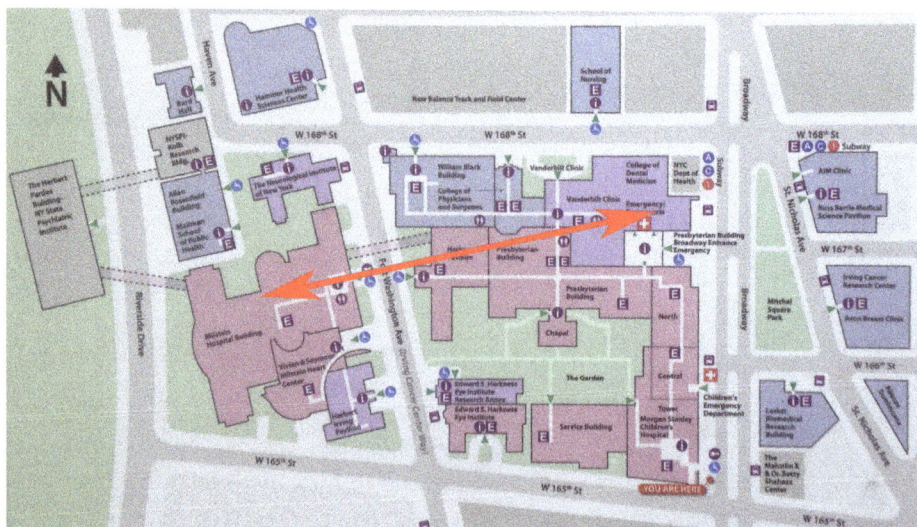

Figure 8. The Columbia University Medical Center campus in New York City illustrates the distance that can occur between inpatient units and the emergency department. Photo: Diana Anderson.

Places of Respite

Perhaps some of the more challenging aspects about being in the trenches are the lack of areas of respite for staff and the shortage of nature and daylight. In design workshops, the patient space is often considered the highest priority, while staff lounges and workrooms are frequently the last areas to be given natural light or situated along the building perimeter. I have often found this to be paradoxical when considering that patient length of stays are decreasing to only a few days, whereas staff will work in the same environment for years.

Critical care units are intense environments for staff and are generally designed in such a way to allow for direct visibility into each patient room from the central work station. Some critical care units allow for an enclosed area with comfortable seating, ambient lighting and music for staff to take a few moments and recharge during long shifts. Having worked in critical care units without this

type of space, I found myself retreating to the clean supply room as a place where I could disappear out of sight between ceiling-high supply shelving units and take a few moments to compose myself during overwhelming clinical moments. Awareness of the need for areas of respite for staff, especially within intensive care, should be included in the planning process and their importance cannot be minimized.

271

Figure 9. Bedside procedures can be challenging given medical equipment in the room and the lack of mobile surfaces for sterile supplies.
Sketch: Diana Anderson.

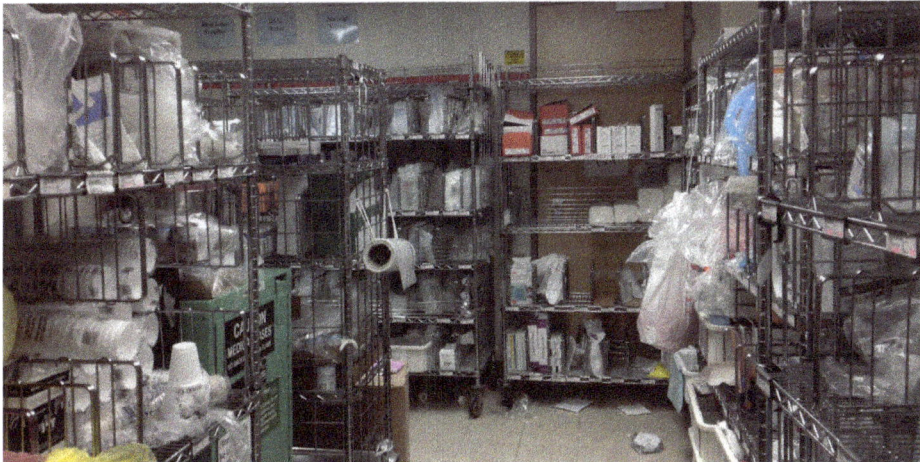

Figure 10. Clean utility supply rooms are often the only locations for staff to be able to gain some privacy for moments of reflection and composure during long shifts. Photo: Diana Anderson.

Design as Influencer of Change

Are there ways in which the design of the environment can soften the metaphor of the hospital as a battleground for trainees? Room layout to promote bedside procedure efficiency can reduce the potential for contamination and needle stick injury. Can better design encourage medical staff to take short breaks and be an influence in the model for behavioral change? Barriers to these moments of respite include individual and community beliefs about work, the operational demands of healthcare work itself, and the quality of the built environment in which that work is being performed.

There is a large window at the end of a corridor on the top floor of my hospital and I will take time to go there, especially after an overnight shift, just to see the sunrise over the city and reflect, leaving behind emotional and physical burdens of the shift. By providing light to staff areas, views to the exterior along wayfinding paths and areas of respite, the training experience can likely be made easier and more humanistic.

THE PROBLEM LIST

When my patients come to see me in the clinic, our structured template that populates within the electronic medical record begins with a "Problem List" for each patient. This is a summary of their medical history and can often provide me with a snapshot into that person's health status prior to seeing them that day. From this list, I can often tell how to prepare my room and if they will enter with assistive walking devices, be accompanied by their children or a home health aide requiring an extra chair, or require the services of an interpreter to help with language. Outpatient or ambulatory medicine requires a particular approach which differs from that of inpatient medicine. Time is often limited and clinics are high-traffic areas, so one must decide on a focus for the brief time period that is allotted. Our role is also to emphasize the importance of preventative m edicine to our patients and record a patient's compliance and maintenance with their screening tests such as flu shots, colonoscopies and cholesterol checks.

Figure 11. Outdoor views should be made accessible to clinical staff for moments of respite and reflection. Photo: Diana Anderson.

272

Design for the Clinical Encounter

As a doctor in-training, I have yet to develop comfort with my own style of interviewing patients in the clinic setting. Some physicians will begin an interview while seated and then ask additional questions during the physical exam, while others prefer to interview entirely during the exam and later chart their notes. I recently shadowed a senior physician in the chronic pain clinic. The room in this instance was set up with a central desk and computer for the provider which faced the door. On one side of the desk there were two chairs for the patient and a family member, set up to face the exam table across the room but not the desk, requiring patients to turn their heads ninety degrees to make eye contact with the physician. The large format computer screen appeared as a barrier to communication as the physician asked questions and typed as the patient answered, frequently looking at the screen or his keyboard. I, too, am guilty of this practice. I began my residency by taking hand-written notes, focusing on my patient, transcribing them at the end of the day, but then my patient list became longer and the time for charting shorter.

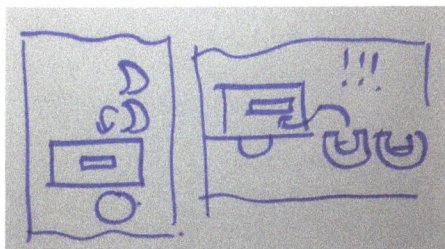

Figure 13. Example of a clinic room where access to the right-hand side of the patient is difficult given the placement of the examination table. Photo: Diana Anderson.

273

Another example from time spent in a dermatology clinic had patient chairs in line with the physician's seat to try and eliminate the computer screen as a barrier. However, this yielded challenges with patients also watching the monitor and noting medical terminology charted by the physician and feeling displeased with the choice of words, thus creating a new barrier to our tool of communication. Can the design of the clinic room encourage flexibility, efficiency, and patient experience? Successful exam rooms make work processes efficient, help alleviate anxiety for patients, and break down barriers through layout, encouraging patients to take greater ownership of their healthcare.

Multidisciplinary Spaces to Promote Collaboration

The physical design of the environment affects individual and organizational performance, including communication and interaction. Locating subspecialty clinics adjacent to one another to promote interdisciplinary collaboration through shared spaces is an area with potential for exploration.

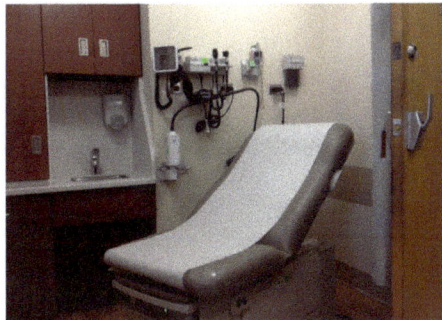

Figure 12. Schematic floor plan layouts of clinic rooms where patients may have difficulty making eye contact with the provider (left), or have visual access to the computer screen (right). Sketch: Diana Anderson.

It has been documented that 80% of scientific breakthroughs occur outside the laboratory environment in social settings (Jen, 2006). The Salk Institute for Biological Studies in La Jolla, California, designed in the 1960s by Louis Kahn, incorporates social spaces into a laboratory setting with the goal of fostering scientific creativity. The Institute was established by Dr. Jonas Salk, developer of the first polio vaccine. His goal was to establish an institute that would make it possible for scientists to work together in a collaborative environment. In planning the design, Kahn recognized the importance of informal and social spaces by separating them from the laboratory spaces. Salk's vision of collaboration can be applied to the hospital environment where design can foster crossing points, supporting the multidisciplinary model of patient care. This is especially relevant in the outpatient primary care setting which often requires input from specialists in addition to social workers, nurses, nutritionists and diabetes educators to provide comprehensive patient care.

In my current hospital we have public elevators, in addition to separate service elevators also used for patient transport. Because of wait times and the inability to discuss cases when inside the elevators, medical teams tend to use the egress stairs. As we walk up and down between floors we often have chance encounters with consultants. Clinicians will frequently stop and review perplexing cases and questions, engaging in real-time discussion rather than communicating through electronic chart notes. Most urban hospitals are vertically stacked with multiple elevator banks. The horizontal or "medical mall" design, although potentially increasing walking distances, also allows for impromptu meetings between multidisciplinary professionals and promotes beneficial face-to-face interactions. Egress stairs are required to be enclosed and usually stripped of any appealing design.

Figure 14. The Salk Institute's outdoor spaces provide chalkboards for scientists to leave their individual laboratories and write notes to be discussed with colleagues, thereby promoting discovery.
Photo: Diana Anderson.

I have often considered a hospital design proposal consisting of a grand open central stair, connecting at least the first few levels of commonly accessed spaces such as the cafeteria, phlebotomy lab and radiology centre. This design feature would promote physical activity and chance encounters between subspecialists, who could then retreat to planned alcoves for further discussion.

274

Breaking Care Barriers through Design

Patients and healthcare providers are beginning to think differently about how they use spaces and about how they want to receive care. The clinic should encourage communication and facilitate the physical examination of the patient at the level of the exam room layout. The ambulatory setting should promote communication between multidisciplinary team members through planned adjacencies, open stairs and strategic social spaces. With increasing emphasis on preventative medicine and minimally invasive surgical techniques, we will likely see a growth in ambulatory care facilities moving forward, helping us to address each patient's problem list and hopefully making it shorter.

Figure 15. An egress stair used by clinical teams on daily rounds to go between floors; staff frequently pause to discuss patient care plans with consultants who may be passing by. Photo: Diana Anderson.

275

CONCLUSIONS

Future trends in healthcare design will likely include the need for areas of respite for staff, supporting the need for short periods of rest given the changing practice of medicine to a shift-work model. In addition, increased time required for computer documentation and decreased time at the bedside with patients will likely have design implications; additional staff work areas and specific documentation zones will need to be planned, allowing for flexibility and acoustic privacy. Finally, with the increasing complexity of chronic illness and an aging population, inter-disciplinary teams are now necessary in caring for patients. This will require a shift from the traditional "M.D." or doctor's lounge to the need for multidisciplinary (MD) spaces where teams can meet and discuss complex patient care plans.

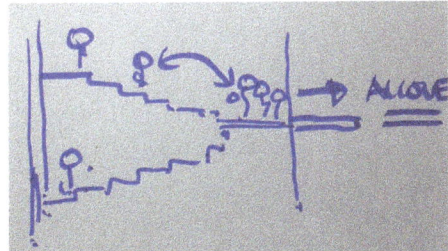

Figure 16. Schematic section of an open staircase design with landings large enough for teams to pause while on rounds and alcoves where providers may retreat and discuss patient care plans. Sketch: Diana Anderson.

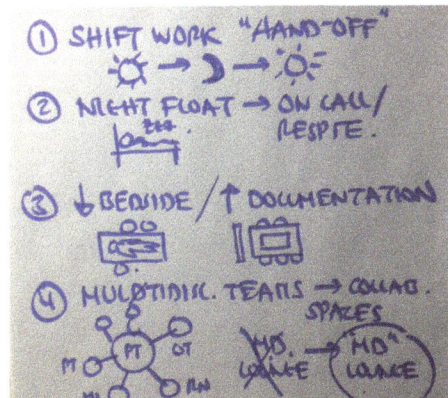

Figure 17. Schematic diagram illustrating predicted design trends for future clinical environments. Sketch: Diana Anderson.

REFERENCES

Jen, L. (2006). Genetic complement. *Canadian Architect,* 51: 28-33.

Lerner, B. H. (March 3, 2009). *A Life-Changing Case for Doctors in Training.* The New York Times.

Twombley, R. (ed.) (1964). Medicine in the Year 2000. *Louis Kahn: Essential Texts. New York,* NY: WW Northon & Co.

Hospital Design in Tropical Malaysia
Towards a Green Agenda

Mohd Nawawi N.[1], Sapian R.[1], Abdul Majid N. H.[1], Aripin S.[1]

norwina19@gmail.com, arazaks@iium.edu.my, hanita@iium.edu.my, srazali@iium.edu.my
[1]International Islamic University, Malaysia

"Sustainability" is a broad concept and a requirement in building designs that tend to be abused by trends and over commercialisation. In the area of hospital design, new is usually associated with being modern, and therefore green. In the quest to distinguish the "tree" from "the forest" with regard to the hundreds of existing hospitals, ranging from colonial to early independence up to the new hospital designs, a yardstick to measure those that are actually "green" and "sustainable" needs to be set. This study intends to provide a qualitative definition and recommended criteria for green hospital designs in the context of the tropical climate of Malaysia and its people. A qualitative approach using case studies of hospital designs from the pre-colonial period to the present day was used. The study includes aspects of the physical architecture that significantly affect health, i.e. the building configuration, form, spatial quality, materials used and culture. Findings indicate that the degree to which green factors are implemented in the different designs varies; intuitive and regulatory approaches to green considerations in the design were seen. The constraints where compromises must be made as a priority include site conditions, costs, construction time, planning time, expertise, experience and procurement methods. The significance of the findings will contribute to the qualitative criteria of the green requirement in healthcare buildings, especially for the tropical climate of Malaysia.

Keywords: tropical, hospital, design, green

INTRODUCTION

The term sustainability may give rise to a variety of understandings and perspectives, depending on the context in which it is used. Sustainability in architecture goes beyond the physical elements of walls, floors and façades; it has spiritual significance and its meaning derives from the continuity of the architecture of the place to the overall built heritage.

The main priority of sustainability for healthcare buildings and design is its ability to function, support operations, and efficiently serve the users, i.e. the patients, staff, relatives, visitors and equipment, around the clock. Healthcare buildings have to be designed for hygiene and infection control, and ease of circulation; they must have adequate space and ventilation, and the capacity to function; and they must be safe and comfortable and provide a supportive healing environment.

In tropical countries like Malaysia, the natural location of hospitals has been idyllic locations such as the sea or hillsides, with windows that can be opened, high ceilings and wide *verandahs* all around (Figure 1).

278

Figure 1. The single-storey colonial hospital architecture of a tropical hospital in a garden. Source: Balik Pulau Hospital, Penang website.

These types of facilities still exist in most parts of the country. Although some have been replaced others are being re-used and are undergoing constant renovations, expansions and refurbishments to meet the current medical needs and demands. Hence the original design intentions of the tropical hospital situated amidst the greenery and fresh air were either ignored due to the pressing priority of functional adjacent spaces and circulation, or mismanaged during renovation work.

Each new wave of the structural planning of urban sites brings proposals for new land uses due to the commercial viability of the land for resorts, residential apartments or any other facility that would bring more economic resources to the city or town as part of its sustainability agenda. Hospitals, with their conflicting roles of centrality and isola-

tion, bringing multi-faceted supplies and disposal in huge quantities, layers of building services, ranges of technologies and energy consumption, contribute to the environmental issue. Hospitals are the second highest energy consumers on a per square foot basis after the food service industry.

Designing new healthcare facilities is not an easy task. Professional architects and health facility planners who plan and design hospitals, a daunting task in itself, need to add the green and sustainable facility to the matrix.

In light of these "movements" across the globe, Malaysia had formulated its own green index under the Malaysian Green Building Index (GBI) for residential, non-residential and industrial buildings to date. As Malaysia is located in the tropics, the GBI is formulated to consider the environmental and developmental context, and the cultural and social needs, specifically for the tropical climate. However, as the GBI for hospital buildings has yet to be formulated, the Malaysian healthcare service provider opted to adapt the foreign standards of LEED, BREAM, or, nearer to home, the Singapore Green Mark, into the building contract brief of requirements.

All hospital designs are subject to the Uniform Building Bylaws (UBBL) 1984. For health and safety purposes the UBBL incorporated the minimum requirements of passive design considerations for users. The design of private hospitals in Malaysia is also governed by the Private Healthcare and Services Act 1998 in addition to the UBBL. The UBBL, however, do not provide mandatory requirements on energy consumption or intangible sustainable issues relating to culture or the clinical procedures required in the holistic make up of a healthcare environment. Specialised buildings such as hospitals have specific design requirements put forward by knowledgeable clients or their advisors. The objectives of this paper are to:

• ascertain the meaning of "green" and "sustainability" in the design of hospital architecture in the tropical climate of Malaysia in view of its architectural sustainability and clinical functionality;

• provide direction for qualitative design guidelines as a rule of thumb in recognising good and practical green hospital designs, in view of the green agenda for hospitals in the tropics.

For the purpose of this paper the scope of the study involves:

• identifying available "green" and "sustainability" standards or criteria for hospital building design in the tropical climate of Malaysia;

• examining the physical and non-physical or humanistic development of selected hospital designs through case studies of hospitals built in Malaysia from the colonial period to the present.

The qualitative method adopted for the study involved data collection executed within a limited time frame. The process involved obtaining both primary and secondary data: primary data from observation, field visits to selected hospital facilities, random interviews with professionals (architects, engineers and green specialists) and clients, as well as personal experiences in the planning and design of hospitals; and secondary data from the content analysis of available literature covering the study of old and new photographs and previous field study notes.

The findings and analyses of the "green" and "sustainability" aspects of these hospitals were based on selected site location, building layout and configuration, built form, internal planning strategy or spatial quality, materials used and construction, as well as culture. The tangible and intangible green elements assessed included each facility's general orientation on site; each building structure's access to natural ventilation, views and daylight; layout or planning designating specific areas of the building for controlled conditions; internal space planning strategies for infection control; natural ventilation; access to views, daylight and family members inside and outside the clinical area; adequate human circulation and orientation; and respect for the local culture and context.

This paper intends to contribute aspects of qualitative considerations in the green planning and design of hospitals for the tropical climate of Malaysia.

ISSUES AND DISCUSSION

This paper discusses exemplar hospital architecture as a universal attribute focusing on the implication of it being located in the tropics. The issue was brought to the forefront with claims that new hospitals are designed with green and sustainable considerations, whereas past hospitals were not. The hypothesis is that these remarks were made without an understanding that the concept of green and sustainability for a hospital goes beyond the passive and active design attributes reflected in the performances of the physical structure and touches on those that embrace the clinical functionality and humane aspects of a healing environment.

279

Hospital Architecture in the Tropics

Each community, depending on where it is located, has different terms for its built facilities, built forms and ways of addressing the sick in accordance with its culture, belief systems and traditions. Asian cultures have not left much evidence behind with regard to hospitals or healthcare buildings, especially in the tropics, that can be studied or emulated. Built structures or shelters to house the sick, such as hospitals in their present-day form, hail from the Western and Middle Eastern evolution of houses of charity, churches, palaces and secular buildings for the sick or Bimaristan, as well as from the training of medical and health professions. Building typologies for hospitals in the tropics are relatively new. Even in the tropics, the early "pavilion plan" hospital design inadvertently came from the same source, i.e. 18th century France (Cook, 2002), so the design of hospital buildings is almost universal worldwide. So how can hospitals built in the tropics differ in order to be sustainable and effective?

Physically, as a shelter for the sick, Kleczkowski (1983) stated that the planning and design of hospitals should consider the local climate and the region's typical approach to architecture, i.e. by providing simple low rise buildings connected by corridors as shown in Figures 2 and 3; utilising local building materials and construction methods; designing to respect local customs and habits: ensuring affordable costs; guaranteeing reliability in terms of operation and maintenance; as well as serving the functions and users of the facility.

280

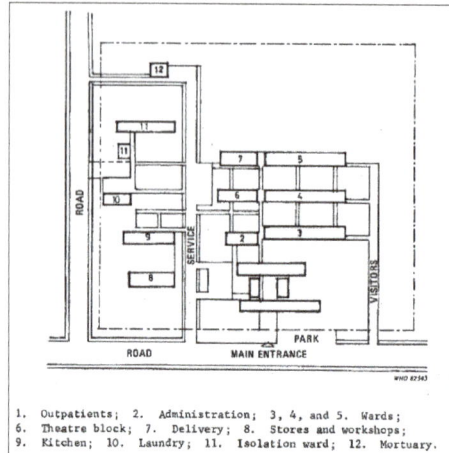

1. Outpatients; 2. Administration; 3, 4, and 5. Wards; 6. Theatre block; 7. Delivery; 8. Stores and workshops; 9. Kitchen; 10. Laundry; 11. Isolation ward; 12. Mortuary.

Figure 2. Typical hospital layout in tropical developing countries. Source: Kleczkowski, 1983.

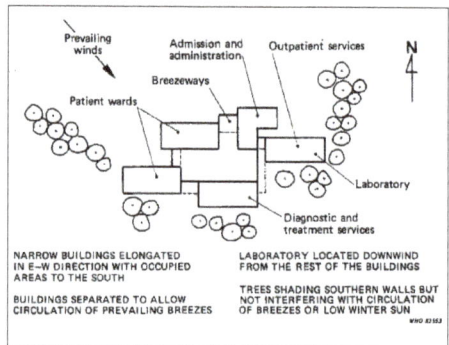

Figure 3. Typical hospital layout for countries with a hot humid climate. Source: Kleczkowski, 1983 .

WHO, following on from the study edited by Kleczkowski (1985), described the different implementation of "standard designs" and "type plans" through case studies of selected healthcare facilities in various countries by looking at their income levels. The study of acceptable internal micro-climates in the physical planning of hospitals in the selected countries, i.e. Venezuela, Cuba, Senegal, Sudan, Zambia and Algeria, all located within the tropics, showed that the design of most of the facilities allowed for artificial ventilation at essential areas with the majority orienting their buildings to capture the prevailing winds. However, most facilities in these countries, except for Cuba, had difficulty in maintaining acceptable levels of artificial ventilation or air conditioning in sensitive areas for several reasons, which included inadequate maintenance and locations within small courtyards that were too small and thus had less air circulation. The study also reveals the importance of site selection as a priority, in compliance with the prevailing local socio-cultural preferences in the making of the design.

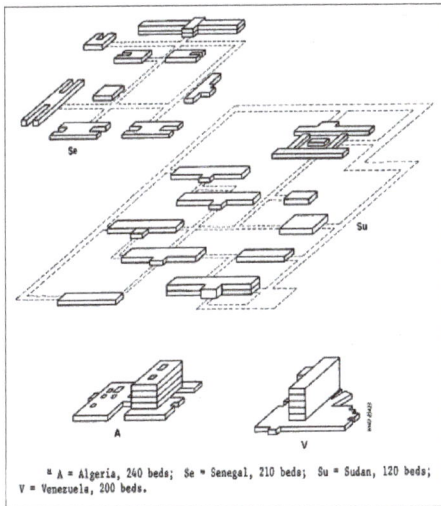

ª A = Algeria, 240 beds; Se = Senegal, 210 beds; Su = Sudan, 120 beds; V = Venezuela, 200 beds.

Figure 4. Comparative evaluation of design efficiency – horizontal and vertical. Source: Kleczkowski, 1991.

The discussion on construction methods and the use of building materials in hot-humid countries highlighted the following issues:

• durability and strength of the building materials used in extreme weather conditions of heat, rain and flooding;
• workmanship due to unskilled labour;

• maintenance culture and skills aside from the passive design discussed earlier;
• availability of constant supplies of water, electricity;
• waste treatment.

Findings by Ziqi Wu (2011) showed that improving the performance of thermal comfort through design sophistication, as found in recently completed hospital buildings, did not necessarily achieve the desired outcomes with respect to simple hospital designs.

In summary, the utilitarian architecture of past hospital designs addressed both functional aspects as well as climatic considerations so as to ensure less maintenance. Today, hospitals are generally designed independently by different architects for different service providers with different philosophies. Hence, present-day hospital designs are not uniform. Old hospitals may not be sustainable or comply with the new requirements of healthcare buildings, but whether the new hospital buildings are sustainable or green, as claimed, has yet to be evaluated.

Hospital Design: Towards a Green Agenda

The hospital represents a building typology with ever conflicting attributes in one cauldron; for those with a green agenda, issues of "architectural sustainability versus clinical functionality" arise.
Definition of Sustainability in the Hospital Context: Architectural Functionality
Sustainability, as defined by Verderber (2010), involves more than the ecological or economic context. It is

281

a holistic approach that incorporates supply-demand tensions, priorities over limited resources such as clean air and water, a livable climate, a healthy standard of living, the community, spiritual and psychological health, meaningful work, intellectual openness, individual and social empowerment, a sense of heritage and history, cultural diversity, art, music, and everyday life.

Yeang (2012) informed designers not to mistake green design as simply focusing on eco-engineering systems and the use of rating systems, although these are an important part of the process and serve as a generic checklist for green design. In the context of designing a hospital, Yeang's principle emphasizes the importance of understanding the very nature of the building as an artificial element; its function, operation, outcomes and impact on the environment will undoubtedly provide insight in the selection of the appropriate site, and into its current and future growth, inter and intra spaces, shapes and configurations.

Both Verderber and Yeang's viewpoints concur with the Islamic perspective of the environment in balance with manmade edifices, be they hospitals or other constructions. The concept of mankind as a stakeholder of development, as a vicegerent on Earth, implies a duty of care in managing the limited resources so as not to waste them but turn them to the benefit of mankind and the environment in a holistic sense, as an act of submission to the Creator for sustainability.

Clinical Functionality: Healthcare Requirements for Hospitals

The clinical functionality of a hospital is based on an environment that places "pathogenic" criteria as a priority. Hospitals include various functions that require different working environments for people, equipment, and pathogens. While there are areas that require low energy and environmental control such as general wards, waiting areas, cafeterias and corridors, due to their location within a bigger envelop these areas are also subjected to environmental control.

The Humanistic Function of a Hospital

Pellitteri and Belvedere (n.d.) introduced aspects that are rarely brought up in hospital design and that relate to the role of hospitals within the city and the community. This role includes recovering values that differ from those of quantity and function characteristic of modern hospitals in the first half of the twentieth century.

The process of humanization involves a holistic vision of people, design environments and spatial distributions that fulfils the needs of the patient (a sense of acceptance and familiarity, respect for privacy, space and sensory comfort, ease of orientation) and at the same time minimizes stress factors. A humanization project can be implemented through the distribution and composition of spaces, the shape of the exterior volume of the building, views to the outside, green areas (gardens) and worship spaces, furnishings, materials, finishes, colours, signage, lighting (both natural and artificial), and elements of visual reference (e.g. art installations).

In the quest for architectural sustainability and clinical functionality, despite the constant dilemma facing hospital planners and designers of how to effectively balance the physical requirements, innovative approaches and outcomes should be constant factors.

MALAYSIAN HOSPITALS: TOWARDS A GREEN AGENDA

Malaysia is located within the tropical equatorial zone, with latitude and longitude at 2° 30' N and 112° 30' E respectively (refer to Figures 7 and 8).
Malaysian general climatic data, retrieved from Malaysian Meteological Department (MMD) 2012, as cited in Norita Johar's (2012) thesis. See Table 1 for temperature and Table 2 for wind direction.

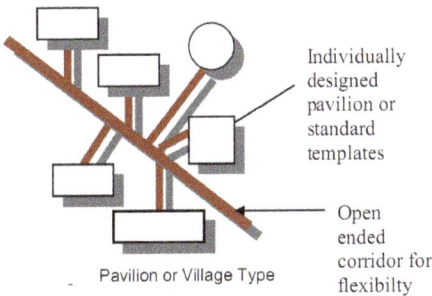

Figure 7. Location of Malaysia in the tropics. Source: Worldmap indicating tropics and subtropics. Retrieved August 12, 2013 from http://en.wikipedia.org.

283

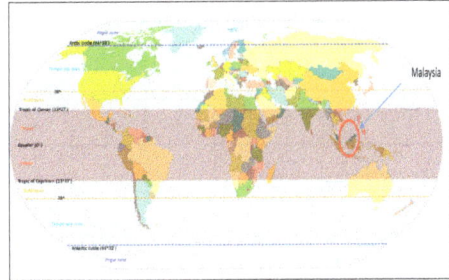

Figure 8. Map of Malaysia in the tropics. Source: Malaysia latitude and longitude map. Retrieved August 12, 2013 from http://www.mapsofworld.com.

Individually designed pavilion or standard templates

Open ended corridor for flexibilty

Pavilion or Village Type

Figure 5. Pavilion building form. Source: Norwina Mohd Nawawi & Srazali Aripin (2004).

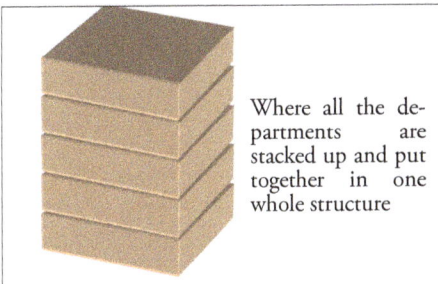

Where all the departments are stacked up and put together in one whole structure

Figure 6. Compact or Stacked Building Form. Source: Norwina Mohd Nawawi & Srazali Aripin (2004).

Climatic Data	
Average Minimum Temperature	24°C or 74°F
Average Maximum Temperature	33°C or 90°F
Average Low Humidity	74%
Average High Humidity	89%
Average Wind Speed	7.7 m/s

Table 1. Malaysian general climatic data. Source: MMD 2012, as cited in Norita Johar's (2013) unpublished thesis.

Factors	Descriptions
Wind direction	Northeast & Southwest
Outdoor wind speed	As measured
Building orientation	Facing wind direction
Building	Shape, depth, size, volume
Openings	Size, location

Table 2. Factors affecting natural ventilation. Source: (NIBS (2011), Ghiaus et al. (2005), Allard & Santamouris (1998), Jiang et al., (2003), as cited in Norita Johar's (2013) unpublished thesis

TESIS Inter-University Research Centre "Systems and Technologies for Social and Healthcare Facilities" University of Florence, Italy

TESIS

284

As regards the disease patterns of the tropics, Malaysia in particular, being hot and humid, is also a haven for vector borne diseases carried, among others, by mosquitoes that cause malaria and dengue fever.

Hence, when focusing on a green agenda, Malaysian researchers, while busy defining and refining the parameters for a green hospital, should also note the conflicting implications the recommendations would make in combating some of the diseases.

The Malaysian authorities, with respect to the nation's green agenda, worked on many aspects of implementation through regulations, best practices and contractual obligations.

The brief and fragmented research on different hospital buildings has provided an idea of what the preferred environmental conditions of hospital design should physically and conceptually "look" like for similar conditions. The guidelines, however, do not spell out the climatic conditions.

Hence detailed studies are required, not only for each hospital building forming part of an entire complex but for each locality in Malaysia. For this brief study, case studies were selected to represent specific periods in which hospitals were built to give insights into what lay behind the decisions of the architects as designers of the time, and the respect and consideration given to the various factors in play at that time and place, for the design of truly complex buildings in the tropics that still exist today.

CASE STUDIES OF SELECTED MALAYSIAN HOSPITAL DESIGNS THROUGH THE AGES

Selected hospitals that represent the periods identified as: Colonial / Pre-independence; Post-Colonial / Independence 1960s and 1970s; Towards Nation Building & Health for All 1980s-1990s; and Towards a Developed Nation 2000s to present, were analysed using a qualitative method based on the criteria listed below:
1. Site location (orientation/organization/topography);
2. Building configuration and layout (compact or sprawling layout, building shape – deep or thin);
3. Built form, materials used and construction details (low rise, high rise);
4. Internal planning strategy (clinical, humanistic);
5. Cultural and humanistic values.

ANALYSES AND FINDINGS

Summary of Analyses

Healthcare facilities including hospitals are not a traditional building typology in old Malaya or present-day Malaysia. Traditionally all illnesses were treated at home. These facilities were brought by colonial masters as early as the 15th century, first from Portugal, then Holland, and most recently Britain, through its East India Company and North Borneo Company. The British deployed similar designs from India and Africa in Malaysia.

The Colonial period witnessed pavilions and climate-friendly building typologies as illustrated in Figure 9, brought over by the British from other parts of the colony with a similar climate and adjusted on site by British soldiers.

Table of Hospital Accommodation.

The date of the construction of the native artillery and European hospital is not known.
The native infantry hospital was erected in 1860.
Total number of wards, 5.
Total regulation number of beds, 46.

Wards. No.	Regulation Number of Sick in each Ward.	Dimensions of Wards.				Cubic Feet per Bed.	Superficial Area in Feet per Bed.	Height of Patient's Bed above the Floor.	Windows.		
		Length.	Breadth.	Height.	Cubic Contents.				Number.	Height.	Width.
		Ft.	Ft.	Ft.				Ft. In.		Ft. In.	Ft. In.
Native Infantry Hospital, 3	14	80	18	19	} 49,590	1,771	93	2 6	{ 27	2 6	5 0
	7	39	15	19					12	7 0	5 0
	7	39	15	18							ventrs.
European Artillery, 1	10	38	19	10	7,220	722	72½	2 6	5	5 0	3 6
Golundauze, 1	8	27	18	10	4,860	607½	27	2 6	4	5 0	3 6

285

Table 3. Statistical table of hospital accommodation in Pinang (Penang). Source: The Commissioners, The Report of the RCSSAI, Vol. 2.

Table 3 demonstrates the standards exercised throughout the British Empire.

Upon independence in 1957, with a view to nation building and meeting the WHO's "Health For All" agenda by 2000, Malaysia embarked on a hospital building programme to replace old hospitals as well as construct new ones at new hospitals sites with "standard" and "type" plans.

In the late '80s and '90s, with the advent of Information and Communication Technology (ICT), mechanical means of transporting goods and information, medical discoveries and changes in medical practices meant that the adjacency of functional departments was no longer critical and they could be placed elsewhere. Similarly passive design requirements, with the advent of medical breakthroughs, considered the welfare of patients in relation to the importance of natural daylight and views in care settings.

The series of hospital designs produced in the year 2000 witnessed the sprouting of more one-off designs for even smaller hospitals, including healthcare centres. With more rural areas becom-

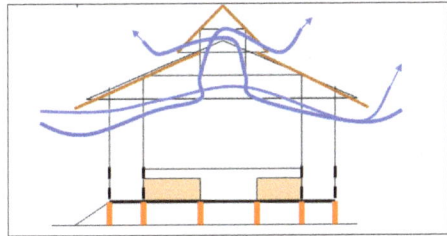

Figure 9. Typical cross section of a single-storey Colonial hospital ward pavilion. Source: Norwina Mohd Nawawi and Srazali Aripin, 2004.

ing urban due to extensive development and the opening up of new areas, architectural structures at district level which were once simple had evolved into more sophisticated structures using more mechanical means. As care was the priority, the introduction of outreach facilities, such as haemodialysis and intensive care units, which require indoor controlled environments, on the doorstep of the people, added to the energy requirement of former low-energy hospitals.

With urban centres becoming heat islands, it became imperative to sustain human comfort in almost all public facilities by using air conditioning systems. Culture had it that air-conditioned spaces in clinics and hospitals

286

were a mark of progress as it signified comfort for both patients and their accompanying relatives. Hence air conditioning was introduced in all waiting areas of hospitals and clinics. Hospitals built during this period, due to their location within cities and the clashing of requirements within the hospital departments themselves, caused many problems among which were condensation issues. This lead to the growth of mould in many hospitals. The government had to address the problem technologically on site for already existing problems and provide guidelines for new ones including the need for design simulation for new projects.

Today, the towards a developed nation approach requires new project briefs to incorporate green requirements. All public hospitals are expected to adhere to these requirements with a certain weightage being given to design evaluation. In the public sector, clinical functionality takes priority in design decisions over everything else after the bottom line has been set. However, implementation and monitoring remain difficult due to the priority of needs when the project commences, the lack of experienced human resources to monitor and make deci-

sions and most of all the will to make it happen on the part of builders under certain procurement methods. Hospitals designed in this period tried their best to avoid deep plans and flat roofs, and to provide wider corridors and patient areas with access to natural daylight, and more space for respite. Being in a tropical climate, the Ministry of Health Malaysia calls for "mosquito free" hospitals. Water and lush plants brought into gardens create a humid environment and thus a haven for mosquitoes. So do designs with water features to a certain degree.

Recently, more private sector healthcare providers answered Malaysia's call for the integration of services and health tourism by complementing the public sector healthcare provisions. The latest project, "healing hands", was introduced as a concept by Nightingale Associates in association with the Malaysian firm M&R Architects. The project promises a green agenda with state-of-the-art technology, materials and the concept of care enveloped in finger-like forms. The project won an international design competition held by leading private healthcare provider KPJ Healthcare Berhad.

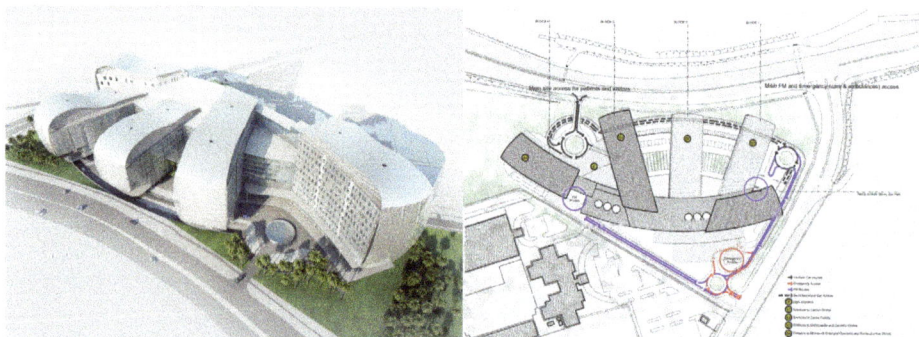

Figure 10. The Healing Hand Hospital, Kumpulan Perubatan Johor. Source: Nick Varey on Aug 3, 2011 from Habitables, Johor Bahru Hospital, Malaysia – Nightingale Associates.

Summary of Findings

A review of the colonial period up to the present day shows that the demand on physical facilities, the environment and medical development have evolved tremendously over time. The idea that a "new" hospital building should be a better building is relative. Location, the level of care, population, site size, planning decisions, project priority and moment in time are among other criteria that define whether a hospital is green and sustainable.

Each hospital analysed has its reasons for being built the way it is which depend on the site orientation or site conditions, despite the north and south facing norms for the Malaysian climate conditions. In the design of the modular block for Colonial and post-independence hospitals, due to the functional requirements of certain buildings that require daylight, ventilation and views, the orientation positioning is compromised according to the best option at the time. The situation is similar for new developments especially in cities, as the sites are islands with minimal space for achieving the best orientation with respect to the evening sun. While newer hospitals have to opt for compact designs, older hospitals can sprawl having the luxury of a site and location either on a hill or at the coast. Similar findings concerning the layout and built form, aside from the standard plan or nucleus hospital, pointed to the site as one of the main factors that shapes its layout.

Older facilities provide simple and effective solutions for protection against the rain, heat and glare through passive and intuitive designs. Newer facilities, due to conflicting requirements, require more technological solutions. With patient and human-centred care in newer hospitals, the duplication of certain service areas for both patient and staff convenience is evident and expected.

The materials used are always the most robust at the time of construction in order to combat the wear and tear of a hospital, infection control containment, and noise abatement, and the colours are symbolic of a place of care; they range from cement render, to tiles and terrazzo. Humanistic values are demonstrated through the culture of use and the indirect provision of a healing environment achieved through orientation, respite spaces, relative waiting areas, staff rest areas and the simple provision of spaces for prayers and meditation, with views, daylight and access to the gardens and therapy spaces.

CONCLUSIONS

The initial purpose of this study was to define "green" and the concept of "sustainability" in the design of tropical climate hospitals for Malaysia with the objective of contributing qualitative attributes for the formulation of the Malaysian Green Building Index for hospital buildings. The study defines sustainability for a hospital, which differs from the general physi-

287

288

cal definition due to clinical requirements and the nature of conflicting spatial requirements with humans as the central users and the healing environment as the supportive aim.

According to Verderber (2010), Yeang (2012), ZiQu Wu (2011), Srazali Aripin (2007), Pellitteri and Belvedere (n.d.) and Burpe (2008), sustainability that embraces the green requirements in healthcare facilities should also embrace the notion of creating a supportive environment (i.e. healing environment) that is physically healthy and psychologically appropriate. The physical aspects should be cleverly designed to achieve the balance and principles of economic, social and ecological sustainability without compromising the functionality of the hospital building (Burnet, 2004). Thus achieving sustainable hospital design through appropriate physical aspects is not an impossible task. The growing research evidence compiled by local researchers and the case studies of Malaysian public hospitals presented above unequivocally suggest that the physical aspects play a significant role in the creation of a healing environment. It is important to note that in the context of hospital buildings, measurable patient health outcomes in a healing environment are the indirect result of the appropriate design of physical aspects. The effort to reduce dependency on artificial lighting would directly contribute to the energy consumption of hospital buildings, subsequently assisting sustainability.

Unlike temperate countries, professionals engaged in healthcare projects and services in Malaysia should be inspired by the availability of the natural environment in the Malaysian climate without sacrificing clinical functionality and design visions. We must accept the fact that the design of a hospital to create a supportive and healing environment as well as a physically healthy and psychologically appropriate one is a multidisciplinary effort that can contribute to a sustainable design. The step towards one-off design for public hospitals in Malaysia through an improved procurement system is a commendable starting point as each location requires a customized design to overcome contextual issues. However, constraints on the physical aspects to meet environmental requirements should be explicitly stated in the design briefs for any hospital development and for the designer to comply with. These requirements must be validated by healthcare designers and approved by the healthcare providers.

In conclusion, the findings of researchers and from the case studies of existing hospitals found that the respective periods provide peculiar and interesting physical solutions derived from the construction details through to the implementation of standards and UBBL. Humanistic requirements derive from the scale, proximity and care requirement and are intuitively woven into the design. These findings could be significantly integrated in a document to reinforce the project briefs provided by the healthcare provider (Ministry of Health Malaysia) as well as the general green guidelines for hospitals in Malaysia for a healthy population.

REFERENCES

Burnet, L. (2004). Healing Environment, *Contract* Vol. 46, Issue 9; Career and Technical Education.

Burpee, H. (2008). *History of Healthcare Architecture, Integrated Design Lab Puget Sound, 1.*

Cook, G. C. (2002). Henry Currey FRIBA(1820-1900): Leading Victorian hospital architect, and early exponent of the "pavilion principle". *Postgraduate Medical Journal,* 78.

Kleczkowski, B. M. and Pibouleau, R. (ed.) (1983). *Approaches to planning and design of health care facilities in developing areas. Vol. 4.* WHO.

Kleczkowski, B. M., Montoya-Aguilar, C., and Nilsson, N.O. (ed.) (1985). *Approaches to planning and design of health care facilities in developing areas. Vol. 5.* WHO. WHO OFFSET 91.

Ministry of Health Malaysia (2012). *Guidelines on Prevention and Management of Tuberculosis for Health Care Workers.* Ministry of Health Malaysia. Occupational Health Unit, Disease Control Division.

Hanita, N., Majid A. et al. (2011). Climate Responsive Strategies versus the Cultural and Religious Dimensions in the Architecture of Malay Traditional Houses. In Nawawi, M. N, (ed.). *Malay Vernacular Architecture-traditional and contemporary expressions.* Kuala Lumpur, IIUM Press.

Hanita, N., Majid A. and Hussaini, I. U. (2011). Islam and the Concept of Sustainable Development. In *The Islamic Quarterly, in the Fourth Quarter* 1432/2011, Vol. 55, No. 4, The Islamic Cultural Centre and London Central Mosque.

Norita Johar (2012). T*he Feasibility of Open Wards For Airborne Infectious Isolation Use During Seasonal Pandemic Crisis: A Case Study of Sungai Buloh Hospital.* A thesis presented to the Kulliyyah of Architecture and Environmental Design of International Islamic University Malaysia in partial fulfilment of the requirements for the Degree of Master of Science (unpublished).

Nawawi, N. M., and Aripin, S. (2004). Comparative Study on Passive Design Considerations on Selected Hospital Designs in Malaysia. Paper presented at a Seminar on *Passive Design Consideration in the Built Environment* from November 22-23, 2004 in KAED, IIUM, Malaysia.

Nawawi, N. M., Hanita, N., Majid, A., Rahim, Z.A., Sapian, A.R., and Denan, Z. (2013). *Configuring The Nature of Colonial Hospital Architecture in Peninsular Malaysia* - Serie 1: Special Studies on The Tuberculosis Ward and Hospital Administration Building Typologies of Kota Bharu Hospital. Unpublished study report.

Pellitteri, G., and Belvedere, F. (n.d.) *Characteristics of the Hospital Buildings: Changes, Processes and Quality. University of Palermo.*

289

Aripin, S. (2007). Healing Architecture: Daylight in Hospital Design, *Proceeding of Conference on Sustainable Building South East Asia*, November 5-7, 2007, Malaysia.

Aripin, S. (2012). The Role of Daylighting in the Green Built Environment. *Proceeding of the International Conference on Green in Built Environment (ICGBE) 2012*: 'Green' Built Environment: Redefined, Kulliyyah of Architecture and Environmental Design, International Islamic University Malaysia.

Verderber, S. (2010). *Innovations in Hospital Architecture*. London: Routledge.

Yeang, K. (2006). *Ecodesign, a manual for ecological design*. London: Wiley-Academy.

Yeang, K. (2012). Green Design and Planning. Keynote paper for Session 3: *International Conference on Green in Built Environment (ICGBE) 2012*: 'Green' Built Environment: Redefined, Kulliyyah of Architecture and Environmental Design, International Islamic University Malaysia.

Ziqi Wu. (2011). *Evaluation of a Sustainable Hospital Design Based on Its Social and Environmental Outcomes*. A thesis presented to the Faculty of the Graduate School of Cornell University in partial fulfilment of the requirements for the Degree of Master of Science.

290

13-Hour Difference: Lessons Learned From the China - US Joint Design Studio

Wachter H.[1], Zhipeng L.[2], Mann G.[2], Zhou Y.[3]

hepw@ou.edu
[1] University of Oklahoma, USA
[2] Texas A&M University, USA
[3] Southeast University, China

291

This presentation will share the experience and lessons learned from the six-party China-US joint design studio collaboration. The six parties include three universities and three advisory design firms, and worked on a 250-bed eye hospital in Puyang, China. Teams were formed, each of which comprised students from the three universities. Students overcame the barrier of the 13-hour time difference and managed to communicate via various forms. By collaborating with a foreign university and international architectural firms, students were exposed to a variety of cutting-edge design practices. Such projects prepared them for a career designing health facilities on an international level and enhanced their opportunities in a competitive job market. The students also gained valuable experience working with alterative design methodologies, which is helpful in a rapidly shifting marketplace.

INTRODUCTION

China and the US are both facing significant challenges in healthcare reforms and striking to provide a higher quality of care to their people. There are many differences in terms of hospital design and planning in the two countries due to different healthcare delivery systems, management models, culture, and other factors. However, designers, researchers, policy makers and students can learn from each other when searching for optimal care environments for patients. In addition, international collaborations have become more important as in recent years more US firms have opened offices in China and Chinese architects are practicing in the US. Therefore, it is important to train young healthcare designers with real collaborative projects and provide them with opportunities to learn from other cultures, broaden their visions and become more internationally competent.

To achieve this goal, the six-party China-US joint design studio was developed. The six parties include three universities and three advisory firms. The three universities are Texas A&M University (College Station, TX), Southeast University (Nanjing, China) and University of Oklahoma (Norman, OK). The three advisory firms include HKS (Dallas & Shanghai), IPPR (Beijing, China) and Miles Associates (Oklahoma City).

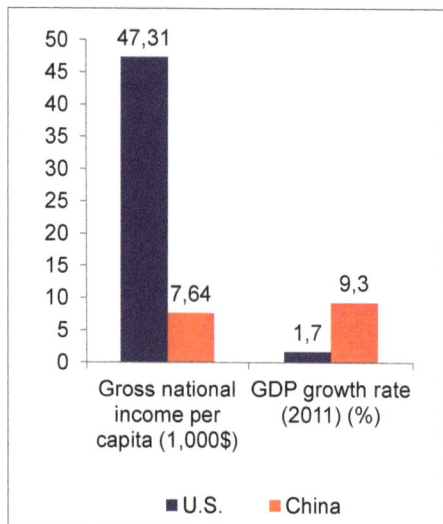

Figure 1. National income.

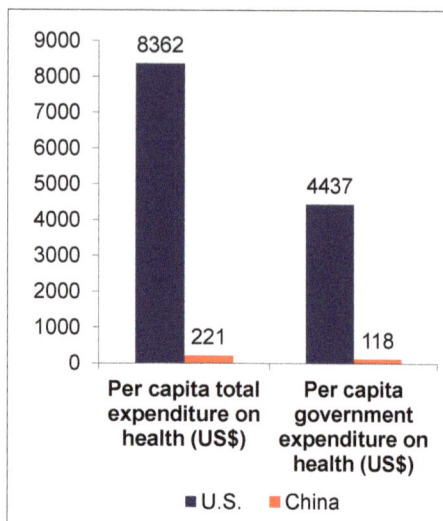

Figure 2. Healthcare expenditure.

All three of the participating universities have an association with their Health Science Centres and College of Medicine and all have the common goal to foster environmental research and create expertise in health facility design (Figure 4). In fall 2011, approximately 60 architectural and interior design students from the three universities participated in the joint studio. The project was a 250-bed eye hospital in Puyang, China, a city with 6,000 years of history. The project for fall 2012 was a 300-bed rehabilitation hospital within a cancer centre in Hainan, China. Approximately 40 students worked on this project. Teams were formed, each of which was comprised of students from three universities. Students communicated with team members via blog (http://hainanrehabilitationcenter.wordpress.com), email, Skype and QQ (a video communication program). Joint group reviews were held using video conference. During the project, US professors visited Nanjing and

met with the collaborators and students. The Chinese students and professors joined the final review at the HKS Dallas headquarter.

In addition to the design studio, Texas A&M organized two sets of "Architecture for Health Lecture Series." The theme of the fall 2011 lecture series was "China: Toward Improved Healthcare and Health Facilities in the Future"; the theme of 2012 was "Pitfalls, Problems and Opportunities in an International Architecture for Health Practice." Multidisciplinary speakers included health administrators, physicians, nurses, politicians, policy makers, designers and researchers.

From the joint studio and the lecture series, students gained not only knowledge of healthcare design, but also learned how to overcome the 13-hour time difference and language barrier to design a project collaboratively in a culturally unfamiliar environment.

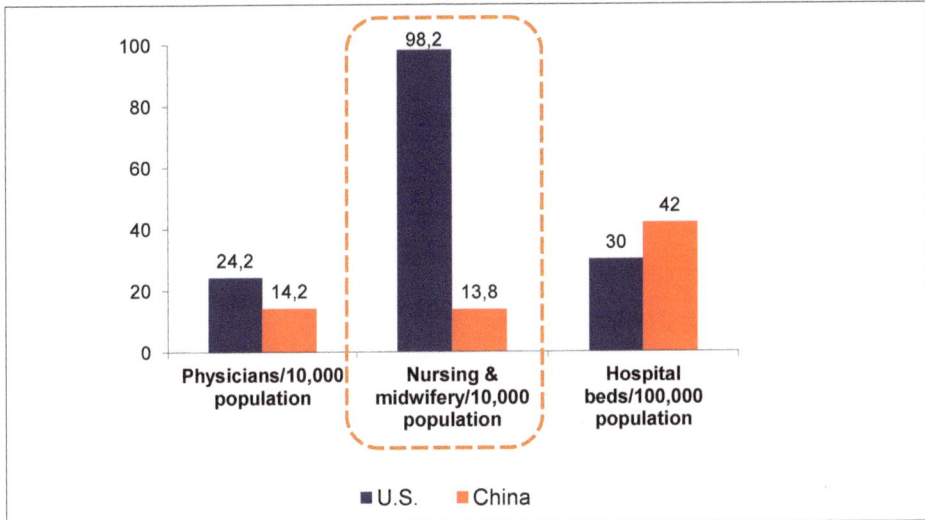

Figure 3. Healthcare workforce & infrastructure.

LEARNING OBJECTIVES AND OUTCOMES

This paper will describe the entire process of the joint studio and share several lessons learned from the previous project.

The nature of a cross-institutional collaboration brings many different viewpoints to the table. The clear advantage of bringing different institutions and multiple disciplines together and sharing pedagogy is the depth of expertise, variety and quality of feedback and the sharing of resources.

Shared resources proved to be the most relevant factor in the cross-institutional collaboration. One single synchronous guest lecture series, available through video conferencing to all participants, minimized organizational efforts, cost, and sustainability in the classroom and insured a single focus on content. The contacts each institution had to affiliated teaching firms and practitioners brought a wealth of expertise into the classroom and enriched student learning otherwise too difficult to accomplish. The student teams also benefited from the participating variety of disciplines and many students would not have access to an interior design perspective otherwise. The mix of expertise and presence of multi-disciplines within the building environment constituted a learning environment for the students that simulated a realistic work environment.

The learning outcomes are: (1) how multiple firms and universities work together on a joint project and get benefits; (2) how to initiate and establish connections among firms and universities; (3) how to select appropriate projects for the design studio; (4) how to promote effective communications among students to ensure the quality of collaboration; (5) how to solve conflicts and problems that emerge during the process; (6) how to enrich students' learning experience; and (7) how to evaluate the collaborative work.

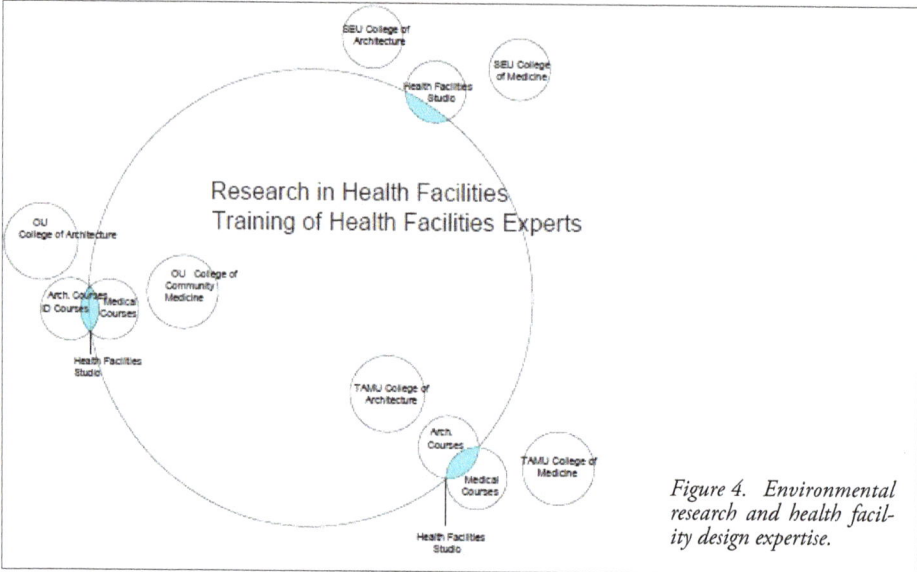

Research in Health Facilities
Training of Health Facilities Experts

Figure 4. Environmental research and health facility design expertise.

294

- 2000-2009: 3,973 new hospitals; 1,287,704 new beds

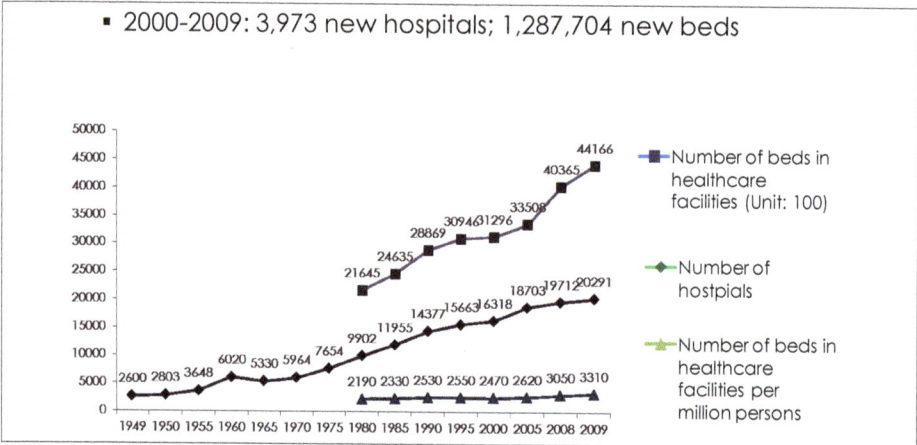

Figure 5. Healthcare construction boom in China. Data Source: Ministry of Health of the People's Republic of China, 2010.

Figure 6. Students' works: rehabilitation hospital in a cancer centre, Haikou, China.

Collective Intelligence: The Impact of Health Predictors

Black S.[1]

s.black@perkinseastman.com
[1] Perkins Eastman Black Architects Inc., Canada

Collective intelligence: a collaborative discussion on the impact of health predictors. We need new thinking! We have health challenges on a global front. By tapping into the root causes of these crises, we can begin to make significant contributions to the direction of global healthcare. In an effort to defeat the odds, we must locally combine our collective IQs into collaborative and highly diverse teams. With the prime consideration of health predictors as the baseline in every project we can ensure, through example and the global reach of technology, a higher standard of living for every man, woman and child on the planet.

INTRODUCTION

Our projects span from "prescriptive" urbanism for a massive medical city to hybrid ORs; from small community wellness facilities to full service hospitals; and from environments for children to those for dementia care. Yet we continually realize the need for research and collaboration in our projects.

Our understanding that some environments, in particular light and nature-filled, view enhancing, temperature modulated and accessible ones, as well as those with clarity in planning and organization, can influence behaviours is supported by evidenced-based design, which uses health-outcome measures, and physiological and ecological data to evaluate decisions. It is also supported by intuition, sometimes more right than we realize, but without scientific fact as confirmation we still do not know the "why."

Let us look at how diverse silos of emerging scientific knowledge can be an important dialogue in the design process towards collective intelligence – collaboratively tapping into the root causes or predictors of these crises in an effort to beat the odds.

IMPACTS OF MEDICAL SCIENCE

Professor Elizabeth Blackburn, a biological researcher, studies telomeres – the structures at the ends of our chromosomes. These "tips" shorten as we age. The process has been scientifically proven to accelerate with stress. Critically short telomeres are evident in age-related diseases, including cardiovascular disease, diabetes, cancer and dementia. Blackburn co-discovered an enzyme (Nobel Prize 2009), called telomerase which has been found to lengthen these tips – seemingly reversing the process.

Studies have indicated that by introducing meditation and other stress-reducing practices into our lives, telomerase increases, confirming that telomere biology supports the need for a much healthier lifestyle.

This is but one medical break-through which flags biological trauma if periods of serenity and wellness-inducing strategies are not inherent in our lives. This information is gleaned from the inside-out; other emerging research is concerned with the outside-in, an environmental expose!

IMPACTS OF ENVIRONMENTAL SCIENCE

The study of epigenetics bridges the gap between scientific discovery and the application of energy efficient design for the distinct purpose of creating health promoting environments. Epigenetics analyzes changes in gene expression caused by the environment, especially in infancy and childhood.

Garnering scientific data through the work of Deborah Burnett, who is on the vanguard of this emerging field, we can make choices for our environment before it is even built.

Figure 1. Trillium Health Partners - Toronto ON. Perkins Eastman Black Architects.

Many possible interventions can be made; an example is the introduction of LED lighting which uses sensors to mimic the colour of natural light throughout the day to complement our 24-hour clock or circadian rhythm – a proven health benefit and correction for "sick" building syndrome, reinforcing the need to integrate this knowledge into building specifications.

This becomes even clearer when we learn that genetics contributes only about 20% to our longevity while the balance is environmental. One looming example is Alzheimer's disease as the numbers are expected to rise to 100 million worldwide over the next decade, long before stem cells will play a part in its mitigation. Healing environments can alleviate merely 1% of the challenges facing us.

The situation is all the more critical as it impacts our families, health systems, and economies. So why not work together to thwart its onset through the full cycle of life, in effect utilizing medical and environmental science in our design processes to respond to known health predictors.

297

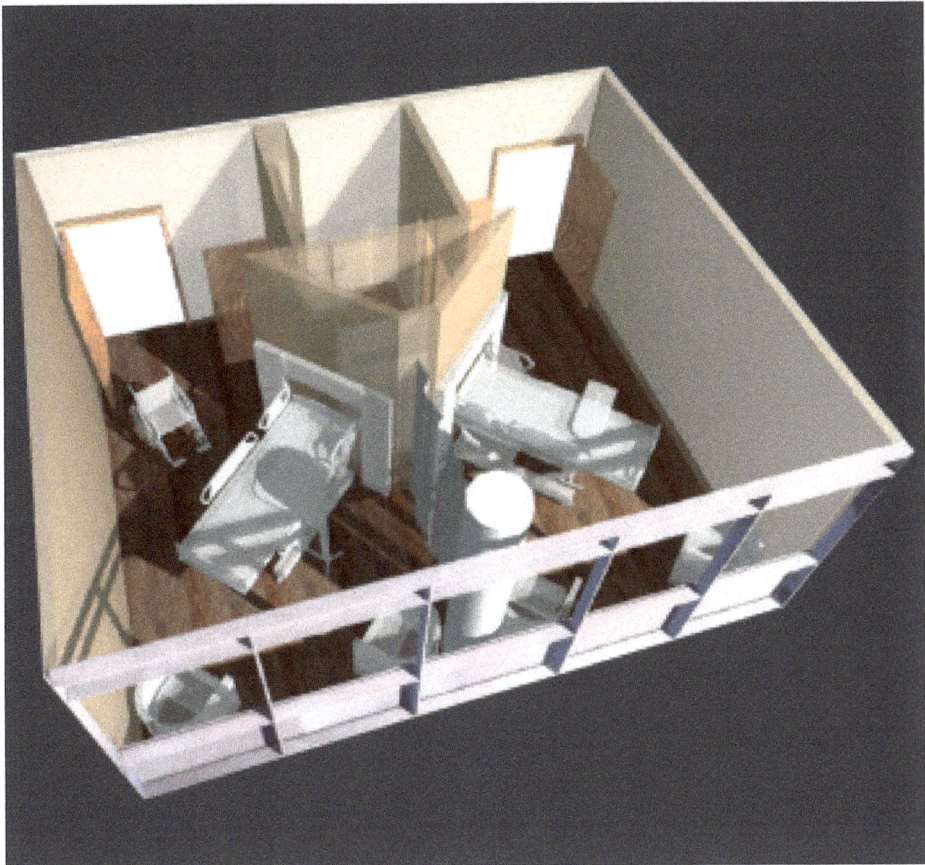

Figure 2. Trillium Health Partners, patient room.

298

Figure 3. Women's College Hospital - Toronto ON. Perkins Eastman Black / IBI Group Architects in joint venture.

Most of the risk factors associated with this disease begin in early childhood. Interestingly, we know that aerobic exercise is the best brain fertilizer and protector against child obesity, diabetes, and even social inequality – all predictors of Alzheimer's. With the scientific data available, we should reflect on how we create daycares, community spaces, and health facilities to alleviate stressors which over time shorten telomeres and may create disease. What if we were proactive in mitigating risk factors before they lead to a pandemic – could this result in prescriptions for design?

A call to action: remember that children are future Alzheimer's patients.

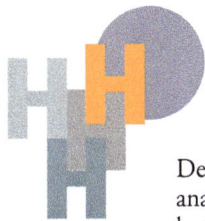

Session introduction

Designing environments for particular types of users requires a detailed analysis of the behavioral and emotional aspects of patients. Thorough knowledge of therapeutic strategies and patient profiles is required in order to rigorously assess the consequences of aspects involving the spatial configuration of care environments.

The absence of specific guidelines on environments for children with autism means that ongoing studies in this area are oriented to a direct research approach designed to gather as much information as possible to give shape to knowledge useful to designers faced with designing these types of facilities.

Patients faced with a cancer diagnosis embark on a course of treatment that sometimes has a strong impact on their life. The design of environments dedicated to cancer care should take into account the particular psychological conditions of the patients, and the environments should be designed according to a patient-centered design approach in order to best accommodate people with this condition.

The aging of the population is a phenomenon that requires careful study, especially at present as it is possible to observe the evolving needs of older people. Improving the quality of life and the desire to remain efficient and active for as long as possible have led to the creation of a new target audience for which new programs and new types of buildings must be devised. Rehabilitation is another key issue that affects a wide range of users from the elderly to children and accident victims. Planning the interior and exterior of rehabilitation centres with ramps and paths helps patients to improve their health conditions. The design of rehabilitation centres can make a significant contribution in stimulating the recovery of patients, in view of their achieving independence and autonomy in daily life.

All of these specific skills can be combined in the design of community centres, and such centres should be able to accommodate, in the same campus, rehabilitation centres, facilities for the elderly and cancer patients, mental health centres, and assisted living and long-term care facilities; alternatively such facilities should be located close to each other in order to provide care for the whole territory. The study of the design of these particular facilities reveals that it was necessary to combine the study of architecture with sociology and epidemiology studies in order to develop spatial patterns that meet the new demands linked to the evolution of society and its changes.

The application of these experiences has highlighted the difficulties inherent in implementing standards and creating architectural works, and the time between the adoption of a standard and the creation of a building. The presence of the standard on the other hand helps to ensure the same level of quality in healthcare buildings throughout the whole territory. The success of such facilities is determined by the ability of the designers to engage stakeholders, to identify needs and to produce benefits that have a positive long-term impact on the community.

Design of a Breast Cancer Centre

Luis P. C. [1]

hedyluis@yahoo.com
[1] Luis & Associates, Philippines

This presentation will focus on describing a patient's point of view, and the processes and procedures experienced by a patient ill with breast cancer. It is important for breast cancer centres to take note of their patients' unique experiences and use them as parameters in the design of patient-centered Breast Centres. The author discusses the unique elements and strategies involved in planning and designing a Breast Centre of this kind in response to the physical, emotional and psychological needs of patients.

INTRODUCTION

About Cancer

In May 2013, Time Magazine featured Angelina Jolie on its cover and devoted 6 pages to discussing her preventive mastectomy in an article entitled "The Angelina Effect." Angelina Jolie, one of the most known beautiful faces in the world, has undergone a double mastectomy after learning that she carried a mutated gene that increased the odds of her getting breast cancer to 87% and ovarian cancer to 50%. Her anxiety was caused by the death of her mother of ovarian cancer at the age of 51. Jolie decided to pre-empt the development of breast cancer in her body by having her two breasts taken off so that "I can tell my children that they don't need to fear they will lose me to breast cancer . . . they know that I love them and will do anything to be with them as long as I can."

In 2010, Siddhartha Mukherjee, a medical oncologist, published the comprehensive book "The Emperor of all Maladies: A Biography of Cancer." It is a well-researched work about the "history of cancer" which is, in a way, a "biography" of this dreaded disease that has plagued the world for centuries. The author defined cancer as ". . . not a disease but a whole family of diseases . . . characterized by . . . occasionally, cells that don't know how to die, but certainly cells that don't know how to stop dividing." It was to answer his patients' questions on what exactly cancer is that propelled the author to write the book.

Cancer is a disease that is most feared because it is associated with dying, and yet so little can be told to a patient about whether or not he or she will recover – or die. It is a long process of treatment that may extend to years while the patient has no recourse but to hope and pray that all will be well and the treatment protocols chosen will eventually lead to that milestone year when he or she is proclaimed "cancer free." Books such as the one authored by Greg Anderson entitled "Cancer: 50 Essential Things To Do" fill very important voids and answer questions nagging in patients' hearts and minds. The book is trusted because the author Greg Anderson is himself a survivor of Stage IV lung cancer, and thus writes about his first-hand experiences.

The above selected reading materials – first, a news item by Time Magazine on a celebrity who had bravely pre-empted the development of breast cancer; second, a comprehensive and reliable book, a source of information about the disease; and third, a book on "how-tos" that can be used by a patient in the journey towards healing – are representative of what patients can hang on to for reference and inspiration.

Objectives of this Presentation

The goal of this presentation is to add its little contribution to the above documents and to the many that have been written about cancer and peripheral matters. This paper aims to contribute to provide comfort in the journey towards healing from the point of view of healthcare architecture.

The following are the specific objectives of this presentation:
1) to describe some of the experiences of a patient ill with breast cancer;
2) to extract from these experiences some considerations for the design of a patient-centered Breast Centre;
3) to describe the planning and design

of a Breast Centre translating the above design considerations.

In the discussion of the planning and design process, this paper will use as its demonstration project a newly completed facility called the Asian Breast Center of the Asian Hospital and Medical Center in Metro Manila, Philippines.

UNDERSTANDING THE PATIENT

A patient-centered facility must have patients at the core of its planning and design. An understanding of the psychological and emotional state of patients results in a design which is receptive to their delicate condition.

Once diagnosed with this dreaded disease, the patient experiences a progression of emotion – what is commonly known as the seven stages of grief: shock, denial, bargaining, fear, anger, despair, and finally acceptance, but not until after the patient has plummeted first into the labyrinth of the previous stages.

The following are excerpts taken from a patient's diary which documents some of her innermost feelings about her experiences as a breast cancer patient:
• I felt crashed, stopped in my direction in life.
• I spent many moments at my dressing table looking at myself in the mirror, assessing how I look, rationalizing my life, and convincing myself that I have done enough to be ready to die.
• The image of life for my family without me kept on recurring and so, privately, I selected and shopped for the gifts that I would leave each of them

which would be meaningful and make them remember me.

• The fear of being forgotten started to plague me and so the idea of legacy suddenly became very important. What could I leave behind in this world that would assure my immortality? I would write a book perhaps. But did I have the time?

• Yes, my mortality suddenly confronted me right in the face. I am not immortal – I would die – and soon!

• After my surgery, I grieved for my lost breast, and imagined it as lying at the bottom of a white can to be thrown away as thrash with other parts of the bodies of other patients. I kept asking, "Where is my breast? Where is she? I did not even have time to say goodbye to her – when I woke up from my surgery, she was gone!"

• Being on my back most of the time, lying on examination tables, operation tables and patient beds, the ceiling became the most important part of a room for me. But how drab and boring they are!

• The lights directly above on the ceiling disturbed me as I was transported from one area to another on the stretcher.

• On the eve of my first chemotherapy, I was very afraid, imagining myself as constantly kneeling before the water closet emptying the contents of my stomach into the bowl in a difficult aftermath of the procedure.

• My veins had been constantly hurt by needles during examination and treatment to draw blood or infuse chemicals. In retaliation, they disappeared and became difficult to find, or when caught they flattened out and became difficult to puncture. And so, drawing blood and infusing chemicals became a very painful and problematic experience.

• The chemotherapy sessions became long drawn-out procedures I could not wait to be finished. I could do very little during the sessions. I spent the whole time looking at the ceiling and being bored.

• It was hard to read and turn the pages with only one hand. I hesitated to watch television because it would disturb my neighbour.

• Connected to the machine that infused the drugs, I felt helpless and not in control, completely dependent on staff and kin.

• Chemotherapy is a very colourful experience! The package of the drug that the oncologist "pushes" into my veins is a glaring electric orange. Urine also becomes orange after the infusion session.

• When I lost my hair, there were colourful head covers available in the women's sports accessories that I delighted in buying and collecting until I had almost 20 of them! My head cover and dress always matched. This made me very happy.

• After my chemotherapy sessions, I was shifted to hormonal treatment. The prescription written by my oncologist was good for five years!

• Upon learning of my illness, many had taken me aside to give advice on what to do, what to eat, what medicine to take and what protocols to follow. Though I feel grateful for their concern, I try my best to focus on the scientific regimen that had been chosen for me through the help of the doctors in the family. I follow the protocols faithfully. But most of all, I follow the greatest and the best protocol of all – trust in a Greater Being Who knows what is best for me. This gives me equanimity and peace.

303

PLANNING AND DESIGNING THE FACILITY

Contents of a Breast Centre in Other Metro Manila Hospitals (Benchmarking and Research)

The Breast Centres of two leading hospitals in Metro Manila were studied and evaluated and were found to contain the following rooms and spaces grouped under four general headings.

In both these centres, the services offered are diagnostic in nature, while therapeutic services such as surgery, chemotherapy and radio-therapy are performed in units in other locations in the hospital.

This is as it should be since these services cut across the requirements for the treatment of diseases other than breast cancer.

COMPARATIVE SPACE PROVISIONS FOR TWO BREAST CENTRES	
CLINIC #1	CLINIC #2
Public area	**Public area**
Reception	Reception/Nurse station
	Cashier
Public waiting area for 10	Public waiting area for 10
Staff area	**Staff area**
Clinic manager's room	
Interpretation room	
Clerical and general work area	Office area
Records and files room – 2 rooms	
Supply room	Medical and general supply storage
Staff toilet	Common toilet
Staff lockers	Staff pantry
Patients/Procedure area	**Patients/Procedure area**
Mammography – 2 rooms	Mammogram with biopsy – 1 room
Biopsy – 1 room	
Ultrasound – 2 rooms	Ultrasound – 2 rooms
Patients' waiting area for 10	Patients' waiting area for 10
Patients' changing area – 5 rooms	Patients' dressing area – 2 rooms
	Consultation room – 1 room
	Examination room – 1 room
Support areas	**Support area**
Server room	
Dark room	

Table 1.   Comparative space provisions for two breast centres.

The Asian Hospital and Medical Center

The Asian Hospital and Medical Center (AHMC) is a private hospital in Muntinlupa, Metro Manila. It was founded in 2002, with a bed capacity of 250 beds. Recently, about 60 beds have been added through new construction, bringing the bed capacity to 310.

AHMC sits on an area of 1.7 hectares and has 3 structures in its complex: Tower 1 and Tower 2 which house the hospital, and the Medical Office Building which houses the doctors' offices. Tower 1 rises up to 10 storeys; Tower 2 to 11 storeys; and the MOB to 7 storeys (see Figures 1 and 2).

Figure 1. AHMC Façade.

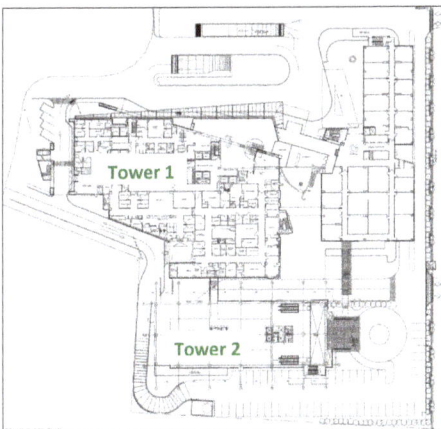

Figure 2. Structures within the AHMC Complex.

AHMC offers cancer treatment services in the following areas: breast cancer, chemotherapy, colon cancer, leukemia, lung cancer, melanoma, ovarian cancer, prostate cancer, cervical cancer and lymphoma.

It was decided that cancer treatment become an area of excellence for AHMC and a Cancer Centre be built in the future. In the meantime, it was also decided that services for breast cancer be strengthened ahead of the rest since breast cancer has a very high incidence among women in the country.

305

The fourth floor of Tower 2 was identified as the new location of the Asian Breast Center. The floor, which has a total floor area of 1,365 sq m, would require a fit out. A short bridge would connect the centre to other ambulatory services on the fourth floor of Tower 1 (see Figure 3).

The Architect's Brief for the Asian Breast Center

The following is a consolidation of the architect's brief developed in a series of meetings by a team composed of officers and end-users from the Asian Hospital and Medical Center and designers from the office of the healthcare architect.

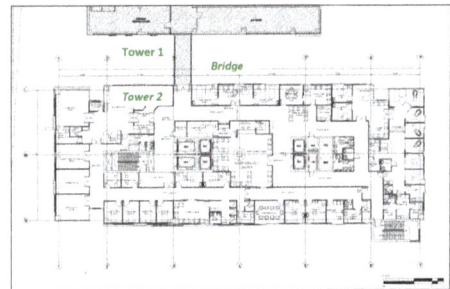

Figure 3. The fourth floor of Tower 2 connected by a bridge to Tower 1.

306

Space / Room	Qty	Unit Area (sq m)	Total Area (sq m)	Design Notes
Public area				
General public waiting area	1	80	80	For the general public to include companions not allowed inside patient areas Provide writing counter for patients and companions for filling in forms while standing
Reception	1	10	10	Space for 2 receptionists; provide counter
Cashier	1	6	6	Space for 1 cashier; provide cashier's window-counter
Releasing	1	6	6	Space for 1 release staff; provide counter
Filing & records room	1	16	16	Adjacent to release area
Patient/Procedure area				
Consult & Exam	2	14	28	For consultation with doctor; provide 1 doctor's table and 1 examination table
Patients' dressing area & toilet	1	18	18	Provide at least 3 dressing cubicles with lockers; provide toilet
Patients' lounge	1	24	24	For at least 10 patients; provide television set and magazine racks
Breast exam	2	12	24	For physical examination of the breast performed by nurses properly trained to examine breasts by palpation; provide 1 office table and 1 bed
Ultrasound	4	14	56	For ultrasound examination and ultrasound-guided biopsy; provide 1 patient bed
Stereotactic biopsy	1	28	28	Provide stereotactic biopsy table (table with hole so that the breast of a patient lying face down protrudes through the hole; provide space for the equipment and all its accessories; provide shielding

Space / Room	Qty	Unit Area (sq m)	Total Area (sq m)	Design Notes
Mammogram	1	24	24	Provide area for patient and a separate protected area for technician and computer; provide shielding for room and technician area.
Mammotome	1	24	24	Provide area for vacuum-assisted image-guided breast biopsy procedure; provide shielding
Operating room Complex composed of: 1 Operating room 2 Recovery bays 1 Reception 1 Patient transfer area 1 Patient dressing area 1 Patient toilet 1 Nurse station 1 Staff changing area 1 Staff toilet 1 Clean utility room 1 Dirty utility room 1 Storage room 1 Janitor's closet	1	150	150	For minor procedures that require anesthesia
Staff area				
Manager's room	1	12	12	Office of person in charge of managing the centre
Meeting room	1	18	18	For staff meetings; also for consultation with patients and relatives
Reading room	1	8	8	For reading results
Admin room	1	8	8	For typing/documentation of results
Staff lounge with pantry and toilet	1	12	12	Amenities for staff
Support/Utility area				
Equipment storage area	1	6	6	For various equipment
Engineering room	1	6	6	For use by electrical & mechanical system maintenance staff
Clean utility room	1	6	6	Clean materials
Dirty utility room	1	6	6	Dirty materials

307

TESIS

308

The floor plate area of the fourth floor of Tower 2 exceeded the space requirements of the Asian Breast Center so other related units concerned with cancer were included in the fit out. The Chemotherapy Infusion Unit was accommodated there. It was also possible to accommodate either the Palliative Care Unit or the Paediatric Chemotherapy Infusion Unit. It was decided that the latter be fitted out beside the Adult Chemotherapy Unit for functional similarity (see Figure 4). This means that in AHMC, the Breast Center not only contains diagnostic areas, but also therapeutic areas.

Patient-Centered Design of the Asian Breast Center

The design of the Asian Breast Center allows for the easy and legible flow of different types of patients.

General Patient Flow (refer to Figure 4):

1. Patient arrives at the centre by elevator from the ground floor;
2. Patient, who is usually accompanied, approaches Reception and is given a form to be filled in;
3. Patient fills in the form on the round writing ledge provided for this purpose, while standing up like in a bank;
4. Patient submits the form and is given a number;
5. Patient enters the patients' waiting area, while companion waits in the main waiting lounge;
6. Patient changes in one of the dressing cubicles, uses the toilet if necessary, and leaves street clothes in a locker;
7. Patient waits for his/her number to be called in the patient's waiting lounge, and watches television in the meantime;
8. Patient proceeds to and is seen in the appropriate procedure room, whether in the Exam room, Ultrasound room, Stereotactic room, Mammography room, or the Mammotome room;
9. Patient may wait for further procedures in the patient's waiting lounge, until released;
10. Patient changes into street clothes in the dressing room;
11. Patient drops by the main waiting lounge to join companion;
12. Patient and companion leave the centre.

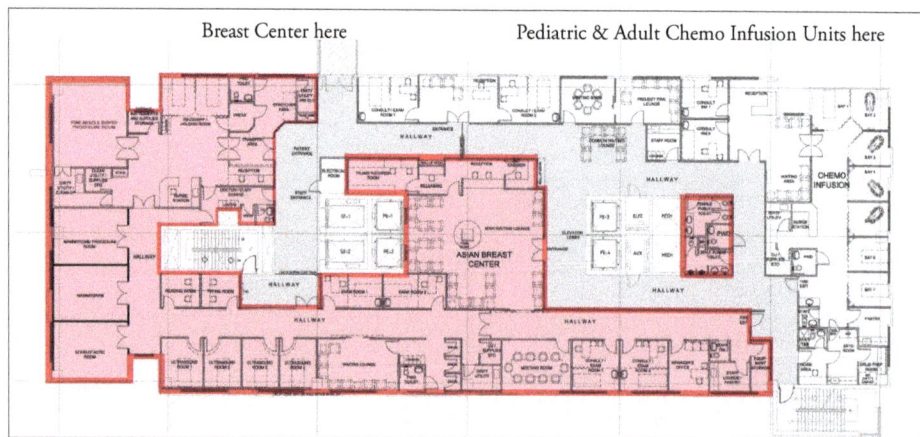

Figure 4. The Breast Center and the 2 Chemotherapy Infusion Units on the fourth floor.

Patient Flow for Ambulatory Operating Room (refer to Figure 4):
(Ambulant Patient)

1. Ambulant patient arrives at the entrance to the OR suite;
2. Patient changes and leaves street clothes in a locker, uses the toilet as necessary;
3. Patient proceeds to the operating room;
4. Patient undergoes procedure with anesthesia;
5. Patient is brought to recovery, rests and recovers;
6. Patient changes into street clothes;
7. Patient is fetched by companion;
8. Patient and companion leave the centre.

Patient Flow for Ambulatory Operating Room (refer to Figure 4):
(Patient on a stretcher)

1. Patient arrives at the entrance to the OR suite on a stretcher;
2. Patient is transferred from a "dirty" stretcher to a "clean" stretcher. The "dirty" stretcher is parked at the entrance area while the patient is wheeled into the operating room on the "clean" stretcher;
3. Patient undergoes procedure with anesthesia;
4. Patient is brought to recovery, rests and recovers;
5. Patient is brought to the transfer area and is transferred to a "dirty" stretcher and wheeled out of the OR suite.

Patient Flow for Chemotherapy Infusion Unit (refer to Figure 4):
1. Patient arrives at the Chemo Infusion Unit by elevator from the ground floor;
2. Patient approaches Reception and submits the results of the pre-chemo laboratory examinations;
3. Patient waits in the waiting area;
4. Patient with companion consults the doctor in the consultation room. The doctor examines the laboratory results and determines if the patient is fit and healthy enough for the procedure;
5. Patient proceeds to one of the infusion bays if fit and healthy. (If the patient is not fit and healthy, the doctor reschedules the procedure for another day.);
6. Patient undergoes the procedure for approximately 2 hours;
7. Patient goes home after the procedure.

Some Design Features for Patient Comfort

Figure 5. A warm and welcoming Reception Area.

Figure 6. An interesting (not boring) ceiling design.

309

310

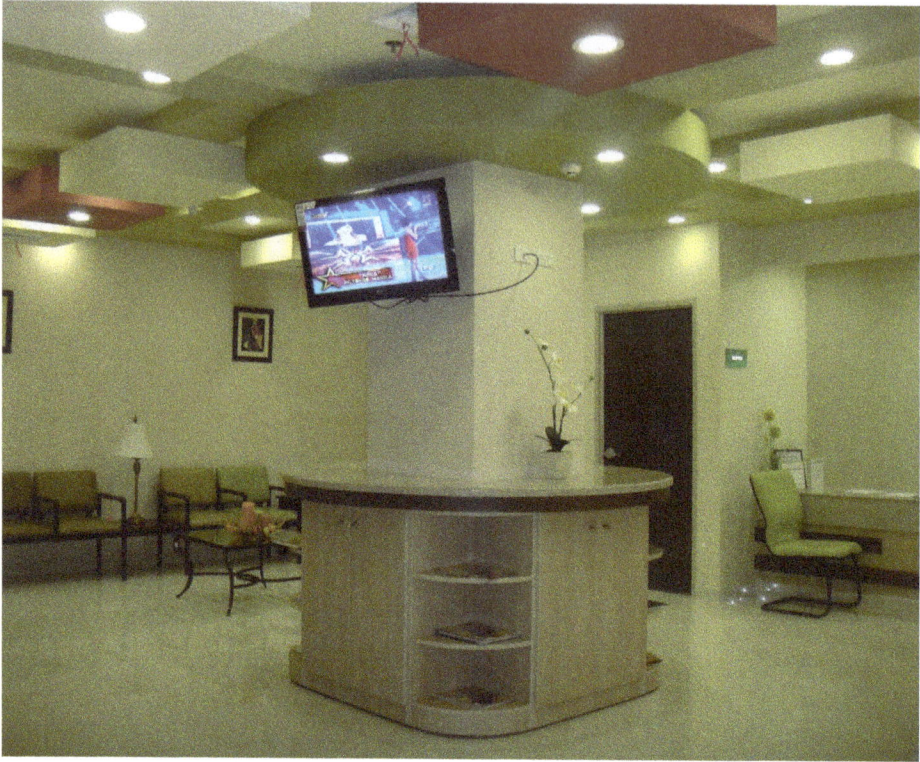

Figure 7. Writing ledge wrapped around a column for filling in forms.

Figure 8. One-sided indirect lighting in corridors to avoid discomfort to patients on stretchers.

Figure 9. Curtain and curtain rail at the door to ensure patient privacy.

THE END OF PHASE 1

The Asian Breast Center is only the initial phase of a bigger plan to make the Asian Hospital and Medical Center a Centre of Excellence for cancer treatment. Plans are afoot for the purchase of therapeutic radiology equipment.

The construction of bunkers in the basement for this equipment is included in the plans for the early part of 2014. With all the sophistication and high technology of the latest equipment, though, there is a consistent concern that it serve the patient who is at the core of all planning and design endeavours.

Have You Heard? Noisy Environments May Affect Learning for Children with Autism!

Kanakri S.M.[1], Shepley M.[2]

Arch1980@neo.tamu.edu, mshepley@arch.tamu.edu
[1]PhD Candidate, Texas A&M University/Department of Architecture College station, TX, USA
[2]Professor, Texas A&M University/Department of Architecture College station, TX, USA

In recent years, research has shown that the educational environment has a profound effect on learning and performance among students, especially those with autism (Mostafa, 2008). Many design solutions that target autistic populations have been introduced for implementation in both mainstream and special education classrooms. Classrooms serve as the major setting for emotional, cognitive, social, and psychological development for all students (Woodcock, Woolner, & Benedyk, 2009). Additionally, for most students with autism, education is centered on learning skills for future independence.

If classrooms and learning environments are not designed to accommodate students with developmental disabilities, it can be assumed that they will not learn these important skills and may struggle to live in our society (Khare & Mullick, 2009). Acoustics is one of the most important issues in the interior design requirements of these children (Caldwell, 2006).

This study consisted of two main stages. The first stage was to evaluate the current situation by distributing a questionnaire to teachers and professionals associated with programs serving children with autism. The second stage involved observing the children's behavior in classrooms with varying noise levels and a short interview with teachers every day of the observation.

The findings led the researcher to recommend a preliminary framework of design guidelines using a quantitative and qualitative analysis to transform the data into tangible knowledge.

Keywords: autism, acoustics, architecture, health, children

INTRODUCTION

Autism is characterized by delayed communication skills, challenges to social interaction, and repetitive behavior. Autism has been excluded from design guidelines for special needs.

Goals and Significance of this Study

This study will be significant for children with autism for five different reasons:

1. Autism has been generally ignored

by the interior design community and excluded from building codes and guidelines, even those developed specifically for special needs individuals. In reference to this exclusion, Baron, from the International Code Council, stated, "I know of no building or accessibility code that incorporates requirements specifically to address children with autism. However, accessibility in general is addressed in the codes developed by the International Code Council" (Baron, 2003), (UN Global Program on Disability, 1993).

Therefore, one of the primary aims of this research is to correct this exclusion by developing a preliminary framework of interior design guidelines for autism. Deasy and Laswell discuss the architect's use of common patterns of cognition to guide and manipulate user behavior in a space (Deasey & Laswell, 1990). If one looks at the meaning, or the cognitive value given to an experience, the way in which a user typically interprets his interior environment becomes clear.

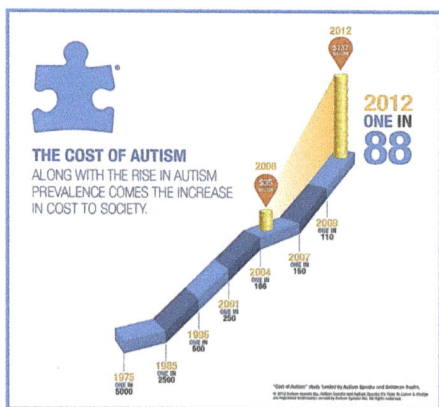

Figure 1. Rise of autism, "Cost of Autism" is a study funded by Autism Speaks and Goldman Sachs.

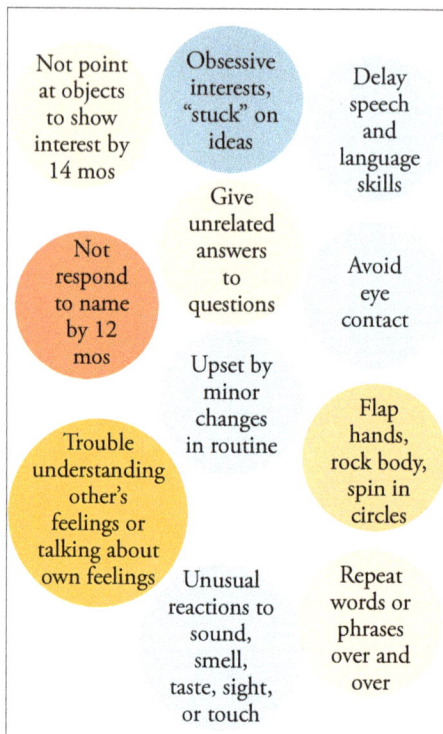

Figure 2. Possible characteristics of people with autism.

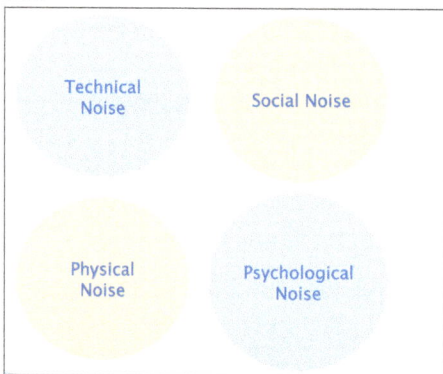

Figure 3. Noise types.

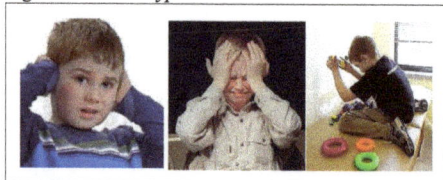

Figure 4. Effect of noise on children with autism.

2. Acoustics is one of the most important issues in interior design. No specific references are made in the mandates regarding individuals with developmental disorders or autism, but the term "consideration" is used in reference to "other communication disorders" (UN Global Program on Disability, 1993).
Individuals with developmental and psycho-social disorders, of which autism is one, have been overlooked (UN Global Program on Disability, 1993).

3. In a study by Mostafa (2008), most parents and teachers (79.3%, 67%, respectively) ranked acoustics as the most significant architectural feature influencing the behavior of autistic children and spatial sequencing as the second most significant (13.19%, 20%, respectively). Lighting, colours and patterns, texture, and smell were ranked lower (Mostafa, 2008).

4. If autistic children are able to understand auditory information they will be more likely to comprehend their environment, both socially and academically. The better we understand the autistic child, the better we can develop ways to intervene in an effective manner (Edelson, 1999).

5. Research indicates that environment is important to the treatment of autism because it influences behavior. The autistic child's environment can be shaped to discourage destructive behaviors and encourage positive behaviors (Edelson, 1999).

PURPOSE OF THE STUDY

The main purpose of this research will be:
• To understand how acoustics impact the behavior of autistic children;
• To generate design guidelines that will support the needs of these children.

METHODOLOGY FOR PHASE 1: TEACHERS' SURVEY

Purpose

The first phase of this research was a survey for teachers of children with autism. The objective of this first phase was to rank the impact of acoustic features such as noise and insulation material on the children's behavior. The results from this ranking would indicate the most influential acoustic factors on autistic behavior, which would become the guide for second phase of this study.

313

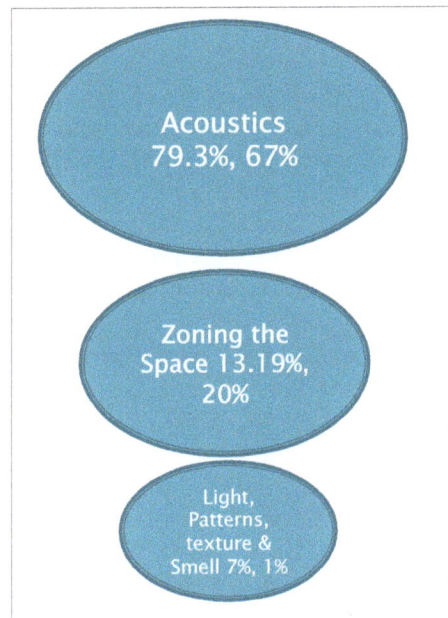

Figure 5. Important features of environments.

METHODOLOGY FOR PHASE 2: BEHAVIOURAL OBSERVATION, BEHAVIOURAL MAPPING, AND VIDEO RECORDING OF CHILDREN

Purpose

To understand how interior space features and spatial environmental characteristics can be used to support the learning and development needs of autistic children.

To compare the behavior of children in noisy classrooms and quiet classrooms so we can understand and define the effect of acoustic features on children with autism behavior. In this way the researcher created a space with minimal sensory stimulation in classrooms which will help children with autism to escape when they feel overwhelmed.

ANTICIPATED RESULTS

In the first phase of the methodology, the researcher documented the teachers' responses to the most significant noise factors that affect children's behavior, the most common behaviors of the children when they have noise in their classroom environment, and their suggestions regarding improving the acoustic environment inside the children's classrooms.

In the second phase of the methodology, the observer documented specific behaviors using the video recorder and sound meter. These tools allowed for a comparison between environmental conditions and the behavior of the children in response to specific noise types. It is expected that rising noise levels in the classrooms would have a negative impact on the behavior of children.

Figure 6. Phase 1: teacher survey and biographies about/by people with autism.

Figure 7. Phase 2: behavioral observation in the field.

	Noises	Behaviors
Teachers	Echoes, air conditioner sounds, sounds from children in the classroom, sounds from other classrooms, traffic noise	Cover ears, hitting, repetitive speech or repetitive behavior
Parents	Air conditioner sounds, traffic sounds	Cover ears, hitting, repetitive behavior
Finding You Finding Me (Book)	Loud sounds, some people voices	Complaining, felt painful
Born on a Blue Day (Book)	Traffic, loud sounds	Cover ears

Figure 8. Noise and behaviors.

The data would be analyzed by using a quantitative method including Freidman tests and Wilcoxon Signed Ranking Tests. Qualitative analyses included descriptive statistics and the recording of interviews with teachers.

314

Figure 9. School 1: classroom 1.

Figure 10. School 1: classroom 2.

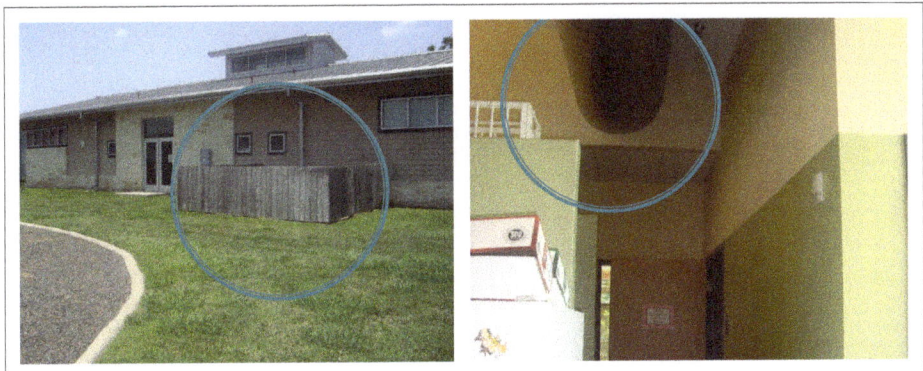

Figure 11. School 1: the picture shows classroom 1, with the HVAC system adjacent to the class, making the environment noisy with high dB readings.

REFERENCES

American Psychiatric Association, (2000). *Diagnostic and statistical manual of mental disorder.* (4th text revision). Washington DC: American Psychiatric Association.

Avondale house, (2011). http://www. avondalehouse.org/

Baron-Cohen, S. (2003). *The Essential differences: Male and Female Brains and the Truth about Autism.* New York: Basic Books.

Baron-Cohen, S. (2007). *The Rise of Autism and the Digital Age.* The World Question Center 2007. New York: Edge Foundation.

Caldwell, P. (2006). *Finding You Finding Me.* Jessica Kingsely Publishers, London, UK.

Centers for Disease Control and Preventation, (2007). *Autism Spectrum Disorders (ASDs) Report.* CDC Division of Media Relations, USA.

Deasy, C.M., and Laswell, T. (1990).

TESIS Inter-University Research Centre "Systems and Technologies for Social and Healthcare Facilities"
University of Florence, Italy

Designing Places for People – A Handbook on Human Behavior for Architects, Designers and Facility Managers. Watson Guptill Publications, New York, USA.

Edelson, J. L. (1999). Children's Witnessing of Adult Domestic Violence. *Journal of Interpersonal Violence,* 14, 8, 839-870.

Haidamous, A. (2011). *Parish School.* www.parishschool.org

Hill, E., and Frith, U. (2003). Understanding Autism: Insights from Mind and Brain. Philosophical Transactions. *Biological Sciences*, 358(1430), 281-289.

Kanner, L. (1943). *Autistic Disturbances of Affective Contact. Nervous Child 2*, 217-250.

Kaplan, A., (1964). *In The Conduct of Inquiry: Methodology for Behavioral Science.* San Francisco: Chandler Publishing Company.

Kaplan, H. et al (2006). *Snoezelen Multi-Sensory Environments, Task Engagements and Generalization.* Research in Developmental Disabilities, 27, 443 – 455.

Khare, R. and Mullick, A. (2009). Incorporating the Behavioral Dimension in Designing Inclusive Learning Environment for Autism. In ArchNet-IJAR: *International Journal of Architectural Research*, vol. 3, issue 3.

Myler, P. A., Fantacone, T. A. and Merritt, E. T. (2003). Eliminating Distractions. The educational needs of autistic children challenge ordinary approaches to school design. *American School and University, special use facilities*, 314-317.

Mostafa, M. (2008). An Architecture for Autism: Concepts of Design Intervention for the Autistic User. *International Journal of Architectural Research*, 2, 189-201

National Institute of Mental Health, (2007). *Autism Spectrum Disorders http://www.nimh.nih.gov/health*

Rimland, B. (1964). *Infantile Autism.* Appleton Century Crofts, New York, USA.

Ulrich, R. S. (1981). Natural versus urban scenes: Some psychological well-being. *Environment and Behavior*, 13, 523-556.

UN Global Program on Disability (1993). Mandates of the UN Global Program on Disability: Standard Rules on the Equalization of Opportunities for Persons with Disabilities. Target Areas for Equal Participation: Accessibility, *United Nations General Assembly resolution* 48/96, annex, 12/20/1993.

Woodcock, A., Woolner, A., Benedyk, R. (2009). Applying the Hexagon-Spindle Model to the design of school environments for children with Autistic spectrum disorders. *Work* 32(3): 249-59.

316

OLD, OLDER, OLDISH – The NEW Elderly and the Impact on Healing Design in Singapore

Bozovic Stamenovic R.[1]

ruzicabozovicstamenovic@gmail.com
[1]Dr.Sc, Associate Professor, Faculty of Architecture, University of Belgrade

This paper tackles emerging issues pertinent to aging in Singapore, and illustrates them with design examples. The public perception of old age is evolving and shifting due to a number of causes such as social and demographic changes, economic considerations, emerging technologies and new cultural habits. The main determining factor affecting all the others, however, is the issue of the character and profile of a different generation of elderly adults. The statistics in Singapore announce the emergence of a more independent and better educated generation of New Elderly. The paper explores the anticipated profound impact of their specific profile, needs and expectations on future better and more affordable design geared towards their wellbeing. One of the objectives is to point to the possible ideological drive in designing for this population, particularly as regards healthcare, housing, and the public domain. Finally, the objective is also to look at trends in the perception of aging and design ideas that transcend the limitations of functionalism and embrace hapticity, embodiment and phantasmagoria in the process.

INTRODUCTION

Singapore shares the problem of an aging population widespread across the developed world. This issue affects urbanized societies regardless of their diverse cultures, social policies or medical resources. Singapore's image of an aging society is bold:
• Today's average age: 36, with a life expectancy of 80;
• Average expected age in 2050: 54 ≥ in Japan and Italy;
• Over 65s make up 8.9% of the population, and are expected to make up 19% by 2030;
• Dependency ratio was 11.4 in 2005 and is expected to be 37.7 in 2030;
• Singapore GDP was 269,97 billion $US in 2005, with 4.5% expenditure for healthcare.
In 2030:
• 13.1% of all those aged 65-74 years old will be university educated = 3 times more than in 2010;
• 62% will have at least secondary education – an important fact since research has already established a strong correlation between educational level and disability.

Many questions arise triggered by the statistics: Who are the new, more educated, demanding and numerous *older adults?* What are their expectations, abilities, fears and dreams? Why might the research based on current 65+ year olds not fit the next senior generation, politically correctly addressed as older adults? Why are these issues of paramount concern and relevance to the society and the healthcare industry?

Public health and the independent elderly population are of paramount strategic interest for any country and even more so for Singapore, a city-state deprived of natural resources. Health and self-reliance are not just private assets but a resource that this country depends upon. Consequently, the attention and the investments poured into maintaining this important national value increase, and as a result an utterly challenging and creative environment also emerges for architects. With the current technocratic policies, issues such as *healthy spaces* for older adults focusing on safety, accessibility, comfort, hygiene, energy consumption and financial returns continue to be addressed as the core objectives. The more advanced, salutogenic approach, however, introduces *healing places for older adults* through a holistic design approach. Academia strives to conceal these sometimes divergent tendencies through theoretical and design research while revealing along the way the commodification of health and imminent manipulation as side-effects. Understanding the changed perception of old age and the emergence of the *oldish*, as they are named in this paper, is crucial for the new design paradigm. The profile, needs and expectations of this new generation of elderly adults are therefore at the core of the discourse.

OLD

A number of issues generated by different platforms persist in shaping the current common perception of old age.

Biological issues transform the previous criterion for senior status, set at the cut-off point of 65 years old, into three distinct categories of seniors: those aged 65-72 are considered elderly adults fully functioning in living and working environments as before, those aged 72-82 may require some assistance with independent living, and those aged 82+ are most likely to require extensive assistance and eventually be institutionalized. Longer life expectancy means that extended years of suffering from chronic deceases may also be expected. However, equality regarding biological status in old age does not necessarily coincide with equal opportunities to improve life conditions.

Social science research has detected that social capital in old people's environments is shrinking mainly due to the inherited cultural idiom *act your age!* Places for the elderly, such as the "seniors' corner" in social housing or typical garage rooftop gardens, are disconnected from social patterns and thus cannot fulfill the need for social integration and building social networks and ties. The inherent social stigma leads to the ghettoization of older communities and even hostility towards them and new facilities for old people in the neighborhood. Stigma against old age is also self-imposed – being old is concealed and often seen as a deficiency in a high-speed working environment.

318

Figure 1. Generation of "the old" caught up between respect and care concerns.

319

Cultural issues address changes affecting the traditional role of old age as respectable and powerful in decision-making terms. The media helps to preserve the respectful image of old age and assists social efforts to support aging. Specific vocabulary develops and terms like *golden age, silver community, peaceful haven* and similar build the image of the noble distinctness of old age. However, an emphasis on support and care also reveals that old people are seen as passive and dependent, and thus a social burden. Demographic issues confirm that with smaller average families and more educated and thus employed women the traditional model of care for older family members is unsustainable. Thus old age is perceived as a burden ultimately affecting many other strata of society such as the economy, workforce policies, productivity and birth rates.

Legislative bodies help social agencies crumbling under the pressure of high numbers by planning more nursing homes and other care facilities. Under these changing conditions, the law regulates family support by obliging children to take care of their parents. Moreover, legislative actions against agism are set to prevent age-related segregation in the workforce. Politics is burdened by the need to sustain social and medical security systems and funds. Political strategies are considering the shrinking and aging workforce, extending the retirement cut-off point while taking into account the impact of the rising number of elderly voters.

Figure 2. Typical ambiences for the elderly in the prevailing social housing environment.

*TESIS Inter-University Research Centre "Systems and Technologies for Social and Healthcare Facilities"
University of Florence, Italy*

At the same time spatial issues focus on providing safe and accessible environments and supporting mobility. The agenda of "aging in place" is recognized, accepted and promoted. However, with a disrupted progressive care system (lacking intermediate facilities between studio apartments for seniors and nursing homes) and limited mobility due to a lack of inclusive urban spaces "aging in place" is not tenable.

320

The newest technologies and IT demand have advanced our abilities to learn new skills. This demand, however, clashes with the declining cognitive capabilities of the elderly. New built-in technologies and gadgets are available to support safety levels and boost independent commuting. However, even simple ones, such as personal alarm devices, have only recently been considered in planning for safety in studio apartments for seniors.

Academic issues focus on finding the right approach in investigating the spatial implications of old age. The transition from barrier-free design to accessibility, universal design and the latest evidence-based design has been established. However, the tendency towards Descartesian scientific rigor in academic research limits the addressed topics to pragmatic, quantifiable ones, while skipping over the qualitative and affective values of space. Research is also compartmentalized in different disciplines and thus only selectively informs us about design requirements for old age. A lack of interdisciplinary research and reliance on behavioral studies in determining the ideal spaces for aged users has lead to other misunderstandings across disciplines. This is why a number of spaces specifically assigned to senior citizens do not serve their purpose and remain abandoned while old people gather in informal locations where social life unfolds (in front of shops or lift lobbies for example), in places where they can see and be seen.

In short, the adjective *old* is a synonym for distinct problems, partial solutions and an unfocused vision regarding the future. Calling someone old sounds judgmental and almost implies a deterministic verdict, something irrevocable and stigmatizing, a condition that requires not only care but also cure.

OLDER

The attribute old has been replaced in research literature by an apparently more acceptable term: older adults. The comparative adjective older loses some of the deterministic condemnation feel of the word old. However, it also announces disguise and even hypocrisy in dealing with aging. The use of the adjective older is not just a persuasive linguistic maneuver to skip incorrectness. We live in a world where linguistic expressions pointing to the equality of social groups seem more relevant than the actual state of, or battle for, this same equality. Therefore, the promotion of the image of older adults best described by the slogan "yes, you can" does not refer to their needs but rather social expectations regarding this group.

Public media is making changes and promoting this older user group too. Marketing, the tourism industry, retail and industrial design are all paying more attention to their existence than ever before since older adults are increasingly becoming their main target group. Social support networks and political decisions in favour of older adults are also set in place. The retirement age has been postponed and social norms regarding the involvement of people over 65

Figure 3. Supportive spaces for exercise and training for the independent living of older adults.

321

years old are tweaked to accommodate the more prominent presence of this age group in public life.

Branding older adults to raise appreciation has been further established through visual media. Film makers, for example, assign roles to older adults roles previously meant for the young (love, sports, action), or promote bonding outside of the family circle as a substitute for weakened family ties. Being older apparently does not suggest deprivation of all the privileges held before (health, social position and economic power), but rather implies certain alterations in lifestyle. The positive aspect of the social change implied by the adjective older is undeniable. The public domain, including public transport, is now fully accessible. Healthcare facilities are built to match the rising needs and stigma is fought through public campaigns.

However being an older adult also implies a dual position for a person categorized as such. Older adults still hold on to the traditional privileges affiliated with old age (respect, support, care), but are also obliged and even subtly pressured to respond to certain expectations:

- to maintain a healthy lifestyle, preserve health and prolong independence in daily life;
- to embrace financial responsibilities linked to a later retirement age and staying longer in the workforce.

In spite of this shift, design for older adults remains trapped in transition from barrier-free to universal, safe and risk-free environments. Playgrounds for older adults are built but they are often not utilized due to the prevailing cultural constraints still holding back the old generation.

The design of salutogenic public spaces as opportunities for multigenerational integration is sporadically rather than systematically addressed. The lack of rest areas and toilet facilities in bustling central areas urges older adults to avoid them. Even the

1-How do you see yourself spending your old age?

	1A1	1A2	1B	1C
Below 50	56	12	4	18
Above 50	32	4	2	2

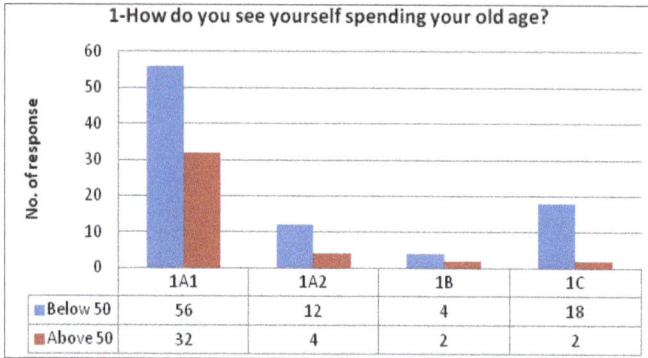

Table 1. Results of the indicative survey on the perception of old age.

322

traditional acupressure stimulation areas in housing estates are rarely utilized. However, new housing typologies, such as studio apartment blocks for independent living, emerge from the very well organized public housing sector. Studio apartment blocks are built according to universal design principles. Showrooms as training centres are organized in community hospitals to help older adults maintain independence even after hospitalization and rehab periods.

Overall, spatial considerations for older adults are more geared towards their positioning in Euclidian space rather than a psychological representation of space, mental mapping and the construction of places.

OLDISH – THE RISE OF THE NEW ELDERLY

The results of the indicative survey on the perception of aging revealed that aging in place (1A1+A2) is still a preferential option compared to specially designed environments such as retirement homes or senior studio apartments (1B) for respondents both under and over 50 years old. However, having many respondents under 50 years old does not necessarily imply that they would age in place living with a family, and many would still also consider living in special homes designed for independent

living in a green, accessible, social, friendly and vibrant environment (1C).

The under 50 group was also much more critical in grading satisfaction levels relating to spaces for the elderly in the HDB[1] environment while the over 50s, the ones actually affected, were more complacent. What caused this difference in views on old age?

Rapid changes in communication technologies and platforms, globalized urban environments that alter traditions and share trends, and the competitiveness of the baby-boomers further change our perspective on older adults. Forever young, as a prevailing mantra of the optimistic post WWII world, lived long enough to be manicured, revamped and adopted in this century too by the bulky strata of the new elderly, or the *oldish*.

The sense of reality has been deliberately removed from this surreal representation of old age. The advertised image of smiling old people, surprisingly active and always surrounded by similarly cheerful companions fetishizes the spirit in old age over matter and bodily experiences that can't cope. *Oldish* is branded as a lifestyle, a target, a permanent state with elusive prospects ahead.

1. *HDB - Housing Development Board, the main provider of social housing in Singapore.*

Never getting old and helpless is subtly implied as a target that, with media enforcements, seems achievable. Altering one's state of mind with regard to aging is not of course going to prevent it from happening. However, it might open up unexpected opportunities to cope with it better and at the same time raise satisfaction regarding the quality of life.

Who benefits from the emergence of the *oldish*?
• The generation of the *oldish* – for them this new position unleashes unforeseen personal strengths to cope with old age and at the same time creates other personal benefits: late-life career change, better social life, self-confidence and respect, etc.
• The society is interested in seeing the new elderly as self-reliant as less social care is anticipated.
• The consumer market is enlarged with the average buyer of commodities pushed to middle age and beyond; this is conveniently the time when their financial strengths and consumer appetites are also higher.
• The benefit of propagating the *oldish* in movies, media campaigns, commercials, tourism, leisure and other entertainment industries is in creating this persuasive realm where the *oldish* feel comfortable, accepted and, more importantly, empowered. However, the message hypocritically delivered to the *oldish* through media is as persuasive as the common "everything will be OK," but without mentioning how exactly.
• By building the optimistic consumer sprit in spite of the other inevitable attributes of old age – declining biological processes and related consequences for cognition and skills – media mes-

323

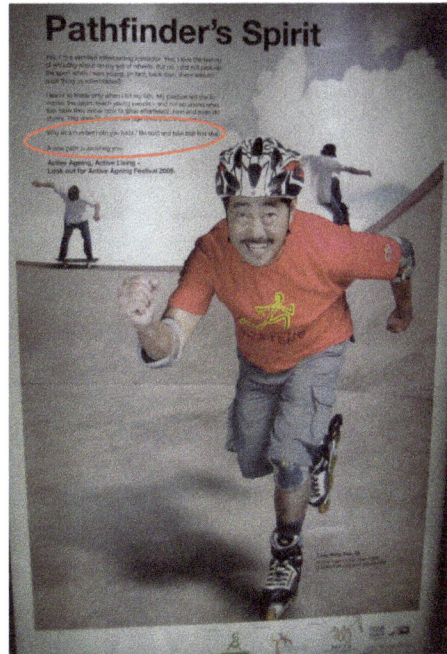
Figure 4. An advertisement at a bus stop promoting an example of an active elderly person.

Figure 5. A multi-generation group of line-dancers regularly exercise in public places.

324

sages are convincing this age group that they are just a little bit off their prime age, –oldish– but nothing more. Thus, the positive aura around old age concurrently and conveniently lessens the burden on social care by partially or fully transmitting it to the senior citizens. The message conveyed through media is: you have to live an active lifestyle, eat and live healthily, exercise, go back to work, socialize, you need to be happy, etc., also hinting that if they do not follow this approach the consequences would not be of societal concern.

• Positive social feedback and approval of the new image of the *oldish* becomes a safe foundation for introducing other policies that might profoundly alter the life of senior citizens in the future. Campaigns such as aging in place are introduced and supported by authorities with incentives and special plans. Considering that the majority of necessary spatial alterations to accommodate the consequences of aging in place are in existing, private homes these plans are, in terms of cost, at best a shared responsibility. On the other hand the responsibility for staying *oldish* and indefinitely postponing the point of becoming old lies entirely with the key protagonists: old people.

• The developers' market may also be impacted since the need and demand for adaptable, customized housing would arise.

To summarize:

Old equals respect and a traditional cultural role set for old people, attention but also pity, stigma, spatial and social isolation and often powerlessness.

Older equals less respect, more stigma, some help and again no power or at best limited control over the institutional-

ized care and social support networks and spaces.

Oldish equals self-help, respect and social praise for not acting old, total control but also total responsibility regarding living circumstances, open-ended social networking with growing and changing tendencies, the ability to trespass into domains reserved for the young such as sports, IT and work; also the power to abandon the old social stereotypes and create new ones.

DESIGN FOR THE *OLDISH - New Tendencies Matching the User Profile and Design*

The new elderly have more confidence, aspirations and hopes, but also declining senses, functional mobility and share social and fiscal concerns. They are open

Figure 6. Social space for social encounters and bonding in a multigeneration housing environment. (Heng Hui Jun Lina, mentor Ruzica Bozovic Stamenovic)

to opportunities, however the common current design response is merely supportive: assistive devices, universally designed spaces and appliances, safety surveillance and even ghettoized facilities with the symbolic resemblance of real living environments. In spite of good intentions the "memory lane" approach carries a certain inherent distortion from reality which further burdens the new elderly. The evidence-based strategies relying on indicators gathered from the old and older cohorts might be anticipated as a confusing betrayal and thus unsuitable for the *oldish* generation. Design solutions too often lack parody, imagination and phantasm while the very construct of *oldish* or the new elderly is paradoxical in its essence.

The mismatch between this new user profile and current design models needs to be addressed with the creative and challenging development of new programs and typologies.
Design needs to encourage bonding and bridging between different social groups in order to raise the social capital value. The new elderly need spaces that foster visual and verbal communication, explicit and implied interactions, and provide choice between these categories. Academia[2] is leading the change by examining advanced design paradigms for the new elderly. For example the Design Studio projects examined the possibility of mixing housing for students and young families with nursing homes for dementia patients. Issues of security, privacy and hierarchical levels of communication between users were particularly addressed.

---

2. *National University of Singapore, Department of Architecture.*

Psycho-Physical Support and Design

The environmental press theory considers design as a motivating force for independent aging. Space acts as a powerful tool in shaping the positive behavioural response and in fostering adaptation skills. Research acknowledges the relevance of competence levels on both behaviour and abilities to adapt. The new, more educated elderly are likely to experience a shorter adaptation time to new and invigorating environments. Therefore, more dynamic environmental changes are required to maintain workable levels of stimuli for the generation of the *oldish*.

In this example (Figure 7) of integrated housing for seniors' independent living a continuous green link is established to guide the elderly from the threshold of the apartments to the ground floor community space.
Green ramps and social spaces stretching alongside the ramp boost the physical and mental activity levels of the elderly commuters.

Balconies and common courtyards placed at regular intervals, and corridors and ramps for walking and exercising, provide interaction among all age groups. The space assures adequate psycho-physical support as well as social protection and commitment. As a result the participation of the elderly in social life or even the workforce is expected to limit their isolation, which is deemed to be the main cause of the mental problems many of them may experience.

325

Due to sheer numbers, the idea of ghettoized, surreal retirement villages will not be feasible for the new generation of elderly, let alone good for their sense of aging in place.

In defining the quality of life, WHO relies on individuals' perceptions rooted in their respective context, culture and value system. In this respect the goals, expectations, standards and concerns of the new elderly ambitiously extend to the urban level too. Design strategies for public spaces cater to the personal mobility of the elderly as a prerequisite for social interactions. In that sense, the Green Link example (Figure 9) is more than part of the urban infrastructure.

The design is innovative and redefines the image of an inclusive environment catering for the entire population so that extended families can visit, exercise or just stroll together. The space of the bridge deck is particularly safe, accessible and comfortable but also empathetic towards the *oldish* in an explorative, intriguing, challenging and joyful manner.

Spatial comprehension of the living environment continuously fades in

Figure 7. Integrated housing for seniors' independent living. (Phuong Oanh Tran, mentor Ruzica Bozovic Stamenovic).

Figure 8. Mixed development – nursing home and housing for students and young families. (Heng Hui Jun Lina, mentor Ruzica Bozovic Stamenovic).

326

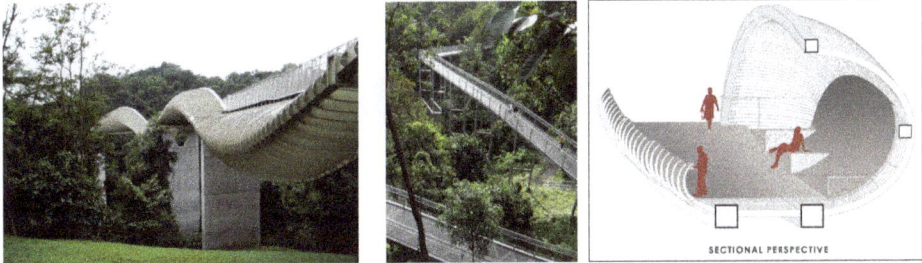

Figure 9. Integrative public space – the Henderson Waves pedestrian bridge and green connector.

327

old age and cognitive maps become less subtle with voids and blind spots. The *oldish* generation will not be spared and the design of the liveable city for their future must balance their hopes and their fading faculties.

Therefore, the role of design for the *oldish* might be to offer accommodative substitutes – spatial escapes, relief spots that rely on reflexes and ancestral behavioural models rather than knowledge or comprehensive skills that decline first. (Kitchin et al, 2002). Differently characterized escape nodes are particularly precious in high density-high rise Singapore.

Figure 10. Escape nodes for the busy city centre (He Yuhang, mentor Ruzica Bozovic Stamenovic), and the escape rooftop gardens on The Pinnacle (50-storey social housing block).

TESIS Inter-University Research Centre "Systems and Technologies for Social and Healthcare Facilities"
University of Florence, Italy

Branding the Design for the Oldish

The *oldish* batch grew up and is currently maturing in an extraordinary urban environment that has changed very quickly and profoundly over the last 50 years acquiring a somewhat phantasmagoric character along the way. The city centre, shopping and entertainment areas are bursting with scenic spots, surreal and theatrical constellations where art and the quotidian intertwine (Figure 11).

Therefore, we assume that the new elderly might be very sympathetic to play and imagination in the spaces they inhabit. The blurred semantic boundaries of non-representational architecture might be interesting to dissect and discuss in relation to the new elderly. The *oldish* might not just tolerate but actually need the sense of phantasmagoria as a sort of mental gymnastics. Therefore, the same principles applied to branding the current image of Singapore should be carried over into branding the spaces for its *oldish* population of the future.

The new elderly might be looking for spaces with a certain flair, environments in which the bold reality of old age seems easy to overcome by immersing oneself into the imaginative. The dream-like, surreal environments where the *oldish* might feel empowered and good actually also fulfill the criteria for healing spaces as they have physical, social, symbolic and environmental qualities. Environmental technologies also make a mark in spaces for the *oldish* (Figure 12). The green brand is particularly applicable as a number of studies confirm the importance of green public areas in the vicinity of housing estates lived in by the

Figure 11. Branding the phantasmagoric image of the urban public spaces.

329

Figure 12. Examples of green technologies and urban agriculture in housing for the elderly. (Lee Hon Bill, mentor Ruzica Bozovic Stamenovic)

elderly (Takano et al, 2002) and connect it to longevity. Contact with nature is also beneficial for mental health (Barton et al, 2010; Groenewegen et al, 2006; Sugiyama et al, 2008). Green building technologies allow for this contact to be more direct and easy to maintain, for instance vertical gardens as green walls.

CONCLUSIONS

In conclusion, the shifting characteristics of the coming generation of elderly will not affect the dominance of essential concerns regarding physical mobility and safety, social integration and spatial stimulation. However, it is the synergy between these aspects that matters the most as it positively affects behavioural plasticity and better adaptation to old age.

The possibility of slowing down if not even reversing the aging process by altering telomere lengths is a thrilling perspective for the future and a challenge for architects and scientists alike. With the prospect of longevity we might expect some profoundly different spatial solutions for the new elderly and consequently some un-

precedented implications for their behaviour and lives.

New developments in design and construction technologies and processes, and the application of BIM, parametric modelling, digital fabrication, adaptive design and robotic/digital construction might result in different design approaches to common issues such as safety and mobility in old age. Anticipation that these technologies might further dehumanize the production of the architectural space is of great concern. However, it is the perception of generic topics such as health and healing, aging and agism, independence and liability that should drive architects to generate context-specific changes in the design of healthcare, housing, work and public spaces alike.

Ultimately, this paper contains predictive rather than conclusive statements. The optimistic spirit in which it is written is fully down to the spirit of Singapore, a city that transforms and reinvents itself at an unprecedented rate and with outstanding results.

REFERENCES

Barton, J., & Pretty, J. (2010). What is the best dose of nature and green exercise for improving mental health? A multi-study analysis. *Environmental science & technology*, 44(10), 3947-3955.

Berkman, L. F., Glass, T., Brissette, I., & Seeman, T. E. (2000). From social integration to health: Durkheim in the new millennium. *Social science & medicine*, 51(6), 843-857.

Chan, A., Ofstedal, M. B., & Hermalin, A. I. (2002). Changes in subjective and objective measures of economic well-being and their interrelationship among the elderly in Singapore and Taiwan. *Social Indicators Research*, 57 (3), 263-300.

Chan, K. M., Pang, W. S., Ee, C. H., Ding, Y. Y., & Choo, P. (1997). Epidemiology of falls among the elderly community dwellers in Singapore. *Singapore medical journal*, 38 (10), 427-431.

Chan, K. M., Pang, W. S., Ee, C. H., Ding, Y. Y., & Choo, P. (1999). Functional status of the elderly in Singapore. *Singapore medical journal*, 40 (10), 635-638.

Groenewegen, P. P., Van den Berg, A. E., De Vries, S., & Verheij, R. A. (2006). Vitamin G: effects of green space on health, well-being, and social safety. *BMC public health*, 6 (1), 149.

Kitchin, R., & Blades, M. (2002). *The cognition of geographic space* (Vol. 4). London: IB Tauris, 87

Lian, W. M., Gan, G. L., Pin, C. H., Wee, S., & Ye, H. C. (1999). Correlates of leisure-time physical activity in an elderly population in Singapore. *American journal of public health*, 89 (10), 1578-1580.

Maas, J., Van Dillen, S. M., Verheij, R. A., & Groenewegen, P. P. (2009). Social contacts as a possible mechanism behind the relation between green space and health. *Health & place*, 15 (2), 586-595.

Sugiyama, T., Leslie, E., Giles-Corti, B., & Owen, N. (2008). Associations of neighbourhood greenness with physical and mental health: do walking, social coherence and local social interaction explain the relationships? *Journal of Epidemiology and Community Health*, 62 (5), e9-e9.

Sugiyama, T., Thompson, C. W., & Alves, S. (2009). Associations between neighborhood open space attributes and quality of life for older people in Britain. *Environment and Behavior*, 41(1), 3-21.

Takano, T., Nakamura, K., & Watanabe, M. (2002). Urban residential environments and senior citizens' longevity in megacity areas: the importance of walkable green spaces. *Journal of epidemiology and community health*, 56(12), 913-918.

330

Normalization of Therapy through Design

Wilson Orr L.[1]

lwo@parkin.ca
[1] Parkin Architects Limited, Canada

As the general population is aging and the number of over 65s is increasing, we are seeing more people requiring rehabilitation following traumatic healthcare events. At the other end of the spectrum, however, there is a cohort of children who need rehabilitation therapy to enhance their capacity to live well. Both groups can benefit from receiving rehabilitation therapy in their home and/or community. New research (McClusky, 2008) is showing that changes in therapy strategies and a physical environment that supports these strategies can influence the success of the outcome. "Normalization of Therapy" is a new approach where therapy is offered in an environment that reflects the "real" world and there is evidence to suggest that the therapy is better absorbed by the patient, resulting in more positive outcomes. New architectural solutions are exploring how evidence-based design can contribute to more effective treatments and earlier discharge. This presentation looks at the work of Patricia Moore and the development of "Easy Street" and "Independence Square" which are the precursors to the Normalization of Therapy approach followed by some recent Ontario rehabilitation facilities that incorporate Normalized Therapy areas.

This presentation looks at the work of Patricia Moore and the development of "Easy Street" and "Independence Square" which are the precursors to the Normalization of Therapy approach followed by some recent Ontario rehabilitation facilities that incorporate Normalized Therapy areas. Patricia Moore, an industrial designer at Moore Design Associates, has developed various environments within medical facilities that simulate real life.

"Independence Way" helps veterans suffering from traumatic brain injuries (TBI) or other neurological or physical conditions train for re-entry into their community (Kaplan, 2011).

"Easy Street" is a 3,500 sq ft rehabilitation facility which looks like a city street. The simulated street is designed to help patients learn skills to ease daily living but also help the client's family and friends learn how to assist them in the real world (Stafford, 1996).

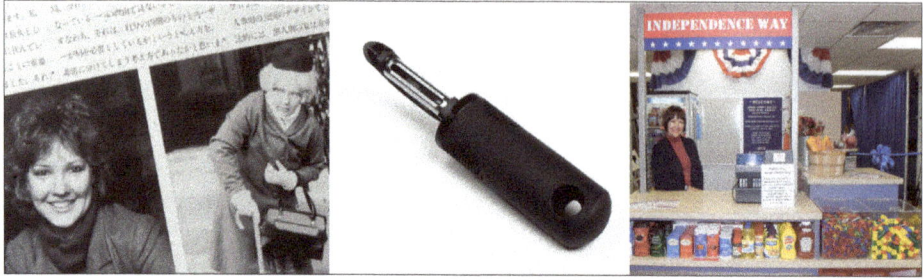

Figure 1. Precedent work: Patricia Moore, industrial designer, gerontologist.

332

Similarly, Hamilton Health Sciences Rehabilitation and Acquired Brain Injury Building by Parkin Architects in association with McCallum Sather Architects includes both centralized and on-unit therapy areas as well as extensive outdoor therapy areas that incorporate a variety of types of walking and wheeling surfaces, varying grades of ramps, different types of outdoor seating and other real world challenges for rehabilitation patients.

The new centre consolidates rehabilitation programs from multiple sites in the Hamilton Region including a specialized Acquired Brain Injury facility in addition to Neuromuscular Rehabilitation and Neurocognitive Rehabilitation outpatient and inpatient programs.

Figure 2. Hamilton Health Sciences, Rehabilitation and Acquired Brain Injury Building, entrance.

Figure 3. Hamilton Health Sciences, Rehabilitation and Acquired Brain Injury Building, masterplan.

Figure 4. Hamilton Health Sciences, Rehabilitation and Acquired Brain Injury Building. Outdoor rehabilitation/social spaces, variable terrain and integrated wheelchair spaces (left); various exercise features integrated into the pool are used to help with rehabilitation (right, above), simple clear wayfinding (right, below).

Recent changes in rehabilitation programs in Ontario mean that inpatients are being returned to their homes much earlier in their recovery path and extensive and intensive outpatient therapy programs have developed to support this early discharge.

Children requiring rehabilitation therapy form a small and consistent percentage of the general population and many are medically fragile, technology-dependent kids while others require less intensive interventions. There are an increasing number of children with Autism Spectrum disorders and these children also benefit from rehabilitation therapy. Many of these children have associated gross motor and/or fine motor deficits in addition to behavioural or cognitive challenges. Within this context, Normalization of Therapy may simulate a junior kindergarten classroom or play area, for example, to teach children the skills that they need to be better integrated, successful and happy. A child's fine motor skills can be improved through using therapeutic manipulatives but can be better improved through using common, everyday household tools and the lessons are then more transferrable to real world situations at home, the playground or other public places.

For example, learning to make cup cakes for a birthday party involves measuring skills, fine motor skills to hold and pour ingredients, and focused attention, all of which can be both challenging and rewarding for children. Since for many of these children invitations to birthday parties are few and far between, integration skills are crucial to their social development. A trip to the playground is a huge

333

334

Figure 5. The garden: steps, grade changes, surface changes, exercise/resting bars, evening lighting with seamless transitions to the interior rehabilitation areas.

challenge for many of these children and a balanced, sensitive universal design approach is required to present challenges that help children develop skills while also respecting capabilities. Those using walkers, for example, are often tired by the time they make the trip from home to the playground and "accessible" playgrounds sometimes require excessive or unreasonable effort to use play elements (e.g. steep ramps, lack of adequate turning spaces or inappropriate surface materials). For other children, the challenge may be playing in an area with others in a way that does not result in tears and arguments.

The new ErinoakKids Centres for Treatment and Development located in Brampton, Mississauga and Oakville are being designed to meet the needs of these children in a new kind of environment. Large therapy rooms are set up as junior kindergarten rooms with sand tables, water play, reading and drama areas so that children can master new skills in an environment very similar to the one they are preparing to enter in the community. Indoor therapy spaces will have equipment that looks like play equip-

ment to encourage climbing, balancing and other skills that could be used in real world applications.

By focusing on meeting the real world rehabilitation needs of adults and children, we can design more effective facilities that help patients achieve optimal independence sooner and at a lower cost to the healthcare system.

REFERENCES

Kaplan, M. D. G. (2011). At the VA, preparing brain-injured veterans for the real world. Smart Planet. Retrieved on August 26, 2013 from http://www.smartplanet.com/blog/pure-genius/at-the-va-preparing-brain-injured-veterans-for-the-real-world/5451

McClusky, J. F. (2008). Creating engaging experiences for rehabilitation. *Topics in Stroke Rehabilitation*. Vol. 15, Issue 2, 80.

Stafford, J. (1996). "Easy St." Therapy. *Chicago Tribune*. Retrieved on August 26, 2013 from http://articles.chicagotribune.com/1996-01-18/news/9601200099_1_easy-street-city-street-outpatient

Towards the Design of a Truly Integrated, Community-Based, Health and Wellness Facility

Colucci G.[1]

gcolucci@dsai.ca
[1]Diamond Schmitt Architects, Canada

Treatment, care and prevention are the cornerstones of most healthcare service delivery providers. This paper describes the theory and practice of accommodating a truly integrated system of community-based health and wellness facilities. An example of this model is one where long-term care, ambulatory care, complex continuing care, life sciences research, education, fitness, learning resource centres and even food markets are co-located within urban, suburban and rural residential communities.

Keywords: *community-based health, wellness facilities*

INTRODUCTION

The idea for this paper came from a competition for an ambulatory care hospital in Ontario. The program brief stressed the importance of wellness and prevention as much as treatment and care.

A study of the allocation of space made it apparent that the wellness and prevention agenda was receiving substantially less floor space than the treatment and care agenda. This prompted the question, "What does it take to design a truly integrated, community based, health and wellness facility?"

This paper is more an inquiry than a proposition. It is intended to stimulate the discussion of a topic that may have profound social and economic implications.

The paper addresses three questions:

– "What is a truly integrated, community-based, health and wellness facility?" Does it have to be facility-based or can it simply be a network of coordinated services?

– "How can it be implemented? What are the economic models and challenges in creating it?"

– "Where is it being built or provided?" What is it? To explain this, the campus of care model will be used.

Campus of Care

Treatment and care (and cure) as well as wellness and prevention, are the cornerstones of most healthcare service providers.

336

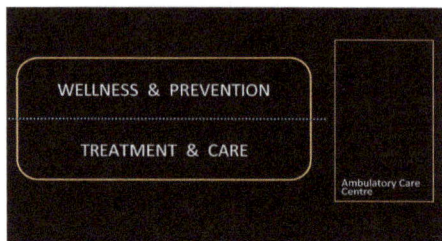

Figure 1. 1st version of the campus plan schematic diagrams.

A campus of care should include a series of facilities:

- *ACC:* an Ambulatory Care Hospital is the facility that anchors the campus, as its purpose is to provide both treatment and care as well as wellness and prevention.

Figure 2 pictures a 300,000 sq ft ambulatory care centre designed as an addition to an existing full services hospital in Medicine Hat, Alberta. All procedures and visits are scheduled and there are no overnight stays in the addition. Clinics include cancer treatment, dialysis, maternal and child health, day medicine and primary care as well as 12 ORs and procedure rooms and a full maternity department.

- *LRC:* a key component on the prevention side is a Learning Resource Centre where health education is provided. This is a locale for seminars and demonstrations, access to resource material, online information and where community specific research can occur (Figure 3).

Figure 2. Medicine Hat Regional Hospital Addition and Redevelopment - Diamond Schmitt Architects.

Figure 3. LRC, Tommy Douglas Library, interiors view - Diamond Schmitt Architects.

Figure 4. Fitness and Community Centre. Cawthra Community Centre, interiors view - Diamond Schmitt Architects.

Figure 5. Complex Continuing Care and Rehab. Bridgepoint Active Healthcare, interiors view - Diamond Schmitt Architects.

- Fitness and Community Centre: exercise and fitness training facilities with plentiful access to outdoor trails (Figure 4).

- CCC Rehab: on the treatment and care side, a centre for the treatment of complex continuing disease and rehabilitation (Figure 5).

- Mental Health: a mental health centre, such as that shown in Figure 6 which is a clinic in Australia specifically designed for children with autism.

- Cancer Treatment: a cancer treatment centre such as the series of purpose-built facilities in the UK known as Maggie's Centre, designed by OMA, at Gartnavel General Hospital, Glasgow (Figure 7).

- Guesthouse: a guest house would provide accommodation for visitors and caregivers serving patients being treated across the campus (Figure 8).

- Assisted Living: those requiring assisted living would benefit from convenient access to all campus facilities (Figure 11).

- Long-term Care: a long-term care facility that enables aging in place for those suffering from Alzheimer's and dementia (Figure 12).

- Market: finally, a marketplace that specializes in locally grown produce, not only to supply food to the campus but also to support dieticians' classes on nutrition and develop healthy eating habits. Foods could be classified according to their nutritional value similar to Loblaw's Guiding Stars program (Figure 13).

337

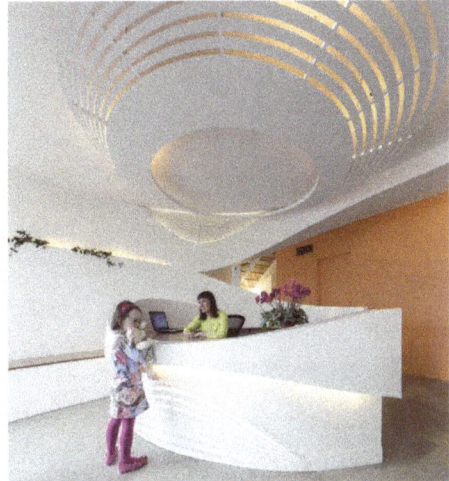

Figure 6. Mental Health, Edgecliff Medical Centre, NSW Australia - Enter Architecture.

Figure 7. Cancer Centre, Maggie's Centre, Gartnavel General Hospital, Glasgow, UK - OMA.

Figure 8. Guest House. Queen's University Residences - Diamond Schmitt Architects.

This gives a picture of a truly integrated, community-focused, health and wellness centre. The idea is to create an integrated network of services and facilities, either collocated on a single campus or within reasonable proximity to support larger residential and commercial zones (Figure 9). This model should be applicable to urban, suburban and rural communities.

HOW CAN IT BE IMPLEMENTED?

If we look at the ownership of these facilities in Ontario, they are a mixture of various public ownerships, particularly on the treatment and care side, private ownership or a combination (Figure10). There are a number of examples of private only, public only and joint facilities. Each has their strengths and limitations.

338

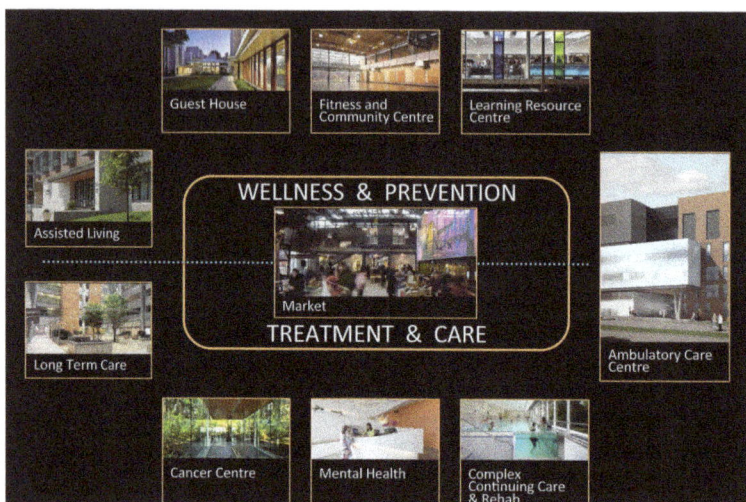

Figure 9. Campus Facility Plan.

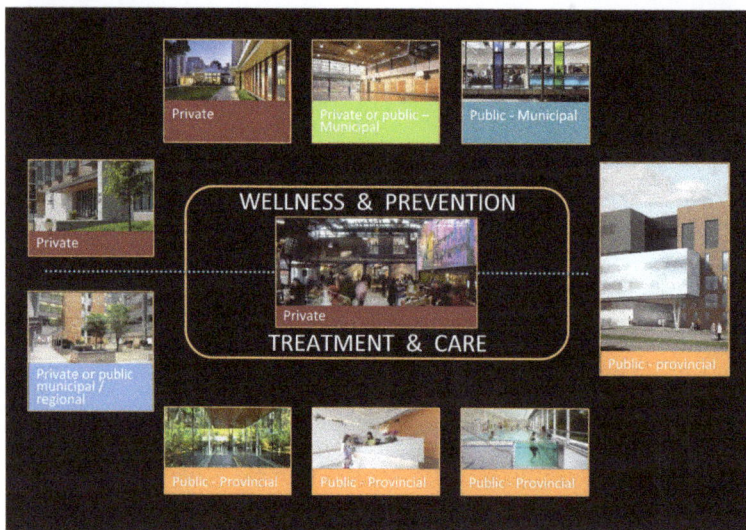

Figure 10. Campus Funding Plan.

Figure 11. Russell Hill Assisted Living - Diamond Schmitt Architects.

Private

Looking at the private side, Kaiser Permanente is a leader in the US with over 9 million subscribers. It operates a very comprehensive network of wellness, treatment and care facilities (Figure 14). As an insurance company as well as a healthcare provider, it is able to carefully manage its clientele's health needs. Its goal is to perfect the management of subscribers' health so that a visit to the emergency room can be avoided. "Any unplanned hospital admissions are a sign of system failure," it says. Like many US care providers and insurers, not everyone qualifies to become a member. KP's services seem to remain largely internally coordinated with few connections to public or non-KP services and facilities.

Public - HealthLinks

On the publically funded side, there are a number of agencies that promote coordinated care delivery and health promotion. Ontario's HealthLinks is a comprehensive program, primarily for seniors and those suffering from complex chronic conditions (Figure 15). Its emphasis is on having various healthcare providers integrate their information and provide each patient with an individualized care and treatment plan. It relies heavily upon electronic health records and aims to reduce duplication of the healthcare service from various service providers. "Patients should receive faster care, spend less time waiting for services and be supported by a team of healthcare providers at all levels of the health care system." It appears to be integrated primarily with other publically funded agencies and, owing to the age of its target population, does not address the prevention side of the equation.

339

TESIS

340

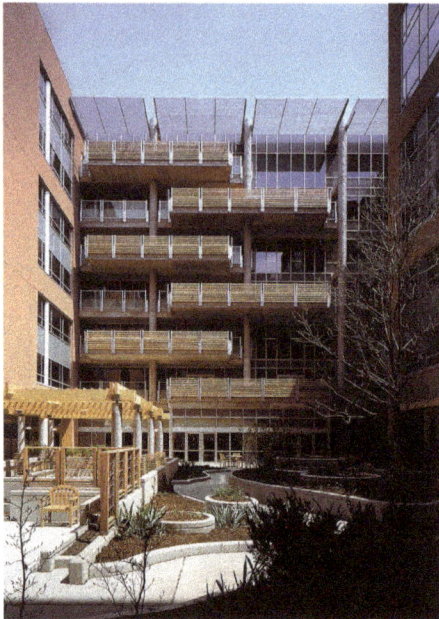

Figure 12. Long-Term Care. Baycrest Centre for Geriatric Care - Diamond Schmitt Architects.

Public – Prevention Research Centres

There is a very interesting association of Prevention Research Centres, close to 40, across the US (Figure 16). These centres tend to specialize in specific areas of disease prevention and are affiliated with the national centres for disease control. They focus on research and appear to be integrated primarily with other research institutes.

Private – Public

About 12 years ago, the UK's National Health Service partnered with Kaiser Permanente to adapt its publicly funded health system to KP's holistic approach to wellness, prevention, treatment and care (Figure 17). A test site was developed in southwest England in a town c alled Torquay.

The objective was to integrate treatment and care at community hospitals with a robust program of social care and healthy lifestyle services. Similar to KP, its objective was to reduce unscheduled care, foster self-care and shift healthcare out of hospitals all together. To date, it claims to have reduced inpatient stays by 20%.

Figure 13. Market. Evergreen Brickworks - Diamond Schmitt Architects.

WHERE IS IT BEING DONE?

The following two projects are striking in their differences but similar in their potential.

Butaro Hospital, Rwanda

The first is a rural, 150-bed community hospital completed in January 2011 (Figure 18). It was built in Burera, one of Rwanda's worst serviced regions. Over 3,000 members of the community were trained in construction techniques to build the facility. They worked multiple shifts around the clock to distribute the opportunity for labour income. The quality stonework shown (Figure 19) is remarkable. In addition to the four basic services (maternity, internal medicine, surgery, and paediatrics), the hospital includes an emergency department, a full surgery ward, a neonatal intensive care unit (NICU), an intensive care unit (ICU), outpatient services and laboratories. The facility features modern measures for infection control including natural cross-ventilation through clerestories, secluded patients wards around courtyards, and an effective spatial triage system allowing for the separation of patients based on their condition.

The vision for the hospital includes creating a scientific community of clinical and non-clinical staff with the hope that people will travel to teach, learn, deliver care, and seek care at the new facility.

While there does not appear to be a prevention and wellness program per se, its significance to the regional community makes it a natural location to expand into this area.

341

Figure 14. Kaiser Permanente.

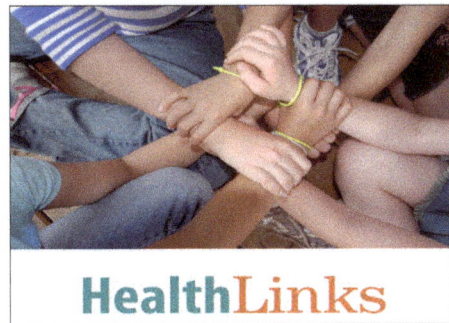

Figure 15. Ontario Health Links.

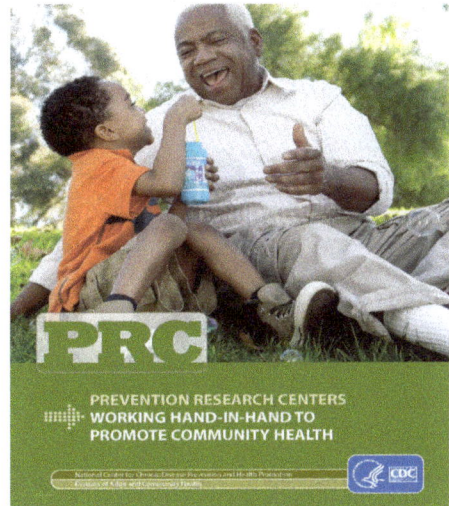

Figure 16. Prevention Research Centres.

342

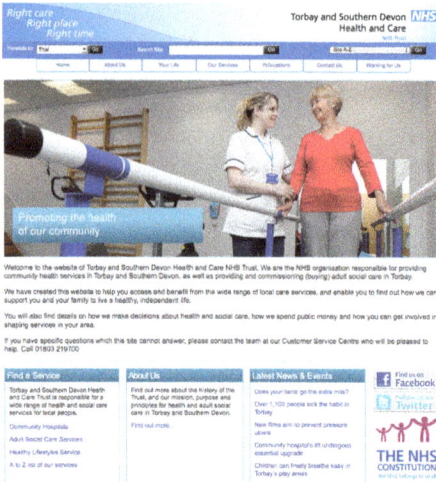

Figure 17. UK's NHS with Kaiser Permanente.

Bridgepoint Active Healthcare

Bridgepoint Active Healthcare is in many ways at the opposite end of the spectrum. Completed in March of 2013, Bridgepoint is a 472-bed complex continuing care and rehab hospital treating those with chronic illness and those recovering from stroke or physical injury. It was designed and build under Ontario's P3 program with Diamond Schmitt and HDR Architecture as the architects of record. Stantec KPMB served as the hospital's Planning Design and Compliance architects.

Like Butaro Hospital in Rwanda, Bridgepoint has the potential to become a campus of care where the full range of wellness and prevention as well as treatment and care services can be provided. Indeed, it is Bridgepoint's ambition to do so. Bridgepoint has a strong community focus, where the lines between public and private properties are blurred.

Figure 18. Butaro Hospital, Burera District, Rwanda - MASS Design Group.

The site is well accessed by public transport and contains a Carnegie funded library, children's palliative care centre, city park, historic former jail and an endless backyard to the north across Riverdale Park. It has four large plots of land earmarked for future development. Services and programs will be compatible with Bridgepoint's CCC, rehab, ambulatory care as well as research, teaching, and disease and injury prevention (Figure 20).

Park View and Street View: at grade, the public is free to enter its outdoor terraces, gardens and pathways en route to the city's network of nature trails and bicycle paths (Figure 21).

Terrace View: its 10th floor terrace has a green roof and provides some of the best views of the city (Figure 22, left).

Room Views: single and double patient rooms are bright, spacious and enjoy spectacular views of the surrounding city and parks (Figure 22, right). The building design is robust and dynamic, intended to stimulate active living within its walls as well as equip patients to enjoy life back in their home communities.

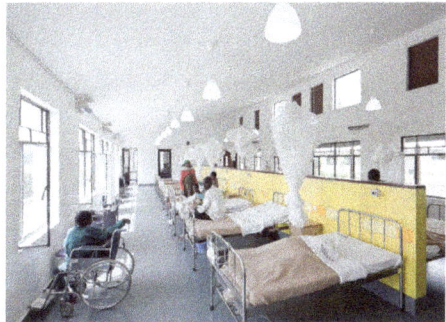

343

Figure 19. Butaro Hospital, Burera District, Rwanda - MASS Design Group.

Figure 20. Bridgepoint Active Healthcare, site plan.

344

Figure 21. Bridgepoint Active Healthcare, street view and park view - Diamond Schmitt Architects.

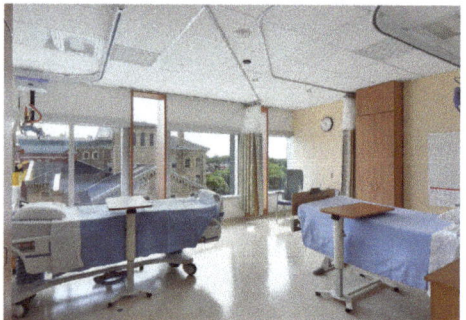

Figure 22. Bridgepoint Active Healthcare, terrace view and room views - Diamond Schmitt Architects.

44 Facilities, 1553 Beds, 3 Years: A Case Study in Design Standards from Nova Scotia

Nycum B.[1], Terauds S.[2]

bnycum@nycum.com, sterauds@nycum.com
[1] NSAA, PMP, C.E.O., William Nycum & Associates Limited, Halifax, NS, Canada
[2] NSAA, Manager, Innovation & Development, William Nycum & Associates Limited, Halifax, NS, Canada

This paper is an examination of unexpected factors that threaten to undermine the implementation and utilization of design standards in health-related facilities using The Province of Nova Scotia's Continuing Care Strategy as a case study. Referencing examples illustrated by drawings and images from real projects from different design teams, working for different clients and using the same standard, this paper examines the impacts of major decisions that had significant capital cost, operations and quality of life impacts. It also examines the variety of outcomes generated despite the strict implementation of one design standard for all 44 facilities. Lastly, it will suggest a process that could be followed to prevent the stifling of innovation during the implementation of a standard.

Keywords: design standard, senior care, architecture

INTRODUCTION

Design Standards are an excellent way to manage a baseline of outcomes in a project construction portfolio. The main challenge with any standard is that it represents a fixed moment in time, while major design and construction projects are usually 2 to 5 years in a standard's future. This fixed moment is typically the product of years of lead-up work, especially for institutional projects where many stakeholders are involved. The result is nearly a decade of time for a standard as it relates to any given project. However, innovation and other reasons for change occur at a higher frequency. For this reason, a standard needs to be able to adapt and include ways to evolve while retaining the integrity of the portfolio of projects following the standard. The alternative is to knowingly commission obsolescence.

The purpose of this paper is to analyse the outcomes of a project portfolio that followed a rigorous design standard in order to understand ways in which standards can be developed to adapt to an ever evolving project environment, and to consider the factors that may lead to differences in outcomes from project to project within a portfolio.

346

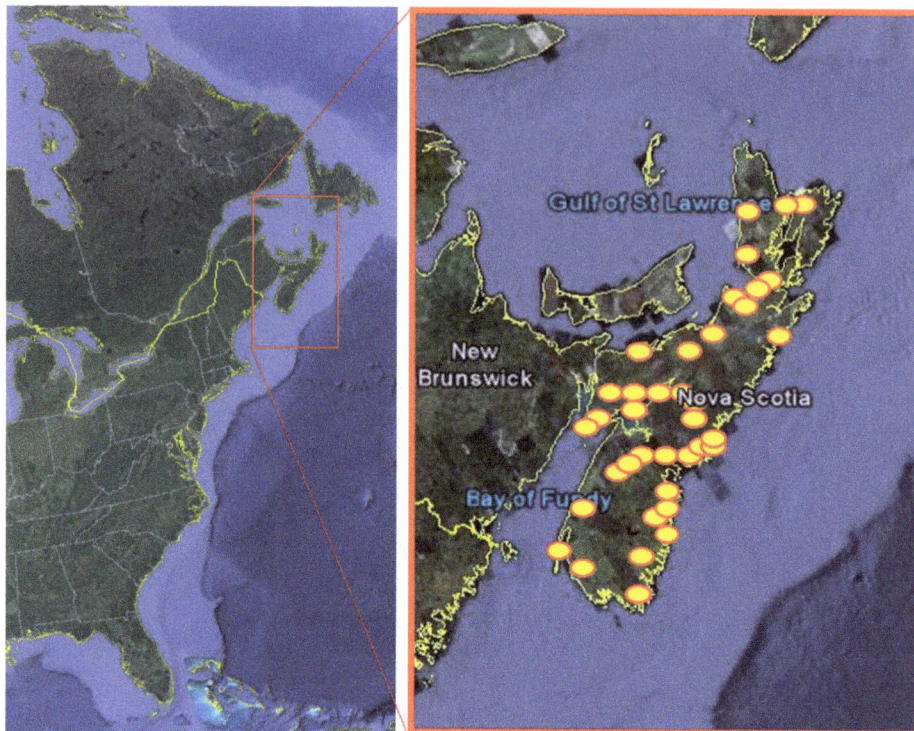

Figure 1. New Nursing Home projects in their geographical context. © 2009 Google, Data U.S. Navy, TerraMetrics, Europa Technologies and Tele Atlas.

Context – Nova Scotia's Geography and Population

Nova Scotia is a province located on the east coast of Canada. It has a population of around 922,000 (2011 Census), 40% of whom live in the county of the capital city of Halifax. It is almost entirely surrounded by water. The combination of its geo-political setting and its population, which easily rounds to a million, provides a reasonably controlled laboratory for the subject of this paper.

Figure 1 shows Nova Scotia in context with the eastern seaboard of North America, and the distribution of the facilities constructed as part of the first round of implementation of the province's new Space and Design Standards under its Continuing Care Strategy.

Context – Nursing Homes in Nova Scotia, Canada

Nursing Homes (also referred to as Continuing Care Facilities or Long-Term Care Facilities) fall under Nova Scotia's Continuing Care Program. Nursing Homes are located in communities across the province, operated by not-for-profit and for-profit private organizations, regulated by the province, and funded by Nova Scotia's taxpayers via the provincial government.

Eligible persons must access a nursing home bed through a single point of entry system, which assigns a bed within 100 km of home. There is a long waiting list, and entrants are not afforded the ability to pick a location.

NOVA SCOTIA'S CONTINUING CARE STRATEGY

In 2007, Nova Scotia embarked on a strategy to replace existing Long-Term Care Facilities and add new facilities throughout the province at a cost of $4.5 billion ($1 billion in Capital Costs and $3.5 billion in operating costs). Existing Nursing Homes badly in need of replacement were prioritized, and communities that were assessed as requiring new beds were identified and ranked by the provincial government for new builds. Replacement facilities were mortgaged and built with pre-existing organizations that were typically already operating the homes being replaced. Private care providers bid on the contracts to construct and operate new facilities with a 25-year resident per diem pay back scheme.

Implementation of the Strategy

1,553 beds were built in 44 new and replacement facilities over a three-year design and construction period, with construction costs ranging from CAD 250 per sq ft to CAD 320 per sq ft.

NURSING HOME DESIGN STANDARDS

Before awarding beds to providers and architects, the province of Nova Scotia created a design standard called *Facility Space and Design Requirements*. The standard was initialized in 2002 and developed further with a pilot project that started design stages in 2007. During the design and construction phases of the new and replacement facilities, regular progress submissions were made to the Nova Scotia Department of Health and Wellness to ensure compliance with the standard.

Standard Highlights

The *Facility Space and Design Requirements Standard* was extensively researched and is based on the "Household" model of care. Highlights include:
• A maximum of 12 residents per household;
• A maximum building gross of 940 sq ft per resident;
• Private resident rooms of 190 sq ft plus a 50 sq ft WC;
• Maximum travel distances from resident rooms to amenities such as dining and bathing areas;
• Access to outdoor garden area from within the household.

ILLUSTRATION OF CHANGES FROM THE PREVIOUS MODEL

In changing from a traditional Nursing Home model, with nursing stations and wards and environments based on medical situations, to a model based on smaller, residentially-scaled environments based on daily life and care, several substantial changes in operating models and physical space were instituted at regulatory level.

Increase in Bedroom Sizes

Whereas most resident rooms were shared in the homes built in Nova Scotia under the traditional model, the new standards required a majority of single rooms, with some larger and/or intended to be flexible enough to be co-joined with adjacent rooms to support more social living environments for couples, family members, or close friends. Every bedroom in the new model is paired with a dedicated toilet room, and has a minimum size of 190 net square feet. Figure 2 illustrates differences with a typical plan under the previous model, a plan based on the new model, and photographs of new and old spaces.

347

348

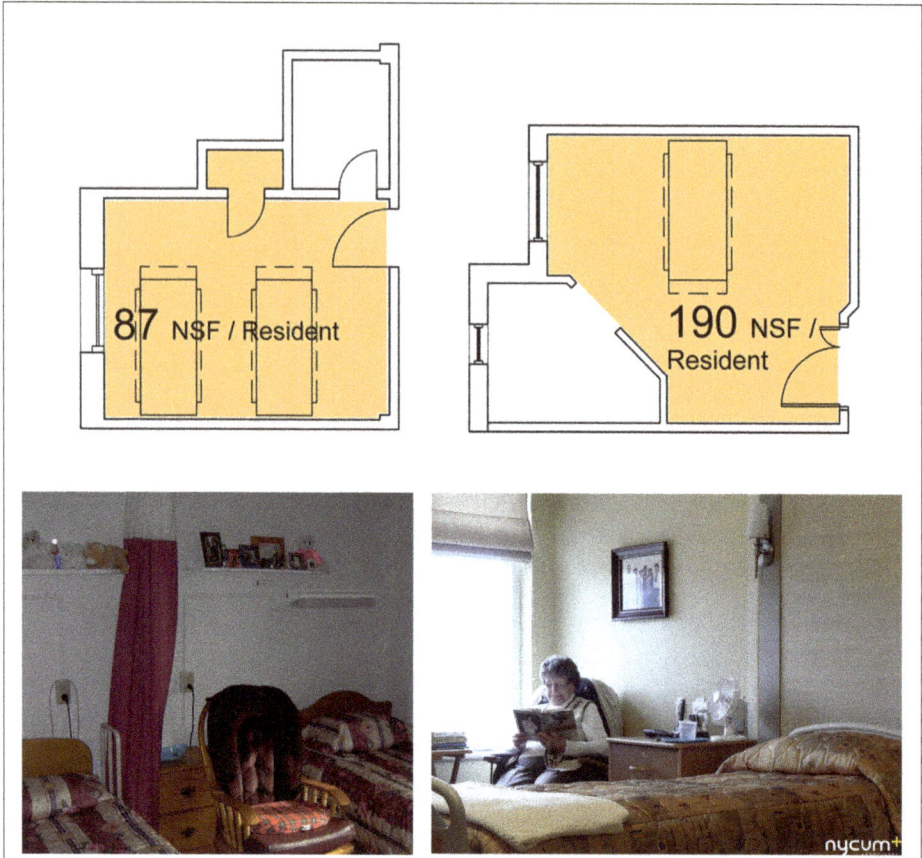

Figure 2. Comparison of bedrooms for the elderly. Clockwise from top left, typical bedroom plan in previous model; typical plan in new model: photograph of typical room in new model, photograph by Deborah Nicholson; and photograph of typical room in previous model.

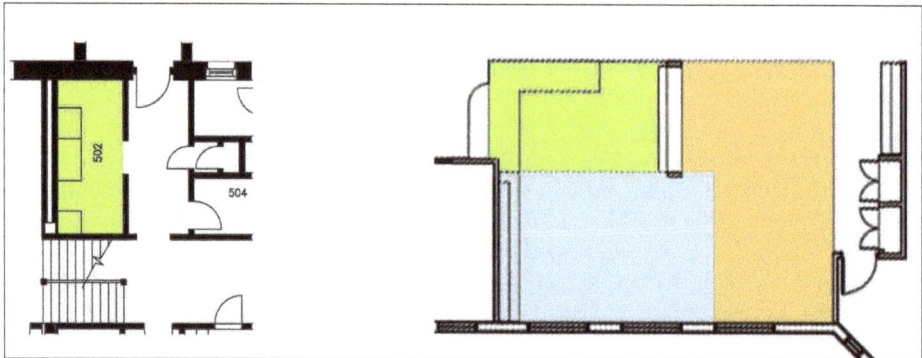

Figure 3. Comparison of living spaces shown at the same scale. Typical former kitchenette (left) and typical new layout for a resident's kitchen, dining and living area (right).

Figure 4. Comparison of travel distances. Typical plan prior to new standard (left) and new layout (right). Above, left : in this pre-standard example, three out of 89 residents are within 50 feet of the dining room and eight are within 75 feet; this is a typical example of a long-term care facility that was slated for replacement in the implementation of the new standard. Above, right : post-standard household design provides all 12 elders with access within 75 feet and half within 50 feet.

Increased Living Spaces for the Elderly

Figure 3 compares a typical former situation and a comparable space in a new residential wing.

The new model assumes the preparation of food is an important part of daily life for elders living in these homes, a value which contributes to the dramatic increase in social spaces for residents.

Decreased Travel Distances to Dining and Living Areas

The new standard mandates a maximum travel distance of 75 feet for up to half the residents, measured from the bedrooms of the elderly to their dining areas, with a preferred travel distance of 50 feet.

OBSERVATIONS FROM IMPLEMENTATION

The following are some examples of implementation of the new standards with projects chosen from the first group of 1,553 beds to be constructed. All projects included here are replacement facilities or additions to existing homes,

and administrative staff approached the new builds with reference to the staffing and physical attributes of their existing situations.

Projects and their design teams included in this paper are:

• Northwood at the Parks, William Nycum & Associates Limited (Nycum)[1];
• Shiretown Nursing Home, Nycum;
• Ivey's Terrace, Nycum;
• Windsor Elms Village, Nycum;
• Annapolis Royal Nursing Home, Nycum;
• Port Hawkesbury Nursing Home, Nycum;
• Tideview Terrace, WHW Architects, with Montgomery Sisam Architect (WHW/MSA) ;
• The Meadows, WHW/MSA;
• Alderwood, WHW/MSA;
• The Admiral, SP Dumeresq Architect Limited (Dumeresq);
• The Heart of the Valley, Dumeresq.

---

1. Northwood at the Parks was the prototype used to develop the standard during design and programming phases. Design began before the standard was finalized.

350

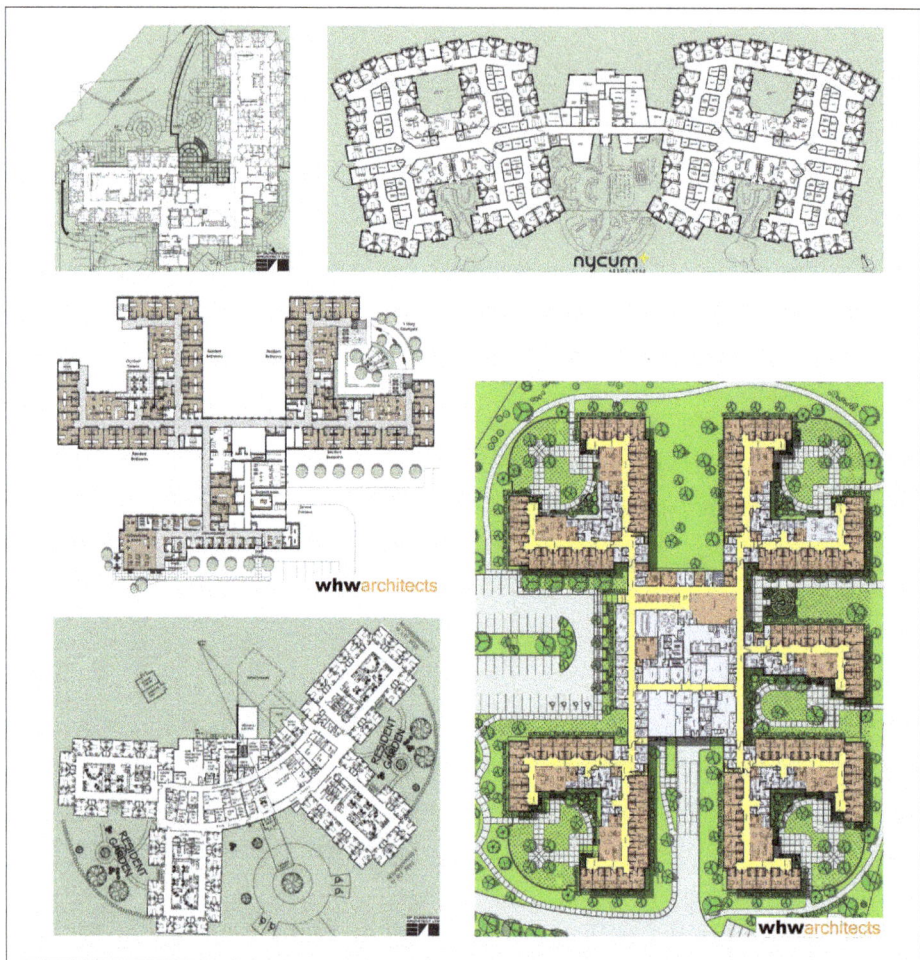

Figure 5. Facility plans. Clockwise from top left: The Admiral, Northwood at the Parks, The Meadows, The Heart of the Valley and Alderwood.

Example Facility Plans: 12-14-Bed Household Model

Courtyards provide access to exterior spaces directly from resident households. Layouts within households themselves tend to vary as follows:

1. Racetrack with household living spaces within the plan;
2. L-shaped wings with living spaces on exterior walls;

3. Hybrid: racetrack plan with living spaces on exterior walls.

Examples of Facility Plans: Nine-Bed Household Model

Nine-bed households are highly self-contained, signifying an operational change from the previous model where staff cared for all residents, as opposed to concentrated household teams. Again, courtyards tend to be shared, one for every two households.

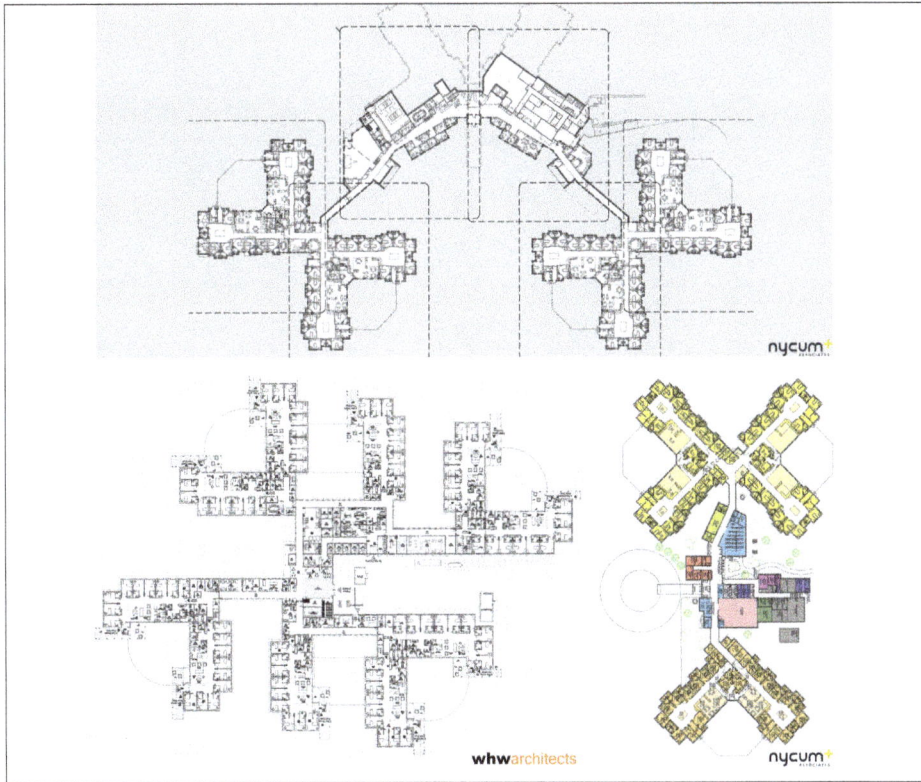

Figure 6. Facility plans. Clockwise from top: Windsor Elms Village, Shiretown Nursing Home and Tideview Terrace.

Facility Scale Versus Residential Scale: Impact of Household Size on Building Massing and Expression of Requirement for "Residential Scale"

Aerial views of three facilities show how the scale of a facility can be manipulated to produce the "residential" aesthetic mandated by the new standard.
• Northwood at the Parks: 156 beds, households of 12-13 residents.
• Tideview Terrace: 90 beds, households of 9 residents.
• The Meadows: 105 beds, households of 11-12 residents.
In the nine-bed household versions, each household can be read as a sepa-rate form. In the 12-bed version at Northwood, the tight and sloping site resulted in a higher-density solution that stacked and closely linked the households, so materiality and modulation became more important. Input from clients can be seen in Figures 8 and 9: Northwood's client wanted the building to look like a "celebration of life", so Nova Scotian vernacular traditions of brightly painted houses were referenced and translated into a larger facility, forming a "village" of houses, each with its own identity, whereas the expression of the other two facilities is more measured, while still evoking a residential scale and feel.

TESIS Inter-University Research Centre "Systems and Technologies for Social and Healthcare Facilities"
University of Florence, Italy

352

Figure 7. Aerial photographs. Clockwise from top left: Northwood at the Parks, photograph by Vision Air Services; Tideview Terrace, photograph courtesy of WHW Architects; and The Meadows, image courtesy of WHW Architects.

Figure 8. Household exteriors. Annapolis Royal Nursing Home, photograph by Deborah Nicholson (left); and Northwood at the Parks, photograph by Chris Reardon (right).

Building exteriors show various interpretations of "residential" in building massing and details.

• *Annapolis Royal Nursing Home:* 12-bed household expressed as a combination of a large unifying gable roof with lower shed roofs.

• *Northwood at the Parks:* two 12-13-bed households shown stacked atop one another. Finishing materials (siding and brick) break up the massing.

• *The Heart of the Valley:* large hipped roof, relieved with gables of varying sizes.

• *Windsor Elms Village:* 9-bed household defined by gable roof and chimney form. Flat roofs identify the portions of the building outside the resident households (mechanical, administrative and common spaces).

• *Tideview Terrace:* mono-pitch or shed roof over households, each with a vent/chimney. Again, spaces outside the households are predominantly flat-roofed.

Household Interiors

In comparison to the variety observed in building exteriors, there is notable similarity across a selection of different facilities, suggesting that a combination of the requirement for residential aesthetic expression and the performance criteria of institutional finishes drove aesthetic outcomes. All of the images in Figure 10 are of the common areas within resident households. Evidence of the careful use of sightlines can be found in the "open" nature of these core shared spaces that co-locate elders' activities and social spaces with staff work spaces (traditionally nursing stations or charting areas).

353

Figure 9. Household exteriors. Clockwise from top left: The Heart of the Valley, photograph courtesy of Dumaresq; Windsor Elms Village, photograph by Chris Reardon; and Tideview Terrace, image courtesy of WHW Architects.

Figure 10. Household interiors. Clockwise from top left: Annapolis Royal Nursing Home, photograph by Deborah Nicholson; Port Hawksbury Nursing Home, photograph by Deborah Nicholson; Windsor Elms Village, photograph by Chris Reardon; The Meadows, photograph courtesy of WHW; Northwood at the Parks, photograph by Chris Reardon; and Tideview Terrace, photograph courtesy of WHW.

Household Plans
12-Beds – Modified Racetrack

The household kitchen/dining/living room is not central to the plan, which impacts staffing and resident travel distances. Some residents must travel significantly greater distances to get from their bedrooms to the common area. Staff ability to observe from a central location without moving around the household is impeded.

354

Visitors to a household must pass a control station prior to entering the more private realms of the elders living there.

Elders' toilet rooms are on the exterior walls, providing staff with a clear view of the resident bed without entering the room. This requires the entry to the toilet to be angled, providing privacy from the corridor (in the event that both doors are left open during toileting) and a clear line of sight from the bed location. This arrangement allows for natural light in the toilet room. There is also sufficient wall area on the partition common to the corridor and bedroom to support a window – allowing the resident to view activity outside their room and have some degree of control over their personal environment by opening or closing the window coverings, while also providing a convenient opportunity for staff to check on residents without entering their personal spaces.

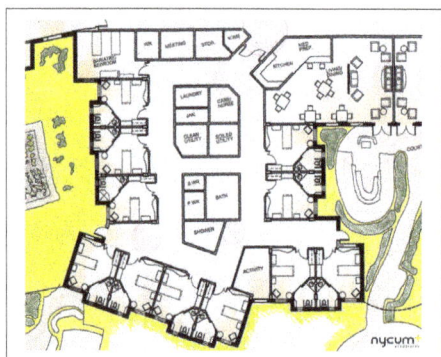

Figure 11. Household plan. Northwood at the Parks.

12-Beds – Perimeter Bedrooms

The household kitchen/dining/living room is central to the plan. Staff ability to observe from a central location is enhanced by co-locating staff work zones with this resident common area.

Visitors to this type of household may encounter a resident room prior to meeting a staff member.

Elders' toilet rooms are on the interior walls. This creates a stronger transition between the semi-private corridor ("owned" by the household) and the private bedroom, providing spatial hierarchy, and a larger window on the exterior wall. This arrangement obstructs the staff's view of residents in their beds or on the floor of the toilet room from the corridor.

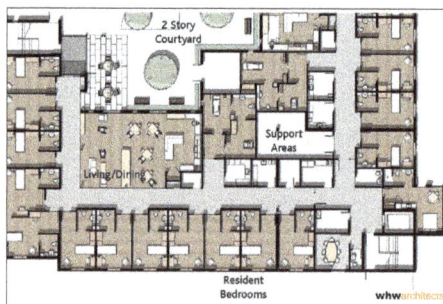

Figure 12. Household plan. Alderwood.

12-Bed Addition to an Existing Facility

In cases where the projects were additions to existing facilities some restrictions were challenging, such as the ability to access the household without passing through other households, which required additional controlled access points.

Staff workspaces in this plan are incorporated within the central kitchen/dining/living space, which is minimally enclosed with few full-height partitions, supporting visual control over the entire household for staff.

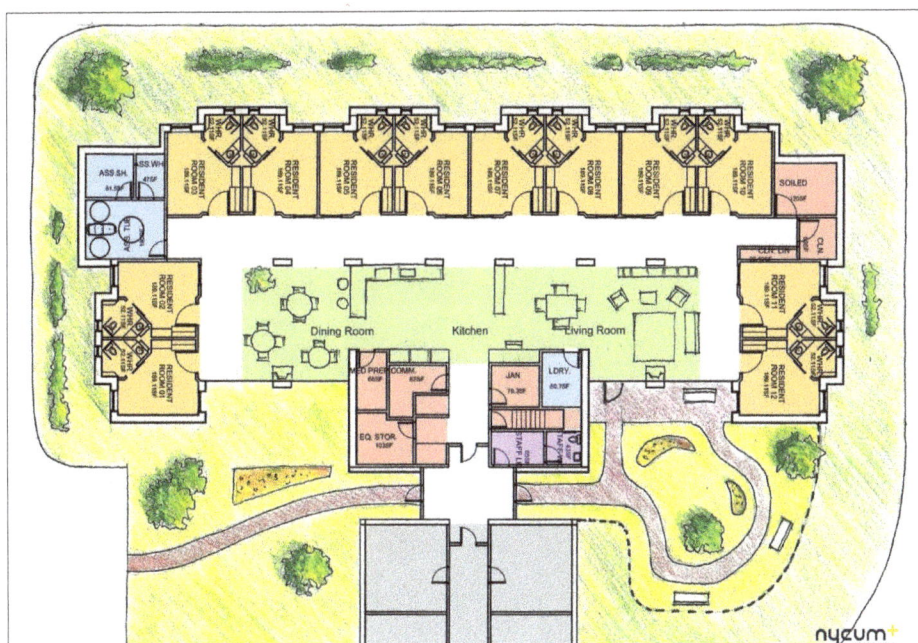

Figure 13. Household plan. Annapolis Royal Nursing Home.

9-Beds – Perimeter Bedrooms

9-bed layouts facilitated an improved balance between interior space and the household perimeter, access to views and natural light over 12-bed versions. The mandated minimums in the Province's design standards did not allow less than 12 beds, and in order to achieve 9-bed layouts an interpretation of the standard was made to view 2 x 9 as an 18-bed household, allowing subdivision into nine beds.

The household kitchen/dining/living room is central to the plan and co-located with staff work zones (charting and medication areas).

Resident households are linked to one another with a shared "spa" area (assisted bathing, showering and associated toilet). Considering these two households as a "super household" lowers capital costs by avoiding a spa for each group of 9 (and recognizes the frequency of use of this expensive equipment). This link, which enters each household via the staff workspace, also helps provide flexibility for staffing, particularly after hours when one staff member may be responsible for two households.

Resident washrooms on exterior walls increase the building perimeter, but help provide efficient building gross by not requiring room width to accommodate an accessible door and accessible toilet room side-by-side (by streamlining the building gross, more area is available for resident amenities).

The version shown in Figure 15 is similar to that in Figure 14 with its centralized elders' common spaces and staff work spaces. In this iteration, resident toilet rooms are on interior walls, providing a flattened and more cost-effective exterior (although this increases corridor length).

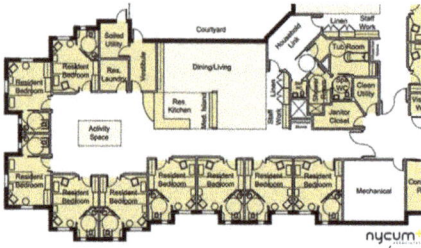

Figure 14. Household plan. Windsor Elms Village.

356

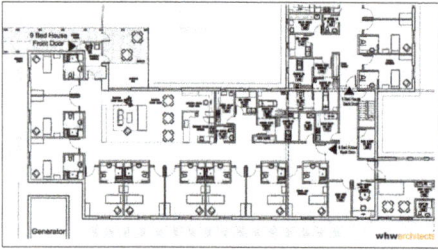

Figure 15. Household plan. Tideview Terrace.

Direct Resident Access to Exterior Space

The standard requires residents to have at-grade access to outdoor spaces directly from their household living groups with the intent of supporting the ability of elders to choose to spend time outdoors. In Nova Scotia, climate and weather conditions often keep elders indoors. There is little guidance in the design standard with respect to providing an attractive space with seasonal interest to support visual use of the space by those unable to access it due to weather or mobility.

Figure 16. Resident courtyard. Port Hawksbury Nursing Home, photograph by Deborah Nicholson.

Raised planting beds allow wheelchair users to reach plants and soil. The shade structure in this garden provides shelter from the sun and is stand-alone, not connected to the building.

Planting flowers in blocks of colour helps maximize visual impact from within the adjacent households. The shade structure in this garden is also separate from the building.

This double-storey courtyard utilizes an elegant layering of balconies, overhangs, and shade structures to shape the edges of the exterior space. Most of the courtyard is hard surface and lawn, and the shade structures are attached to the building, helping the transition from interior to exterior lighting conditions while providing a spot to escape from the hot summer sun.

Figure 17. Resident courtyards. Left and right. Windsor Elms Village, photograph courtesy of Windsor Elms Village.

Figure 18. Resident courtyard. Alderwood, photograph courtesy of WHW Architects.

357

CONCLUSIONS

The outcomes of this standard-driven simultaneous multi-facility design and construction initiative are highly congruous. The facilities conform to the standard with a high degree of rigour. This is largely thanks to a high level of commitment to the development review process which addressed non-conformance at each stage-gate of programming, design, construction and licensing before proceeding to subsequent stages. Maintaining regulatory and licensing control with the provincial body that developed the standard appeared to assist the ability to enforce it.

A few exceptions were made to the standards if they could be comfortably applied to all the projects. Generally, if an exception had the potential to cause a dangerous precedent (such as increase the cost of the program or add risk to care delivery) it was not allowed.

Although not studied, the experiences of the authors of this paper suggest that a clear process to manage requests for deviations from the beginning could have supported innovations, leading to cost savings or care improvement. The following explores some highlights where this could be the case.

Reasons for Deviation from the Standards

Site & Local Climate: Like any building type, continuing care facilities have unique requirements that impose limits on the appropriateness of a building site. These include building servicing, barrier-free accessibility, easy visitor access, high ratio of window perimeter, and easy outdoor access. The Design Standards reflected most of these requirements in specific terms, resulting in specific site demands. For example, a site needed to be relatively flat and expansive, be ser-

358

viceable, have manageable access and integrate with community traffic patterns. The inflexibility of standards meant that in a community where a new facility was mandated to be built, there may have been few available sites. Once sellers were aware that they possessed property that was of high value, the availability of affordable sites narrowed even more. In some cases, a simple easing of the standards or redefinition of a requirement to meet the same objectives may have substantially decreased site development costs and/or purchase prices.

Local and Provincial Politics: As with any government initiative, the work of politicians and bureaucrats to achieve project delivery and meet community needs added pressure to the standard. For example, a political promise to complete a facility within a certain time frame might conflict with the fulfillment of the standard. Political pressures should be factored into the creation of a standard.

Care Provider Organization: Different care providers were awarded the right to design, construct, and operate the projects built under the new standard. Care providers were not-for-profit or for-profit enterprises, each with its own corporate ethos and cultural history. Many had an operational culture that was deeply rooted in outdated practices that needed to be quickly converted to the thinking of the future in a newly designed facility. Some wanted to push the standard beyond its maximum limits to improve quality for residents, families and staff. Others wanted to push the standard beyond its minimum requirements to work around specific

challenges or to increase profitability. For all, the standards represented change. The approach could have benefited from a process that incorporated change management. In any case, corporate culture and influence, a willingness to innovate, and the presence of change champions within the organization willing to commit the time, effort and personal risk to push for culture change affected the degree to which that culture change was effective and sincere.

New vs Replacement Facilities: Some facilities were new, requiring new operators. Others were replacements or extensions of existing facilities and were dependent on a transfer or expansion of operations. This difference was compounded by different procurement methods for each type. The replacements were offered the opportunity to carry on their existing practice in a new facility with most of the project risk burden being carried by the province. The new facilities were awarded based on a 25-year per diem payback scheme that placed the risk burden of design and construction on the care provider. The result was a different approach to the standard from each of the two groups.

Unexpected Factors

As can be expected, many unexpected factors emerged throughout the project portfolio rollout. These are summarized as follows:

• Not everyone interprets standards in the same way as they were intended to be read. *Recommendation: explain intent of each standard.*

• The meaning and influence of a standard is not widely understood. What is a "standard" and what does it actually mean? (Is it official? Is it a guideline? A law?) *Recommendation: be clear and upfront about the enforceability of the standard.*

• Procurement processes can impact – and possibly curtail – opportunities for innovation. *Recommendation: develop mechanisms in procurement processes that empower modifications at client/regulator discretion.*

• Culture change has to occur quickly and within the premise of "what will be". This is difficult when the impacts of the standard are not well understood. *Recommendation: implement a structured parallel culture change process.*

• Designing/constructing many facilities simultaneously reduces opportunities to learn from project to project and improve iteratively (this is not a factor of the standards, rather the timing of the projects.) *Recommendation: for many reasons and especially in a smaller region where resources are scarce, rollout projects in sequence. In this case, a minimum of three months between the award of each project would have been highly beneficial.*

• Interdepartmental conflicts may emerge within the government. For example the Department of Agriculture had concerns over food delivery, floor finishes, and the tasks of the front line workers as outlined in the standard, but did not become involved until the projects were in the final stages of design or later. In another example, the Office of the Fire Marshal objected to "open" floor plans for the kitchen and living areas, and an untimely workaround had to be created to adhere to the standard while addressing fire concerns. *Recommendation: in early stages of writing the standard, cast a wide stakeholder engagement net.*

• Methods of measurement (e.g. floor area) are not consistent. One example occurred when a thicker wall system with a higher "R-value" increased the gross square footage. Thus an energy efficient building was penalized. *Recommendation: include measurement methodology and expect a process to work around cases where that methodology is not in the best interest of anyone.*

• Mandated square foot room areas resulted in inflexible design options. *Recommendation: in order to allow for efficiencies to be realized by design, allow margins of variation provided the intents of the room are met.*

• As the projects evolve and costing information emerges, it becomes very difficult to do a fair cost comparison between facilities. *Recommendation: be aware that uniform standards do not result in uniform costs when regional, labour, geographical and other factors are involved.*

• Operating costs are much greater than upfront capital construction costs, however if operating costs are not contemplated in the standard, they will be sacrificed. *Recommendation: consider standards in light of the life-cycle performance of the building, not just on opening day.*

359

• Several other factors were impacted by, or impacted, the implementation of the standard on a smaller scale. These included the minimum number of beds per household, floor finishes, administrative spaces, accessibility, building systems, lighting and anything not included in the standard. *Recommendation: embrace the concept that a standard is not a static document. Recognizing that when a great amount of risk is involved (financial, political, etc.), standards are subject to all kinds of pressure, so embed processes to evaluate, permit, and support innovation at any scale.*

Supporting Innovation within a Standard

The tendancy is to include all possible innovation prior to finalizing a standard. Everyone works to complete a wide and deep research and writing exercise and finally (often after many years have passed) arrive at the completed document: the Official Standard.

An improvement would be to accept that innovation is natural and must be anticipated after finalization of the standard. If this has been accepted, then typically the standard is re-issued as a new version. This can be very confusing because it results in many official or "final" versions (including the inevitable "final final" version).

A better model may be to create a process-driven (as opposed to product-driven) document that includes standards and how to meet them, rather than a standards-driven document that processes must work around. The National Building Code of Canada, with its Objective-Based Solutions provides a way to address intents when the prescriptive solutions stand in the way of an innovation, may be a helpful guide.

Standards should be written to address or embrace the inevitable: innovation occurs in our information-based society faster than a standard can be issued and followed. Standards should not hinder innovation and excellence. Embracing innovation is imperative to achieving excellence in projects.

Acknowledgments

Drawings and photographs of projects realized under the adoption of a new standard provided by William Nycum & Associates Limited (Shiretown, Pictou; Ivey's Terrace, Trenton; Windsor Elms Village, Falmouth; Annapolis Royal Nursing Home, Annapolis Royal; Port Hawkesbury Nursing Home, Port Hawkesbury), WHW Architects with Montgomery Sisam Architect (The Meadows, Yarmouth; Tideview Terrace, Digby; Alderwood, Baddeck), and SP Dumeresq Architect Limited (The Heart of the Valley, Middleton; The Admiral, Dartmouth).

References

Nova Scotia Department of Health and Wellness (NSDHW), Continuing Care Policies and Standards: http://novascotia.ca/dhw/ccs/policies-standards.asp

NSDHW, Long Term Care Facility Requirements (Space and Design): http://novascotia.ca/dhw/ccs/policies/Long-Term-Care-Facility-Requirements-Space-and-Design.pdf

Community Health Centres – Community, Renewal and Partnerships

Rosenberg C. [1]

charles@hilditch-architect.com
[1] B.Arch., Hilditch Architect, Toronto, Canada

Community Health Centres (CHCs) are a healthcare model that combines primary healthcare services with a wide range of other health promotion and community development services. They subscribe to the definition of health adopted by the World Health Organization (WHO): "Health is a state of complete physical, mental, social and spiritual well-being and not merely the absence of disease or infirmity."
A case study of a newly completed CHC will demonstrate how interprofessional teams and community partners are successfully incorporating and focusing on the social determinants of health.
Emerging partnerships, challenging sites, community engagement and providing access to underserved communities are all hallmarks of this new project.
The paper will focus on the Unison Community Health Care Centre and Bathurst Finch Community Hub highlighting the architectural response to program, community, and site specific constraints.
Because CHCs are relatively small projects within the healthcare system they face extraordinary development challenges: site selection and the challenges of securing a site or building, approval processes, challenges of balancing partnerships and multiple funding envelopes, community consultation and building community capacity.
The objective is to demonstrate the importance of CHCs within the continuum of care model, the challenges to develop such projects and the success of these projects in not only providing services but contributing to the renewal of neglected and under-serviced communities.

Keywords: *community health centres, partnerships, renewal.*

INTRODUCTION

The most valuable assets the architectural firm offers are the ability to listen well, communicate simply and effectively, facilitate constructive discussions between stakeholders, balance their many needs, observe, and interpret and transform ideas into creative, accessible and sustainable built form.

The aim is to foster community development through the projects, and to empower the projects' end users. Larger scale projects are framed into smaller, more familiar groupings based on an understanding of how people operate.

The wonderful thing about Community Health Centres is that, while in theory they all deliver similar care and programs, in practice they are all quite different, reflecting the diverse communities that they serve. This difference and the community are embraced to produce a building that truly reflects the community's unique and diverse needs and culture in order to foster health, support, respect, dignity and pride.

A review of the client list and CHC projects illustrates experience in working with large and diverse communities from youths to elders, individuals with mental health issues, individuals and families living in poverty, homeless and underhoused people, people with disabilities, people escaping abuse, the Gay and LGBT community, the non-insured, members of racialized communities and people with addictions.

This paper will demonstrate how inter-professional teams and community partners are successfully incorporating and focusing on the social determinants of health.

Emerging partnerships, challenging sites, community engagement and providing access to underserved communities are all hallmarks of this project.

Outcome of this paper:

1 Understanding of CHCs and their role in primary care;

2 The challenges of developing a CHC;

3 Developing partnerships and hubs within the CHC model.

Community Health Centres

CHCs were established to provide care to those populations that have traditionally faced barriers accessing healthcare. A typical CHC will offer primary clinical care from doctors, nurse practitioners, nurses, social workers and dieticians. Frequently a CHC will provide other services such as dental, chiropody, physiotherapy and health promotion.

Community Health Centres are non-profit organizations and they are community governed by boards made up of clients, community members, health providers and community leaders, ensuring a community-focused response for services. CHCs are funded by the Ministry of Health and Long-Term Care of Ontario (MOHLTC) for both operating and capital expenditures. Staff are paid by salary rather than a fee-for-service system. There are approximately 80 CHCs operating in Ontario and in 2005 the Province of Ontario announced a major expansion of the CHC model as a key component of Ontario's healthcare strategy.

They offer culturally-adapted programs for the needs and preferences of the communities they serve including delivering services in many different languages. Working in partnership with other social services and community members CHCs provide an integrated model of care and address and raise awareness of the broader determinants of health such as employment, education, environment, isolation and poverty.

CHCs play a critical role in providing a continuum of care for a large sector of people that have traditionally faced barriers to healthcare.

Part of the strategy is to provide a variety

of services within the CHC so that the patient can receive services from a multi-disciplined team of practitioners. Many clients have faced multiple obstacles in accessing care including cultural and linguistic barriers, transportation, arranging for child care, following up with appointments and the complex services that may be required for treatment. The goal is to engage with and make clients feel comfortable to continue their treatments within a familiar and supportive environment, and to provide counselling and life skill programs.

CHCs subscribe to the World Health Organization's definition of health: "Health is a state of complete physical, mental, social and spiritual well-being and not merely the absence of disease or infirmity."

Social Determinants of Health can include: Income and income distribution; Education; Unemployment and job security; Employment and working conditions; Early childhood development; Food insecurity; Housing; Social exclusion; Social safety network; Health services; Aboriginal status; Gender; Race; Disability.

CHCs are an important piece of the continuum of care model and in order to fulfil this role they are facilities that:
- Encourage care, treatments, counselling and participation;
- Connect people to complimentary services;
- Provide a familiar, dignified, supportive, culturally responsive and professional environment;
- Offer engagement rather than efficiency;
- Are readily identifiable to their community.

Additionally from a design perspective they should be places that:
- promote health by designing spaces that facilitate active design, walking, cycling, using the stairs, and by providing program areas that support active participation in social activities such as cooking, gardening, etc.;
- are not about efficiency but rather engagement by providing open spaces which may have a community kitchen, child minding program and community spaces;
- are identifiable and interconnected with the community, a facility to be proud of and for users to take ownership of and to feel that there has been an investment made in their community.

PARTNERSHIPS

In 2005 the United Way of Greater Toronto reported in a research paper entitled "Poverty by Postal Code" that there was a growing concentration within Toronto's inner suburbs of low income families and individuals. In response to these findings they launched their Building Strong Neighbourhood Strategy in 2006 by strengthening these communities through targeted efforts that included resident involvement, the revitalization of neighbourhoods, promoting community partnerships and recognizing and leveraging existing strengths.

The 2006 hallmark United Way study reported: "Healthy neighbourhoods are the hallmark of Toronto's civic success. Their strength comes from the rich mixture of cultures of residents, safe streets, abundant green space, diversity of shops and cultural amenities, and the social infrastructure of community services and programs. The increase in the number

363

of higher poverty neighbourhoods had been especially acute in the inner suburbs."

Perhaps their most telling message was about growing community stigmatization, and their fear that the rest of Toronto might "write off" their neighbourhoods.

These became known as Priority Neighbourhoods and what resulted from this was a new strategy and partnership to reinvest in those communities.

Community Reinvestment/Community Partnerships

A number of United Way strategies were initiated including:
- Action for Neighbourhood Change;
- Resident Action Grants;
- Community Hubs.

All of them were created to fund innovative service partnerships in neighbourhoods across the inner suburbs, direct more donor dollars to these areas, strengthen social service agencies and to work strategically and in partnership with CHCs.

The Community Hub is modelled on the idea of providing community services under one roof for improved access to a variety of resources and space for both formal and informal "gathering," greater synergy between participants, partners and providers, and benefiting from a more sustainable operating model.

CHCs were a logical partner for this new paradigm. The following Unison CHC and United Way Hub makes an excellent case study.

CASE STUDY: INVESTING IN SOCIAL INFRASTURE—PUTTING NEIGHBOURHOODS ON THE PUBLIC AGENDA

This project represents the first partnership between the Toronto District School Board (TDSB), owner of the land, a health services provider and a Community Hub. This unique relationship has been pivotal to the success of the project. Unison Community Health Centre was first established in 1974 as the Lawrence Heights Medical Centre with one doctor and one nurse-receptionist. Residents formed a non-profit Board of Directors and lobbied the Ontario government for more accessible healthcare with added services and new programs to better serve their communities. The name was changed to New Heights CHC and after a recent merger with another CHC it was renamed as Unison CHC.

Unison CHC Mission Statement: "Working together to deliver accessible and high quality health and community services that are integrated, respond to needs, build on strengths and inspire change."

To accommodate the ongoing growth, in 2006 the MOHLTC funded the addition of a satellite and community services hub to be located within one of the priority neighbourhoods of Bathurst/Finch, also known as Westminster-Branson, identified in the United Way Report. The project was approved to include approximately 10,000 sq ft of primary healthcare space including dental, diabetes, health promotion, social work, and chiropody facilities. The clinical space criteria was developed based on needs, funding and MOHLTC capital development templates for Community Health Centres.

Through community, partner and stakeholder consultations it was determined that approximately 8,000 sq ft of shared partner hub spaces would be needed. This included office space for legal aid, employment services, youth programs, childminding, and settlement service agencies. It was also determined in the consultation process that the future space should have a variety of shared spaces including a community kitchen, a variety of meeting and program spaces, staff areas and a shared counselling and communication room. There was also consensus that it would be of benefit if it could have a secure outdoor space for community gardens.

An exhaustive two-year search for a site or building within the catchment area ensued. Securing a site through a private developer and landlord was difficult as they were unwilling to let

Unison conditionally hold a property for the duration of the MOHLTC approval period. In 2009 a local school trustee invited Unison to explore the option of developing a portion of an existing school site into a CHC and United Way Hub, suggesting a unique partnership between the Toronto District School Board (TDSB), The Ministry of Health and Long-Term Care, The United Way of Greater Toronto as well as additional funding partners. The proposed site was located in the Bathurst/Finch neighbourhood at the north edge of the city, within a neighbourhood that struggles with poor access to services, isolation, and lower socio-economic indicators in comparison to the Greater Toronto Area.

The Toronto District School Board's 16-acre Northview Secondary School site presented many challenges. It was detached from its surroundings, with

365

Figure 1.   City of Toronto: the shaded area represents the catchment area for this facility.

TESIS Inter-University Research Centre "Systems and Technologies for Social and Healthcare Facilities"
University of Florence, Italy

no direct or meaningful connection to the larger community, and included a large public stadium and recreation conservation area to the rear. The community and students made little use of the site as it was disjointed by large parking areas, fencing, poorly articulated pedestrian routes and large gaps in the urban fabric. Early on it was recognized that the building could play a role in ameliorating some of these larger urban issues.

Figure 2. *Proposed site, looking north towards the conservation area and existing school.*

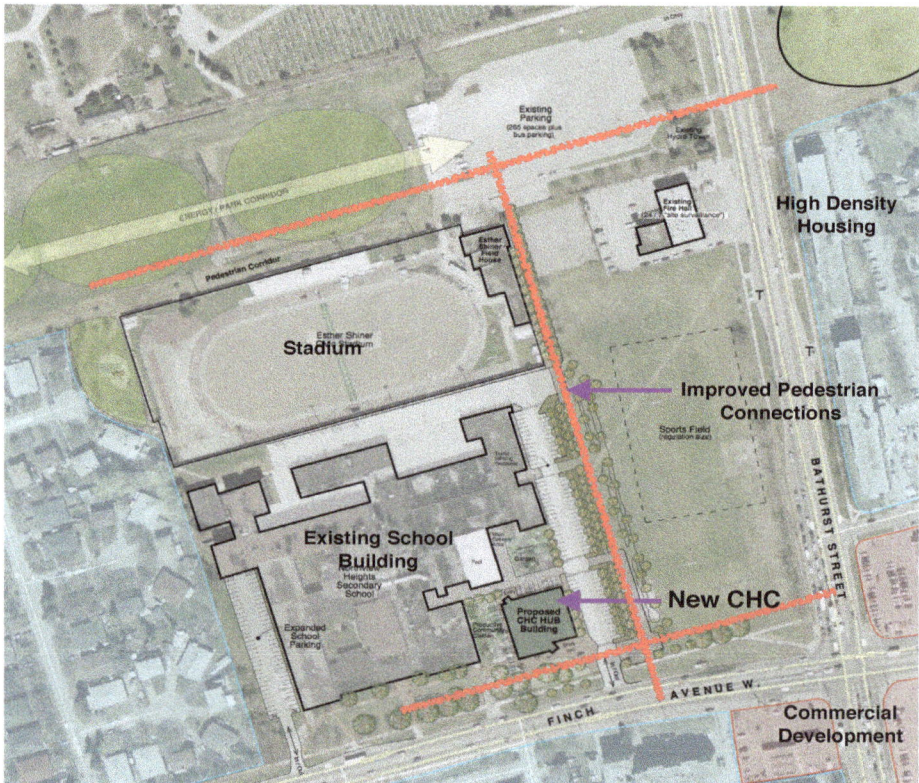

Figure 3. *Proposed site plan indicating the location of the CHC, the existing school to the west, the conservation area to the north and the "greened" parking area to the east adjacent to the playing field.*

The design process included many consultations with the larger community, the school and students, hub partners and the municipality including:

MOHLTC: involving a comprehensive review of programs and a functional program within a staged process from conceptual design through to tender. This included spatial, technical, costing and infection prevention control reviews and approvals;
The City: city planning, development control, public works, roads and traffic, storm water management and building permits;

United Way of Greater Toronto and its hub partners: a number of in-depth collective and individual consultations to develop private and shared spaces, including governing and management;
Unison CHC: staff, board, stakeholders, and Functional Program Consultant;
Consultations with providers: doctors, dentists, nurses, health promotion, diabetes team, social workers, general staff, reception, facility management, Information Technology, and administration;
TDSB: trustees, teachers, students, parents, facility management, TDSB staff architects, planners and management;
Public Health: City of Toronto jurisdiction, funding for Dental Clinic, approval of community kitchen;
Funders: Federal Government (Infrastructure Action Plan), Ontario Trillium Foundation and private donors.

DESIGN

The consultations with stakeholders reinforced the need to create an environment that would foster collaboration and provide bridges between organizational silos. Good design should promote interaction and collaboration between practitioners. There was also an opportunity to improve the urban and natural fabric, pedestrian routes, safety, and to foster activities in and around the site.

From the early stages it was decided that the building should meet high energy efficiency standards with optimized orientation and solar shading. For occupant comfort, operable windows for a mixed-mode ventilation system and enhanced indoor air quality were decided on.

A functional plan was concurrently developed for the hub partners during the design stage, which involved establishing common interests and dovetailing it into the CHC program. Meetings were held with all the partners to determine their individual space needs and to encourage them to move from their "silos" of operation to other ways of providing services.

Ensuring the building was grounded to the site and the community connections was very important for the team. Particular attention was paid to maintaining short cuts that had been imbedded into the site by thousands of students over the past 50 years. Improvements were made to on-site vehicular traffic, student drop-off zones, pedestrian movement and short cuts improving walkways from the community through the site to the conservation area. There was also a wish to encourage other activities at the site and the parking areas were designed to be accessible for weekend activities such as farmers markets.

367

TESIS Inter-University Research Centre "Systems and Technologies for Social and Healthcare Facilities"
University of Florence, Italy

368

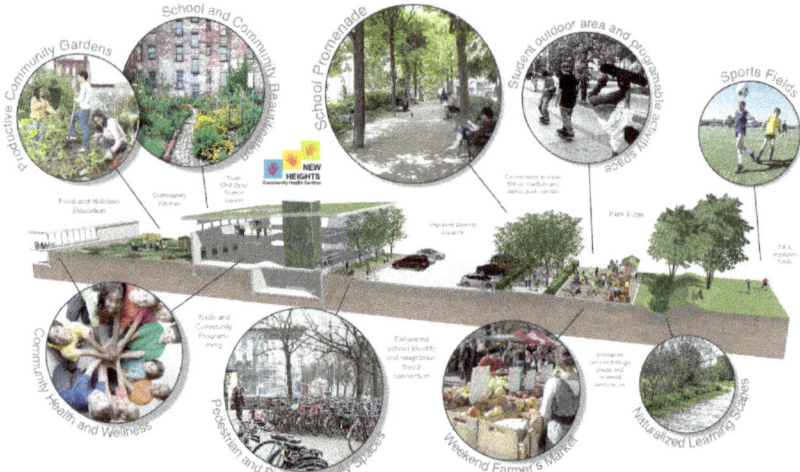

Figure 4. Conceptual design: section through site demonstrating engagement and active areas.

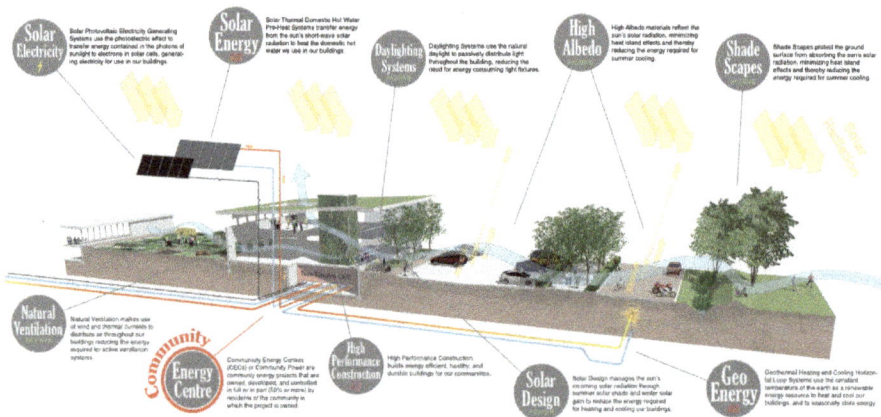

Figure 5. Conceptual design: section through site demonstrating green features.

The lower story of the building accommodates all the community program spaces including the community kitchen and child minding area. All these spaces open onto a covered porch overlooking the community gardens; moreover they all connect back to the main street making them an integral part of the community. The community is encouraged to make use of the large community gardens and community veranda. Programs spill out onto these areas, students linger or have their lunch there.

No one partner dominates the space; the hub partners are tucked below the clinical area giving the impression that building is mostly public. There is a shared photocopier, meeting area, counselling room, and staff lounge with hot desks. There has been a positive emotional response to the building, the natural materials incorporating a rich palette

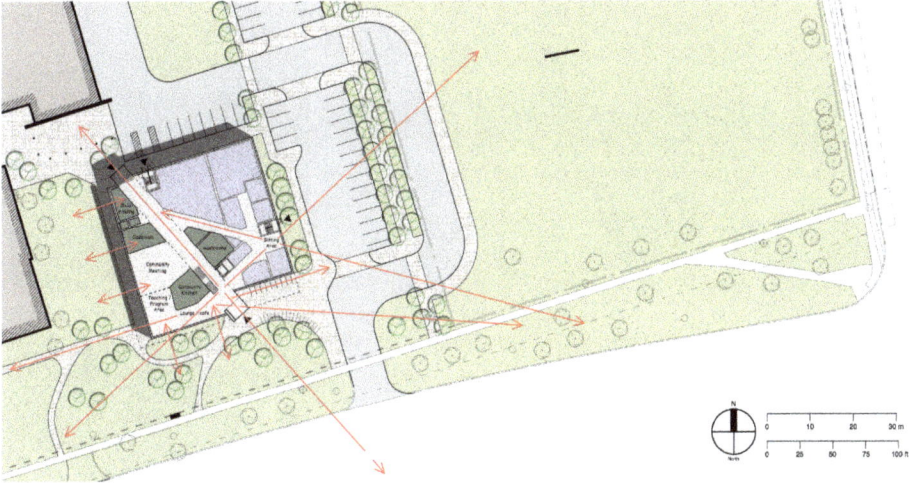

Figure 6. Proposed site and building plan. Indicating links inside and outside the building, green space and rationalized parking layout.

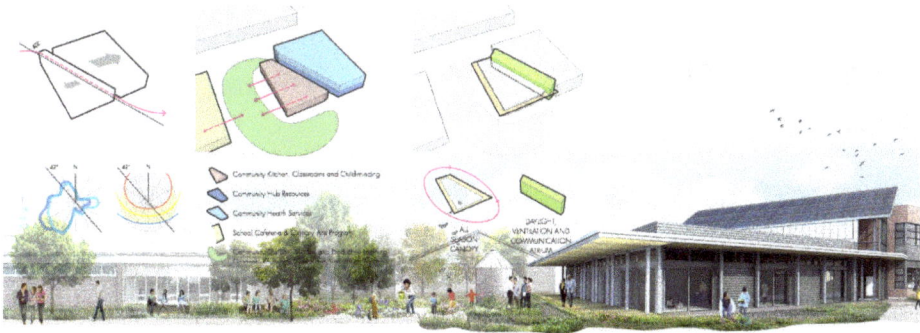

Figure 7. Top: Study demonstrating both the organization of the building parts and the solar orientation. Bottom: front (south) elevation with the existing school on the left, the community garden centre and proposed building with porch and adjacent community rooms and kitchen.

of colours (which were developed with the stakeholders) and the setting. The funders are delighted by the outcome; private donors in particular took a special interest in the project returning often to see its progress, and they continue to show interest in its success.

The building is well used and new programs have been developed in response to the community needs.

The extensive landscaping and new productive garden, which provides produce for the community kitchen, also acts as a social meeting area and activity space for students and members of the local community. The school's cafeteria and cooking program look onto this space. It is hoped that the school will eventually install connecting doors to this area so it can be utilized further.

Over the course of 6 months the landscaping started to mature and students started to actively use the outdoor areas. A remarkable reinvestment.

370

Figure 8. Left: shared program room with connecting covered porch (right).

Figure 9. Community kitchen and informal sitting area that also connects to the covered porch and community gardens.

Figure 10. Natural light and materials along with colour create an inviting environment. The community is particularly proud of this building. A large interior street connects all the main public spaces as well as the second floor clinical space which overlooks the program spaces below. Large windows provide natural light deep into the building and are planned along with fans that open or turn on to naturally ventilate the space.

CONCLUSIONS

There cannot be conclusive evidence of the success of this project until a follow up study measuring the project outcomes in relation to health accessibility and equity, community vitality, efficiency and integrated services has been initiated. What can be observed is that a sustainable, accessible multipurpose building with an extensive green and community space has been built on public land that was once used for parking.

Every opportunity was explored to engage the community during the development process. An extensive consultation process invited community voices to be heard; many ideas were incorporated into both the building and the programs that addressed issues of neglect, safety, health and community services. Working with the community, building on strengths and hopefully inspiring change promoted a sense of pride and ownership. Thirteen social agencies are now cooperating with Unison CHC to provide synergy between partners and convenience and efficiency for clients and staff.

The inviting, bright new building appears to have been embraced by the community as a place for local health services as well as an expression of the neighbourhood. The community garden and kitchen are actively used by a range of participants. The local high school students regularly volunteer their services, and routinely use the grounds and the building demonstrating that it has been accepted as an inviting and familiar part of the urban fabric.

Figure 11. South views showing the community garden and building with porch beyond.

Figure 12. Before and after photographs of the site.

371

REFERENCES

Poverty by Postal Code
Prepared by United Way Toronto
The number of poor Toronto neighbourhoods is rising at a rapid rate.
In the past two decades, Toronto has changed dramatically and not all for the good. The income gap is widening and neighbourhood poverty has intensified. As the numbers of high poverty neighbourhoods increase—especially in the inner suburbs—everyone's quality of life suffers. United Way Toronto explored the changing geography of neighbourhood poverty in Poverty by Postal Code. Poverty by Postal Code encourages public debate and action—the first steps in preserving Toronto as one of the best places in the world to live. See maps of the changing geography of neighbourhood poverty over the last 20 years.
Read the report and the executive summary: Poverty by Postal Code 2004

A Report on the Strong Neighbourhood Task Force
Prepared by United Way Toronto

In April 2003, the Toronto City Summit Alliance released its report, Enough Talk, which called upon the Prime Minister and Premier to implement a new fiscal deal for municipalities, and to immediately address the need for new physical infrastructures in the Toronto area. It also pressed government to address the urgent need for more affordable housing, improved access to post-secondary education, quicker economic integration of newcomers, and new social infrastructures in the city's poorest neighbourhoods.
The Strong Neighbourhood Task Force was formed in April 2004 to take up the challenge of Enough Talk. A joint initiative of United Way Toronto and the City of Toronto, with the support of the Government of Canada and the Province of Ontario, the goal of the Strong Neighbourhood Task Force was to build an action plan for revitalizing Toronto neighbourhoods. The Task Force made 10 recommendations within the report.
Read the report: Strong Neighbourhoods 2005, Steenkamp, J.-B. E. M. (1997). Dynamics in consumer behaviour with respect to agricultural and food products. In Wieringa, B., Tilburg, A. van, Grunert, K., Steenkamp, J.-B. E. M. and Wedel, M. (eds), Agricultural Marketing and Consumer Behaviour in a Changing World. Dordrecht: Kluwer Academic Publishers, 143-188.
Swinnen, J. F. M. (ed.) (1997). Political Economy of Agrarian Reform in Central and Eastern Europe. Aldershot, UK: Ashgate.

Ontario Community Health Centres
Every One Matters, Who We Are and What We Do. March 2008
http://www.ontariochc.org/index.php?ci_id=2341&la_id=1

Community Orientation in Primary Care Practices
Results from the Comparison of Models of Primary Health Care in Ontario Study – 2010

Laura Muldoon, MD MPH FCFP
Clinical Investigator for the C.T. Lamont Primary Health Care Research Centre (CTLC) of the Élisabeth Bruyère Research Institute in Ottawa, Ont, a Lecturer in the Department of Family Medicine at the University of Ottawa, and a clinician at the Somerset West Community Health Centre
http://www.cfp.ca/content/56/7/676.full.pdf+html

All graphics and photographs by Hilditch Architect

www.ingramcontent.com/pod-product-compliance
Lightning Source LLC
Chambersburg PA
CBHW041601260326
41914CB00011B/1348